D0805818

Crosslinguistic Research in Syntax and Semantics

Georgetown University Round Table in Languages and Linguistics series
Selected Titles

CROSSLINGUISTIC RESEARCH IN SYNTAX AND SEMANTICS
Negation, Tense, and Clausal Architecture

Raffaella Zanuttini, Héctor Campos, Elena Herburger, and Paul Portner *Editors*

GEORGETOWN UNIVERSITY PRESS
Washington, D.C.

As of January 1, 2007, 13-digit ISBN numbers will replace the current 10-digit system.
Paperback: 978-1-58901-080-2

Georgetown University Press, Washington, D.C.

Library of Congress Cataloging-in-Publication Data

Georgetown University Round Table on Languages and Linguistics (2004)
Crosslinguistic research in syntax and semantics : negation, tense, and clausal architecture / Raffaella Zanuttini . . . [et al.], editors.
   p. cm. — (Georgetown University round table on languages and linguistics series)
   Papers from the Georgetown University Round Table on Languages and Linguistics (GURT), held March 26–29, 2004.
Includes bibliographical references and index.
   ISBN-13: 978-1-58901-080-2 (pbk. : alk. paper)
   ISBN-10: 1-58901-080-9 (pbk. : alk. paper)
   1. Grammar, Comparative and general—Clauses—Congresses. 2. Grammar, Comparative and general—Negatives—Congresses. 3. Grammar, Comparative and general—Tense—Congresses. 4. Grammar, Comparative and general—Syntax—Congresses. 5. Semantics—Congresses. I. Zanuttini, Raffaella. II. Title. III. Georgetown University round table on languages and linguistics series (2004).
P297.G46 2004
415—dc22   2005027252

Contents

Introduction

RAFFAELLA ZANUTTINI, HÉCTOR CAMPOS,
ELENA HERBURGER, AND PAUL PORTNER
Georgetown University

1. The Event: GURT 2004

This volume in the 2004 Georgetown University Round Table on Languages and Linguistics (GURT) series comes from the conference that took place March 26–29, 2004, with the theme *Comparative and Crosslinguistic Research in Syntax, Semantics, and Computational Linguistics.* While the conference was open to any research within this broad theme, the conference announcement noted that presentations focusing on the following issues were especially welcome: the syntax and semantics of clause types; syntactic variation across varieties of English; the internal structure of the noun phrase; negation, negative polarity, and negative concord; tense and aspect in formal and/or computational semantics; microvariation in the left periphery of the clause; and linguistic typology for machine translation.

The main session in the conference had space for thirty-two presentations chosen from 126 submitted abstracts, in addition to seven presentations by the following invited speakers: Paola Benincà, Marcel den Dikken, Liliane Haegeman, James McCloskey, Toshiyuki Ogihara, Colin Phillips, and Henriëtte de Swart. The presentations were evenly chosen from the abstracts submitted in the areas of syntax and semantics, with a small number in computational linguistics (reflecting the small number of abstract submissions in this area). In addition to the talks in the regular sessions, other conference events included two well-attended poster sessions, where twenty-four posters were displayed; a lively panel discussion on methodological issues in the study of English dialects, led by Judy Bernstein (William Paterson University), Ralph Fasold (Georgetown University), Simanique Moody (New York University), and Christina Tortora (College of Staten Island, CUNY); a tutorial on computational tools for linguists, organized and conducted by Inderjeet Mani (Georgetown University); and a postconference workshop on clause typing and the left periphery, which included the presentation of six papers and ample time for discussion.

In preparing this volume for publication in the Georgetown University Press's longstanding GURT conference series, we took upon ourselves the difficult task of selecting only a few contributions from the many high-quality presentations. We envisioned a volume that would reflect the balance of syntax and semantics seen at the conference and that would touch on at least some of the topics that were highlighted during that engaging weekend. To achieve this goal, we solicited the submission of contributions from all the invited speakers and from a handful of other presenters. Needless to say, there were numerous other excellent papers that would have allowed

1

us to reach our goal equally well and that we regretfully could not accommodate in the volume.

2. The Contributions

In what follows, we will provide a brief overview of the issues discussed in the contributions to this volume. The chapters can be placed into three groups: clausal architecture, negation, and tense and aspect, with one, that by Colin Phillips, falling outside of these groups.

Colin Phillips's chapter, "Three Benchmarks for Distributional Approaches to Natural Language Syntax," addresses the role of linguistic theory in computational models of language learning, in particular questioning the optimism (widespread in certain computational circles) that the discovery of the right statistical learning procedure will ultimately provide an adequate account of human linguistic abilities. Is it really possible to do away with the richly articulated structures widely assumed by linguistic theory and to account for human linguistic abilities simply on the basis of a statistical learning procedure? In other words, would an "ideal" statistical learner capture human knowledge of language? With impeccable coherence and clarity, the chapter summarizes a series of findings (from language acquisition, crosslinguistic typology, and language processing) that illustrate the challenges that any serious model of natural language syntax must meet. Phillips's goal is not to argue that statistics plays no role in models of language learning but rather to show that speakers' knowledge of constraints on language involves much more than just surface co-occurrence patterns, and that computational models of language learning can only succeed if they incorporate the richer representations provided by linguistic theory.

2.1 Clausal Architecture

Among the chapters on syntax, three address issues concerning the left periphery of the clause. Liliane Haegeman's "Argument Fronting in English, Romance CLLD, and the Left Periphery" builds on Rizzi's (1997) seminal work and focuses on arguments interpreted as topics. The chapter addresses the question of whether topics in English and topics resumed by a pronominal clitic in so-called clitic left-dislocation (CLLD) constructions in Romance and modern Greek share the same properties and thus should receive the same analysis, as is sometimes assumed. Haegeman starts out from the observation due to Hooper and Thompson (1973) that topicalization in English is restricted to root clauses and does not occur in clauses with uninflected verbs. She combines this with observations from her own recent work on adverbial clauses. In this recent work, she shows that adverbial clauses fall into two classes, "peripheral" and "central" adverbial clauses, distinguished because they make different interpretive contributions and also because they have different structural representations, the former exhibiting a full and the latter a reduced CP structure. Given these distinctions, the paper is then positioned to make its empirical and theoretical contributions. On the empirical side, Haegeman provides a more refined statement of the distribution of topicalization in English, pointing out that the clauses allowing topicalization are the same as those that may also contain expressions of epistemic modality, speaker-oriented adverbs, and tag questions. In contrast, CLLD topics in Romance and Greek are not restricted to occurring in root clauses or in sentences that exhibit this cluster of properties. Based on this evidence, she makes two theoretical claims. First, she argues that English topicalization occurs in clauses that encode in the syntax the notion of speaker. Second, working on the assumption that the notion of speaker is encoded in a high projection in the left periphery, she proposes that English topicalization targets a high projection and, therefore, like the other properties that involve reference to the speaker, is restricted to clauses that have a full CP structure. In contrast, CLLD topics target a lower structural position, one that is present even in reduced clauses. This leads to the conclusion that clauses contain a higher and a lower structural position for topics, and this point corroborates the results independently obtained in other recent work in the literature.

Paola Benincà's chapter, "A Detailed Map of the Left Periphery of Medieval Romance," uses the hypothesis of a highly articulated structure of CP as a magnifying glass with which to examine certain aspects of the syntax of Romance languages from the twelfth to the early fourteenth century. The languages under analysis are Old French, Old Spanish, Old Portuguese, Old Provençal, and several varieties spoken in what is now Italy (Old Florentine, Old Milanese, Old Piedmontese, Old Sicilian, Old Tuscan, Old Umbrian, and Old Venetian). Because these languages show common properties, Benincà proposes to view them as variants of an abstract "Medieval Romance," which differs from most contemporary Romance languages in exhibiting more movement to CP, both of the verb and of other constituents. The chapter offers many novel and insightful generalizations that are certain to form a solid and useful basis for further investigations and analyses. We will mention only two here. One concerns verb movement: in Medieval Romance, the verb always raises to CP in main clauses; it may or may not raise in embedded clauses, depending on the content of CP; and the only context where it cannot raise is that of embedded interrogatives. Having formulated this generalization, Benincà can then offer an account of the complex word order patterns exhibited by the varieties under investigation, as well as the distribution of null subjects (always possible in main clauses, but more restricted in embedded clauses); the possibility of a null subject is argued to correlate with the possibility of having the verb in C. Another generalization concerns the distribution of enclisis, that is, the word order verb-clitic: enclisis is never found when the verb is in C° and the XP that precedes it is in a specifier of the Focus Field; rather, it is found when the verb is in C° and the XP that precedes it is in a higher projection, within the Topic or Frame Fields. Noting also that enclisis is impossible in embedded clauses with overt complementizers, Benincà then speculates that it might result from the movement of the verb to a position past the Focus Field, possibly the one that hosts the topic in its specifier. The chapter is a beautiful example of how theoretical tools can take our understanding of language farther than pretheoretical descriptions can, especially when combined with the skills of a linguist who can analyze difficult and complex data.

In "Questions and Questioning in a Local English," James McCloskey compares so-called standard English with those Irish varieties of English where inversion of subject and auxiliary is found not only in matrix but also in embedded questions, as exemplified in (1):

(1) a. I wondered would I be offered the same plate for the whole holiday.

   b. The baritone was asked what did he think of Mrs. Kearney's conduct.

What makes standard English, where sentences of this type are ungrammatical, different from Irish English? And why are sentences like the ones in (2) ungrammatical in both standard and Irish English?

(2) a. *I found out how did they get into the building.

   b. *The police discovered who had they beaten up.

First, a correlation is uncovered: predicates like *wonder, ask,* and *inquire* allow not only inversion in embedded clauses (1), but also adjunction of an adverbial phrase to their CP complement, as in (3):

(3) a. ?He asked me when I got home if I would cook dinner.

   b. ?I wonder when we get home what we should do.

In contrast, predicates like *discover, find out,* and *establish* disallow both inversion (2) and adjunction of an adverbial to their CP complement, as shown in (4):

(4) a. *It was amazing while they were out who had got in to their house.

   b. *The police established while we were out who had broken in to our apartment.

The distinction between these two classes of predicates corresponds to a distinction that is important in the work on the formal semantics of questions, where the literature has argued that the complement of predicates like *wonder* (*question predicates,* following Ginzburg and Sag 2000) is semantically of the same type as a root question, whereas the complement of predicates like *discover* (*resolutive predicates*) is a kind of proposition. McCloskey takes the differences uncovered by his work to be the syntactic correlate of the semantic differences between these two classes of predicates. He proposes that the syntax of the two classes differs as follows: question predicates, but not resolutive predicates, embed clauses with a double layer of CP structure. The additional layer of CP structure is where the difference between the denotation of the two classes of predicates is syntactically encoded. It is also what makes adjunction to CP possible in the complement of a question predicate, as in (3) above: the adverbial phrase is adjoined to the lower of the two CPs; since this is not an argument of the matrix verb, there is no violation of the well-known prohibition against adjunction to complements of lexical heads. This option is not available in the complement of resolutive predicates, which do not have two layers of CP structure. While the difference between the two classes of predicates is deep and affects both the syntax and the semantics, the microsyntactic variation observed between standard English and Irish English within the class of question predicates is argued to be rather superficial: in Irish English, but not in standard English, the head of the lower CP triggers verb movement, which results in subject-auxiliary inversion, as in

(1) above. The chapter is exemplary for the clarity and coherence of the argumentation and the discussion of the theoretical issues raised by the data.

Lisa deMena Travis's contribution, "VP-, D°-Movement Languages," asks us to reflect on the nature of movement. Consider two familiar kinds of movement, verb (V) movement and DP movement, which can be seen as triggered by a V-feature and by a D-feature on T, respectively. V-movement proceeds from head to head, is confined to the extended project of the verb, and builds a bigger syntactic object by picking up inflectional material on the way (what Travis calls "the snowball effect"). DP movement, in contrast, proceeds from specifier to specifier (Spec-to-Spec), is not sensitive to the boundaries of an extended projection, and does not build a bigger object by picking up material as it moves. Are these asymmetries a reflection of a deep distinction within the grammatical system or simply an artifact of the languages that have been studied so far? Is the snowball effect exhibited by verb movement determined by the affixal nature of the elements to which the verb adjoins, or is it a property related to the categorical nature of the element that moves, namely the verb? Are there languages that exhibit the opposite combinations of movement possibilities, that is, head movement of D° and Spec-to-Spec movement of VP? The chapter provides compelling answers to these novel and challenging questions through a sophisticated analysis of certain word order properties of several languages. Malagasy, a Western Malayo-Polynesian (WMP) language, overtly exhibits the unexpected combination of movement possibilities: D° incorporates into T° and the VP fronts, moving from specifier to specifier. Malay, another WMP language, overtly exhibits D-to-T movement and is convincingly argued to have covert VP movement. In fact, Travis argues that a typology emerges, which contrasts V°-, DP-movement languages with D°-, VP-movement languages: whereas in the former class (which includes English and other widely studied languages) XP movement can target arguments, in the latter, XP movement targets only predicate projections. The latter class of languages (which includes Malagasy and Malay, Breton and Irish, and Yatee Zapotec and Quiavini Zapotec) is characterized by the following cluster of properties: fronting of the predicate, V-initial word order, D°-movement, and the use of a cleft to form *wh*-constructions. Interestingly, in languages of this class, fronting of the predicate exhibits the snowball effect, since the VP creates a bigger syntactic object as it moves from Spec to Spec. This suggests that the effect is not due to the affixal nature of the elements to which the verb adjoins in instances of V-movement. Rather, Travis suggests that it stems from the fact that movement targets the largest unit that contains the relevant categorical feature; since the elements along the extended projection of V contain a V-feature, they get picked up in the movement process.

2.2 Negation

Three of the chapters in this volume deal with some aspect of the syntax and semantics of negation. In "Parasitism, Secondary Triggering, and Depth of Embedding," Marcel den Dikken furthers our understanding of the licensing conditions on polarity items (PIs) by continuing the in-depth investigation of the properties of the Dutch polarity item *heel* begun in den Dikken (2002). In particular, the chapter focuses on the notion of parasitic licensing, examining cases where *heel* occurs in an environment where the conditions on its licensing are not met, and yet where it does not give rise to ungrammaticality because of the presence of another PI that is properly licensed. Based on the analysis of a novel set of data, the chapter makes two observations that show that depth of embedding plays an important role in parasitic licensing: (1) the negative marker cannot be more than one clause boundary removed from polar *heel* and the PI on which it is parasitic, and (2) polar *heel* and the PI on which it is parasitic must occur in the same clause. To account for the facts, den Dikken proposes a distinction between two kinds of PIs: those that are inherently negative and those that are indefinites licensed by a clausemate licenser. This distinction makes possible an account of the observed distributional restrictions by sharpening the notions of primary direct licensing, secondary direct licensing, and parasitic licensing. Primary direct licensing involves A′-movement of the noun phrase containing polar *heel* into the specifier of the NegP projection that contains the clausal negative marker. Secondary direct licensing, or "secondary triggering" (see Horn 1996), also involves A′-movement of the noun phrase containing polar *heel* into Spec, NegP, but this time it is a NegP projection whose head contains the negative component of the PI on which polar *heel* is parasitic, which adjoins to Neg° as it raises from head to head to the matrix NegP. Finally, parasitic licensing does not involve movement but rather holds when polar *heel* can link up to a relationship that has been established between another PI (of the nonnegative, indefinite type) and a clausemate licenser (Neg or C). These mechanisms all share the property that the relation between the licenser and the PI is syntactically local.

The contribution by Bernhard Schwarz and Rajesh Bhatt, "Light Negation and Polarity," deals with light negation in German and the bearing it might have on the semantics of "rescuing" positive PIs under negation. Though light negation employs the same morpheme as regular sentential negation (*nicht*), its syntactic distribution is shown to be quite different. The sentential negative marker *nicht* in German does not normally precede definite descriptions, indefinites, or disjunctions: definite descriptions generally scramble across *nicht,* the combination of *nicht* and indefinites results in a form of *kein* plus noun, and the equivalent of disjunction under the scope of negation is expressed in terms of a negative disjunction (*weder. . . noch* 'neither . . . nor'). However, under certain circumstances *nicht* can appear preceding definite descriptions, indefinites, and disjunctions, and this is what the authors call *light negation.* Its distribution is discussed in detail in the chapter. It can be found in negative polar questions, in the antecedent of conditionals, in the scope of negative quantifiers, and in the scope of the German equivalent of *surprised.* This distribution leads to the claim that light negation is a kind of negative polarity item (NPI). At the same time, the authors note that light negation can appear in a context that normally does not license NPIs, namely in the main clause of a subjunctive conditional if the antecedent is interpreted counterfactually, for example, in *If Fritz were stupid, he wouldn't have answered question 3,* on the interpretation that Fritz answered question 3 and he is not stupid. Finally, the authors also show that light negation appears as an instance of expletive negation in combination with *bevor* 'before.'

Regarding the semantic properties of light negation, the authors carefully show that it takes scope over the entire clause in which it surfaces but immediately under its licenser (under the assumption that light negation is an NPI). Moreover, the licenser must be of the antiadditive kind. Since light negation appears both as a contentful negation and as an expletive negation, which seemingly makes no semantic contribution, no unified semantic characterization is said to be possible. It is further shown that, unlike regular negation, light negation is not an antilicenser for positive polarity items in its scope. This observation leads to another important concern of the paper, that of the analysis of rescuing. Instances of rescuing are cases like those in (5): here, the PPI *some* is interpreted in the scope of negation, and this is somehow made possible by the presence of the NPI licensers *no one* and *surprised:*

(5) a. There is no one here who didn't find some typos.

　　b. I am surprised they didn't find some typos.

Two possible accounts of rescuing are considered. Both assume that rescuing involves the licensing of an NPI. Where they differ is with respect to what this NPI is. On one view, inspired by observations in Ladusaw (1979), the negation itself is the NPI. On the other view, recently advocated in work by Anna Szabolcsi, the NPI is a "derived" one, consisting of the combination of *n't* and *some* in (5a), for instance. The authors argue that the distribution of light negation in German bears on this issue, favoring the first approach.

　　Henriëtte de Swart's "Marking and Interpretation of Negation: A Bidirectional Optimality Theory Approach" analyzes negative indefinites, a term that includes, for instance, English *nobody,* French *personne,* Polish *nikt,* and Spanish *nadie.* Building on earlier work in collaboration with Ivan Sag (de Swart and Sag 2002), de Swart regards negative indefinites as inherently negative, that is, as negative quantifiers. In order to account for negative concord, she assumes that multiple occurrences of negative indefinites do not necessarily result in the same number of semantic negative indefinites or negative quantifiers; although this is a possibility ("iteration"), it is also possible to interpret multiple occurrences of negative indefinites by "resumptive" quantification. This amounts to saying that *No x, No y, No z R(x, y, z)* is interpreted as *No x, y, z R(x, y, z).* Building on de Swart and Sag (2002), this chapter aims to account for the crosslinguistic variation in the distribution and interpretation of negative indefinites by using the tools of Optimality Theory (OT). To this end, de Swart proposes a series of often functionally motivated constraints that are argued to be ordered differently in different languages. These constraints are used both to generate the relevant structures and to interpret them.

　　A central constraint is FaithNeg, which requires that the nonaffirmative nature of the input is reflected in the output. This constraint is ranked the highest across languages. In particular, it is always ranked higher than *Neg, which demands avoiding negation in the output. A third important constraint is MaxNeg—mark the arguments of a negative chain. If *Neg is ranked higher than MaxNeg, the optimal way to express a meaning of the sort 'it is not the case that somebody saw anything' is in terms of indefinites under negation. The reverse order (MaxNeg higher than *Neg) results in the opposite: the optimal output to express the desired meaning being a series of negative indefinites. To account for the possibilities of interpretation of a series of negative indefinites, a further constraint is introduced, namely IntNeg, according to which every negative expression in the input form is interpreted as contributing a semantic negation in the output. If *Neg, which also has a semantic application, is ranked higher than IntNeg, then a sequence of multiple negative expressions leads to a single negation in the semantics. The opposite order forces a double negation interpretation.

Since the constraints are ordered relative to individual languages, one would expect that in a given language, either negative indefinites are interpreted as giving rise to negative concord or they are interpreted as giving rise to multiple negations. As de Swart observes, however, the facts are more complex: as the relevant literature makes clear, there are various patterns across languages that would seem like "mixed" cases. One such mixed case arises when a preverbal negative indefinite gives rise to ambiguity. For instance, a sentence like *personne n'est le fils de personne* in French is ambiguous between 'no one is the son of anyone' or 'everyone is the son of someone.' Apart from ambiguities of negative indefinites, another mixed case that seems to pose a challenge to an OT perspective is given by languages where preverbal negative indefinites are said to differ from postverbal ones in that the preverbal ones do not give rise to negative concord, but the postverbal ones do (e.g., Italian, Spanish, or Portuguese; New Testament Greek; and older varieties of several Slavic languages). De Swart resolves the problems posed by mixed cases in two ways. The ambiguity of the preverbal negative indefinites is argued to stem from an overlap between the range of two constraints, meaning that in some contexts their order can be reversed. As for the asymmetric distribution of negative indefinites in languages like Italian, it is attributed to the workings of a highly ranked constraint that requires that some negative element (be it a negative indefinite or a sentential negation) appear preverbally. Why do these languages differ from languages that require preverbal negative indefinites to co-occur with a sentential negation (e.g., modern Slavic languages, Greek)? De Swart suggests that in strict negative-concord languages there is a constraint, MaxSN, that requires that a negative clause must contain an overt marker of sentential negation. This constraint is similar to but not identical with NegFirst, which requires that a marker of sentential negation occur in preverbal position; this is clearly shown by Afrikaans, which has an overt marker in sentential negation that occurs postverbally, thus satisfying MaxSN but not NegFirst. De Swart's contribution raises the standard for approaches to negation and negative concord in that it aims to explain fine-grained variation that has not been accounted for in other theories.

2.3 Tense and Aspect

Alice ter Meulen's chapter, "Cohesion in Temporal Context: Aspectual Adverbs as Dynamic Indexicals," discusses the role of aspectual elements, in particular the adverbials *not yet, still, already,* and *not anymore,* in dynamic semantics. According to ter Meulen, the goal of dynamic semantics is to integrate a theory of sentence content with accounts of the complex structuring of information in discourse and in reasoning. This is a broad and sophisticated perspective on the role of dynamic interpretation, and she shows that aspectual information has a complex and subtle role to play.

The basic meanings of the adverbials can be captured in a simple static semantics. For example, as ter Meulen puts it, *John is already asleep* means that John has fallen asleep in the past and been asleep since. She then discusses two different ways in which this basic meaning can be made more complex as it is integrated into dynamic semantics. The first way is that it can be modified, in English through the use of prosody, to indicate "the speaker's attitude regarding the flow of events or its perceived speed." (Other languages may use different mechanisms, as ter Meulen points out.) For example, *John is alREADY asleep* can indicate that the speaker didn't expect John to be asleep yet. The second way in which the basic meanings of the aspectual adverbials can be modified as they are integrated into dynamic semantics concerns the partitioning of the information they convey into asserted and presupposed components. For example, *John is still asleep* presupposes that he was asleep and asserts that he is now asleep. This division into presupposed and asserted information allows an explanation of the patterns found in question-answer sequences like the following:

(6) a. A: Was John *still* asleep when Mary arrived?

    b. B: No, he was *not* asleep *anymore.*

    c. B: *No, he was *already* asleep.

    d. B: No, he had *not* (even) fallen asleep *yet.*

Because *not anymore* in (6b) asserts an answer to (6a), and otherwise presupposes the same things (6a) does, it is a simple coherent answer. The incoherence of (6c) is due to the fact that *already* fails to match the partitioning induced by *still,* because *still* is basically about the end point of an event while *already* is about its initiation. (6d) shows that marked constructions are able to bring presupposed information into the foreground in such a way that it can be denied. This reasoning is represented in an explicit and formal way in the chapter.

This chapter also discusses the contrast between the perfect and past in asserting presupposed information. It is typically possible to use a sentence in the perfect to assert what is presupposed, but this is not possible with the past:

(7) a. John was already asleep. He had fallen asleep.

    b. ??John was already asleep. He fell asleep (again).

Ter Meulen takes this contrast to be due to a difference in how the two tenses affect the reference time. This contrast presents another example of how important semantic contrasts only come to the fore when aspectual elements are viewed in a dynamic setting.

In "Tense, Adverbials, and Quantification," Toshiyuki Ogihara studies the interaction of tense and quantified temporal PPs such as *during every meeting* and *on a Sunday.* Examples like (8) pose a problem for compositional semantics:

(8) John cried during every meeting.

In (8), the adverbial has scope over *John cried,* but the past tense of *John cried* seems to restrict the interpretation of *every meeting* in such a way that it only quantifies over past meetings. Ogihara's solution is to say that the temporal anteriority of a past tense sentence is not contributed by its tense; rather, tense reflects the presence of a (covert or overt) higher temporal adverbial. In the case of (8), *during every meeting* is actually represented at LF as *during every meeting in the past,* and the past tense has no direct effect on the interpretation. This idea is similar to that of Vlach (1993) and can be connected to other literature such as Carlson and Spejewski (1997).

Ogihara's chapter lays out in a very clear way some of the important lessons of thirty years of work on temporal semantics. In particular, he reviews arguments that show that tensed sentences do involve existential quantification over times, but that this quantification does not come from the tense itself. The quantification can be seen as coming from a covert or overt adverbial (Bäuerle and von Stechow 1980) or existential closure (Stump 1985, improving on Dowty 1979). Ogihara adopts Bäuerle and von Stechow's approach.

Ogihara argues against one intuitively appealing way of dissolving the problem posed by (8), namely the possibility that the set of meetings being quantified over is limited to past meetings by pragmatic contextual restriction such as that which occurs in every quantified sentence (the familiar fact that *everybody arrived on time* doesn't quantify over everyone in the world). Such an approach incorrectly predicts that example (9) (Ogihara's [19]) can describe a situation in which not every meeting was past. For example, (9) cannot be used to describe the situation in (10), because meeting 3 is still in the future.

(9) Mary kissed John before every meeting.

(10)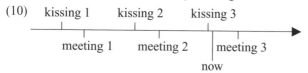

(Interestingly, one could utter the present perfect sentence *Now Mary has kissed John before every meeting* at the time indicated by *now.*)

Pratt and Francez (2001) have presented a successful analysis of the phenomenon in (8). They include a temporal context variable *during I* in the interpretation of every temporally dependent expression, including temporal adverbials and tensed clauses. The temporal context variable of the widest-scope temporal expression is linked to the reference time, and this allows the pastness of (8) to affect the wide-scope adverbial's interpretation. Ogihara reviews their account and then criticizes it on conceptual grounds. He then goes on to present his own account; Ogihara's analysis is based on the earlier insights of Bäuerle and von Stechow, as mentioned above, but adds to it by attributing not only the existential quantification of past tense sentences to a wide-scope adverbial, but also the temporal anteriority itself. This means that the anteriority will be introduced into the semantics in such a way that any expressions that need to be dependent on it can be. Ogihara's analysis of tense and temporal adverbials, in particular his idea that tense itself plays an indirect role while the adverbials play a more major role, is likely to be extremely fruitful in future work on temporal semantics.

ACKNOWLEDGMENTS

We are very grateful to the following Georgetown University institutions for providing funds towards the conference and for their overall support that made it possible, fruitful, and pleasant: the Graduate School, the College of Arts and Sciences, the Faculty of Languages and Linguistics, the Department of Linguistics, the Department of Spanish and Portuguese, and the Center for the Brain Bases of Cognition. We would also like to extend a most sincere thank you to the graduate assistants who worked on the planning of the conference: Corinne Brandstetter, Amy Pogoriler, and Jennifer Spears. We are particularly grateful to Corinne, who participated in every stage of the planning and running of the conference; for her willingness to take on a great share of the responsibility and the burden of decision making; and for the patience, grace, and generosity she maintained through many, many hours of work. Finally, we are deeply indebted to Michael Diercks, who served as our graduate assistant in the production of this volume; we very much admire the thoroughness, carefulness, and patience with which he prepared the manuscript for publication. We are delighted to be able to deliver to Georgetown University Press a manuscript that is of high quality not only in content but also in form.

REFERENCES

Bäuerle, R., and A. von Stechow. 1980. Finite and non-finite temporal constructions in German. In *Time, tense, and quantifiers,* ed. C. Rohrer, 375–421. Tübingen, Germany: Niemeyer.

Carlson, G., and B. Spejewski. 1997. Generic passages. *Natural Language Semantics* 5: 101–65.

Dikken, M. den. 2002. Direct and parasitic polarity item licensing. *Journal of Comparative Germanic Linguistics* 5:35–66.

Dowty, D. 1979. *Word meaning and Montague grammar: The semantics of verbs and times in generative semantics and in Montague's PTQ.* Dordrecht: D. Reidel.

Ginzburg, J. and I. A. Sag. 2000. *Interrogative investigations.* Stanford, CA: CSLI.

Hooper, J., and S. Thompson. 1973. On the applicability of root transformations. *Linguistic Inquiry* 4: 465–97.

Horn, L. 1996. Flaubert triggers, squatitive negation, and other quirks of grammar. *Tabu* 26. Repr. in *Perspectives on negation and polarity items,* ed. J. Hoeksema, H. Rullman, V. Sanchez-Valencia, and T. van der Wouden, 173–200. Amsterdam: John Benjamins, 2001.

Ladusaw, W. A. 1979. *Polarity sensitivity as inherent scope relations.* PhD diss., University of Texas at Austin.

Pratt, J., and N. Francez. 2001. Temporal generalized quantifiers. *Linguistics and Philosophy* 24: 187–222.

Rizzi, L. 1997. The fine structure of the left periphery. In *Elements of Grammar,* ed. L. Haegeman, 281–337. Dordrecht: Kluwer.

Stump, G. 1985. *The semantic variability of absolute constructions.* Dordrecht: D. Reidel.

Swart, H. de and I. Sag 2002. Negation and negative concord in Romance. *Linguistics and Philosophy* 25: 373–417.

Vlach, Frank. 1993. Temporal adverbials, tenses and the perfect. *Linguistics and Philosophy* 16: 231–83.

1

Three Benchmarks for Distributional Approaches to Natural Language Syntax

COLIN PHILLIPS
University of Maryland, College Park

1. Complexity

There has been a good deal of recent interest in statistical learning models for language (Manning and Schütze 1999) and in evidence that humans can learn and use at least some distributional statistics (MacDonald, Pearlmutter, and Seidenberg 1994; Saffran, Aslin, and Newport 1996). Although it has been shown that there are some quite simple statistical patterns that humans are not good at tracking (Newport and Aslin 2004; Pena et al. 2002), there appears to be widespread optimism in some circles that discovery of the right statistical learning procedure will ultimately provide an adequate account of human linguistic abilities and obviate the need for the richly structured representations widely assumed in the linguistics tradition.

Rather than discussing the successes and limitations of current statistical models of language, the goal of this chapter is to draw attention to problems that will remain even if it is possible to construct an "ideal" learner of surface distributional facts. These problems can be divided into three types of challenges, each of which is likely to encompass a large variety of linguistic phenomena. *Complexity* refers to the fact that human linguistic abilities extend far beyond what one finds in the corpora that appear to be the standard benchmarks for current statistical learning models. Speakers are able to make fine-grained judgments about sentence structures that they have encountered rarely or never at all before. I will not discuss specific examples of the complexity of human syntactic abilities in this section, since the cases discussed in sections 2 and 3 already serve this role. *Consistency,* discussed in section 2, refers to the contribution of linguistic typology. Crosslinguistic variation is surprisingly limited, particularly when one looks beyond the simplest and most frequent phenomena, and it is unclear how powerful statistical learning models can explain this consistency or the evidence for early emergence of universal constraints in language development. *Causality,* discussed in section 3, refers to the fact that humans appear to be very sensitive not only to the fact that a reliable statistical co-occurrence obtains, but also to why it obtains.

2. Consistency

Linguists tend to be impressed by the consistency of crosslinguistic variation. Many properties or constraints appear to hold in all languages, and other sets of properties show consistent covariation across languages (e.g., if a language has property X it also has property Y). Human languages seem to carve out just a small part of the space of conceivable languages. If this crosslinguistic consistency is matched by consistency in surface distributional phenomena, then it may be possible to develop a learning model that relies on surface statistics. However, if crosslinguistic consistency occurs in the face of very diverse surface distributions, then it is more likely that the consistency reflects constraints that are built into the learner (whether these are language-specific constraints or general cognitive constraints—my current arguments do not distinguish between these alternatives). Therefore, it is important to determine whether crosslinguistic consistency is matched by consistent surface statistics, and whether children's learning of constraints is better predicted by the consistency of their surface patterns or by the consistency of their crosslinguistic variation.

2.1 Backward Anaphora

A pronoun stereotypically appears in a context where it is preceded in discourse by a full NP that serves as its antecedent. There are also fully natural cases where the pronoun precedes its antecedent, known as *backward anaphora,* as in (1a), where coreference is indicated by coindexation. However, there are specific environments where backward anaphora is ruled out, as in (1b). A standard account of the impossibility of (1b) is that the pronoun c-commands its antecedent, in violation of Condition C of the Binding Theory (Chomsky 1981).[1]

    (1) a. While he$_i$ was eating an apple, John$_i$ read a book.

       b. *He$_i$ ate an apple while John$_i$ was reading a book.

    This constraint is very real and can be demonstrated without reliance on conscious grammaticality judgments. For example, we have recently shown that Condition C applies immediately in language processing, using a series of self-paced reading studies (Kazanina et al. 2005). When the gender of the second subject NP *John* is manipulated in sentences like (1), such that it mismatches the gender of the pronoun (e.g., . . . *he* . . . *Mary* . . .), there is an immediate slowdown in reading times at the mismatching NP in sentences like (1a), suggesting that speakers expect to find an antecedent for the pronoun in that position, as previously shown by van Gompel and Liversedge (2003). However, the same speakers show no similar gender mismatch effect at the corresponding NP in examples like (1b), which suggests that the NP is not even considered as a potential antecedent, as expected if Condition C acts as an immediate filter on structure building.

    In language development studies, Condition C appears to be active as early as it is possible to test children. English-speaking three-year-olds allow coreference in sentences like (1a) but not in sentences like (1b) (Crain and McKee 1985). In addition, Condition C is a good candidate for a crosslinguistic universal, appearing in languages as diverse as English, where the surface facts are relatively straightforward, and Mohawk, where the facts of free word order and liberal argument omission make the effects of Condition C rather more difficult to detect (Baker 1991).

Many linguists are impressed by the correspondence between the early emergence of Condition C in development and the fact that its crosslinguistic distribution is more consistent than its surface realization across languages, and they conclude from this that it is a constraint that need not be learned. An alternative possibility is that future advances in statistical learning tools might someday succeed in deriving the contrast between (1a) and (1b) from the input available to two-year-olds and will also succeed in deriving similar contrasts in Mohawk and other languages. Since universals of language have no privileged status for this putative learner, we can suppose that it would be sophisticated enough to also rapidly learn constraints on backward anaphora that are very similar to Condition C but not universal. Russian provides an interesting case that we have investigated in a project led by Nina Kazanina. Russian has similar word order properties to English, and like English, it disallows coreference in Condition C contexts (2b), but unlike English, it also disallows coreference in (2a), which is the counterpart of (1a). There is no across-the-board ban on backwards anaphora in Russian (Avrutin and Reuland 2002; Kazanina and Phillips 2001).

(2) a. *Poka on$_i$ chital   knigu,   Pooh$_i$ s'el   yabloko.
     while he was reading.IMP the book Pooh ate.PERF the apple

    b. *On$_i$ s'el   yabloko, poka Pooh$_i$ chital   knigu.
     he   ate.PERF the apple while Pooh was reading.IMP the book

In a truth-value judgment task study with Russian three- to six-year-olds (Kazanina and Phillips 2001), similar to that conducted previously in English, we found that five- to six-year-olds reliably respect both the universal constraint (100 percent) and the language particular constraint on backwards anaphora (78 percent), just like Russian adults. More interestingly, the Russian three-year-olds gave judgments that were almost identical to those of their English-speaking contemporaries. They consistently disallowed coreference in (2b) (85 percent), as required by Condition C, but they consistently allowed coreference in (2a) (13 percent), in violation of the Russian-specific constraint. Four-year-olds gave a mixed pattern of judgments.

The substantial developmental delay between mastery of Condition C and the Russian-specific constraint is not surprising in an approach where universals need not be learned but language specific constraints clearly must be. The developmental delay is rather more surprising if the two similar constraints must be learned by the same sophisticated statistical mechanism. There are no viable current proposals about how Condition C effects might be inferred from the input to learners by age three, but if such an account were found, it would run the risk of predicting that Russian children would also master the Russian-specific constraint at a similar age.

2.2 Verb Argument Structure

It is well known that verbs with similar meanings have similar syntactic properties (argument structure). Children and adults are able to use knowledge about these links between syntax and semantics to infer information about novel verbs (Gillette et al. 1999; Gropen et al. 1991). Importantly, detailed studies of English show that the syntactic classification of verbs follows very specific semantic parameters, such as transfer of possession, manner of motion, or change of state (Levin 1993), rather than general notions of semantic similarity. While some have suggested that the specificity of these semantic parameters reflects built-in biases in the learner (Pinker 1989), others have argued that these generalizations can be learned from surface statistics (Seidenberg 1997), and that the existence of crosslinguistic variation makes this necessary. In a project led by Meesook Kim, we tested these ideas using a detailed survey of the syntax of locative verbs, such as *pour, fill,* and *load,* in twenty languages (Kim 1999; Kim, Landau, and Phillips 1999; Phillips, Rabbin, and Kim 2001). We found that there is indeed crosslinguistic variation but that it is restricted and rather systematic. More importantly, languages appear to consistently group verbs along the same semantic parameters.

For example, change-of-state verbs like *fill, cover,* and *decorate* in English disallow the "figure" frame (3a), but allow the "ground" frame (3b). Many languages treat these verbs in the same way that English does, but in many other languages (e.g., Japanese, Turkish, Luganda, Hindi, Thai), these verbs are alternators, allowing both of the constructions in (3). Although these languages diverge from English in their more liberal treatment of the *fill* class, we have found no languages that diverge from English in their treatment of the *pour* class, the members of which encode manner-of-motion meanings (e.g., *spill, drip, shake*) and allow only the figure frame (4). Thus, the association between manner-of-motion verbs and the figure frame appears to be a universal.[2] Furthermore, those languages that allow change-of-state verbs in the *fill* class to alternate are all languages that allow verb compounding (serialization) and null objects, whereas none of the English-type languages allow these. Thus, variation in this verb class is quite systematic and appears to reflect what linguists call a *parameter,* that is, a set of properties that consistently co-occur across languages (Baker 2001).

(3) a. *He filled water into the glass.

   b. He filled the glass with water.

(4) a. He poured water into the glass.

   b. *He poured the glass with water.

Furthermore, we have often found that distinctions among verb classes that seem to disappear in the most common surface verb phrase forms sometimes reemerge in more obscure corners of the grammars of individual languages. To take just one example, verbs like *pile, scatter,* and *load* are alternators in English, allowing either the figure or the ground frame (5).

(5) a. He piled the books onto the shelf.

   b. He piled the shelf with books.

In Korean, the counterpart of (5b) is unavailable, and thus the distinction between the *pour* class and the *pile* class appears to be lost. However, the distinction reemerges in Korean verb-compounding constructions. When Korean verbs from the *pile* class are compounded with *put* to form compounds such as *pile-put,* both figure and ground frames become available. Note that neither *pile* nor *put* allows the ground frame when the verb is used alone. Meanwhile, compounds involving verbs from the *pour* class, for example, *pour-put,* do not allow alternation (Kim 1999). In other words, compounding recreates exactly the same distinction seen in English between the *pour* class and the *pile* class. We have found other instances in which a language appeared at first sight to conflate a verb class distinction found in English but turned out to preserve the distinction in constructions that we had good reason to believe are not frequent in the input to learners.

The fact that languages consistently classify verbs using the same semantic parameters, even when this is obscured in the frequently occurring constructions of the language, suggests that something other than classification based on surface statistics is at work. The crosslinguistic regularities observed in our survey are expected under an approach that views syntax-semantics links in argument structure as reflections of fixed constraints on language learners. On the other hand, under the view where verb classes reflect distributional analyses of frequently occurring surface forms in individual languages, the crosslinguistic consistency is more surprising.

3. Causality

A dependency between two elements in a structure may be viewed in purely statistical terms, encoding the fact that the two elements reliably co-occur. Let us assume for the sake of discussion that statistical models are good at extracting such regularities and can readily make use of observations of the form "after an X occurs, a Y is sure to follow (at some point) thereafter." However, structural dependencies are generally much more than statistical regularities. Most reliable co-occurrences exist for a reason, and a number of results indicate that speakers are very sensitive to the causes of structural regularities. A statistical model that is able to extract regular co-occurrences but is not able to encode the causes of the regularities will miss important generalizations.

3.1 Wh-*Questions*

Wh-dependencies are the most widely investigated type of unbounded linguistic dependency. The head of the dependency is a fronted *wh*-phrase, and the tail of the dependency is a gap in an argument position in some models (Gibson and Hickok 1993; Haegeman 1994) or a predicate that selects the fronted phrase in other models (Pickering and Barry 1991; Sag and Fodor 1994). For ease of exposition, I will adopt the terminology of gap-based approaches here. It is likely that in English and other languages, most naturally occurring *wh*-dependencies span just a single clause, for the simple reason that most questions contain only one clause. A well-known generalization about the processing of English *wh*-questions is that after encountering a fronted *wh*-phrase, speakers actively attempt to construct a gap in the first available position without waiting for confirmation that the position is available. This is shown by the occurrence of a processing disruption when speakers encounter an overt NP in a position where a gap may have been anticipated, highlighted in (6) (Crain and Fodor 1985; Stowe 1986). In other words, it appears that speakers try to construct short *wh*-dependencies.

(6) My brother wanted to know who Ruth will bring **us** home to _____ at Christmas.

The preference for shorter *wh*-dependencies could be explained in a number of ways. It may reflect a specialized subroutine of the parser that favors short dependencies (Frazier and Clifton 1989), or it may reflect statistical biases accrued from large amounts of experience with short dependencies. Alternatively, it may reflect the more abstract property that in English a short *wh*-dependency allows the *wh*-phrase to receive a thematic role and enter into compositional semantic interpretation more quickly (Pritchett 1992). This last alternative specifically makes reference to the cause of the gap in a *wh*-dependency: the gap marks the thematic position of the *wh*-phrase and allows it to enter into compositional interpretation with the verb.

In a project led by Sachiko Aoshima, we have found that the online processing of Japanese *wh*-fronting constructions looks strikingly different from English when viewed in terms of surface structures, but it looks very similar to English when viewed in terms of the cause of *wh*-dependency formation. Japanese *wh*-phrases canonically appear in situ in argument positions, but fronting of *wh*-phrases is also possible, in a process known as *wh-scrambling.* Short-distance scrambling creates a dependency that spans just one clause; long-distance scrambling creates a dependency that spans multiple clauses, as in a sentence like (7). In (7) the fronted dative *wh*-phrase is an argument of the embedded verb *ageta* 'gave.' The fact that the *wh*-phrase occurs in sentence-initial position does not mark the sentence as a direct question, as would be the case in English. Rather, the presence of the question particle *-ka* on the embedded verb marks the sentence as an indirect question.

(7) Dare-ni   John-wa [Mary-ga _____ sono hon-o   ageta-ka] itta.

whom-DAT John-TOP Mary-nom ____gap that book-ACC gave-Q   said

'John said who Mary gave that book to.'

In a series of four different experiments using Japanese biclausal sentences with a fronted *wh*-phrase, we have found that Japanese speakers show a consistent bias for the long-distance scrambling construal of the fronted phrase (8) (Aoshima, Phillips, and Weinberg 2004; Yoshida, Aoshima, and Phillips 2005). Furthermore, our experiments show that this is not simply a consequence of the need to satisfy argument structure requirements of the embedded verb, as might be argued based on examples like (7). The same bias was found to be present in a comprehension task where the embedded verb does not require a dative argument, and also in a generation task where the participants were left to generate the embedded verb for themselves. Furthermore, online reading time profiles suggest that a gap is posited in the embedded clause before any verb is encountered.

(8) *wh*-DAT NP-NOM ____potential main clause gap site [NP-NOM ____preferred gap site · · · V] . . . V

The bias for long-distance scrambling is unexpected under an account that incorporates a specific principle favoring gaps that are close to their antecedents. It is

highly unlikely that the bias for long-distance scrambling reflects a predominance of long-distance scrambling in corpora of Japanese questions, although we have not specifically checked this statistic. The relevant configurations are quite rare in naturally occurring Japanese. However, the bias is expected under an approach that takes into account the syntactic and semantic motivation for completing a *wh*-dependency. The strongly verb-final property of Japanese means that a gap in the embedded clause provides the first opportunity for grammatical constraint satisfaction and compositional interpretation of the fronted phrase. Thus, there is good reason to posit a gap in the embedded clause where possible in Japanese. Under this approach, the same mechanism can account for generalizations in English and Japanese that appear quite different on the surface.

Although a statistical model that simply tracks surface co-occurrence probabilities is unlikely to capture the Japanese generalization (however sophisticated its learning algorithm might be), this does not mean that there is no role for a statistical model that uses sufficiently rich representations. It is probably true that in the majority of Japanese *wh*-questions, the grammatical requirements of the *wh*-phrase are satisfied at the first available opportunity, either because the question contains just one clause or because the *wh*-phrase appears in situ in an embedded clause. A model that can abstract the motivation for *wh*-dependency formation in this way may be able to appropriately generalize to our findings about long-distance scrambling. On the other hand, a model that simply registers the frequent occurrence of local *wh*-dependencies will wrongly predict a bias for local scrambling. Furthermore, a model that attempts to explain our findings by ignoring the structural configurations of Japanese and blindly linking a sentence-initial *wh*-phrase with the first verb will also fail. The bias for long-distance scrambling is absent in configurations where Japanese grammar blocks long-distance scrambling, such as when the *wh*-phrase bears nominative case (Miyamoto and Takahashi 2003) or when the embedded clause is a relative clause (Yoshida, Aoshima, and Phillips 2005).

3.2 Tense

Linguistic dependencies give rise to situations where the occurrence of one element reliably predicts the subsequent appearance of another related element, often many words later in the sentence. Many statistical models are rather good at picking out such regularities; we will assume for the sake of discussion that there will be statistical models that are able to pick out any reliable co-occurrence. However, models that detect reliable co-occurrence do not typically encode why certain elements co-occur. In contrast, this is something that humans are quite good at. A recent event-related potentials (ERP) study of Hindi sentence processing provides a clear example of this (Nevins, Dillon, Austin, and Phillips 2005). In this study, we were interested in two environments in Hindi that give rise to the same prediction but for different reasons. The goal of the study was to test whether during sentence comprehension speakers carry forward just information about what material is predicted, or whether they also carry forward information about why that prediction was generated.

Like Japanese, Hindi exhibits primarily verb-final word order. This means that prior material in a clause may provide a variety of cues to the form of the verb. We investigated two types of reliable cues for the tense marking on the verb. As in other languages, the occurrence of a past-tense adverbial in Hindi, such as *last week,* reliably predicts a past-tense verb. This is a semantic cue. In addition, in transitive past-tense clauses, the case marking on the subject NP serves as a predictor of past tense. Hindi has a split-ergative case system, in which present and future tenses are associated with nominative-accusative case marking, but past (perfective) tense is associated with ergative-absolutive case marking. Therefore, the appearance of ergative case on a subject NP is a reliable predictor of past tense. This is a syntactic cue. The statistical properties of both dependencies appear to be the same. Adverbials and ergative case both reliably predict an upcoming past-tense verb, and neither the adverbial nor the ergative case is necessary in a past-tense clause. However, when speakers are presented with sentences containing tense violations, in which a past-tense verb is substituted with a future tense verb, the ERP responses differ markedly, depending on whether the past tense was predicted by a semantic cue (9) or by a syntactic cue (10). Sentences were presented visually using Devanagari script in a rapid serial visual presentation (RSVP) paradigm (600 ms/word). ERPs were recorded from thirty scalp electrodes in twenty native speakers of Hindi. Violations of a syntactically cued past tense elicited a large P600 response, which is characteristic of syntactic violations (Hagoort, Brown, and Osterhout 1999). In contrast, violations of a semantically cued past tense elicited a much weaker P600 response and a significant N400 response, which is characteristic of semanatic violations (Kutas and Federmeier 2000; Kutas and Hillyard 1980).

(9) Haalanki pichle shaam vo   rahgiir   pathaar ke-upar giraa/   giregaa,
     although last   night that traveler-ABS stone   upon   fall-PST/ fall-FUT
     lekin use   choT   nahiin aayii
     but   to-him injuries not   happen
     'Although last night that traveler fell upon a stone, he was not injured.'

(10) Haalanki us   bunkar-ne   ek baRaa sveTar jaldi   bunaa/
     although that weaver-ERG one big   sweater quickly weave-PST/
     bunegaa   lekin graahak-ne   sabhii-ki kimaat ek-hi dii
     weave-FUT but   customer-ERG all-of   prices same gave
     'Although that weaver wove one big sweater quickly, the customer paid the same for all of them.'

Previous ERP studies of English have shown that locally cued violations involving tense-aspect morphology elicit a P600 response (e.g., *was eat;* Allen, Badecker, and Osterhout 2003), and there have been numerous studies that have contrasted N400 and P600 responses associated with semantic and syntactic violations, respectively (e.g., Friederici, Pfeifer, and Hahne 1993; Hagoort 2003; Neville et al. 1991). What is unusual about the Hindi study is the fact that the content of the violation is identical in both conditions, and that other potentially interfering factors are matched (e.g., distance from predictor to predicted, number of referents). Thus, the results suggest that Hindi speakers encode not only what they are predicting as they process a sentence but also why they are predicting it.

The challenge that the Hindi results present is similar to the challenge provided by the example from Japanese *wh*-fronting. They show that a model that accurately captures the surface statistics of Hindi sentences will still fall short as a model of how speakers process sentences. On the other hand, a model that incorporates more abstract representations and that can therefore encode the causes of structural dependencies may be able to attain far greater success using simpler statistics.[3]

4. Conclusion

Any model of language that aspires to account for human abilities rather than simply to solve an engineering task needs to take seriously the full range of human language abilities, many of which are not apparent in everyday speaking and writing. Although corpora can provide a reasonable first approximation to the training data available to the human learner, the ability to parse similar corpora is a rather poor criterion for a model of the end state of language learning.

There are a number of reasons why the full complexities of human language may tend to be overlooked in current statistical models. In part, this may reflect the attraction of the objectivity of corpus-based benchmarks, such as the Penn Treebank, which allow for simple quantitative scoring of competing models. Another factor may be that there is skepticism about the reality of the complex phenomena that linguists describe. Finally, part of the problem may be that linguists and psycholinguists tend to focus on knowledge of constraints, which describe what a speaker cannot do. It is easy to assess whether a model successfully parses an individual sentence but much harder to assess whether a model captures the effects of a constraint, since this requires detailed analysis of what structures the model systematically avoids building. However, none of these can justify ignoring the richness of natural language syntax. The complexities described by linguists are very real, and speakers' knowledge of constraints on language involves much more than just surface co-occurrence patterns, as the studies described above show.

In presenting the challenges offered by complexity, consistency, and causality, my goal is not to argue that statistics play no role in models of language learning, nor is it my goal to argue against the use of objective benchmarks for testing of models. The point is that the objective benchmarks that are used need to more accurately represent the scope and complexity of human language abilities, and that models are unlikely to succeed on stronger tests of this kind unless their designers are willing to incorporate richer representations. ▪

ACKNOWLEDGMENTS
This chapter is based upon a talk originally presented at the Workshop on Syntax, Semantics, and Statistics at the Neural Information Processing Systems meeting in Whistler, British Columbia, in December 2003, and I thank the editors of this volume for allowing me to include it here. This work was supported in part by grants from NSF, #BCS-0196004; the Human Frontier Science Program, #RGY-0134; the McDonnell-Pew Cognitive Neuroscience Program, #99-31; and the University of Maryland General Research Board. Thanks to Sachiko Aoshima, Brian Dillon, Nina Kazanina, Meesook Kim, Barbara Landau, Ellen Lau, Moti Lieberman, Andrew Nevins, Beth Rabbin, Amy Weinberg, and Masaya Yoshida for their major contributions to the studies described here, and thanks to Raffaella Zanuttini and Héctor Campos for comments on an earlier draft.

NOTES

1. There are examples that appear to violate this generalization, e.g., *He$_i$ then did what John$_i$ always did in such situations*. . . . Discussion of such cases goes back more than twenty years (Evans 1982; Reinhart 1983), and it is generally understood that they involve situations where multiple mental representations or "guises" of the same individual are being compared, indicating that the constraint really applies to reference in a mental model and not to objects in the world. Minimally different examples still disallow coreference, e.g., **He$_i$ did what John$_i$ had done half an hour earlier*. . . .

2. Some languages do allow the equivalent of (4b), for example, German and Russian. However, when they allow this, they use different verb roots for (4a) and (4b); for example, for 'pour', German uses *giessen* in (4a) but *begiessen* in (4b).

3. Note that there have been attempts to capture the difference between syntactic ungrammaticality and semantic anomaly in the literature on simple recurrent backpropagation networks (e.g., Allen and Seidenberg 1999). However, such efforts rely on the assumption that syntactic and semantic violations will have different contents, an assumption that is contradicted by the Hindi examples.

REFERENCES

Allen, J., and M. Seidenberg. 1999. The emergence of grammaticality in connectionist networks. In *Emergentist approaches to language,* ed. B. MacWhinney, 115–51. Mahwah, NJ: Erlbaum.

Allen, M., W. Badecker, and L. Osterhout. 2003. Morphological analysis in sentence processing: An ERP study. *Language and Cognitive Processes* 18: 405–30.

Aoshima, S., C. Phillips, and A. Weinberg. 2004. Processing filler-gap dependencies in a head-final language. *Journal of Memory and Language* 51: 23–54.

Avrutin, S., and E. Reuland. 2002. Backward anaphora and tense interpretation. Unpublished manuscript, Utrecht University.

Baker, M. 1991. On some subject-object non-asymmetries in Mohawk. *Natural Language and Linguistic Theory* 9: 537–76.

Baker, M. 2001. *The atoms of language.* New York: Basic Books.

Chomsky, N. 1981. *Lectures on government and binding.* Dordrecht: Foris.

Crain, S., and J. D. Fodor. 1985. How can grammars help parsers? In *Natural language parsing: Psycholinguistic, computational, and theoretical perspectives,* ed. D. Dowty, L. Kartunnen, and A. M. Zwicky, 94–128. Cambridge: Cambridge University Press.

Crain, S., and C. McKee. 1985. The acquisition of structural restrictions on anaphora. In *Proceedings of NELS 15,* ed. S. Berman, J. Choe, and J. McDonough, 94–110. Amherst, MA: GLSA, University of Massachusetts.

Evans, G. 1982. *The varieties of reference.* Oxford: Oxford University Press.

Frazier, L., and C. Clifton, Jr. 1989. Successive cyclicity in the grammar and the parser. *Language and Cognitive Processes* 4: 93–126.

Friederici, A. D., E. Pfeifer, and A. Hahne. 1993. Event-related brain potentials during natural speech processing: Effects of semantic, morphological, and syntactic violations. *Cognitive Brain Research* 1:183–92.

Gibson, E., and G. Hickok. 1993. Sentence processing with empty categories. *Language and Cognitive Processes* 8: 147–61.

Gillette, J., H. Gleitman, L. Gleitman, and A. Lederer. 1999. Human simulations of vocabulary learning. *Cognition* 73: 135–76.

Gropen, J., S. Pinker, M. Hollander, and R. Goldberg. 1991. Syntax and semantics in the acquisition of locative verbs. *Journal of Child Language* 18: 115–51.

Haegeman, L. 1994. *Introduction to government and binding theory.* 2nd ed. Oxford: Blackwell.

Hagoort, P. 2003. Interplay between syntax and semantics during sentence comprehension: ERP effects of combining syntactic and semantic violations. *Journal of Cognitive Neuroscience* 15: 883–99.

Hagoort, P., C. M. Brown, and L. Osterhout. 1999. The neural architecture of syntactic processing. In *Neurocognition of language,* ed. C. M. Brown and P. Hagoort, 273–316. Oxford: Oxford University Press.

Kazanina, N., E. Lau, M. Lieberman, C. Phillips, and M. Yoshida. 2005. Use of grammatical constraints in the processing of backward anaphora. Manuscript submitted for publication.

Kazanina, N., and C. Phillips. 2001. Coreference in child Russian: Distinguishing syntactic and discourse constraints. In *Proceedings of BUCLD 25,* ed. A. Do, L. Dominguez, and A. Johansen, 413–24. Somerville, MA: Cascadilla Press.

Kim, M. 1999. A cross-linguistic perspective on the acquisition of locative verbs. PhD diss., University of Delaware.

Kim, M., B. Landau, and C. Phillips. 1999. Cross-linguistic differences in children's syntax for locative verbs. In *Proceedings of BUCLD 23,* ed. A. Greenhill, H. Littlefield, and C. Tano, 337–48. Somerville, MA: Cascadilla Press.

Kutas, M., and K. D. Federmeier. 2000. Electrophysiology reveals semantic memory use in language comprehension. *Trends in Cognitive Sciences* 4: 463–70.

Kutas, M., and S. A. Hillyard. 1980. Reading senseless sentences: Brain potentials reflect semantic anomaly. *Science* 207: 203–5.

Levin, B. 1993. *English verb classes and alternations.* Chicago: Univ. of Chicago Press.

MacDonald, M. C., N. J. Pearlmutter, and M. S. Seidenberg. 1994. The lexical nature of syntactic ambiguity resolution. *Psychological Review* 89: 483–506.

Manning, C. D., and H. Schütze. 1999. *Foundations of statistical natural language processing.* Cambridge, MA: MIT Press.

Miyamoto, E. T., and S. Takahashi. 2003. Typing mismatch effects in the processing of wh-phrases in Japanese. Unpublished manuscript, Tsukuba University and Massachusetts Institute of Technology.

Neville, H., J. Nicol, A. Barss, K. I. Forster, and M. I. Garrett. 1991. Syntactically-based sentence processing classes: Evidence from event-related brain potentials. *Journal of Cognitive Neuroscience* 3: 151–65.

Nevins, A., B. Dillon, A. Austin, and C. Phillips. 2005. Syntactic and semantic predictors of tense in Hindi: An ERP study. Manuscript submitted for publication.

Newport, E. L., and R. N. Aslin. 2004. Learning at a distance I: Statistical learning of non-adjacent dependencies. *Cognitive Psychology* 48: 127–62.

Pena, M., L. L. Bonatt, M. Nespor, and J. Mehler. 2002. Signal-driven computations in speech processing. *Science* 298: 604–7.

Phillips, C., B. Rabbin, and M. Kim. 2001. Principles and parameters of locative verb syntax. Paper presented at Mid-Atlantic Verb Meeting, University of Maryland, October 2, 2001.

Pickering, M. J., and G. D. Barry. 1991. Sentence processing without empty categories. *Language and Cognitive Processes* 6: 229–59.

Pinker, S. 1989. *Learnability and cognition: The acquisition of argument structure.* Cambridge, MA: MIT Press.

Pritchett, B. L. 1992. *Grammatical competence and parsing performance.* Chicago: Univ. of Chicago Press.

Reinhart, T. 1983. *Anaphora and semantic interpretation.* London: Croom Helm.

Saffran, J. R., R. N. Aslin, and E. L. Newport. 1996. Statistical learning by 8-month-old infants. *Science* 274: 1926–8.

Sag, I. A., and J. D. Fodor. 1994. Extraction without traces. In *Proceedings of the 13th Annual Meeting of the West Coast Conference on Formal Linguistics,* ed. R. Aranovich, W. Byrne, S. Preuss, and M. Senturia, 365–84. Stanford, CA: CSLI.

Seidenberg, M. 1997. Language acquisition and use: Learning and applying probabilistic constraints. *Science* 275: 1599–1603.

Stowe, L. A. 1986. Parsing *WH*-constructions: Evidence for on-line gap location. *Language and Cognitive Processes* 1: 227–45.

van Gompel, R. P. G., and S. P. Liversedge. 2003. The influence of morphological information on cataphoric pronoun assignment. *Journal of Experimental Psychology: Learning, Memory, and Cognition* 29: 128–39.

Yoshida, M., S. Aoshima, and C. Phillips. 2005. Relative clause prediction in Japanese. Manuscript submitted for publication.

I

Clausal Architecture

2

Argument Fronting in English, Romance CLLD, and the Left Periphery

LILIANE HAEGEMAN
UMR 8163 STL du CNRS, Lille III

1. Argument Fronting in the Left Periphery

This chapter explores the syntactic distribution of fronted arguments. The focus will be on the contrast between English argument fronting and clitic left dislocation.

1.1. The Unified Account of English Topicalization and Romance Clitic Left Dislocation

In a seminal paper on the composition of the left periphery of the clause, Rizzi (1997) proposes that the CP layer is decomposed into a number of articulated projections which are hierarchically organized as in (1). Summarizing his analysis and simplifying somewhat, Rizzi proposes for English that focalized constituents move to the specifier of FocP (2a), topicalized arguments without a resumptive element occupy the specifier of TopP and are associated with an empty operator in Spec, Fin (2b), and fronted adjuncts are TopP adjoined (2c). For details and motivation see Rizzi (1997).[1] Furthermore, Rizzi proposes that the topicalized constituent in Romance clitic left dislocation (CLLD) constructions also targets the specifier of TopP (2d).

(1) Force > Topic > Focus > Fin[2]

(2) a $[_{ForceP} [_{FocP}$ YOUR book $[_{FinP} [_{IP}$ I bought t last year.]]]]

    b $[_{ForceP} [_{TopP}$ This book $[_{FinP}$ OP $[_{IP}$ I bought t last year.]]]]

    c $[_{ForceP} [_{TopP}$ Last year $[_{TopP} [_{FinP} [_{IP}$ I bought your book.]]]]]

    d $[_{ForceP} [_{TopP}$ Ton livre $[_{FinP} [_{IP}$ Je l'ai   déjà   lu.]]]]

        your book   I it have already read

In much recent literature on the left periphery inspired by Rizzi's paper, it is also assumed that fronted topics uniformly occupy a designated position, the specifier of TopP. This assumption is found, for instance, in Grewendorf (2002), Grohmann (2003), and Platzack (2004). (But see, among others, Benincà 2001; Benincà and Poletto 2003; Frascarelli and Hinterhölzl 2004; Lopez 2003; and Pereltsvaig 2004 for different views.) The assumption that the position of topics is identical across various languages often goes hand in hand with the tacit assumption that these topics are interpretively similar. Delfitto (2002, 61) says explicitly that "topics are inter-preted in essentially the same way in English topicalization and Italian CLLD."

In this chapter, I want to highlight some distributional differences between Eng-lish topicalization patterns without a resumptive pronoun, as in (2a), and Romance CLLD arguments. The chapter is organized as follows. The remainder of section 1 presents the idea that English argument fronting, that is, both topicalization and focalization, is a root transformation, or a main clause phenomenon. Section 2 dis-cusses the syntax of adverbial clauses. Two types of adverbial clauses must be distin-guished, which I will label central adverbial clauses and peripheral adverbial clauses. Sections 3 and 4 show how adverbial clauses, and embedded clauses in general, dif-fer with respect to the composition of their left periphery: specifically, it is proposed that the CP of central adverbial clauses, as well as that of factive complements, of subject clauses, and of infinitival clauses, is structurally reduced and lacks the pro-jection that licenses argument fronting. Section 5 shows that Romance CLLD has a wider distribution than topic fronting in English, occurring also in the domains asso-ciated with a reduced CP. It is proposed that there is a lower topic position in the left periphery which can host CLLD constituents in Romance. The section examines a number of proposals for locating this position in the left periphery. Section 6 is a summary of the chapter.

1.2. Main Clause Phenomena
In a rich literature going back to the 1970s, a range of syntactic phenomena associ-ated with the left periphery of the clause has been identified whose domain of appli-cation is restricted to root clauses and to embedded clauses with root properties. Among such "root transformations" or "Main Clause Phenomena" (MCP) is ar-gument fronting in English (Emonds 1970, 2004; Rutherford 1970; Hooper and Thompson 1973; Andersson 1975; Green 1976; Davison 1979; Heycock 2002; Haegeman 2002; Maki, Kaiser, and Ochi 1999).[3] Hooper and Thompson (1973) ar-gue that MCP are restricted to what they call asserted clauses. They claim that the relevant restriction cannot be syntactically represented, or if it could be, that such syntactic representation would not be explanatory (1973, 495).

1.3. Root Phenomena and the Split CP
It may be true that at the time that Hooper and Thompson were writing, a syntactic account for the restricted distribution of main clause phenomena was not available, but already the authors themselves give a hint as to what the syntactic distinction should rest on when they say "R[oot] T[ransformation]s . . . may never apply in any complements that are *reduced clauses.* By reduced clauses we mean infinitives, ger-unds, and subjunctive clauses, i.e., those complement types which have uninflected verbs." (Hooper and Thompson 1973, 484–5, italics mine).[4]

At an intuitive level, we can reinterpret this to mean that MCP are licensed in domains with more functional structure and that any domain lacking the relevant layer of structure will not allow MCP. A similar intuition is expressed in, among oth-ers, Emonds (2004), Larson and Sawada (forthcoming, 5) and McCloskey (this vol-ume). In the first part of this chapter, I will present some arguments for diversifying the functional structure of embedded clauses. Using a modified version of Rizzi's split CP, I will elaborate this point on the basis of a distinction between two types of adverbial clauses: those that I call central adverbial clauses resist MCP and those that I label peripheral adverbial clauses allow them.

2. Adverbial Clauses and Root Phenomena

This section shows that adverbial clauses in English are not a homogeneous group. Two types will be distinguished: *central* adverbial clauses, which are tightly connected with the clause they modify, and *peripheral* adverbial clauses, which have a looser connection to the main clause and display MCP.

2.1 Two Types of Adverbial Clauses

Based on English data, I distinguish between central adverbial clauses, whose function is to structure the event expressed in the associated clause, and peripheral adverbial clauses, which structure the discourse (Haegeman 2002, 2003a, 2003b). The latter type expresses propositions that are to be processed as part of the discourse background for the proposition expressed in the associated clause. Central adverbial clauses are closely integrated into the associated clause; peripheral adverbial clauses have a looser connection with the associated clause. The two types are illustrated by the examples in (3) and (4). Adverbial clauses introduced by the conjunction *while* provide either a temporal specification of the event, as illustrated in (3a), or a background proposition which, combined with the proposition expressed by the associated clause, will yield contextual implications and thus enhance the relevance of the associated clause (in the sense of Sperber and Wilson 1986), as in (3b):

(3) a. These men worked for Clinton <u>while</u> he was governor.

   b. <u>While</u> [Dr Williams'] support for women priests and gay partnerships might label him as liberal, this would be a misleading way of depicting his uncompromisingly orthodox espousal of Christian belief.
   (*Guardian* 2.3.2, 9, col. 1–2)[5]

Similarly, clauses introduced by the conjunction *if* either express a condition for the realization of the event expressed in the main clause (4a) or have an evidential reading and provide a privileged background for the speech act of the associated clause (4b).

(4) a. <u>If</u> your back-supporting muscles tire, you will be at increased risk of lower-back pain.   (*Independent on Sunday, Sports* 14.10.1, 29, col. 3)

   b. <u>If</u> we are so short of teachers ('Jobs crisis grows as new term looms,' August 30), why don't we send our children to Germany to be educated?
   (Letters to the editor, Eddie Catlin, Norwich, *Guardian* 31.8.1, 9, col. 5)

Some conjunctions can embed the two types of clauses (*since, when, while, if*); other conjunctions introduce adverbial clauses that have only one reading: either they always modify the event (*before, after, until*), or they always contribute to discourse structuring (*although, whereas, given that*).

2.2 The Internal Structure of Adverbial Clauses

Central and peripheral adverbial clauses display a number of differences which can be reduced to one essential contrast: peripheral adverbial clauses express propositions and are directly anchored to the speaker; central adverbial clauses express events and are not directly anchored to the speaker.

2.2.1 Epistemic Modality and Adverbial Clauses

Peripheral adverbial clauses can, and central adverbial clauses cannot, contain expressions of epistemic modality:

(5) a. *Mary accepted the invitation without hesitation after John <u>may</u> have accepted it.   (based on Verstraete 2002, 149)

b. ??John works best while his children are <u>probably/might be</u> asleep.

c. The ferry will be fairly cheap, while/whereas the plane <u>may</u>/will <u>probably</u> be too expensive.

d. If Le Pen will <u>probably</u> win, Jospin must be disappointed.

(Nilsen 2004, 811)

Epistemic modality is by definition anchored to the speaker: it expresses the speaker's stance concerning the likelihood of the state of affairs or the event, as suggested, for instance, in the following quotation from Tenny (2000, 319):

> Epistemic modality, which addresses a state of knowledge of something, must involve a sentient mind that is in the state of knowing; at the sentential level it is the speaker who is represented as holding that knowledge.

Note also that epistemic modality is always anchored to speech time. As signaled by Verstraete:

> Epistemic modals can be morphologically associated with a past tense, . . . *this morphological marking does not express the speaker's past judgement.* Either it is used for tentativeness, . . . or it occurs in a context of indirect or free indirect speech. (Verstraete 2002, 152; italics mine).

2.2.2 Expressions of Illocutionary Force

The availability of epistemic modality in peripheral adverbial clauses and its absence in central adverbial clauses suggest that peripheral clauses are anchored to the speaker in a way that central adverbial clauses are not. This distinction is confirmed by the observation that peripheral adverbial clauses may contain indicators of illocutionary force, a point signaled by Declerck and Reed (2001, 131) for conditional clauses. Central adverbial clauses do not have this independent illocutionary potential and are integrated in the speech act conveyed by the associated clause. Example (4a) above expresses one single prediction of the cause-effect relation between tired back muscles and the risk of back pain. Example (4b) contains two speech acts: the assertion that we are short of teachers is contextually salient and is singled out as supportive evidence for (jokingly) making a suggestion to send our children to Germany. In (3a) above, the *while* clause is merely a time specification of the event expressed in the clause on which it depends; example (3b) contains two assertions, one of which is the *while* clause. This is illustrated more clearly in (3c):

(3) c. (i) [Dr Williams'] support for women priests and gay partnerships might label him as liberal.

    (ii) This would be a misleading way of depicting his uncompromisingly orthodox espousal of Christian belief.

I assume that peripheral adverbial clauses encode a syntactic representation of the speaker, while central adverbial clauses do not encode speaker representation. As a result, peripheral adverbial clauses have rootlike properties and allow for MCP.

2.2.3 Tags Some additional evidence for the relation to the speaker in peripheral adverbial clauses and its absence in central adverbial clauses comes from the observation that the former may, and that the latter may not, have their own question tags associated with them.[6] Question tags typically encode the speaker's attitude: by means of a tag, the speaker asks for the hearer's response to the content of the utterance.

    Example (6) illustrates that tags cannot be related to central adverbial clauses. In (6a), the tag *didn't she* is related to the matrix clause; a tag *hadn't they* related to the central temporal adverbial clause is not possible, as seen in (6b).

(6) a. Mary went back to college <u>after/before</u> her children had finished school, <u>didn't she</u>?

    b. *Mary went back to college <u>after/before</u> her children had finished school, <u>hadn't they</u>?

Temporal *while* clauses show the same restrictions (7).

(7) a. Bill took a degree at Oxford while his children were still very young, <u>didn't he</u>?

    b. *Bill took a degree at Oxford while his children were still very young, <u>weren't they</u>?

The situation is different for peripheral adverbial clauses. Sentence-final peripheral *while* clauses cannot normally be followed by a tag relating to the host clause. Such a tag would have to precede the contrastive *while* clause (8a, b). On the other hand, a peripheral *while* clause may have its own tag; by means of the tag in (8c), the speaker asks for confirmation of the assertion in the *while* clause.

(8) a. *Bill took a degree at Oxford, while his daughter is studying at UCL, <u>didn't he</u>?

    b. Bill took a degree at Oxford, <u>didn't he</u>, while his daughter is studying at UCL.

    c. Bill took a degree at Oxford, while his daughter is studying at UCL, <u>isn't she</u>?

Verstraete (2002, 146) signals that some peripheral adverbial clauses may also contain imperatives (9). I refer to his work for discussion.

(9) The students should have enough money, although remember we are expecting a drop in the department funding.

Languages with distinctive markers of illocutionary force offer further evidence for the contrast between the two types of adverbial clauses. Example (10) illustrates conditional clauses in Korean. A central conditional clause does not contain an illocutionary force marker such as declarative *ta* (10a); this marker occurs in the peripheral evidential conditional in (10b), which expresses a premise entertained as a background for the associated clause.

(10) a. (ku-ka)   i   chayk-ul ilk-<u>umyen</u>/ilk-ess-<u>umyen</u>[7]
       (he-NOM) this book-ACC read-if/   read-PAST-if
       ku-nun ama   ku yenghwa-lul poko siphe hal kes-i-ta.
       he-TOP probably that movie-ACC see want will-DEC
       'If he reads/read this book, he will probably want to see that movie.'

     b. ku chayk-ul cohaha-n-<u>ta</u>-<u>myen</u> way kukes-ul ca-ci   anh-ni?
       that book-ACC like-PRES-<u>DEC</u>-if why that-ACC buy-NMZ not-do-Q
       'If you like that book, why don't you buy it?'

Along the lines of Tenny (2000), I assume that the fact that peripheral adverbials may contain speech act markers implies that such clauses are syntactically anchored to a speaker. Tenny (2000, 319) says that "we cannot have a point of view without a sentient being to hold it. A speech act, of course, necessarily involves the speaker as a participant."

2.2.4 Speech Act Adverbials   Peripheral adverbial clauses may contain speaker-oriented adverbials (11a). Such adverbials are not possible in central adverbial clauses.

(11) a. [A referendum on a united Ireland] . . . will be a good thing, because <u>frankly</u> they need to be taken down a peg and come down to earth and be a little bit more sober in their approach to things.

                                              (*Guardian* 22.7.2, 4, col 4)

     b. *I didn't drop the class because <u>frankly</u> I didn't like it, I dropped it because it was too expensive.

I assume that the fact that peripheral adverbial clauses may contain speech act adverbials also implies that they are syntactically anchored to a speaker.

2.3 Argument Fronting in Adverbial Clauses
This section is concerned with the distribution of argument fronting in adverbial clauses: while argument fronting is disallowed in central adverbial clauses, it is possible in peripheral adverbial clauses.

2.3.1 English   In the left periphery, we need to distinguish argument fronting from local adjunct fronting (Haegeman 2003a). This contrast is not always made. While in English, argument fronting is restricted to root clauses or embedded clauses with root properties, adjunct fronting is not subject to such a restriction; specifically, argument fronting is banned in central adverbial clauses, while adjunct fronting is possible:[8]

(12) a. *If these exams you don't pass you won't get the degree.

b. If next week you cannot get hold of me, try again later.

(13) a. *While this book Mary was writing this time last year, her children were staying with her mother.

b. While around this time last year Mary was writing this book, her children were staying with her mother.

The differences between argument fronting and adjunct fronting in adverbial clauses do not follow from Rizzi's (1997) analysis as summarized in section 1. In particular, if fronting of argument topics and fronting of adjuncts target the same projection, TopP, then it is not clear how, in the same context, argument topicalization can be ruled out while adjunct fronting is grammatical. Elaborating an alternative analysis suggested by Rizzi himself (1997, 331n26, 333n30, 333n32), Haegeman (2003a) proposes that some fronted adjuncts need not be adjoined to TopP. Specifically, adjuncts may also be associated with a projection Mod(ifier)Phrase (see Bowers 1993) somewhat lower in the left periphery. Central adverbial clauses have an impoverished CP in which the lower projection for fronted adjuncts is available while the higher functional projections that constitute the articulate CP are missing.

Argument fronting is (marginally) possible in peripheral adverbial clauses. The examples (14) provide some illustrations of this: (14b) through (14e) are attested examples, (14a, f, g) are constructed examples.

(14) a. His face not many admired, while <u>his character</u> still fewer felt they could praise. (Quirk et al. 1985, 1378)

b. I think we have more or less solved the problem for donkeys here, because <u>those we haven't got</u>, we know about.
(*Guardian* G2, 18.2.3, 3, col. 2)

c. We don't look to his paintings for common place truths, though <u>truths</u> they contain none the less. (*Guardian* G2, 18.02.3, 8, col. 1)

d. It is amazing how this view could have spread about someone who changed the image of causes like Aids and landmines, and in doing so showed a possible new role for the royals. It is particularly ironic since <u>so much of what Diana did for her fellow humans</u> she did with no concern for publicity whatsoever. (*Guardian* G2, 31.8.4, 9, col. 2)

e. Naturally, my carrots, peas, beans, potatoes, lettuces and tomatoes have a taste beyond compare, although <u>whether it is because they are organic or just mine</u> I am not sure. (*Guardian* 6.11.3, page 2, col. 1)

f. If <u>these problems</u> we cannot solve, there are many others that we can tackle immediately.

g. If <u>anemones</u> you don't like, why not plant roses instead?

The fronted arguments have a range of different readings. In (14a) and in (14b), the fronted element is a contrastive topic; in (14c, d) the fronted constituent picks up an entity salient in the context; in (14e) an embedded interrogative clause is focused. In the constructed examples (14f, g), the fronted argument is also a contrastive topic. The differences in interpretation are not relevant at this point (see discussion in section 5.2.3.). What is crucial is that central adverbial clauses do not allow argument fronting.

2.3.2 Comparative Data   The contrast in argument fronting between the two types of adverbial clauses is also found in Japanese, in Korean (see Whitman 1989), and in Gungbe, which I will illustrate below, and it has been reported for Chinese (Lu Peng 2003, 232–34).[9] In Japanese, *wa* topicalization is not possible in central conditional clauses (Maki, Kaiser, and Ochi 1999), but it is licit in peripheral (evidential) conditional clauses which express a premise for the processing of the host clause.[10]

(15) a. *Mosi sono yoona zassi-wa,   (anata-ga) yome-<u>ba</u>,

      if   that like   magazine-top (you-NOM) read (CONDITIONAL)-if

      (anata-wa) yasai-ga   sukini narimasu.

      (you-TOP) vegetable-NOM like   become

      'If these magazines, you read, you will come to like vegetables.'

   b. Mosi sono yoona zassi-wa   (anata-ga) sukide-nai (CONCLUSIVE)-

      if   that like   magazine-TOP (you-NOM) like-not

      <u>naraba</u>, naze (anata-wa) (sorera-o)   kai-tuzukerunodesu ka?

      if   why (you-TOP)   (them-ACC) buy-continue-Q

      'If such magazines you don't like, why do you keep buying them?'

Observe that *ba* in the central conditional clause alternates with *nara ba* in the evidential conditional clause. Concerning the conditional sentence pattern [[S1 *nara*] S2], Kuno says "it is usually said that this pattern has a strong degree of assertion about the statement represented by S1" (Kuno 1973, 168).

Korean shows a similar contrast between central conditionals, which do not allow topicalization, and peripheral ones, which do (see Whitman 1989):

(16) a. *I   <u>chayk-un</u> (ku-ka)   ilk-<u>umyen</u>/ilk-ess-<u>umyen</u>[11]

      this book-TOP (he-NOM) read-if/   read-PAST-if

      ku-nun ama   ku   yenghwa-lul poko siphe hal kes-i-<u>ta</u>.

      he-TOP probably that movie-ACC   see   want will-DEC

      'If this book, he reads/read, he will probably want to see that movie.'

   b. <u>Ku chayk-un</u> (ney-ka)   cohaha-n-<u>ta</u>-<u>myen</u> way kukes-ul

      that book-Top (you-NOM) like-PRES-DEC-if   why that-ACC

      ca-ci anh-ni?

      buy-NMZ not do-Q

      'If that book, you like, why don't you buy it?'

The contrast is also found in Gungbe: only *ni* conditionals with evidential reading allow *ya* topicalization. Example (17) "implies that speaker and hearer are not at the Procure, but in another bookshop where they have found a book that the hearer had seen at Procure and told the speaker about" (Enoch Aboh, pers. comm.).

(17) (*) Ni <u>wema ehe lo   ya</u>, a   mon e   to Procure, xo e   na mi.
       if book this DET TOP 2SG see   3SG at Procure buy 3SG for me
       'If you saw that book at Procure, buy it for me.'

3. RT/MCP and the Internal Makeup of CP

In this section, it is proposed that the difference between central and peripheral adverbial clauses can be related to the amount of functional structure in the left periphery.

3.1 *"Structural Reduction"*

My account for the difference between central and peripheral adverbial clauses is inspired by Hooper and Thompson's own observation that MPC are generally excluded from "reduced" clauses. I propose that central adverbial clauses are reduced clauses in that they are structurally deficient, while peripheral adverbial clauses display the full clausal structure available in root clauses. I assume that anchoring to the speaker is encoded in the syntax (see Tenny 2000 for arguments to this effect). In root clauses (and clauses embedded under speech act verbs or propositional attitude verbs), a functional projection in the CP-area encodes anchoring to the speaker. The CP of central adverbial clauses lacks the functional projection that ensures anchoring to the speaker. The speaker-related projection, I contend, is projected in peripheral adverbial clauses. The proposed structural distinction is semantically motivated. Central adverbial clauses are part of and modify the proposition with which they are associated; peripheral adverbial clauses express independent propositions, associated with their own force, that serve as the immediate discourse background to the associated clause.

3.2 *RT/MCP and the Internal Makeup of CP*

This section proposes a syntactic account for structural truncation, using Rizzi's (1997) split CP as a basis.

3.2.1 *"Reduction" and Speaker-Related Projections*   The structural distinction between the two types of adverbial clauses proposed here is analogous to that postulated elsewhere to differentiate between complement clauses. Citing Benincà and Poletto (2003), for instance, Grewendorf (2002, 53) refers to "the idea that embedded clauses vary as to which portions of the CP-layer may be projected, and that this has to do with the selectional properties of the matrix verb . . . it may be a property of non-bridge verbs that their complement does not project the whole CP-layer while bridge verbs select a complete CP-layer with all projections of the left periphery available." (For similar ideas, see also, among others, Emonds 2004; McCloskey, this volume; Meinunger 2004). My proposal is that the dual selectional behaviour of conjunctions is not restricted to conjunctions introducing complement clauses but extends to other subordinating conjunctions. For instance, *while* selects a different type of projection depending on its interpretation: temporal *while* selects a reduced variant of CP, contrastive *while* selects the full CP. In order to make this idea more precise, I will explore Rizzi's (1997) split CP.

3.2.2 The Split CP: Sub versus Force (Rizzi 1997)   Following Bhatt and Yoon (1992), Rizzi (1997, 328n6), Roussou (2000), and others, I propose to decompose the head which Rizzi labels Force in (1), repeated here for convenience as (18a):

(18) a. Force > Topic > Focus > Fin

Conjunctions are inserted in the position Sub; Sub serves to subordinate the clause, to "make it available for (categorial) selection independently of its force" (Rizzi 1997). The head (provisionally) labeled Force syntactically represents the anchoring of the proposition to the speaker and is implicated in the licensing of, among other things, illocutionary force and epistemic modality.

Both central adverbial clauses and peripheral adverbial clauses are introduced by the position Sub, which hosts the subordinating conjunction. Central adverbial clauses refer to events and states of affairs, and lack Force; peripheral adverbial clauses contain Force. Root clauses obviously also contain Force. We end up with the following functional hierarchies in the left periphery of finite clauses:

(18) b. Central adverbial clause:	Sub				Mod*	Fin
c. Peripheral adverbial clause:	Sub	Top	Focus	Force	Mod*	Fin
d. Root clause:		Top	Focus	Force	Mod*	Fin

Epistemic modality, which I take to be licensed by anchoring to speaker, is licensed through the presence of the head Force. For a similar proposal relating epistemic modality and illocutionary force, I also refer to Bayer (2001, 14–15).[12]

I should underline here that the label Force is a shorthand. The idea is that a functional head, here labeled Force, serves to syntactically encode the fact that the proposition is directly related to a speaker and a speech time. There are a number of alternative implementations, among which, at the moment, I find it hard to choose the best option. It is, for instance, conceivable that Force is reinterpreted in terms of a functional layer in the CP area, consisting of speaker-related projections, such as those hosting Cinque's (1999) high adverbials, namely, speech act adverbials, evidential adverbials, evaluative adverbials, and epistemic adverbials. For some proposals, see Tenny (2000) and Speas (2004) and the papers cited there. Alternatively, Force could be said to encode the external logophoric center (pace Bianchi 2003). Along the lines of Tenny (2000, 318), Force might also be relabeled as Speaker Deixis (while the lower head Fin might be associated with her Temporal Deixis). Finally, Force could be seen as the head that encodes speech time, in contrast with Fin, which encodes reference time. At this point, it is not clear to me how best to characterize the projection(s); what is crucial is that I assume that speaker anchoring is syntactically encoded through one or more functional projections and that it is available in peripheral adverbial clauses and absent from central adverbial clauses. I refer to the relevant projection(s) as *Force*.

3.3 Topicalization and Force

In a discussion of Bavarian emphatic topicalization, Bayer (2001, 14–15) postulates a link between the presence of illocutionary force and the availability of topicalization.

In the same vein, I assume that English argument fronting (topicalization and focalization) in the left periphery depends on the presence of Force. The unavailability of argument fronting in English central adverbial clauses is a consequence of the absence of Force.[13]

The differentiation between two types of adverbial clauses in English is to be related to the more general distinction between clauses that express mere events and states of affairs and those that are assertions associated directly with a speaker. In the next sections, I review other embedded domains that can also be characterized in terms of a reduced CP structure (see Hooper and Thompson 1973).

3.4 Complements of Factive Predicates

Complements of factive predicates (which I refer to as *factive complements*) are not assertive: the truth of the proposition is taken for granted. In terms of my analysis, such complements lack Force (and TopP and FocP, projections which are, by hypothesis, licensed by Force) while nonfactive complements encode Force.

(19) a. Nonfactive complements: *that* (Top)(Focus) Force Mod* Fin

b. Factive complements *that* Mod* Fin

Because of their reduced structure, factive complements are correctly predicted to resist topicalization, while nonfactive complements admit it:

(20) a. The inspector explained that <u>each part</u> he had examined very carefully. (Hooper and Thompson, 1973, 474; their [48])

b. (%)*John regrets that <u>this book</u> Mary read.[14] (Maki, Kaiser, and Ochi 1999, 3; their [2c])

An assertion is anchored to the speaker, and the clause contains an extra layer of functional structure in the CP (see also Meinunger 2004); presupposed complements, not being asserted, lack that layer of the structure. My analysis thus contrasts rather sharply with Zubizaretta (2001, 201), who assumes an Assertion operator for factive predicates. Similarly, my analysis is not compatible with that proposed by Barbiers (2002), who seems to assume that factive complements have more structure than nonfactive ones. He says that with factive complements "Force is complete" (Barbiers 2002, 50), whereas (nonfactive) "propositional clauses are defective" (Barbiers 2002, 51). I do not exclude in principle that factive complements might involve additional structure, but if they do, then it would be in terms of, for instance, being selected by a D-head, rather than there being additional CP-internal structure.

3.5 Sentential Subjects

That subject clauses resist argument fronting (Hooper and Thompson 1973, 476; Authier 1992, 332–33) can be interpreted as a consequence of their reduced structure:

(21) a. *That this book, Mary read thoroughly is true. (Authier 1992, 332; his [17b])

b. It is true that this book, he read thoroughly.

(Authier 1992, 333; his [18b])

This structural hypothesis reconciles the claims that sentential subjects do not exist at all (Koster 1978) with those that have argued that they do exist (Davies and Dubinsky 1999, 2001; Miller 2001). To the extent that sentential subjects occupy the canonical subject position, my proposal is that they have a reduced CP (without Force). Sentential subjects with a full CP (including Force) could then be argued to occupy a peripheral position (Koster 1978; see Meinunger 2004). I hope to elaborate this conjecture in future work.

4. Romance CLLD Is Not a Root Phenomenon

In the preceding sections, the nonoccurrence of topicalization and focalization in English in specific clause types was presented as the result of the impoverished structure of their CP domain. If Romance CLLD were interpretively and structurally identical to English topicalization (as assumed by, among others, Rizzi 1997 and Delfitto 2002), we would predict that CLLD should be disallowed in contexts disallowing argument fronting in English, namely in central adverbial clauses, factive complements, sentential subjects, and infinitival clauses.[15] This prediction is not borne out. I provide a survey of these contexts in the next sections.

4.1 Central Adverbial Clauses

In examples (22) through (26), CLLD occurs in central adverbial clauses. It would appear that these clauses also refer to events and states of affairs and cannot be plausibly argued to differ interpretively from their English counterparts.[16, 17]

(22) It   Se <u>gli esami finali</u> non <u>li</u>   superi,   non otterrai

          if   the final exams NEG them pass-2SG, NEG obtain-FUT-2SG

          il   diploma.

          the diploma

          'If you don't pass the final exams, you won't obtain the diploma.'

(23) Ca   Si <u>aquest examen</u> no <u>l'</u>aproves   amb un cinc, perdràs   el

          if this exam   NEG it pass-2SG with a   five, lose-FUT-2SG the

          curs   sencer.

          course entire

          'If this exam you don't pass with a five, you'll lose the whole year.'

(24) Sp   Si <u>este examen</u> no <u>lo</u> apruebas   con un cinco, perderás

          if this exam   NEG it finish-2SG with a five,   lose-FUT-2SG

          el   curso   entero.

          the course entire

          'If this exam you don't pass with a five, you'll lose the whole year.'

(25) Fr[18] % Si <u>ce livre-là</u>   tu   <u>le</u> trouves à la   Fnac, achète-le.

            if this book there you it find   at the Fnac, buy it

            'If this book here you find it at the FNAC, buy it.'

(26) MG[19] An <u>afto to vivlio</u> <u>to</u> vris   stin   dhimotiki vivliothiki,
           if   this the book it find-2SG in-the local   library
           boris   na to paraggilis tin   kentriki vilviothiki.
           could-2SG PRT it order-2SG in-the central   library
           'If you find this book at the local library, then you can order it in
           the central library.'

4.2 Factive Complements

Factive complements resist topicalization in English (and in Japanese, see Maki, Kaiser, and Ochi 1999); factive complements allow CLLD in Romance:[20, 21]

(27) a. It   Mi dispiace   che <u>questo problema</u> gli studenti non
             me displeases that this problem   the students NEG
             l'abbiano potuto risolvere.
             it have-SUBJ-3PL can solve
             'I regret that the students have not been able to solve this
             problem.'

     b. Ca   Lamento   que <u>aquesta pregunta</u> els meus estudiants no
             regret-1SG that this   problem the my   students NEG
             l'hagin   contestat correctament.
             it have-SUBJ-3PL answered correctly
             'I regret that my students have answered this question
             correctly.'

     c. Fr   C'est bizarre que <u>ce texte-là</u>   personne ne <u>le</u> connaisse.
             it is strange   that that text-there no one   it knows-SUBJ-3SG
             'It is strange that no one knows that text.'

     d. MG[22] Lipithike   pu <u>tin diatrivi tu</u> dhen <u>tin</u> ixan   paraggili
             resented-3SG that the thesis his not   it have-SUBJ-3PL ordered
             sti vivliothiki.
             in-the library
             'He resented that they had not ordered his thesis in the library.'

4.3 Sentential Subjects

In Italian, CLLD is licensed in sentential subjects:

(28) It[23] Che <u>questo problema,</u> i   professori non l'abbiano   potuto
          that this   problem, the professors NEG it have-SUBJ-3PL can
          risolvere mi sembra improbabile.
          solve   me seems unlikely
          'That the professors should not have been able to solve this problem
          seems implausible.'

Modern Greek also allows CLLD in sentential subjects:

(29) (To) oti <u>tin Ellada</u> <u>tin</u> kritikaroun sinexia me enoxli.
     (The) that the Greece it   criticize-3PL always me-bothers
     'It always bothers me when they criticize Greece.'
                                        (Anagnastopoulou 1997, 163; her [27]).

For Catalan and Spanish, the judgments are less clear: sentential subjects analogous to those in (28) for Italian give marginal results and are even more marginal with CLLD. But my informant did not consider them to be ungrammatical.[24]

(30) Sp   ??Que <u>este problema</u> los profesores no <u>lo</u> hayan   podido
              that this problem   the professors NEG it have-3PL can
           resolver me parece improbable.
           solve   me seems unlikely
           'That the professors should not have been able to solve this
           problem seems implausible to me.'

(31) Ca   Que <u>aquest problema</u> els professors no <u>l'</u>hagin   pogut resoldre
              that this   problem   the professors NEG it have-3PL can   solve
           em sembla improbable.
           me seems unlikely
           'That the professors should not have been able to solve this
           problem seems implausible to me.'

Though this suggests there are important crosslinguistic differences which one would like to further explore, I conclude that CLLD is at least more easily available in sentential subjects than topicalization would be in English, again showing CLLD is not subject to the same licensing requirements.

4.4 CLLD in Infinitival Complements
That CLLD has a wider distribution than argument fronting in English also becomes clear when we consider Hooper and Thompson's own "reduced" contexts. Infinitival control complements resist topicalization and focalization in English:

(32) *I have decided <u>your book</u> to read.

On the other hand, CLLD is (at least marginally) possible in Italian infinitival control clauses, as shown by the following data from the literature. The CLLD constituent precedes the complementizer *di,* which Rizzi (1997) assumes spells out the head Fin.

(33) a. Gianni pensa, <u>il tuo libro</u>, [$_{Fin}$ di] conoscer<u>lo</u> bene.
        Gianni thinks, the your book,   *di* know-it   well
        'Gianni thinks that he knows your book well.'   (Rizzi 1997, 309)
     b. Mi sembra, <u>il tuo libro</u>, [$_{Fin}$ di] conoscer<u>lo</u> bene.
        me seems, the your book,   *di* know-it   well
        'It seems to me that I know your book well.'   (Rizzi 1997, 309)

Significantly, though, Italian raising complements disallow CLLD. I return to this point in section 5.2.1.

(34) *?Gianni sembra, <u>il tuo libro</u>, conoscer<u>lo</u> bene.

     Gianni seems the your book know-it well

With respect to French, there is speaker variation (see also Tellier 2001, 356–57); Rizzi says that "speakers of French are reluctant to accept CLLD with infinitives. Nevertheless, a detectable contrast exists between control and raising (Christopher Laenzlinger, pers. comm.)":

(35) a. ??Je pense, <u>ton livre</u>, pouvoir <u>le</u> comprendre.

     I think, your book, to-can   it understand.

     'I think that I can understand your book.'

    b. *Marie semble, <u>ton livre</u>, pouvoir <u>le</u> comprendre.

     Marie seems, your book, to-can   it understand (Rizzi 1997, 331n24)

Spanish is more restrictive than Italian.[25] Anticipating the discussion below, observe that there is no filler for Fin in the examples in (36), which might suggest that Fin is not projected and hence that there is less structure in the Spanish infinitival complement than in its Italian or French counterpart.

(36) a. *Juan piensa, <u>tu   libro</u>, conocer<u>lo</u> bien.

     Juan thinks, your book, know-it   well

    b. *Me parece, <u>tu   libro</u>, conocer<u>lo</u> bien.

     Me seems, your book, know-it   well

4.5 CLLD in French Complex Inversion

Further evidence to distinguish CLLD from topicalization is that in spoken French CLLD constituents may intervene between the constituent that triggers inversion and the inverted verb or auxiliary, as discussed by Laenzlinger and Musolino (1995):

(37) a. Où   <u>ce livre</u> (Jean) l'a -t-il   acheté?   (Laenzlinger and Musolino

     where this book John   it-has-he bought   1995, 83)

     'Where did John buy this book?'

Once again, fronted arguments cannot intervene between the trigger for inversion and the inverted auxiliary in English (see Haegeman 2000):

(37) b. *Not only many of these things do I agree with, but urgent action is needed to solve the problems.

4.6 Preliminary Conclusion

The data discussed above suggest quite clearly that the CLLD argument in the left periphery is found in environments that resist topicalization in English. See also Cinque (1990, 58) for Italian, Hirschbühler (1997, 62) for French, Anagnostopoulou (1997, 160) for Modern Greek, Zubizaretta (1998, 187) for Spanish, and Wiltschko

(1997, 328) for CLLD in general. While topicalization in English is related to the availability of anchoring to speaker (which I represent by means of the functional head Force), this restriction does not apply to CLLD, which has a significantly wider distribution. These findings cast doubt on the assumption that topicalized arguments as well as CLLD constituents invariably target Spec,TopP.

5. A Lower Topic Position in the Left Periphery

In this section, I will examine some accounts for the distribution of CLLD topics.

5.1 CLLD Topic Is Higher than the Preverbal Subject

To account for the distribution of CLLD arguments, one might propose that such arguments are IP adjoined or even that they are IP internal. Zubizaretta (1998), for instance, suggests that CLLD constituents may occupy Spec, IP:

> Spanish to some extent resembles some of the Germanic languages—
> specifically, Yiddish and Icelandic [references omitted]. . . . Languages with a
> generalized TP may be said to allow a certain amount of feature syncretism.
> More precisely, in these languages a discourse-based functional feature, such
> as 'topic,' 'focus,' or 'emphasis,' may combine with the feature T(ense),
> giving rise to the syncretic categories T/'topic,' T/'focus,' T/'emphasis.' A
> topic, focused, or emphatic phrase may therefore be moved to [Spec, T] for
> feature-checking purposes. . . . This of course is possible only to the extent
> that the nominative subject can be licensed in these languages in some way
> other than via specifier-head agreement with T. (Zubizaretta 1998, 100)

However, though the IP domain may arguably contain constituents with a topic reading (see Meinunger 2000; Belletti 2001), one cannot assume that all CLLD arguments in central adverbial clauses are IP internal nor that they occupy Spec, IP, because CLLD arguments in central adverbial clauses can precede the subject even when the latter is in an IP-initial position, by assumption Spec, IP.[26]

(38) a. It   Se <u>queste cose</u>   Maria non le   sa,   non supererà l'esame.
           if these   things Maria NEG them knows, NEG will pass the exam
           'If Maria does not know these things, she won't pass the exam.'

      b. Ca   Si <u>aquest examen</u> el Josep no   l'aprova amb un cinc, perdrà
           if this   exam   Josep   NEG it pass   with a   five, he'll lose
           el   curs   sencer.
           the whole year
           'If Josep does not have a five for this exam, he will lose the whole year.'

      c. Sp   Si <u>este examen</u> Juan no   lo aprueba con   un cinco, perderá
           if this exam   Juan NEG it pass   with a   five,   he'll lose
           el   curso   entero.
           the whole year.'

'If Juan does not have a five for this exam, he will lose the whole year.'

Moreover, we have seen that in Italian control infinitives (33), the topicalized argument precedes *di,* which Rizzi associates with the lowest head Fin of the CP domain. The topicalized constituent cannot follow *di:*

(39) *Mi sembra, [_{Fin} di] il   tuo   libro, conoscer<u>lo</u> bene. (Rizzi 1997, 309)
     me seems   *di* the your book know-it   well

5.2 A Lower TopP
The discussion above leads to the conclusions that (i) CLLD constituents are IP external and (ii) that they do not depend on the presence of Force. One way of interpreting this is to propose that in addition to the higher topic position licensed by Force, there is a lower topic position that can host CLLD constituents. Various proposals have been elaborated along these lines. I will discuss three of them here.

5.2.1 Rizzi (2001)   To accommodate the distribution of topicalized DPs and the fronted adjuncts in Italian illustrated by the positions of the adverbial of manner *rapidamente* 'quickly' and the DP *i libri* 'the books' in (40), Rizzi (2001) postulates the hierarchy in (41) with a recursive topic position lower than the Focus projection and also lower than the Mod position for fronted adjuncts. (On recursion of Top, see below.)[27]

(40) Rapidamente, i   libri,   li hanno   rimessi a posto.
     quickly,   the books, them have put   to place
     'They have put the books quickly back in the right place.'
                                                       (Rizzi 2001; his [49])
(41) Force Top* Int Top* Focus Mod* Top* Fin

We expect the lower topic position to be available in reduced structures, which contain Fin and Mod (see section 2.3.1). In particular, the presence of the infinitival complementizer *di* in Italian control structures provides evidence for the presence of Fin. We predict that CLLD is licit in such control structures, which are arguably reduced CPs with Fin still available. We also predict that the lower topic will not be available in Raising structures, which are deficient CP-less structures, lacking Fin altogether. The prediction is borne out, as shown by the contrast in between Italian (33) and (34) and by the contrast in French (35).

While CLLD is licit in central conditional clauses in Romance, focalization is not possible. This suggests that the reduced CP structure is truncated above Mod.

(42) *Se GLI EXAMI FINALI non superi,   non otterrai   il diploma.[28]
     if THE EXAMS FINAL NEG pass-2SG, NEG obtain-FUT-2SG the degree
     'If you don't pass the FINAL exams, you won't get the degree.'

As expected, focalization leads to a degradation in sentential subjects, where CLLD was seen to be possible (28).[29]

(43) ?(?)Che QUESTO PROBLEMA i   professori non abbiano   potuto
        that THIS   PROBLEM   the professors NEG have-SUBJ-3PL can
    risolvere mi sembra improbabile.
    solve   me seems   unlikely
    'That the professors should not have been able to solve THIS PROBLEM
    seems implausible to me.'

Similarly, focalization leads to strong degradation in control complements:[30]

(44) ?(?)Gianni pensa IL TUO LIBRO di conoscere bene, non il suo.
         Gianni thinks YOUR BOOK   to know   well, not his
    'Gianni thinks that he knows YOUR book, not HIS.'

Rizzi's paper is essentially based on Italian, and he does not discuss whether the
structure in (41) extends to English. If we postulate a lower position for licensing
CLLD constituents in Romance, dominating FinP, and if we assume that this position is not available for topicalization in English, we can relate the difference in distribution in the different clause types to the structural proposals elaborated above
concerning CP structure. English topicalization depends on the availability of the
head Force; similarly, Focus in the CP domain is anchored to Force. In Romance,
CLLD can be licensed in a lower position. This suggestion entails that there should
be some further interpretive differences between the two types of topics. I return to
this point presently.

One prediction of Rizzi's hierarchy in (41) is that the lower topic or the fronted
adverbial adjunct in Mod should be able to follow a focalized constituent or an interrogative *wh*-constituent (assumed to occupy Spec, FocP). This prediction is not
borne out. Concerning this problem, Rizzi (2001, 16) says the following:

> Preposed adverbials can't naturally occur in a position lower than the *Wh*
> element either, a property plausibly related to the obligatory adjacency
> between the *Wh* element and the inflected verb, whatever its ultimate
> theoretical status . . . :

(45) *Che cosa, rapidamente, hanno fatto?
        what,   rapidly,   did they do

A particularly clear indication of the peculiar distributional properties of
preposed adverbs emerges with *Wh* elements not requiring inversion, such as
perché in Italian . . . : the preposed adverb can follow but cannot precede
perché, while a topic can occur in both positions:

(46) a. Perché, improvvisamente, Gianni è tornato a casa?
         why,   suddenly,   Gianni went   home
        'Why did Gianni go home all of a sudden?'
     b. *Improvvisamente, perché Gianni è tornato a casa?
         suddenly,   why Gianni went   home

(47) a. Perché, il mio libro, Gianni lo ha portato via?

        why,   my book, Gianni took it   away

    b. Il mio libro, perché Gianni lo ha portato via?

        my book, why   Gianni took it   away

        'Why did Gianni take away my book?'

5.2.2 Benincà and Poletto (2004)

An alternative proposal postulating a lower topic position is elaborated by Benincà (2001) and Benincà and Poletto (2004), who propose that the left periphery be decomposed as in (48):[31]

(48) a. ForceP . . . Hanging Topic . . . Left Dislocated Topic . . . Focus   FinP

This hierarchy introduces a distinction between a higher topic position, which hosts the Hanging Topic (HT), and a lower one, which hosts the Left Dislocated (LD) Topic. There is only one HT per clause, while there may be multiple LD topics. In Italian, multiple CLLD constituents are indeed possible (49a) (see Rizzi 1997, 290; Wiltschko 1997, 328; Delfitto 2002), and they are also possible in central adverbial clauses (49b):[32, 33]

(49) a. Il libro, a Gianni, glielo daro   senz' altro.

        the book, to Gianni him-it give-FUT-1SG without doubt

        'I will certainly give Gianni the book.'   (Rizzi 1997, 290; his [21])

    b. Se a Gianni questo libro non glielo mostro,   sarà   molto

       if to Gianni this   book *non* him-it show-1SG, be FUT-3SG very

       deluso.

       disappointed

       'If I don't show Gianni this book, he'll be very disappointed.'

As English tends to allow only one topic per clause (see Rizzi 1997), we could equate Benincà and Poletto's HT position with the high TopP which is licensed by Force and which is implicated in English topicalization. The lower LD topic position could then arguably be taken to correspond to the position associated with the lower CLLD arguments.

    This analysis correctly predicts that LD topics do not occur to the right of focalized constituents. However, if we adopt a truncation analysis to account for the properties of central adverbial clauses, sentential subjects, and infinitival clauses, then in order to allow LD topics in reduced structures, these clauses would have to be truncated just under the HT:

(48) b. Reduced structure

       Left Dislocated Topic . . . Focus   FinP

    c. Full structure

       ForceP . . . Hanging topic . . . Left Dislocated Topic . . . Focus   FinP

This does not give the right predictions: focalized constituents lead to ungrammaticality in reduced structures (examples [42] through [44]).

5.2.3 Froscarelli and Hinterhölzl (2004)   Frascarelli and Hinterhölzl (2004) distinguish three types of topics:

(i) The *Aboutness topic* occupies the highest Topic position in the left periphery. "It is cognitively speaking important for such Topics to occur at the beginning of the sentence" (Frascarelli and Hinterhölzl 2004, 6). Aboutness topics are in a higher position with respect to *wh*/Focus constituents.

(ii) The *Contrastive topic* is "an element that induces alternatives which have no impact on the Focus value and creates oppositional pair(s) with respect to another Topic" (Frascarelli and Hinterhölzl 2004, 1).

(iii) The *Familiarity topic* occupies the lowest TopP projection. Familiarity topics are lower than *wh*/Focus constituents, and they can be realized in either peripheries. (Frascarelli and Hinterhölzl 2004, 6).[34]

The structure these authors propose for the left periphery is the following:

(50) a. $[_{AboutP} [_{ContrP} \quad [_{FocP} \quad [_{FamP} \quad [_{IP}$

In terms of the analysis elaborated here, the Aboutness topic and the Contrastive topic would be associated with Force. "ABOUTNESS topics and CONTRASTIVE topics are unique, while multiple FAMILIAR Topics are allowed (different elements can be part of background information)" (Frascarelli and Hinterhölzl 2004, 6).[35] The Familiarity topic is not dependent on Force and is licensed in a lower position. "FamP is recursive (they can be iterated): a major difference with respect to Aboutness and Contrastive Topics" (Frascarelli and Hinterhölzl 2004, 7).

The hierarchy postulated is similar to that proposed by the revised split CP in Rizzi (2001): the lower Familiarity topic follows the focalized constituent. Assuming truncation above FamP for the reduced clauses, we predict that these will allow Familiarity topics though not focalized constituents nor Aboutness topics or Contrastive topics. The fact that multiple topics are possible in Romance (49) is expected, since Familiarity topics are recursive. Multiple (Familiarity) topics are hence also predicted to be possible in the reduced structures.

(50) b. Reduced structures   Sub $[_{FamP} \quad [_{IP}$
     c. Full embedded structures   Sub $[_{AboutP} \quad [_{ContrP} \quad [_{FocP} \quad [_{FamP} \quad [_{IP}$

In the full structures, the nonoccurrence of a Familiarity topic with a higher focalized constituent remains to be accounted for. Perhaps one can invoke the adjacency constraint referred to by Rizzi (see section 5.2.1).

5.3 Fin and CLLD

This section explores the role of the functional head Fin in the licensing of CLLD topics.

5.3.1 Fin as the licenser of CLLD   The three proposals discussed above all distinguish at least two topic positions, one of which is low enough so as to survive in truncated clauses. This would be the position that can be targeted by CLLD topics in Romance.[36] The implication of the analysis is that this lower position is not available for topics in English.

Based on the observation that control complements allow the (low) topicalized constituent and raising complements do not, I propose that the lower topic position depends on Fin, the lowest position of the left periphery. The analysis raises the question why the lower topic position is not available to English (and similar languages). One option is to directly associate the low topic position with the content of Fin. Possibly the rich mood system of Romance is encoded in Fin and contributes to the licensing of the lower topic position.

Such an analysis implies a prominent role for Fin in the left periphery. I can only speculate here. Additional interpretive aspects of Fin that could be explored could be that it encodes reference time (along the lines of Reichenbach 1947; Hornstein 1990). Speech time could then be related to Force. Proposals that are similar to this are that Fin encodes the "perspective point" (Bianchi, Bertinetto, and Squartini 1995; Bianchi and Bertinetto 1996). Boeckx (1998; 2001, 50) links FinP and point of view. One might also relate the CP domain to the logophoric center of the clause and propose that while Fin encodes the "internal logophoric center" (Bianchi 2003), Force encodes the external logophoric center (pace Bianchi 2003). Topicalization in English would necessarily be associated with the external logophoric center, while CLLD could be either realized through the external logophoric center or through the internal logophoric center. As mentioned above, in terms of Tenny (2000, 318), Force might be correlated with Speaker Deixis while Fin might be correlated with Temporal Deixis. English topicalization would then be associated with Speaker Deixis, while CLLD can also be associated with Temporal Deixis.

5.3.2 A Problem: Pied-Piping and Adverbial Clauses (Munaro 2004)   There is one remaining problem for the account of CLLD elaborated here. In his discussion of CLLD in Italian conditional clauses, Munaro (2004) points out that "a constituent can be felicitously topicalized inside a conditional *only when the if-clause precedes the main clause, that is, when it is itself a topic*" (Munaro 2004, italics mine). Example (51) illustrates the restriction (Munaro 2004; cf. [38] above).

(51) *Non supererai   l'esame   se <u>queste cose</u>   non le sai.
     non pass-FUT-2SG the exam if these   things *non* them know-2SG

The restriction applies to the other Romance languages examined here. One way of reconciling this restriction with the account elaborated above is to propose the following (Munaro 2004):

1. Romance CLLD topics may target a lower landing site in the CP domain.
2. However, such topics still require anchoring to the discourse. The position the topic occupies in the central adverbial clause is inadequate to license the topic

in central adverbial clauses because central adverbial clauses lack the projection to ensure anchoring to the discourse.

3. Pied-piping of the adverbial clause to the topic projection of a matrix CP makes up for the internal deficiency of the central adverbial CP and guarantees the licensing of the (lower) topic.

A similar pied piping analysis has been proposed to account for emphatic topicalization in central adverbial clauses in Bavarian (Bayer 2001) and for the licensing of Verb Second patterns in complement clauses in German (Meinunger 2004). I hope to return to this issue in future work.

6. Summary
In this chapter, I examine some of the differences between English argument fronting (topicalization and focalization) and Romance (and Modern Greek) CLLD. English argument fronting is a MCP: it is excluded from central adverbial clauses, factive complements, subject clauses, and infinitival complements. I propose that English argument fronting is to be related to the functional head (or the functional layer) Force in the left periphery. Whenever the left periphery is structurally reduced, Force is not projected and topicalization becomes illicit. CLLD is not an MCP. CLLD does not depend on Force but is licensed through the lower head Fin. In contexts in which Force is not projected but in which Fin is projected, CLLD remains licit. The fact that focalization, unlike CLLD, is not available in the reduced structures suggests that this too depends on Force.

ACKNOWLEDGMENTS
This chapter was presented in various forms at, among others, the Workshop on Dislocated Elements in Discourse: Syntactic, Semantic, and Pragmatic Perspectives (ZAS, Berlin), and the Georgetown University Round Table. Thanks to the audiences at both conferences for comments. Thanks also to Carlo Cecchetto, Luis Lopez, Philip Miller, Nicola Munaro, Josep Quer, Luigi Rizzi, and Anna Roussou for judgments. Thanks to Paola Benincà, Valentina Bianchi, Luis Lopez, Enriqueta Perez Vazquez, Cecilia Poletto, Ben Shaer, and Raffaella Zanuttini for comments on an earlier version of the chapter. Needless to say, they cannot be held responsible for the way I have used their comments.

NOTES
1. Rizzi does not make a distinction between different interpretive classes of topics (see Frascarelli and Hinterhölzl 2004, and section 5.2.3).
2. Mainly on the basis of Romance data, Rizzi (1997) introduces a lower topic position to the right of Focus. I will argue in section 5 that this position is not generally available.
3. Note that in the 1970s, the term *topicalization* was used to refer to both fronting of topic arguments and fronting of focalized arguments. Hooper and Thompson (1973, 468) simply distinguish what they call topicalization as in (i) from left dislocation as in (ii). I assume that for them topicalization subsumes focalization.
   (i) This book you should read.
   (ii) This book, it has the recipe in it.
4. See Emonds (2004, 77).
5. I use attested examples, as this brings out the different readings more clearly.
6. See also Hooper and Thompson (1973, 471).

7. Thanks to Shin-Sook Kim for the judgments for Korean. Abbreviations: NMZ = nominalizer, Q = question/interrogative, DEC = declarative. The alternation *umyen/myen* depends on whether the word preceding it ends in a consonant or a vowel.

8. As pointed out by McCloskey (this volume), not all temporal clauses allow adjunct fronting. See also Emonds (2004, 77).

9. Lu Peng distinguishes an external topic from an internal one. The latter appears to the right of the subject and is arguably IP internal. It can occur in all types of adverbial clauses. The external topic is restricted to what would be peripheral adverbial clauses.

10. Thanks to Hideki Maki (pers. comm.) for the Japanese data. See also Larson and Sawada (forthcoming, sec. 1.2).

11. I thank Shin Sook Kim for the judgments.

12. Meinunger (2004) proposes that embedded clauses displaying Verb Second in German are characterized by the presence of an assertion operator in the CP domain. This proposal is obviously compatible with postulating a Force projection in CP.

13. Whitman (1989) postulates a link between topicalization and the availability of modal markers.

14. On factive and semifactive verbs, see Hooper and Thompson (1973, 480–81). For discussion of variable judgements on topicalization in factive complements, I refer the reader to Maki, Kaiser, and Ochi (1999).

15. For a survey of the movement versus base generation debate and an analysis of CLLD in terms of the Big DP analysis, see Cecchetto (2000).

16. The data are complex, though. Carlo Cecchetto (pers. comm.) signals that though CLLD is possible in central adverbial clauses in Italian, it certainly is not as good as it would be in peripheral adverbial clauses.

17. In (22) through (26), *It* = Italian, *Ca* = Catalan, *Sp* = Spanish, *Fr* = French, *MG* = Modern Greek. Judgements in Catalan and Spanish come from Josep Quer (pers. comm). However, judgments seem to vary. Escobar (1997, 248) seems to consider CLLD as a root phenomenon.

18. See also Ashby (1988), Barnes (1985), Lambrecht (1981). There is considerable variation among French informants.

19. Thanks to Anna Roussou for the Modern Greek data. For similar observations and discussion see also Anagnostopolou (1997, 163).

20. Factive complements are subjunctive in Romance. English subjunctive complements resist topicalization, as already pointed out by Hooper and Thompson.
    (i) *It's important that the book he study carefully. (Hooper and Thompson 1973, 485; their [166])

21. CLLD is slightly more marked there than it would be in bridge verb complements. Its status is comparable to CLLD with infinitives (Luigi Rizzi, pers. comm.).

22. Thanks to Anna Roussou for the Modern Greek data.

23. Thanks to Nicola Munaro and Luigi Rizzi for the judgments on these sentences.

24. Judgments come from Josep Quer. Note that both (30a) and (30b) are acceptable for Luis Lopez.

25. Judgments come from Enriqueta Perez Vazquez. See also note 17. There may be variation among speakers.

26. Thanks to Gunther Grewendorf for bringing the relevance of these data to my attention.

27. For the projection Int, see discussion in Rizzi (2001).

28. The judgments are no different if the adverbial clauses occur sentence finally. Thanks to Nicola Munaro for this judgment.

29. As expected, the degradation is far less when the clause is extraposed; recall example (21) in the text.

30. Thanks to Nicola Munaro for judgments.

31. I have adjusted their hierarchy for easier comparison with Rizzi's hierarchy.

32. For Modern Greek, see Anagnostopoulou (1997, 160).

33. Thanks to Nicola Munaro for the data. Observe that multiple topicalization is also possible in temporal adverbial clauses in Italian. Larson and Sawada (forthcoming) point out that in some temporal adverbial clauses only one CLLD constituent is possible. This suggests that a subset of temporal adverbial clauses impose some additional restriction. See also McCloskey (this volume), who shows that some temporal adverbial clauses disallow even fronted adjuncts.

34. Lopez (2003) points out that Catalan CLLD arguments are contrastively stressed. Italian or Spanish CLLD arguments do not have to be contrastively stressed.
35. Gill and Tsoulas (2004, 129) point out that the topic is unique in Korean. Since I assume that the Korean topic depends on Force (see section 2.2.2.), the uniqueness of the topic follows, since it must be either an Aboutness topic or a Contrastive topic. See their paper for an alternative analysis, though.
36. Inspired by Delfitto (2002), we can assume that the relation between the CLLD constituent in the left periphery and the clitic in the IP domain is one of agreement and that it does not require feature checking.

REFERENCES

Anagnostopoulou, E. 1997. Clitic left dislocation and contrastive left dislocation. In *Materials on left dislocation,* ed. E. Anagnostopoulou, H. van Riemsdijk, and F. Zwarts, 151–192. Amsterdam: John Benjamins.
Andersson, L.-G. 1975. *Form and function of subordinate clauses.* Gothenburg Monographs on Linguistics, 1. Department of Linguistics, University of Göteborg, Sweden.
Ashby, W. 1988. The syntax, pragmatics, and sociolinguistics of left- and right-dislocations in French. *Lingua* 75: 203–29.
Authier, J.-M. 1992. Iterated CPs and embedded topicalization. *Linguistic Inquiry* 23: 329–36.
Barbiers, S. 2002. Remnant stranding and the theory of movement. In *Dimensions of movement,* ed. A. Alexiadou, E. Anagnostopolou, S. Barbiers, and H.-M. Gaertner, 47–69. Amsterdam: John Benjamins.
Barnes, B. 1985. *Left detachment in spoken Standard French.* Amsterdam: John Benjamins.
Bayer, J. 2001. Asymmetry in emphatic topicalization. In *Audiatur Vox Sapientiae,* ed. C. Féry and W. Sternefeld. *Studia Grammatica* 52: 15–47.
Belletti, A.. 2001. Aspects of the low IP area. Unpublished manuscript, University of Siena, Italy.
Benincà, P. 2001. The position of topic and focus in the left periphery. In *Current studies in Italian linguistics offered to Lorenzo Renzi,* ed. G. Cinque and G. Salvi, 39–64. Dordrecht: Foris.
Benincà, P., and C. Poletto. 2004. Topic, focus and V2: Defining the CP sublayers. In *The structure of CP and IP.* Vol. 2 of *The cartography of syntactic structures,* ed. L. Rizzi, 52–75. Oxford: Oxford University Press.
Bhatt R., and J. Yoon. 1992. On the composition of Comp and parameters of V-2. In *WCCFL 10: Proceedings of the tenth West Coast Conference on Formal Linguistics,* ed. D. Bates, 41–53. Stanford, CA: CSLI.
Bianchi, V. 2003. On finiteness as logophoric anchoring. In *Temps et point de vue/Time and point of view,* ed. J. Guéron and L. Tasmowski, 213–246. Paris: Publidix, Université Paris X.
Bianchi, V., and P. M. Bertinetto. 1996. Temporal adverbs and the notion of perspective point. In *Semantyka a konfrontacja jezykowa,* ed. V. Koseska-Toszewa and D. Rytel-Kuc, 11–21. Nauk: Warszawa Polska Akademia.
Bianchi, V., P. M. Bertinetto, and M. Squartini. 1995. Perspective point and textual dynamics. In *Temporal reference: Aspect and actionality.* Vol. 1 of *Semantic and syntactic perspective,* ed. P. M. Bertinetto, V. Bianchi, M. Squartini, and J. Higginbotham, 309–24. Turin: Rosenberg and Sellier.
Boeckx, C. 1998. Raising in Romance. Unpublished manuscript, University of Connecticut.
———. 2001. On the co-occurrence of expletives and definite subjects in Germanic. In *Issues in formal German(ic) typology,* ed. W. Abraham and J.-W. Zwart, 45–64. Amsterdam: John Benjamins.
Bowers, J. 1993. The syntax of predication. *Linguistic Inquiry* 24: 591–65.
Cecchetto, C. 2000. Doubling structures and reconstruction. *Probus* 12: 1–34.
Cinque, G. 1990. *Types of A'-dependencies.* Cambridge, MA: MIT Press.
———. 1999. *Adverbs and functional heads.* Oxford: Oxford University Press.
Davies, W., and S. Dubinsky. (1999). Sentential subjects as complex NPs: New reasons for an old account of subjacency. In *CLS 34-1: Papers from the Main Session,* ed. M. C. Gruber, D. Higgins, K. S. Olson, and T. Wysocki, 83–94.
———. 2001. Functional architecture and the distribution of subject properties. In *Objects and other subjects,* ed. W. Davies and S. Dubinsky, 247–80. Dordrecht: Kluwer.
Davison, A. 1979. Some mysteries of subordination. *Studies in the Linguistic Sciences* 9: 105–28.

Declerck, R., and S. Reed. 2001. *Conditionals: A comprehensive empirical analysis.* Berlin: Mouton de Gruyter.

Delfitto, D. 2002. On the semantics of pronominal clitics and some of its consequences. *Catalan Journal of Linguistics* 1: 41–69.

Emonds, J. 1970. Root and structure-preserving transformations. PhD diss., Massachusetts Institute of Technology.

———. 2004. Unspecified categories as the key to root constructions. In *Peripheries,* ed. D. Adger, C. de Cat, and G. Tsoulas, 75–120. Dordrecht: Kluwer.

Escobar, L. 1997. Clitic left dislocation and other relatives. In *Materials on left dislocation,* ed. E. Anagnostopolou, H. van Riemsdijk, and F. Zwarts, 233–74. Amsterdam: John Benjamins.

Frascarelli, M., and R. Hinterhölzl. 2004. Types of topics in German and Italian. Handout for presentation at the Workshop on Information Structure and the Architecture of grammar: A Typological Perspective, Tübigen, Germany, February 1–2, 2004.

Gill, K.-H., and G. Tsoulas. 2004. Peripheral effects without peripheral syntax: The left periphery in Korean. In *Peripheries,* ed. D. Adger, C. de Cat, and G. Tsoulas, 121–41. Dordrecht: Kluwer.

Green, G. 1976. Main clause phenomena in subordinate clauses. *Language* 52: 382–97.

Grewendorf, G. 2002. Left dislocation as movement. In *Georgetown University working papers in theoretical linguistics,* ed. S. Mauck and J. Mittelstaedt. Vol. 2, 31–81.

Grohmann, K. 2003. *Prolific domains.* Amsterdam: John Benjamins.

Haegeman, L. 2000. Inversion, non-adjacent inversion and adjuncts in CP. In *Transactions of the Philological Society. Specialissue: Papers from the Salford Negation Conference,* ed. P. Rowlett. 98 (1), 121–60.

———. 2002. Anchoring to speaker, adverbial clauses and the structure of CP. In *Georgetown University working papers in theoretical linguistics,* ed. S. Mauck and J. Mittelstaedt. Vol. 2, 117–80.

———. 2003a. Notes on long adverbial fronting in English and the left periphery. *Linguistic Inquiry* 34: 640–49.

———. 2003b. Speculations on adverbial fronting and the left periphery. In *Temps et point de vue/Tense and point of view,* ed. J. Guéron and L. Tasmowski, 329–65. Paris: Publidix, Université Paris X.

Heycock, C. 2002. Embedded root phenomena. Unpublished manuscript. University of Edinburgh.

Hirschbühler, P. 1997. On the source of lefthand NPs in French. In *Materials on left dislocation,* ed. E. Anagnostopolou, H van Riemsdijk, and F. Zwarts, 55–66. Amsterdam: John Benjamins.

Hooper, J., and S. Thompson. 1973. On the applicability of root transformations. *Linguistic Inquiry* 4: 465–97.

Hornstein, N. 1990. *As time goes by.* Cambridge, MA: MIT Press.

Koster, J. 1978. Why subject sentences don't exist. In *Recent transformational studies in European languages,* ed. J. Keyser, 53–64. Cambridge, MA: MIT Press.

Kuno, S. 1973. *The structure of the Japanese language.* Cambridge, MA: MIT Press.

Laenzlinger, C., and J. Musolino. 1995. (Complex) inversion and triggers. *GenGenP* 3 (1): 77–96.

Lambrecht, K. 1981. *Topic, antitopic and verb agreement in non-standard French.* Amsterdam: John Benjamins.

Larson, R. K., and M. Sawada. Forthcoming. Presupposition and root transforms in adjunct clauses. In *Proceedings of NELS 34,* Ed. M. Wolf and K. Moulton. Amherst: GLSA, University of Massachusetts.

Lopez, L. 2003. Steps for a well-adjusted dislocation. *Studia Linguistica* 57: 193–232.

Lu, Peng. 2003. *La subordination adverbiale en chinois contemporain.* PhD diss., Université Paris VII.

Maki, H., L. Kaiser, and M. Ochi. 1999. Embedded topicalization in English and Japanese. *Lingua* 109: 1–14.

McCloskey, J. 2006. Questions and questioning in a local English, this volume.

Meinunger, A. 2000. *Syntactic aspects of topic and comment.* Amsterdam: John Benjamins.

———. 2004. Verb Second in German(ic) and mood selection in Romance. Paper presented at the Workshop on Clause Typing and the Left Periphery. Georgetown University Round Table, Washington, D.C., March 29, 2004

Miller, P. 2001. Discourse constraints on (non) extraposition from subject in English. *Linguistics* 39: 683–701.

Munaro, N. 2004. Computational puzzles of conditional clause preposing. In *UG and External Systems,* ed. A. M. Di Sciullo, 73–95. Amsterdam: John Benjamins.

Nilsen, Ø. 2004. Domains for adverbs. In Adverbs across frameworks, ed. A. Alexiadou, special issue, *Lingua* 114: 809–47.

Pereltsvaig, A. 2004. Topic and focus as linear notions: Evidence from Italian and Russian. In Focus and the interaction between syntax and pragmatics, guest ed. D. Bury, K. Froud, R. Horsey, and K. Szendroï, special issue, *Lingua:* 114: 325–44.

Platzack, C. 2004. Cross-linguistic word order variation at the left periphery: The case of object first main clauses. In *Peripheries,* ed. D. Adger, C. de Cat, and G. Tsoulas, 191–210. Dordrecht: Kluwer.

Quirk, R., S. Greenbaum, G. Leech, and J. Svartvik. 1985. *A comprehensive grammar of the English language.* London: Longman.

Reichenbach, H. 1947. *Elements of symbolic logic.* New York: Free Press.

Rizzi, L. 1997. The fine structure of the left periphery. In *Elements of grammar,* ed. L. Haegeman, 281–337. Dordrecht: Kluwer.

———. 2001. Locality and left periphery. Unpublished manuscript, University of Siena, Italy.

Roussou, A. 2000. On the left periphery. Modal particles and complementizers. *Journal of Greek Linguistics* 1: 65–94.

Rutherford, W. 1970. Some observations concerning subordinate clauses in English. *Language* 46: 97–115.

Speas, M. 2004. Evidentiality, logophoricity and the syntactic representation of pragmatic features. *Lingua* 114: 255–77.

Sperber, D., and D. Wilson. 1986. *Relevance.* Oxford: Blackwell.

Tellier, C. 2001. On some distinctive properties of parasitic gaps in French. In *Parasitic gaps,* ed. P. Culicover and P. Postal, 341–67. Cambridge, MA: MIT Press.

Tenny, C. 2000. Core events and adverbial modification. In *Events as grammatical objects,* ed. C. Tenny and J. Pustejovsky, 285–334. Stanford, CA: CSLI.

Verstraete, J.-C. 2002. Interpersonal grammar and clause combining in English. PhD diss., University of Leuven, Belgium.

Whitman, J. 1989. Topic, modality, and IP structure. In *Proceedings of the third Harvard workshop on Korean linguistics,* ed. S. Kuno et al. Seoul: Hanshin.

Wiltschko, M. 1997. Parasitic operators in German left-dislocation. In *Materials on left dislocation,* ed. E. Anagnostopoulou, H. van Riemsdijk, and F. Zwarts, 309–39. Amsterdam: John Benjamins.

Zubizaretta, M. L. 1998. *Prosody, focus and word order.* Cambridge, MA: MIT Press.

———. 2001. Preverbal subjects in Romance interrogatives. In *Subject inversion in Romance and the theory of Universal Grammar,* ed. A. Hulk and J.-Y. Pollock, 183–204. Oxford: Oxford University Press.

3

A Detailed Map of the Left Periphery of Medieval Romance

PAOLA BENINCÀ
Università di Padova

1. Introduction

A line of research that has received a strong impulse from recent empirical work is the so-called cartographic program, which aims to provide a map of the functional projections in the structure of the clause. In the framework of this project so far, a highly articulated functional structure has been drawn, where specialized positions appear to have the same respective order across languages. Some of the results of this research can be found in Cinque (2002), Rizzi (2004), and Belletti (2004). In this chapter, I present some descriptive generalizations based on medieval Romance as a contribution to the outline first proposed by Rizzi (1997) on the "fine structure of CP." I will try to show that these languages allow us to draw a more precise picture of the functional structure of the CP area and provide further evidence in favor of the proposals I made in Benincà (2001).

The general assumptions and the procedure I adopt are inspired by Cinque's (1996, 1999) extensive investigation of IP functional structure: no variation is assumed to be allowed by Universal Grammar in the number and type of functional projections and their relative order in natural languages; determining the hypothetical hierarchy is a matter of empirical investigation, based on observed order restrictions between the occupants of the functional projections (heads and/or specifiers).[1]

I will use data from medieval Romance varieties, including medieval dialects of Italy, dating from the twelfth to the early fourteenth century.[2] Some of the phenomena are well known to Romance philologists, some are even part of the knowledge of nineteenth-century Romanists. Syntactic theory gives us a way to see in all of them some new and interesting regularities, which confirm or add further precision to the conclusions reached so far on CP structure.

I will argue that the whole of medieval Romance languages share important features of sentence structure and properties of the lexical constituents and functional elements, so that they can be considered a set of variants of an abstract Medieval Romance. On the basis of these common characteristics, we can at least try to exploit what is clear and evident in one variety in order to enlighten what is more obscure or elusive in another. I first briefly summarize the general framework sketched in Rizzi's (1997) work on the left periphery, together with the revisions that have been suggested in Benincà (2001) and further developed in Benincà and Poletto (2004b), mainly on the basis of modern Italian and Italian dialects (section 2). In section 3, I present the main properties of medieval Romance languages, which lead us to consider them a homogeneous linguistic group in this respect, that is, a set of dialects sharing syntactic features relevant to our investigation. I will also point out the peculiar characteristics that distinguish subareas of this linguistic family and present the first generalizations. In section 4, I concentrate on the rich articulation of the left periphery that appears in the medieval Romance varieties spoken in Italy. The fact that CP is open to more than one constituent in these varieties permits us to observe ordering constraints and make hypotheses on the organization of the functional structure. The generalizations can be formulated adopting the theory of an articulated series of functional projections, thus supporting the structure proposed in Benincà (2001). The focus of the analysis will be the position of complement clitics in main clauses. I will show that it is possible to state a set of generalizations that are valid for all medieval Romance if we make reference not to surface positions or roughly to a CP/IP distinction but to specific functional positions in an articulated CP structure. In particular, I will motivate the following generalizations concerning the position of the clitic with respect to the verb:

1. Enclisis and proclisis are sensitive to verb movement and the content of CP.
2. When the verb moves to C, we have enclisis if and only if the Focus field is empty.

Finally, in section 5, I point out what these phenomena can further indicate with respect to the processes we assume to happen in CP, giving rise to the data we have been observing.

It is important to emphasize that I use the labels Topic and Focus to refer to syntactic objects, putting aside their precise pragmatic values. It appears that the relation between syntactic phenomena of the left periphery and their pragmatic interpretation is not obvious. Unfortunately, these phenomena have inherited labels that seem to refer to pragmatics more than to syntax and misleadingly suggest an overlapping of these two levels. Here, I use these labels only as a way of referring to syntactic positions, bearing in mind that their pragmatic and semantic interpretation is in certain respects language specific (or depends on other language-specific characteristics).

The medieval Romance data are meant just to illustrate the phenomena under investigation, since positive evidence is insufficient to prove a generalization and since it is impossible to get grammaticality judgments on dead languages. The generalizations are then necessarily tentative; nevertheless, I will assume that what has not yet been found is ungrammatical.

2. The Fine Structure of CP: Evidence from Modern Italian
Rizzi (1997) proposes a first articulation of CP as shown in (1):

(1) [ForceP   [TopP*   [FocP   [TopP*   [FinP]]]]]

The leftmost projection (ForceP) encodes the force of the sentence; as Rizzi suggests, this projection "looks outside," connecting the sentence with the context or marking it with respect to the clause type.[3] In contrast, the rightmost projection (FinP) "looks inside," towards the content of the IP; the choice of the complementizer, for example, has to do with the modality and tense in IP, a sort of agreement between C° and I°, as it has been traditionally seen. TopP in Rizzi's system can appear in two different positions and is recursive in both cases; it can contain many arguments, without ordering restrictions.

In Benincà (2001), I argued that Topics can only be inserted to the left of FocP. Furthermore, the area of topics is articulated in two distinct fields, with distinct syntactic properties; the higher one is called FrameP. The structure can be synthesized as follows:

(2) [ForceP   [FrameP   [TopP   [FocP   [FinP]]]]]

The recursivity of TopP has also been challenged in Benincà and Poletto (2004b), where it is proposed that these projections stand for fields, that is, sets of projections sharing specific semantic and syntactic characteristics. Data are provided showing that different kinds of topics can appear in the Topic field, in distinct and strictly ordered functional projections, and that the same holds for different kinds of foci in the Focus field.

Reaching a characterization of these projections in terms of their semantic interpretation and pragmatic felicity is beyond the scope of the present research. I will more simply try to identify their exact structural position on the basis of their semantic properties and given a prototypical semantic and pragmatic characterization. The traditional labels can be misleading, and judgments are often elusive and slippery. Even phonological properties like stress or intonation do not strictly determine the nature of preposed constituents; for example, intonational pitch is neither a necessary nor a sufficient feature to determine whether an element is in the Focus field or not.[4] Moreover, when dealing with languages only accessible through written records, it is obviously impossible to get judgments or prosodic evidence, and in spoken languages, judgments can vary depending on local varieties.

Looking for purely syntactic evidence to identify projections and fields, we can start by considering a *wh*-element (or an emphatic Focus) as a Focus par excellence, a typical occupant of the Focus field, and take Italian Hanging Topic (HT) and Clitic Left Dislocation (LD) as typical Topics in the Frame field and in the Top field, respectively. Extending the properties of these prototypical elements, I propose that the Focus field hosts elements with operatorlike properties that undergo movement. Topics of various kinds are, on the contrary, base generated and hosted in fields all located above the Focus field. [5] These properties are connected with different surface phenomena, which can be exploited in order to reconstruct the hierarchy of functional projections.[6]

An argument in CP is in the specifier position (Spec) of a functional projection strictly of the X-bar form (one head, one Spec); a head in the Romance CP can be occupied either by a complementizer or by the verb (depending, first of all, on the nature of the sentence, as a main or a dependent clause). More than one Focus and more than one Topic can appear, in their respective fields, even if the possibility for them to co-occur is subject to language-specific restrictions, which in some languages can be very strong. The functional projections are strictly ordered, and this is part of Universal Grammar.

As we shall see, the hypothesis that the Focus field can host various kinds of Foci is very relevant for medieval Romance languages. This part of the structure appears to be more easily activated in medieval languages than in modern Italian, so that we find there not only emphatic Focus or *wh*-elements but also less marked elements (an identificational, informational, or unmarked focus; an anaphoric operator; or even elements with the pragmatic characteristics of a topic "put into relief"). At the moment, we have very limited means to order the possible occupiers of Focus, as there are strong restrictions on the possibility of them occurring together; nevertheless, we are able to localize them in this field, using various types of evidence. A firm conclusion, though, is that the *wh*-projection is below all other projections in the Focus field (see sections 2.2 and 5.1).

Some of the elements identified as occupants of precise positions in the fields hosting topics have been identified in modern Italian: they are circumstantial adverbs and HTs in the Frame field, and Listed topics and LD topics in the Top field. As they can more freely co-occur in Italian than in other Romance languages, we are able to provide an order of these functional projections (the order in which I have listed them, going from left to right). In the following sections, I will introduce the properties that permit us to identify, in the appropriate cases, the various kinds of topics in modern Italian and to localize them in CP with respect to other heads and specifiers. We will then explore medieval Romance using—where possible—the same properties to distinguish constructions and identify positions.[7]

2.1 A Typology of Italian Topics

Italian has two different types of thematized arguments: HT (Hanging Topics) and LD (Left Dislocated topics). They differ in four respects:

(a) While in the case of LD topics, an entire argument appears on the left (3a), HTs can only be DPs (3b). The two constructions are distinguishable in this way only when a prepositional phrase is involved, as in the following cases:

(3) a. Di Mario/di questo libro, non (ne)   parla più   nessuno.   (LD)
       of Mario/of this book,   NEG (of.him) talks anymore nobody

    b. Mario/questo libro, non ne parla più   nessuno.   (HT)
       Mario/this   book, NOT of.him talks anymore nobody
       'Nobody talks about Mario/this book any more.'

(b) LD topics require a resumptive pronoun only with direct and partitive objects, while the clitic is optional in the other cases (obviously impossible if that type of argument has no appropriate clitic). If present, the clitic agrees with the LD topic in gender, number, and case (4a). In contrast, HTs necessarily require a resumptive pronoun, which expresses the syntactic relation of the preposed argument with the sentence; case is only marked on the pronoun, which is not necessarily a clitic (4b, c):

(4) a. Mario, *(lo) vedo domani. (LD)
    Mario, (him) see tomorrow
    'Mario, I'll see him tomorrow.'

   b. MARIO, (*lo) vedo domani. (Focus)
    'MARIO, I'll see tomorrow.'

   c. Mario, nessuno parla più   di lui/ ne   parla più. (HT)
    Mario, nobody talks anymore of him/of.him talks anymore
    'As for Mario, nobody talks about him anymore.'

(c) There can only be one HT, while there can be more than one LD element:

(5) a. *Mario, questo libro, non ne hanno parlato a lui. (*HT-HT)
    Mario, this book, NEG of.it have talked to him

   b. A Gianni, di questo libro, non gliene   hanno mai parlato (LD-LD)
    To Gianni, of this   book, NEG to.him-of.it have never talked
    'To John, about this book, they've never talked to him about it.'

(d) HTs can co-occur with LD; the relative order is HT-LD:

(6) a. Giorgio, ai nostri amici, non parlo mai di lui. (HT-LD)
    Giorgio, to our   friends, NEG talk never of him
    'As for Giorgio, to our friends, I never talk about him.'

   b. *Ai nostri amici, Giorgio, non parlo mai di lui. (LD-HT)
    to our   friends, Giorgio, NEG talk never of him

Having drawn a distinction between HTs and LD topics, let us now examine the relative order of LD topics and focalized elements. In Benincà (2001), I concluded that a syntactic Topic cannot appear below Focus.[8] The following examples show that the order LD-Focus is grammatical, while the opposite order is ungrammatical. For some still unclear reason, the contrast is stronger if the sequence is tested in the left periphery of a dependent clause:

(7) a. Il tuo amico, A MARIA, lo presenterò! (LD-Foc)
    the your friend, TO MARIA, him will-introduce
    'Your friend, TO MARIA I'll introduce him.'

   b. *?A MARIA, il tuo amico, lo presenterò! (*? Foc-LD)
    TO MARIA, the your friend, him will-introduce

   c. *IL TUO AMICO, a Mario, gli   presenterò! (*Foc-LD)
    THE YOUR FRIEND, to Mario, to.him introduce

   d. *Ho deciso che A MARIA, il tuo amico, lo presenterò. (*Foc-LD)
    have decided that TO MARIA, the your friend, him introduce
    '*I have decided that TO MARIA, your friend, I'll introduce him.'

Crucially, if the resumptive clitic is missing, (7a) becomes ungrammatical (8a) as expected, because a clitic is obligatory if the LD element is a direct object. If we change the order of Topic and Focus, the omission of the clitic corresponding to the hypothetical topic renders (7b, c) grammatical (8b, c); there is no difference in this case between main and dependent clauses:

> (8) a. *Il tuo amico, A MARIA, presenterò!
>
> b. A MARIA, il tuo amico, presenterò!
>
> c. Ho deciso che A MARIA, il tuo amico presenterò.

A possible conclusion is that the sequence of elements in CP in (8b, c) is not [Focus LD], as the pragmatic interpretation would suggest, but [Focus Focus], as indicated by their syntactic behavior. This conclusion is a natural one if Focus is not a single projection but a field in which more than one element can be moved, binding a variable. Inside the field, the elements appear to be ordered, since only one can be intonationally focalized, namely the leftmost one: this instantiates the "emphatic focus" position (I Focus).[9]

The hypothesis is, then, that we are locating fields containing several projections: the following scheme shows the fields in braces and the projections in square brackets:

> (9) {$_{\text{Frame}}$ ... [HT] ...} {$_{\text{Topic}}$ ... [LD] ...}{$_{\text{Focus}}$ ... [EmphFocus] ...
> [UnmFocus] ...}

2.2 Interrogatives, Relatives, and Complementizers

Further evidence in favor of the ordering of the elements appearing in the left periphery comes from the observation of their relative order in relation to interrogative and relative *wh*- phrases and with respect to heads located in CP, such as complementizers and verbs. In a main question, a lexicalized *wh*-element cannot be separated from the verb; an HT or an LD must precede the sequence *wh*-element–verb:

> (10) a. Questo libro, a chi   l'hai   dato?   (LD-*wh*-V)
>
>   this   book, to whom it-have given
>
>   'This book, who did you give it to?'
>
> b. *A chi   questo libro, l'hai   dato?   (*wh*-LD-V)
>
>   to whom this   book, it-have given
>
> (11) a. Mario, quando gli   hai   parlato?   (HT-*wh*-V)
>
>   Mario, when   to.him have spoken
>
>   'Mario, when did you talk to him?'
>
> b. Questo libro, a Mario, quando gliene   hai   parlato? (HT-LD-*wh*-V)
>
>   this   book, to Mario, when   to.him-of.it have spoken?
>
>   'This book, to Mario, when did you talk to him about it?'
>
> (12) *Quando questo libro, ne   hai   parlato?   (*wh*-HT)
>
>   when   this   book of.it have spoken

The resulting sequence is then (13).

(13) {Frame ... [HT] ...} {Topic ... [LD] ...} {Focus ... [wh] V}

As shown in Rizzi (1997), the relative wh-element occupies a section of the functional field that is higher than that of the interrogative wh-element; in the same area we also find the relative complementizer che:

(14) a. Il ragazzo a cui il libro lo porterò domani.

   the boy to whom the book it will.bring tomorrow

   'The boy to whom I'll bring the book tomorrow.'

   b. *Il ragazzo il libro a cui lo porterò domani

   the boy the book to whom it will.bring tomorrow

   c. Il libro che a Mario non regalerò mai ...

   the book that to Mario NEG will.give never ...

   'The book that I'll never give Mario ...'

   d. *Il libro a Mario che non regalerò mai ...

   the book to Mario that NEG will.give never ...

It is interesting to compare indefinite relative clauses with normal (restrictive and appositive) relative clauses on the one hand and interrogative sentences on the other. Indefinite relatives, in Italian as in many other languages, use wh-elements of the interrogative paradigm as relative pronouns; nevertheless, the position of the wh-element in indefinite relatives is in the Spec of the projection in which the relative complementizer appears when present (quite a high position; it precedes LD) and not that of the interrogative wh-element:

(15) a. Lo chiederò a chi queste cose le sa bene. (rel wh-LD)

   it will.ask to whom these things them knows well

   'I will ask this of those who know these things well.'

   b. *Lo chiederò queste cose a chi le sa bene. (*LD-rel wh)

   it will.ask these things to whom them knows well

   c. *Mi chiedo a chi queste cose le hai dette. (*interr wh-LD)

   SELF wonder to whom these things them have said

   d. Mi chiedo queste cose a chi le hai dette. (LD-interr wh)

   SELF wonder these things to whom them have said

   'I wonder to whom you said these things.'

This observation will help us understand the behavior of a particular class of interrogatives in medieval Romance (see below, section 5.1). The complementizer introducing a subordinate clause also occupies a head in the higher portion of CP: it precedes LD (see Rizzi 1997) and can be preceded by an HT:[10]

(16) a. *Sono certa di questo libro che non (ne) ha mai

   am certain of this book that NEG (of.it) has never

   parlato nessuno. (*LD-che)

   spoken nobody

b. Sono certa   questo libro che non ne ha mai
   am   certain this   book that NEG of.it has never
   parlato nessuno.   (HT-*che*)
   spoken nobody
   'I am certain that nobody ever talked about this book.'

c. Sono certa   che di questo libro non ne ha mai   parlato
   am   certain that of this   book NEG of.it has never spoken
   nessuno.   (*che*-LD)
   nobody
   'I am certain that nobody ever talked about this book.'

The co-occurrence of interrogative-*wh* and Focus is highly restricted in Italian (as in many languages); I will not try to determine whether they share the same position or not, but it is possible to conclude that the *wh*-projection is the lowest one in CP. The evidence (which will be dealt with below) is the fact that in dependent interrogatives in all Romance languages, any access to the CP system is blocked. If we hypothesize that the *wh*-head is the lowest one, its involvement in dependent interrogatives blocks all the higher projections. The *wh*-head appears overtly in those Romance dialects (Northern Italian in particular) that require a lexical complementizer to introduce dependent interrogatives (see Benincà and Poletto 2004a).

2.3 The Recursivity in TopP Is Only Apparent

In the previous section, the apparent recursivity of TopP* assumed by Rizzi (1997) was scaled down. There is a syntactic difference between HT and LD that allows us to isolate two distinct and ordered projections; HT is probably in a field (call it Frame) where scene-setting adverbs (ScSett) also find their location (ordered above HT; [17a]). However, with respect to LD, recursion does not appear to be completely reduced. In Benincà and Poletto (2004b), we pointed out some semantic-pragmatic differences among LD arguments that appear together, identified a particular kind of topic with List Interpretation (LI), and showed that its position is below the ordinary LD (17b, c). The resumptive clitic has the same distribution with both the LD and the LI topic, which leads us to locate them in the same Topic field.

(17) a. [$_{ScSett}$ In quel momento [$_{LD}$ Gianni [$_{IP}$ non lo   vedevo.]]]
           in that moment   Gianni   NEG him saw
        'At that moment, Gianni, I couldn't see him.'

     b. [$_{LD}$ Agli   amici,[$_{LI}$ la prima [$_{IP}$ gliela vendiamo, (la   seconda
           to-the friends, the former   him-it sell,   (the latter
        gliela   regaliamo).]]]
        him-it give)
        'To friends, the former we sell, the latter we give for free.'

    c. *[$_{LI}$ La prima [$_{LD}$ agli amici [$_{IP}$ gliela vendiamo, (la seconda
        the former, to-the friends him-it sell,   (the latter
    gliela regaliamo).]]]
    him-it give)

The pragmatic differences between the various categories of topics are in most cases hard to detect but can be brought out in particular contexts. This suggests that recursion could be completely eliminated once observation and grammatical description lead us to a fuller understanding of this part of grammar.

    On the basis of the arguments briefly outlined here and discussed in more detail in Benincà (2001) and Benincà and Poletto (2004b), we can sketch the following structure of the left periphery: braces include fields, square brackets include single projections; a slash separates arguments whose relative order is unclear; C° indicates any head in the CP system (I have only marked the C°s for which we have some evidence, even if all Specs are supposed to be accompanied by a C°):

    (18) [Force C°][Relwh C°]/{$_{Frame}$[ScSett][HT] C°}{$_{TOPIC}$[LD] [LI] C°}
        {$_{Focus}$[I Focus][II Focus]/[Interrwh] C°}[Fin C°]

3. Medieval Romance: Common Syntactic Features

As shown by syntactic research on these languages, all the varieties of Romance languages in the Middle Ages (until the beginning of the fourteenth century at least) present characteristics in their syntax that have been explained hypothesizing that they share Verb Second (V2) syntax. Note that by *V2,* I refer to the obligatory activation of CP in all main clauses and not simply to the verb being in second position.[11]

    By virtue of sharing a V2 syntax, these languages exhibit subject-verb inversion in main clauses when a constituent different from the subject appears in first position (see section 3.1). But since all of them are pro-drop languages (some have an asymmetric pro-drop, licensed by V-movement: see section 3.2), this surface sign of V2 syntax is not always immediately visible.[12] In what follows, some aspects of Romance V2 syntax are illustrated with examples from some medieval Romance languages.

3.1 V2 Syntax: Subject-V Inversion in Main Clauses

In a V2 main clause, an object, an adverb, or a filler in first position is immediately followed by the verb. In this context, the subject can be omitted (see below); otherwise, it appears immediately after the inflected verb.[13] We analyze this structure as resulting from movement of the verb to a head in CP; any constituent (including the subject) can appear in (one of) the specifiers of CP. In the following examples, the inflected V is in small capitals while the inverted subject is italicized (clitics and negation are not to be taken into account in this respect):

    (19) a. Autre chose NE POT   *li roi* trouver.
          other thing NEG could the king find
          'The king couldn't find anything else.'   (OFr.; *Artu,* 101)

b. Un pou aprés eure de prime FU   *Mador* venuz   a   cort.
   a   bit   after   hour of first   was Mador   arrived to court
   'Mador arrived to court a little after the hour of first hour
   (i.e., 6:00 a.m.).'   (*Artu*, 103)

(20) a. Mal cosselh DONET   *Pilat*
   bad   advice   gave.3SG Pilatus
   'Pilatus gave bad advice.'   (OProv.; *Venjansa*, 106)

   b. Si SAI   *eu* la   meillor razon.
   so know I   the best   reason
   'So I know the best reason.'   (OProv.; Gaucelm Faidit, 47)

(21) Este logar MOSTRO *dios* a Abraam.
   this place showed God to Abraham
   'God showed Abraham this place.'   (OSp.; Fontana 1993, 64)

(22) Con tanta   paceença SOFRIA   *ela* esta enfermidade.
   with so.much patience   suffered she this disease
   'She suffered this disease so patiently.'   (OPort.; Ribeiro 1995, 114)

(23) a. Bon vin   FA   *l'uga   negra.*
   good wine makes the-grape black (SUBJ)
   'Black grapes make good wine.'   (OMil.; Bonvesin, 96)

   b. Et   così LO MIS *e'* ço
   and so   it-put   down
   'And so I put it down.'   (OVen.; *Lio Mazor*, 31)

   c. Ciò TENNE *il   re*   a grande maraviglia
   this held   the king to great   marvel
   'The king was astonished at that.'   (OFlor.; *Novellino*, Tale 2)

The examples above represent the clearest cases. Sometimes the verb is in first, third, or fourth position. We will come back to this variation, which is typical of medieval varieties spoken in Italy; we will see that it leads us to discover other interesting syntactic properties and restrictions.

3.2 V2 Syntax: The Asymmetric Pro-Drop of Northern Italian and French

Another type of evidence for V2 syntax in Romance is provided by those Romance varieties (distributed in a continuous area going from France to Northern Italy) that exhibit what I will call *asymmetric pro-drop:* main clauses allow pro-drop, whereas in dependent clauses, the subject has to be expressed (Vanelli, Renzi, and Benincà 1985). The following sample of sentences shows the asymmetry. In the main clause, the subject is expressed only if semantically necessary; in the dependent clause, a subject pronoun is inserted even when it is coreferential with the subject of the main clause and is not required for semantic reasons:

(24) a. Or   poez __ veoir a   terre   un des   freres   del   chastel d' Escalot
       now can.2PL see   on ground one of-the brothers of-the castle   of-Escalot
       'Now you can see on the ground one of the brothers of the castle of
       Escalot.'   (OFr.; *Artu*, 14)

   b. Ceste merveille poés __ veoir
       this   marvel   can.2PL see
       'You can see this marvel.' (*Artu*, 186)

(25) a. Si errerent __ tant   en tele maniere qu'*il*   vindrent en la praerie
       so wandered so.much in such way   that-*they* came   in the prairie
       de Wincestre
       of Winchester
       'They wandered so much in such a way that they arrived in the prairie
       of Winchester.'   (OFr.; *Artu*, 13)

   b. Or   avoit __ tant les doiz   gresliz Qu'il   s' en issi
       now had   so   the fingers frozen that-*he* cl-cl went
       'He had the fingers so frozen that he left.'   (OFr., Béroul, 63)

(26) Quand *tu*   veniss al   mondo, se *tu*   voliss   pensar, negota
    when   you came to-the world,   if you wanted to.think, nothing
    ge   portassi __ , negota n   poi __ portar
    there brought.2SG, nothing from.there can.2SG to.take
    'When you came into the world, if you think about it, you didn't bring
    anything, and nothing can you take away.'   (OMil.; Bonvesin, 179)

(27) et   levà __   lo rem et de-me __ sulo col et menà-me __ ço per
    and raised.3SG the oar and hit.3SG-me on-the neck and struck.3SG-me down
    lo braço, sì ch'*el*   me lo   scaveçà
    the arm,   so that he to.me-it broke.3SG
    'And he raised the oar and hit me on the neck, and struck my arm so that
    he broke it.'   (OVen.; *Lio Mazor*, 18)

(28) E   così ne   provò __   de' più cari ch'*elli* avea.
    and so of.it tested.3SG of.the most dear that-he had
    'So he tested some of the best friends he had.'   (OFlor.; *Testi fiorentini*,74)

This asymmetry can be taken as evidence for V-movement to C° in main clauses
by making the following hypothesis. When the inflected verb moves to C° (as it does
in main clauses), it locally governs the subject position, so it transmits its features to
pro and licenses it as a subject. But when the verb doesn't raise to C° (as is typically
the case in subordinate clauses), it cannot license *pro* as a subject. This hypothesis
accounts for the asymmetry of pro-drop, as V-movement to C° is primarily a root
phenomenon.

This description is an idealization, because in a number of cases the subject is
dropped in dependent clauses as well. The theory of an articulated structure of CP

makes possible a more complex hypothesis which accounts for the apparent counter-examples in an interesting way. V-movement to C° is not obligatory in dependent clauses, but it is possible provided that the lowest head is not occupied; the only case in which V-movement is prohibited is in a dependent interrogative.[14] In dependent clauses involving portions of the structure higher than the locus of *wh*-movement, the verb is allowed to move at least to the FocusP head, licensing a *pro* in subject position. In medieval Romance languages that do not show the asymmetry of pro-drop, a *pro* subject is always licensed in Spec, IP.

As movement to the CP system (in both main and dependent clauses) is much freer in Old Italian varieties than in other medieval Romance languages, data from medieval Italy will be used in sections 4 and 5 to test the consequences of this hypothesis on a wider database.

3.3 V2 Syntax: Preverbal Elements

In this subsection, I will focus on two classes of elements that appear in preverbal position and adjacent to the verb in medieval Romance varieties: high-frequency words like *so* and *then,* and preposed objects. I make the hypothesis that all these elements occupy the Spec of FocusP, or better, a Spec in the Focus field, as sentential operators or moved arguments.

A few high-frequency lexical elements, when preverbal in a main clause, always appear strictly adjacent to the inflected verb (and its clitics)—for example, Venetian *an,* French *(ain)si* 'so', *lors* 'then', and *ainz* 'on the contrary.'[15] Complement clitics, if present, are always proclitic in this context. Occurrences are innumerable, with no exceptions (clitic elements are in italics):

(29) a. Ainz   *n'en*   osastes __ armes   prendre
        on.the.contrary not-cl dared.2SG weapons to.take
        'On the contrary you didn't dare to take up arms.'   (OFr. ; Béroul, 94)

      b. An'   *me*   credev-eo servirte.
         on.the.contrary myself thought-I to.serve-you
         'I rather thought I was your servant.'   (OVen.; *Rainaldo,* 172)

      c. an   *lo* dies tu   ben!
         on.the.contrary it said you well
         'On the contrary, you said it well!'   (OVen.; *Lio Mazor,* 18)

(30) a. Si *se*   conseillierent __ entr'ex   comment il   feroient
        so SELF consulted   among-them how   they would do
        'They consulted each other on what to do.'   (OFr. ; *Artu,* 253)

      b. il conut bien icele beste, si *en*   crola   .ii. foiz la teste
        he knew well that beast, so of.it shaked.3SG two times the head
        'He recognized that beast and shook its head twice.'
                         (OFr. ; Pierre de Saint-Cloud, *Renart,* 3)

      c. Si *en*   fu la reïne moult corrociee.
        so of.it was the queen very   upset

'The queen was very upset about that.'   (OFr.; *Artu,* 166)

d. et   enaysi, senher, fo   tot lo tezaur   de Iherusalem maniatz e

   and so,   sir,   was all the treasure of Jerusalem touched and

   gastats par las gens.

   spoiled by the people

   'And in that way, sir, was all the treasure of Jerusalem touched and

   spoiled by the people.'   (OProv. ; *Venjansa,* 117)

e. et   così cors-e' là   e   sì *g'* entremeçaj _.

   and so   run-I   there and so them pulled.apart

   'And I rushed there and pulled them apart.'

                                          (OVen.; *Lio Mazor,* 30)

There is also another class of elements that always appear adjacent to the main verb: preposed direct objects without a clitic copy. Pragmatically, these objects can have various interpretations: they can represent an emphatic or an unmarked focus, a "relevant" theme, or an anaphoric theme. They do not seem pragmatically marked, as in modern Italian and other modern Romance languages. In the following examples, the preposed object is italicized, and the Romance verb (with clitics, if present) is in small capitals (some examples given above are repeated here):

(31) a. *La traison* LI   A   CONTÉ que li   vasals a   apresté.

     the treason him has told   that the vassal has prepared

     'He told him about the treason that was planned by the vassal.'

                                    (OFr.; *Enéas,* 23–24)

    b. Mes *Lancelot* ne CONNUT   il mie, car   trop   estoit enbrons

     but Lancelot NEG recognized he NEG, because too.much was   sullen

     'But he didn't recognize Lancelot, as he was too sullen.'

                                    (OFr.; *Artu,*11, 3)

(32) *Mal cosselh* DONET Pilat.

    bad advice gave   Pilatus

    'Pilatus gave bad advice.'   (OProv.; *Venjansa de la mort de Nostre Senhor*)

(33) *Este logar* MOSTRO dios a Abraam.

    this place showed God to Abraam

    'God showed Abraham this place.'   (OSp.; Fontana 1993, 64)

(34) *Tal serviço* LHE   PODE fazer hûn homen pequenho.

    such service to.him can do   a   man   short

    'A short man can do this service for him.'   (OPort.; Huber 1933)

(35) *una fertra*   FEI   lo reis Salomon . . . *Las colones* FEI   d'argent

    a   sedan.chair made the king Solomon . . . The columns made of-silver

    e   *l'apoail*

    and the-support

FEI   d'or;   *li   degrai per   unt   hom i   montava* COVRÌ
made of gold the steps   through which man there mounted covered
de pur pura.
of purple
'King Solomon made a sedan chair. He made the columns of silver and
the support of gold; he covered the steps on which one climbed up with
purple.'   (OPied.; *Sermoni,* 232)

(36) *Questa obedientia de morire* REGUIRIVA lo Padre a lo   Fiolo
this   obedience of to.die   demanded the Father to the Son
'The Father exacted this submission to die from the Son.'
                                                              (OMil.; *Elucidiario,* 123)

(37) et   *lo pan   ch' e aveva en man* DÉ   per la   bocha a Madalena.
and the bread that I had   in hand slammed on the mouth to Madalena
'And I slammed the bread that I had in my hand on Madalena's mouth.'
                                                              (OVen.; *Lio Mazor,* 27)

(38) *L'uscio* MI   LASCERAI   aperto istanotte
the-door to.me will.leave.2SG open   tonight
'You will leave the door open for me tonight.'   (OFlor.; *Novellino,* 38)

(39) *Guiderdone* ASPETTO   avere   da   voi.
guerdon   expect.1SG to.have from you
'I expect compensation from you.'   (OSic.; Scremin 1984–1985)

The pattern that emerges from the examples above has some apparent counter-
examples: cases can be found in which the preposed object, even if adjacent to the
verb, has a clitic copy, which is always enclitic. In the following sentences, the preposed object is in square brackets and the copy is italicized:

(40) a. [Lo primo modo] chiamo*lo* estato temoruso
         the first   mode call.1SG-it state timorous
         'I call the first type (of love) timorous state.'   (OUmbr., Jacopone)
     b. A voi [le mie poche parole ch'avete   intese] hol*le*   dette
         to you the my few   words that-have.2PL heard have-them said
         con grande fede
         with great   faith
         'The few words that you heard from me I pronounced with great faith.'
                                                              (OFlor.; *testi fiorentini,* 282)
     c. e [a los otros] acomendo-*los*   adios.
         and to the others commended.3SG-them to god
         'And he commended the others to God.'   (OSp.; Fontana 1993, 153)

The generalization based on surface order is the following:

Generalization on Preverbal Objects (Part 1):

In a main clause, an object can precede the verb and lack a clitic copy only if no lexical material intervenes between the object and the verb (except for clitics and the negative marker).

If, as anticipated above, we make a formal hypothesis on the structural position an object occupies when it is preposed without a clitic copy, we can formulate an absolute generalization as follows. Let us hypothesize that when a direct object moves leaving a trace, it can only move to the Spec of one of the projections in the Focus field. More precisely, let us assume that it can move only to the specifier immediately preceding the head to which the verb moves in a main clause. This hypothesis predicts that we should never find a preverbal object connected to a trace if some other XP intervenes between it and the verb. This is because the intervening XP would be in the specifier of the FocP headed by the verb, and thus the object would be in the Topic field. If the object is in the Topic field, it is not connected to a trace, but rather to a clitic copy in the clause.

When no XP intervenes between the preposed object and the verb, the structure is ambiguous, and the pragmatics determines where the object is located in the structure. We assume that the syntactic correlate of the pragmatic choice is the presence or absence of the clitic copy. One piece of syntactic evidence for disambiguating between the two possible structures—one with the preposed object in the Focus field and one with the preposed object in the Topic field—comes from the position of the clitic copy. This will be discussed in the following section.

3.4 The Position of Clitics (Tobler-Mussafia Law)

The law formulated in the nineteenth century by Adolf Tobler and Adolfo Mussafia (see Tobler 1875/1912; Mussafia 1886/1983) states that complement clitics cannot appear in first position in a sentence in medieval Romance languages. Since they must be adjacent to the verb,[16] when the V is in first position they become enclitic. Enclisis is also found sentence internally; it is then supposed to be an option, obligatorily adopted to avoid clitics in first position. This corresponds to a first approximation of an accurate description of clitic syntax in medieval Romance. We will see that the description can reach a more detailed and interesting level. The Tobler-Mussafia law is based on data like the following (the verb is in small capitals, enclitics are italicized):

(41) REMANBRE *li*   de la   reine.
     occurred   to.him of the queen
     'He remembered the queen.'   (OFr.; Chrétien, *Erec et Enide,* 28)

(42) RESPONDIO *les*   el que lo non farie.
     answered   them he that it neg would-do
     'He answered that he wouldn't do it.'   (OSp.; Fontana 1993, 110)

(43) TORNÉ-*s-en*,   sì ané a l'autre so ami (. . .), sì li   ai

went3SG-back.*clit.clit,* so went to the-other his friend,   so to-him has

coità so desasi.

told his trouble

'He went back and went to the other friend and told him his troubles.'

(OPied.; *Sermoni Subalpini,* 238)

(44) et he li   tras   la fosina de   man et BRANCHAI-*lo*

per li caveli et TRAS-*lo*   en   la sentina . . .

and I   to-him snatched the harpoon from hand and seized.him

by the hair   and pulled.him down into the bilge

'And I snatched the harpoon from his hands and caught him by his hair

and pulled him down into the bilge.'   (OVen.; *Lio Mazor,* 18)

(45) LEVÒ*ssi*   questa femmina e   AIUTO*llo*

raised.herself this   woman   and helped.him

'The woman stood up and helped him.'   (OFlor.; *Novellino,* 38)

(46) GRAVA*me*   forte   lo balestrire.

burdens.me heavily the arbalester

'The arbalester burdens me heavily.'   (OUmbr.; Jacopone)

(47) PURRIA*mi*   laudari d'Amori bonamenti.

could1SG.myself praise of-love kindly

'I could praise Love.'   (OSic.; Scremin, 44; Stefano Protonotaro)

The distribution appears very regular: if something precedes the verb, clitics are generally proclitic; if the verb is initial, clitics are enclitic. If we try to push the generalization further, we face an asymmetrical situation: with no exception, in all the written Romance texts until at least the fourteenth century, if the verb is initial in a main assertive clause, there is enclisis.[17] However, enclisis cannot completely depend on the impossibility for clitics to appear in first position, because we find cases of sentence-internal enclisis. Even if the latter case is quite rare outside Italy, it is found in all Romance languages of the Middle Ages:

(48) a. [Quelgli il quale andasse per   Firenze in die di lavorare],

he   the which would-go through Florence in day of working,

*debbia*l*gli*   essere soddisfatto . . .

must.to-him to-be paid

'Who happens to go through Florence in a working day must be

paid . . .'   (OFlor.; *Testi fiorentini,* 54)

b. E   [despues] *mando-lo* fazer a sus discipulos

and afterwards gave.it   to-do to his disciples

'And afterwards he asked his disciples to do it.'

(OSp.; Fontana 1993, 53)

Using as a diagnostic test the properties of topics established on the basis of modern Italian, and anticipating in part what is to come, the examples in (48) are to be analyzed as follows. In (48a), the constituent preceding the verb is an HT, as there is no Case-matching between it (a bare DP) and the clitic that resumes it (a dative). In (48b) as well, the constituent in first position (followed by a V with an enclitic pronoun) is an HT, as it is one of the few elements (a circumstantial adverb) that allows V3 in Old Spanish. At a more abstract level, we can reach the following conclusion:

Generalization on Enclisis (Part 1):

Enclisis is found when the verb has moved to C°, and the XP which immediately precedes it is not in the Focus field, but rather in the Topic field or in the Frame field.

The examples in (48) are cases of sentence-internal enclisis in which a V is in second position but the Focus field is empty. With this formulation, which will be illustrated below for other cases, the generalization has no exception.

4. Medieval Romance of Italy: The Multiple Accessibility of CP

The V2 syntax of Romance varieties spoken in Italy appears less rigid than that of other Romance languages: V1, V3, and V4 are very common in all the languages of medieval Italy. These options are not totally impossible in other Romance languages but are governed by stronger textual and pragmatic requirements.[18]

The multiple accessibility of CP in Italian Romance is illustrated by the following examples:

(49) a. [L'altre   ami]   [si] est la   moiller.
         the-other friend so is the wife
         'The other friend is the wife.'   (OPied.; *Serm. Sub.,* 238)

    b. [A lè] [per tug li tempi] me rend   e   me consegno
         to her for all the times me surrender and me-deliver
         'I surrend and submit myself to her forever.'   (OMil.; Bonvesin, 163)

    c. E   [Pero Capel] [en la fiata]   branchà uno uiger de pes
         and Pero Capel   immediately seized   a hamper of fish
         'And Pero Capel   immediately seized   a hamper of fish.'
                                                            (OVen.; *Lio Mazor,* 35)

    d. [Allora] [questi] andò e   ricombatté.
         then   this   went and fought-again
         'Then he went there and began to fight again.'   (OFlor.; *Novellino,* 37)

    e. [Ad ogni matto] [i savi]   paiono matti, [sì come] [ai savi]
         to each madman the sane.men seem   mad,   so as to   the sane-men
         [i matti]   paiono veramente matti.
         the madmen seem   truly   mad

'To each madman the sane men seem crazy, just as the madmen seem
truly crazy to the sane men.'   (OFlor.; *Novellino,* 40)

f. Et [chi facesse   contra]   [la prima volta] gli   sia imposta
   and who should-act contrarily, the first   time   to-him be imposed
   penitença, et   la   seconda sia cacciato
   penance,   and the second   be expelled
   'And to anyone who may act contrarily, the first time he should be fined,
   the second time he should be expelled.'   (OFlor.; *Testi fiorentini,* 46)

g. [La speranza che avìa   de lo   tuo   gran perdonare] [a peccar]
   the hope   that had.1SG of the your great forgiving   to sin
   me conduca.
   me drove
   'The hope that I had of your great forgiveness led me to sin.'
                                                              (OUmbr.; Jacopone)

h. [La figura piacente] [lo coro] mi   diranca.
   the figure pleasant   the heart to-me wrenches
   'The pleasant figure tears my heart.'
                                        (OSic.; Scremin, 34, Jacopo da Lentini)

Note that this phenomenon does not represent a late evolution of Italian syntax, as
the oldest Italian text (*Placitum* from Capua, 960) shows it, in a dependent clause:

(50) Sao   ko [kelle terre per kelle fini   que ki   contene], [trenta anni]
     I.know that those lands for those boundaries that here contains, thirty years
     le possette   parte Santi   Benedicti.
     them-owned party of.Saint Benedict
     'I know that the party of Saint Benedict owned for thirty years those
     lands between the boundaries that are here contained.'

Two constituents precede the inflected verb in a dependent complement clause.
Since the complementizer *ko* is in a very high position in CP (see above, section 2),
access to the lower projections is open for moved and base-generated constituents.[19]

This freedom of Italian allows us to refine our understanding of the properties of
the elements in the left periphery. We can conclude that, even if the verb can frequently be initial and more than one constituent can precede it in main (and even dependent) clauses, the syntax continues to be what we call V2 syntax. That is, it is
characterized by obligatory movement of the verb to a head position within the CP.

5. The Structure of CP in Medieval Romance
5.1 The Accessibility of CP in Main and
Dependent Clauses
We can map the sentence of the *Placitum* into the structure that was proposed in (18)
on the basis of modern Italian:[20]

(51) Sao [ForceC° ko [TOPPkelle terre per kelle fini que ki contene [FocP trenta anni [C° le possette [IP[SPECparte Sancti Benedicti]]]]]

Italian varieties, if viewed (with all possible caution) as a coherent subgroup of Romance, show us with greater clarity what in other varieties appears harder to detect. I will express it with the following generalization (see below for discussion of a systematic exception):

Generalization on Verb Movement:

In Romance, the CP is blocked for V-movement only in dependent interrogatives.

In other dependent clauses—in which only higher functional projections are involved—constituents can be moved to CP if pragmatics require it and, as the data of the asymmetry of pro-drop shows, the V can move to C°. Old Spanish, Old Portuguese, and Old French have very few cases of V3; in most of these cases, the first constituent is a circumstantial adverb or phrase (see Fontana 1993, sec. 3.4.3, for Old Spanish), which in our structure occupy a very high position in Frame.

In the varieties of Romance spoken in Italy, we can find two noun phrases preceding the verb; if neither has a clitic copy, the leftmost one is the subject, and the object is adjacent to the verb:

(52) [La mia cattivanza] [l'alma] ha menata.
     the my wickedness the-soul has led
     'My wickedness led my soul.'   (OUmbr., Jacopone)

There is no ambiguity in the interpretation of this kind of sentence. The subject precedes the object; were the first DP an object, it would have a clitic copy.

As stated in the generalization, the only type of subordinate clauses in which the access to CP is blocked is a dependent *wh*-interrogative (I discuss an apparent exception below). This is again consistent with the functional structure we have outlined: the projection hosting a *wh*-element is the lowest in the structure. As can be deduced from modern varieties, a dependent interrogative involves not only a Spec but also a head (in modern dialects of northern Italy, a lexical complementizer *che* 'that' also appears, accompanying the *wh*-element). Neither a phrase nor a head can move to C° in a dependent interrogative, as exemplified by the following sentences:

(53) a. Sire, ge sai   bien [qui ceste demoisele fu.]
        Sir, I   know well who this damsel   was
        'Sir, I know well who this damsel was.'   (OFr.; *Artu,* 89)

     b. Et sez   tu   [de quel part Booz et Lionnaix et Estors se   son mis?]
        and know you in   what part Booz and Lionnaix and Estors SELF are put
        'And do you know where Booz and Lionnaix and Estors went?'
                                                              (OFr.; *Artu,* 12)

     c. Domandà lo dito Pero   [que eli deveva far del   pes]
        asked   the aforementioned Pero what they should do of-the fish

'The aforementioned Pero asked what they should do with the fish.'
(OVen.; *Lio Mazor,* 37)

In dependent complement clauses governed by bridge verbs, and even in dependent relatives, the accessibility of CP appears more restricted than in main clauses. But this restriction applies only to quantity, not to quality: the structures are allowed, even if they are not very frequent. We could informally conclude that the accessibility of CP in noninterrogative dependent clauses is the same in all Romance languages as in Italian, and the differences are governed only by pragmatics.

Some examples follow; the ones in (54) are complement subordinate clauses, those in (55) are relatives:

(54) a. v'aven   noi scritto che ['l fornimento che vi   bisongniasse]

to.you-have we written that [the supply   that to.you was.necessary]

traeste   di   Bari e   dell'altre   fiere.

should.get2PL._ from Bari and from other fairs

'We have written you that the supply you needed you should get from Bari and other fairs.'   (OFlor.; *Lettera,* 1)

b. mes ge croi   qu'[encor] le fera   il mieuz en la fin.

but I think that even it will-do *he* better in the end

'But I think that in the end he will do it even better.'   (OFr.; *Artu,* 16)

c. vos poez bien dire (. . .) que [riens   qu'il   me requiere] je ne   feroie.

you can well say   that nothing that-he me asks   I NEG will-do

'You can say that I will not do anything that he asks me to.'   (ibid., 142)

(55) a. . . . cil qui [meint   grant cop]   avoit doné.

he who numerous big   strokes had   given

'He who had given many strokes.'   (OFr. ; *Artu,* 255)

b. . . . li   chevalier qui [a la   guerre] devoient aler.

the knights   who to the war   had-to   go

'The knights who had to go to war.'   (ibid., 138)

A class of apparent exceptions to the generalization above (which states that V-movement is blocked in a dependent interrogative) involves dependent interrogatives introduced by *come* 'how':[21]

(56) a. Vedi tu (. . .) *come* [per   le dette vie] *fa/*   Avarizia/le sue

see you   how through the said ways makes Greed   its

operazioni (. . .)?

operations?

'Can you see how Greed in the aforesaid ways makes its operations?'
(OFlor.; Bono Giamboni, *Trattato,* 46)

b. Pregoti   che mi   dichi *come* [queste cose] tu   le   sai.

pray1SG.you that to-me tell how   these   things you them know

'I pray you that you tell me how you know these things.'

(OFlor.; *Novellino*, 2)[22]

The object *queste cose* 'these things' in (56b) is in TopP, as is revealed by the presence of the resumptive clitic; the subject is in the Focus field. In (56a), the subject follows the inflected V, which has moved to C°. I assume, without strong motivation, that the preposed PP in (56a) is in Focus (the adjective *dette* '(afore)said' suggests this possibility, in analogy with modern Italian Anaphoric Anteposition; see Benincà 2001); nothing changes if one prefers to consider it a Topic.

There are reasons to hypothesize that these interrogatives have in fact the structure of a headless relative. The structure of (56a, b) would be as in (57a, b), respectively:

(57) a. [Rel*wh* come C°] {$_{Frame}$}{$_{TOPIC}$} {$_{Foc}$ per le dette vie C° fa }
[$_{IP}$ Avarizia t_V le sue operazioni t]

b. [Rel*wh* come C°] {$_{Frame}$ } {$_{TOPIC}$ queste cose} {$_{Foc}$ tu C° le sai } [$_{IP}$ t_V t]

With respect to modern Italian, the structural location of the *wh*-pronoun in headless relatives was briefly illustrated above; in particular, it occurs in the same position as the *wh*-element of a regular relative clause (i.e., in a very high projection in CP).[23]

5.2 Arguments in CP and Their Clitic Copies

From the analysis of Italian varieties we concluded that an object can be in CP and separated from the verb by another constituent; in this case it is obligatorily doubled by a clitic:

(58) a. [La mia gran pena   e   lo   gravoso affanno c'ho
the my great sorrow and the grievous pain   that-have1sg
lungiamente per amor
long   for love
patuto], [madonna] lo m'ha   in   gioia ritornato
suffered, my-lady   it to-me-has into joy   turned
'The great sorrow and grievous pain I have suffered for a long time, my
Lady turned into joy for me.'   (OSic.; Scremin, 89, Guido delle Colonne)

b. [Madonna per cui   stava   tuttavia in allegranza], [or] no   *la*
my.lady   for whom was.1SG always in happiness   now NEG her
veggio né   notte né   dia.
see.1SG neither night nor day
'My Lady, who always used to make me happy, I see her now neither
day nor night.'   (ibid., 88, Giacomino Pugliese)

c. [La vertude ch'ill'ave   d'auciderme e   guarire], [a lingua dir]
the virtue   that-he-has of-kill-me and heal,   to tongue to-say
non *l'*auso.
NEG it.dare.1SG

'I don't dare to tell the virtue he has to kill me and heal me.'

(ibid., 88, Re Enzo)

In the structure we have hypothesized, an object that precedes the verb can either be in the Focus field (via movement) or be base generated in the Topic or Frame field, even if nothing intervenes between the object and the verb. In the former case it behaves like a *wh*-element and there is no resumptive clitic; in the latter case, it is a base-generated Topic, and so it must be doubled by a clitic.

On the basis of data from all Romance languages (examples are scarce in some languages, but there is virtually no exception), the following generalization holds:

Generalization on Preverbal Objects (Part 2):

A direct object that immediately precedes the verb and is doubled by a clitic requires enclisis.

This completes the generalization on preposed objects given in section 3.3 (some of the examples are repeated here for convenience):

(59) a. [Lo primo modo] chiamo*lo* estato temoruso, [lo seconno] pare*me*
        the first   mode call.1SG.it state timorous, the second   seems.me
        amor medecaruso,   [lo terzo amore] pare*me*   viatico   amoruso,
        love medicamentous, the third love   seems.me viaticum amorous
        'I call the first type (of love) timorous state, the second seems to me
        medicinal love, the third love seems to me amorous viaticum.'

                                                              (OUmbr., Jacopone)[24]

     b. A voi [le mie poche parole ch'avete   intese] hol*le*   dette con
        to you the my few   words that-have.2PL heard have-them said with
        grande fede
        great   faith
        'The few words that you heard from me I pronounced with great faith.'
        (OFlor.; *Testi fiorentini*, 282)

     c. e   [a los otros] acomendo-los   a dios.
        and to the others commended.3SG.them to god
        'And he commended the others to God.'   (OSpan.; Fontana 1993, 153)

In these examples, we find enclisis of the clitic to a verb that is not in first position. The element in first position is one of those that permit V3; that is, in our view, one of those that can be inserted in the Frame field. This means that, though the verb is not first, it is still the case that the Focus field is empty. This configuration triggers enclisis.

5.3 Reformulating the Tobler-Mussafia Generalization

In the light of a theory that hypothesizes an articulated functional structure of CP, we can formulate several descriptive generalizations mapping surface phenomena to an abstract sequence of positions in CP.

Generalization on Enclisis (Part 2):

When the verb is in C° and an XP is in a Spec of the Focus field, enclisis is impossible.

The XPs in a specifier of the Focus field can be preverbal *sì, così, ainsi, assi*, and so on; 'so'; preverbal objects without a clitic copy (general Romance); *or* (OFr.); and *an* (OVen.). After these elements, clitics, if present, are always proclitic:

(60) a. et   *così* lo mis e' ço.
       and so   it put down
       'And so I put it down.'   (OVen.; *Lio Mazor*, 31)

     b. An'   *me*   credev-eo servirte.
        on-the-contrary myself thought-I to-serve-you
        'I rather thought I was your servant.'   (OVen.; *Rainaldo*, 172)

     c. . . . e   *sì* la lavé   e   forbì e   retorné-*la* en sen loc
              and so it washed.3SG and wiped and put-back.it in its place
        'And he washed it and wiped it and put it back in its place.'
                                                         (OPied.; *Serm. Sub.*, 252)

     d. E *così* ne provò __ de' più cari ch'*elli* avea.
           and so of-it tested.3SG of-the dearest that he had
        'So he tested out some of the best friends he had.'
                                                         (OFlor.; *Testi fiorentini*, 74)

     e. *Sì* en   est li rois moult a malese
         so of-it is the king very at unease
         'The king was very troubled about that.'   (OFr.; *Artu*, p. 100)

(61) a. *tutto ciò   che m'hai   chiesto* t'ho dato.   *La*
        all   which that to-me-have.2SG asked   to-you-have.1SG given. The
        signoria   di Roma t'ho   data. *Signore t*'ho
        domination of Rome to.you-have.1SG given. Master you-have.1SG
        fatto di molte dilizie
        made of many delights
        'I gave you everything you asked me. I gave you the domination
        of Rome. I made you the master of many delights.'
                                                         (OFlor.; *Novellino*, 124)

     b. *Tal serviço* lhe   pode fazer hûn homen pequenho.
        such service to-him can do   a   man   small
        'A short man can do this service to him.'   (OPort.; Huber 1933)

Generalization on Enclisis (Part 3):

If a verb is preceded by an XP in a Spec higher than the Focus field, and this verb has clitics, they are obligatorily enclitic.

Elements that have to be higher than Focus are HTs and preposed objects with a clitic copy:

(62) [Quelgli il   quale andasse   per   Firenze in die di lavorare],
     he   the which would-go through Florence in day of working,
     debbialgli   essere soddisfatto . . .
     must.to-him be   paid
     'Who happens to go through Florence in a working day must be paid . . .'
                                                        (OFlor.; *Testi fiorentini,* 54)

The constituent preceding the verb is an HT, which can only be base generated in the Frame field; as no lexical material intervenes between it and the verb, there is enclisis.

Circumstantial adverbs, too, have their natural location in a Spec in Frame, but this is not a strong syntactic constraint; whether they receive a Frame, Topic, or Focus interpretation depends on pragmatics. In the following sentence, we have enclisis to a verb immediately preceded by a circumstantial adverb; this implies that this adverb is not in Focus but base generated in Frame:

(63) E   *despues*   MANDO-LO fazer a sus discipulos
     and afterwards gave.it   to.do to his disciples
     'And afterwards he asked his disciples to do it.'   (OSp.; Fontana 1993, 53)

In other cases, adverbs of the same kind are immediately followed by clitic and verb (proclisis); they are examples of the other option, a circumstantial adverb located in FocusP.

A similar treatment is required for circumstantial clauses, a long-standing puzzle: if a V with clitics follows a circumstantial clause, we can find both enclisis and proclisis. The position of clitics depends on the pragmatic interpretation; the following sentences show the two options, in the same text. In the first, the circumstantial clause is in a Spec of TopP or FrameP, in the second it is in FocP:

(64) a. ed essendo poveramente in arnese,   *misesi*   ad andare ad Alessandro
        and being   poorly   in condition, set.himself to go   to Alessandro
        'And being in poor condition, he set out to go see Alessandro.'
                                                        (OFlor.; *Novellino,*4)

     b. la famiglia volendoli   bene, *l'insegnaro*   a campare
        the family   wanting.him good, him.taught.3PL to get-by
        'As the family loved him, they taught him how to get by.'   (ibid.)

The following structure, the same that we have proposed in (18) for modern Italian, accounts for the subtle facts we have pointed out in medieval Romance:

(65) [Force C°[Rel*wh* C°]/{$_{Frame}$ [ScSett][HT] C°}{$_{TOPIC}$[LD] [LI] C°}
     {$_{Focus}$[I Focus][II Focus]/[Interr*wh*] C°}[Fin C°

There is a particular fact that deserves some reflection here:

Generalization on Enclisis (Part 4):

Enclisis is never found in dependent clauses with overt complementizers.[25]

This is not an immediate consequence of what we have argued so far; since V2 is possible in dependent clauses (apart from interrogatives) and enclisis is triggered by an empty focus, enclisis should in principle be possible in dependent clauses, too. Interestingly, the absence of enclisis in all dependent clauses can instead be linked to the fact that V-movement to C° in dependent clauses is in fact possible but not obligatory; the requirement is that the complementizer be in a head higher than that of the interrogative. In main clauses, enclisis is triggered by an empty Focus. My hypothesis is that, while enclisis is fed by V-movement to C°, it is the effect of a further movement that is required in main clauses, but rendered unnecessary—in fact, impossible—if a C° head (and a Spec) is realized higher in CP. I will briefly elaborate on this idea in the following, concluding section.

5.4 Some Consequences and Speculations

The descriptive generalizations on medieval Romance pointed out in this chapter are accounted for if we assume that the lowest field in CP—the Focus field—is reserved to constituents that move there leaving a trace. In contrast, the higher fields host elements that are base generated (or moved with a different kind of movement, see note 5) and resumed by a clitic. The requirements for clitic doubling in medieval Romance are identical to those of modern Italian (see above, section 2): only direct objects in Topic or Frame are obligatorily doubled; HTs are distinguished from LD by the lack of Case-matching. Direct objects in Focus are moved and cannot be clitic doubled.

In the light of an articulated structure of CP, we have obtained a unitary description of enclisis of complement clitics in Romance, which accounts for enclisis and proclisis on purely syntactic grounds. Enclisis is a phenomenon—still to be understood as a morphosyntactic process—triggered by a V in C° and an empty Focus. It seems reasonable to suppose that it is the result of a further movement of the V to the left, to reach the head in whose Spec a Topic (LD or HT) is base generated.

In dependent clauses, enclisis is not attested;[26] as such, we conclude that this further movement is not required (and thus not possible). If we think of the empty topic as a *pro,* this context recalls various cases in Romance of *pro*-licensing via government; in dependent clauses, a null topic can be licensed via government by a higher head with features. A sentence beginning with a V is not, in fact, a sentence without a Topic but a sentence whose Topic is interpreted by default. When nothing precedes a V, an argument is necessarily supplied in a Spec in the CP system (possibly to satisfy some version of EPP). While a "null topic" can be inserted and interpreted on the basis of the linguistic context or general knowledge, a "null Focus" seems impossible on various grounds: being a moved element, it must not be inserted as a last resort; being relevant information, it cannot be interpreted by default. An inflected verb in a main clause is then supposed to obligatorily create a Spec-Head configuration with a constituent in Spec, CP, which can either be overt (in the Focus or Topic field) or a null element; a null element can only be in the Topic field. Even if more than one element (overt or null) can coexist in the various CP specifiers, the requirement is satisfied with the lowest one. As a set of V2 languages, Old Romance shows that V2 requirements can be fulfilled at different functional levels in CP. In the framework of this hypothesis, a V-initial sentence is then a sentence that has a Topic (superficially empty) and has nothing in the Focus field, and as such the position of the clitics—if present—conforms to the generalization: they must be enclitic.[27] In Benincà (1989), enclisis was described as the result of a further movement of the V to the Spec of Top;[28] with an articulated structure, the verb can be thought of as moving to a higher head, thus preserving head movement in its classical version. The enclitic position of complement clitics that results from this further movement of the V suggests the existence of a position for clitics in CP; this completes the map of clitics that are being identified in (the functional structure of) IP and VP.[29]

Let me try to sketch a very rough typology of the three layers of clitics I am proposing. In the VP functional area, we find clitics for complements and, in very few cases, clitics for subjects; in the IP area we find the complete series, complements and subjects; only clitics corresponding to subjects have been located in CP for modern Romance (namely, northern Italian dialects). It should not be surprising to find that complement clitics also used to be realized in CP in medieval Romance, in particular cases; this characteristic was lost together with other features of the old syntax.

In a restrictive theory of parameters (see Chomsky 1995, 160; Kayne 2005), parameters are seen as properties of functional elements. If we compare medieval Romance languages with their modern descendants, it seems to be the case that the V2 phenomena we have been dealing with—shared by all varieties and simultaneously lost or modified by all of them—are to be accounted for by a change in parameter setting. Two sorts of phenomena can be recognized that may depend on parametric features: the first is V-movement to $C°$ when the lowest $C°$ is free, and the second is V-movement to higher $C°$ heads in CP. Both phenomena appear to be a consequence of properties of verbal inflection, which in the medieval stage of Romance could be assumed to be endowed with features to be discharged in CP and with features able to licence an argument in its Spec. The relative independence of these two types of features appears reflected in the varieties of Romance that still preserve some residue of the older syntax. These are the Rhaeto-Romance varieties, which are still V2 but have no residue of the medieval clitic syntax, and Portuguese, which maintains the medieval clitic syntax but has a limited V2 phenomenology (no inversion after Focus, etc.). The higher frequency of V-initial word order in the medieval languages of Italy corresponds to a wider range of "dropped" Topics that the V is able to legitimize in the corresponding Spec in this set of languages, that is, to a "stronger" V-inflection.[30]

All that I have been saying makes sense only if we restrict the possible orders of constituents appearing in CP. Topics are merged in the Topic field or in the Frame field; the Focus field is the lowest one and hosts only moved elements. This is consistent with what we had independently concluded on the basis of modern Italian. ■

ACKNOWLEDGMENTS

Various parts of this work have been presented and discussed in class lectures and seminars at the University of Padua (2001–2002, 2004); at the Department of Linguistics, University of Konstanz (2002); at the meeting *Italiano. Strana lingua* (Sappada, July 2002); at the *IV Incontro di Dialettologia* (University of Bristol, September 2002); at the Graduate Center, CUNY (2004); and at the Doctoral School in Cognitive Sciences in Siena (2005). Thanks to those audiences and to the participants in GURT 2004 for stimulating observations, and to Guglielmo Cinque, Lidia Lonzi, Nicola Munaro, Hans Obenauer, and Cecilia Poletto, who provided relevant comments on the first draft. Finally, I thank Raffaella Zanuttini and Héctor Campos, who carefully read the manuscript and provided invaluable suggestions.

NOTES

1. This position can be integrated in the Minimalist Program as outlined in Cinque (1999, sec. 6.3): the full structure is itself part of the numeration; an element is merged (or "base generated") via feature checking; empty functional heads receive a default interpretation (see Cinque, 1999, sec. 6.1). Cinque (2003) discusses in detail the idea that the order of functional projections cannot be accounted for in terms of semantic scope, even if in some particular instances this could seem to be the case (for example, the relative order of Tense and Aspect projections). The order of functional projections is a construct of the computational system, as is the choice of particular modalities and functions among all those that could be linguistically encoded in the system.

2. It is not possible to include Rumanian in the set of languages considered because in its first written texts, which are from the sixteenth century, there is no trace of the phenomena that characterize Old Romance. It was probably too late, as by then all other Romance languages had already undergone a change in this part of the grammar. It is interesting to underline, in relation to this, that the Romance languages seem to change at the same pace in this part of syntax. The only partial exceptions are some Rhaeto-Romance dialects, which are still V2 today, and European Portuguese (with Galician and dialects belonging to that area), which preserve till today, though simplified, the general pattern of the relation between the syntax of clitics and V2 (see a brief discussion in Benincà 1995; more details and theoretical proposals can be found in Costa 2000, in particular the articles by Barbosa, Duarte and Matos, and Raposo).

3. The theory concerning the location of "clause typing" has been recently developed by Nicola Munaro, Hans Obenauer, Cecilia Poletto, Jean-Yves Pollock, Paul Portner, and Raffaella Zanuttini, in various papers on Romance languages and dialects, showing that clause typing markers seem to appear in different positions in the CP system, not just in the leftmost field. It could be the case that the explicit markers are secondary offspring of an abstract primary marking, located in ForceP. More work is needed to further explore this topic.

4. See Benincà (2001) for the case of syntactic topics (LD) that are intonationally focalized. An interesting, more restrictive, analysis of focalized topics as syntactic focuses is discussed in Bocci (forthcoming). Lonzi (2005) presents a very detailed and insightful discussion of the various pragmatic values a syntactic focus can have in spoken Italian.

5. I am oversimplifying the difference between all kinds of Topics on the one hand, and Focus on the other, in terms of base generation for the former versus movement for the latter. Cinque (1990) has proposed an analysis of LD in terms of base generation; the problem remains as to how to account, even in descriptive terms, for the syntactic differences between the two classes of Topics, namely HT and LD (which will be discussed in section 2.1 below). It seems straightforward to analyze a HT as base generated, as the sentence to which it belongs is always a closed sentence, whereas LD is connected to a sentence that in certain cases can be an open sentence, with gaps corresponding to, for example, LD PPs. Even if we were to adopt a movement analysis for LD (as proposed by Cecchetto 1999), we would have to hypothesize a type of movement different from Focus/*wh*-movement. It could be the case, for example, that LD involves a kind of movement that leaves behind functional material, which is either realized as a clitic or remains silent depending on the grammatical relation the element entertains with the sentence (see also, for similar properties of resumptive clitics in Celtic relative clauses, the solution proposed by Rouveret 2002). This problem is however not directly relevant to the issues examined in this paper. I maintain that different kinds of elements

occupy specific fields within CP, and only those elements that are legitimately moved as operators leaving a trace occupy the lower field. The others, which for the sake of simplicity are all claimed to be base generated, occupy higher fields.

6. Rizzi (2002) has approached some restrictions on sequences of arguments in CP as consequences of Relativized Minimality, blocking movements of operators in particular cases. It would be very interesting to do a detailed comparison of his theory and the one adopted in this paper. The ordering of base-generated elements seems, however, to remain outside of its explanatory scope.

7. One interesting aspect of Romance comparative syntax is that having identified the distinctive properties on the basis of modern Italian, we can use them in the analysis of Old Romance and obtain consistent results.

8. In Benincà (2001), evidence is given to identify a position in IP for certain kinds of (apparently topicalized) adverbs, as in the following example:

(i) [CP La casa [IP Gianni domani   la compra]
      the house   Gianni tomorrow it buys
      'The house, tomorrow Gianni will buy it.'

A consequence is that a subject appearing on the left of adverbs of this kind is not necessarily in CP (TopP or FocP) but can be in subject position in IP.

9. More evidence comes from cases in which weak crossover effects can be observed, showing that the alleged Topic appearing on the right of Focus has the properties of a moved element, not of a base-generated topic. See Benincà (2001), section 1.2.1.2, and Benincà and Poletto (2004b), section 2. Recent works present interesting results that are consistent with ours. Krapova (2002) analyzes Bulgarian phenomena that provide very clear evidence against the idea that proper topics (base-generated themes) can also appear below Focus. Interesting data from Russian (Jacopo Garzonio, pers. comm.) show that elements that cannot be topics but only focus in CP (indefinite operators such as *some, some kind of*) can appear to the right of an emphatic Focus ([ia] through [ic]). The same can be observed with respect to Italian *nessuno* 'nobody' ([iia] through [iic]):

(i) a. *kakujuto knigu IVAN kupil   (some book IVAN bought)
    b. KAKUJUTO KNIGU Ivan kupil   (SOME BOOK Ivan bought)
    c. IVAN kakujuto knigu kupil   (IVAN some book bought)
(ii) a. *A nessuno Mario parlava   (to nobody Mario spoke)
    b. A NESSUNO parlava   (TO NOBODY he-spoke)
    c. MARIO a nessuno parlava   (MARIO to nobody spoke)

In a different framework, Dryer (2003) argues for the existence of double Focus preposing in English, which is consistent with the proposal that some apparent cases of Focus followed by a Topic pointed out by Rizzi are double Focus cases, individuating a Focus field where moved elements appear. Some of the examples of Dryer (2003) are in fact to be interpreted as emphatic topics in the light of Italian (our List Interpretation). In Italian, the distinctive feature of this construction is the obligatoriness of the clitic, a piece of evidence not available in English. Even leaving these cases aside, the evidence provided by Dryer remains sufficient and convincing.

10. HTs are not taken into account in Rizzi (1997; see also Rizzi 2001). The example of LD Rizzi uses, where the LD element is a direct object, cannot be distinguished from an HT; this probably explains, at an abstract level, the apparent disagreement between my data and his, for example, with respect to a sentence like the following, which is for me colloquial but grammatical:

(i) Maria dice il   tuo libro che lo leggerà   domani.
    Maria says the your book that it will-read tomorrow
    'Maria says that, your book, she'll read it tomorrow.'

The example is a case of HT and as such it does not falsify the generalization that LD follows the sentential (and relative) complementizer, as can be immediately established using a PP:

(ii) Maria crede,   il tuo libro, che non ne   parlerà nessuno.
     Mary believes the your book, that NEG of-it will-talk nobody
     'Mary believes that, your book nobody will talk about it.'
(iii) *Maria crede,   del tuo libro, che non ne   parlerà nessuno.
      Mary believes of-the your book that NEG of-it will-talk nobody

11. This means that German-type V2 is just a special case of V2 syntax, which entails the requirement of having one and only one overtly filled Spec.

12. See Adams (1987), Benincà (1983/1984), Benincà (1989), Benincà (1995), Vanelli, Renzi, and Benincà (1985); the hypothesis has been developed and refined in works on single Romance languages. See, for example, among others, Vance (1989) on French, Salvi (1990) on Iberian languages, Fontana (1993) on Spanish, Ribeiro (1995) on Portuguese, Paul Hirschbühler's works on Old and Middle French, for example, Hirschbühler and Junker (1988).

13. I will not consider the cases of subjects (DP only) in final position, which have to be considered instances of lexical subjects linked to an expletive *pro* subject licensed by the V in C°: the issue is tangential to the present concerns. A sentence like (20a) is in fact ambiguous as for the position of the subject, while the sentences in (20b; 21a, b), where the subject precedes the object, are more transparent. Sentences with tensed auxiliaries would be even more explicit in this respect, but given the tense system of these languages, we have a relative scarcity of compound tenses.

14. This conclusion is consistent with generalizations on V2 in Germanic languages: the last case in which a Germanic language extends V2 in subordinate clauses is in a dependent interrogative (see Vikner 1995). If a language presents embedded V2 in an interrogative, it will present V2 in any other type of dependent clauses. An apparent exception in Old Romance will be briefly dealt with below, in section 5.1.1.

15. These elements are also used as nominal or adverbial modifiers; in such cases, they obviously have a different distribution. Moreover, in the manuscripts, *si* is written without the accent, which makes it a homograph of the reflexive clitic and the complementizer 'if.' This must be kept in mind because the form of the edited texts depends on the decisions of the editors (and in some edited texts all types of *si* are written without the accent).

16. It is necessary to set aside cases of interpolation, that is, the occurrence of lexical material between the clitic and the inflected verb. Interpolation is found in Old Spanish and Old Portuguese and—in my view—the phenomenon occurs in CP. It is interesting to observe (see Raposo 2000, 279) that the lexical material is found only if the clitic is on the left of the verb. Interpolation is also found in ancient varieties of Italian and modern Romance languages—including modern Spanish and Portuguese; this type is limited to a very restricted class of adverbs and occurs in IP. For interpolation in Old Portuguese, see Rivero (1986), Martins (1994), Raposo (2000, 277); for the type found in modern Italian dialects (which corresponds to what is found in Old Italian and modern Portuguese) see Ledgeway and Lombardi (2002). More reflection is needed on this interesting topic, which can be kept separate from other aspects of clitic syntax.

17. This specification is necessary, as some medieval Romance languages (Old Venetian, Old French, etc.) systematically show proclisis in initial position in *yes-no* questions. Moreover, some varieties treat differently the first position of coordinate sentences: Old Florentine, Old Venetian, and all the medieval varieties of southern Italy behave like Old Spanish and Old Portuguese and have obligatory enclisis if the verb appears immediately after a coordinating conjunction (irrespectively of the syntactic nature of the clause to which they are coordinated, whether a main or a dependent clause). Old French, Old Piedmontese, and Old Lombard do not have obligatory enclisis in this context. I will not further comment here on this difference, which involves the syntax of coordinated structures. I will not examine these particular cases (even if they can easily be accounted for in the proposed framework), as they do not directly bear on the object of our investigation.

18. See, for example, Fontana (1993, sec. 3.4.2) for V1, who points out that V1 appears to be a means of getting a strong textual cohesion, as in the Germanic V2 languages that admit it. This can be related to the hypothesis I will make that V-initial sentences have a null topic; Fontana (1993, sec. 3.4.3) shows that V3 sentences in Old Spanish and Old French admit only a certain type of elements in first position (see below).

19. Given the early date of this text, we cannot be sure that *ko* has already developed into a complementizer head; it is possible that it still retains its original nature of a neuter pronoun, occupying a Spec and marking the associated complementizer head (complementizers introducing complement clauses developed from pronouns in all Indo-European languages).

20. The constituent in TopP is probably an HT, as often is the case in other examples with a DP or PP containing a relative clause (or other material) that renders it "heavy." If so, the presence of an HT after a complementizer in this early text is notable. We cannot be sure of the exact categorial status

of the complementizer at this stage of the development of Romance languages: an element such as *ko* (in contrast with the following *que*) could still have pronominal features; it could have the function of a pro-sentence and structurally be a sister of the entire clause.

21. I am grateful to Nicola Munaro for sharing the data, taken from his chapter on interrogative clauses in Old Florentine (in Renzi and Salvi, forthcoming), and for discussing the analysis with me. As Paul Portner suggested to me (pers. comm.), relative clauses with *come* may represent instances of base generation of the relative pronoun in Topic or Frame with subsequent movement to the higher relative *wh*-projection.

22. It is interesting that in a different version of the *Novellino* the order appears as "normal": *come tue sai queste cose.*

23. In support of this hypothesis, we can consider cases of relative clauses introduced by *come* 'how' in other Old Romance languages, in which we observe that the subject appears in postverbal position. This means that we have V in C° in a dependent clause; so, even if the *wh*-element belongs to the interrogative paradigm, its position is very high, and access to CP is open to the V:

(i) a. de   si lointeingnes terres comme sont les parties de Jerusalem
       from so far   lands how   are the parts of Jerusalem
       'From lands as far as the parts of Jerusalem.'   (OFr. ; *Artu,* 1)
   b. aisi com es amors
       so   as is love   (OProv.; Bertran Carbonel, 54)

The idea that interrogatives can be structurally ambiguous is confirmed by the fact that we find dependent interrogatives using an indefinite relative pronoun or being coordinated with nonambiguous (indefinite) relatives, as exemplified by sentences like the following:

(ii) a. vedutala   così crucciata, la dimandò, quello ch'ella avesse.
       seeing-her so upset,   her asked.3SG that   that-she had
       'Seeing her so upset he asked her what she had.'   (OTusc.; Fr. Da Barberino)
   b. egli è talora   difficile e   grave veder ciò ch'ave alchuno   e   chi
       it   is sometimes difficult and grave to-see that that-has somebody and who
       è quello, a che e   come a ragion   si   move ello.
       is that,   to what and how following reason self moves he
       'It is sometimes difficult and grave to see what somebody has and who he is, why and how reasonably he operates.'   (OTusc.; Fr. Da Barberino)

24. The sentence appears to be a sequence of List Interpretation Topics (see above, section 2.3); the topic of the first clause is an object, the following ones are subjects, and the clitics are always enclitic.

25. This conclusion was already reached by Schiaffini (1954, 68), who asserted that in Old Italian enclisis is never observed after a *che.*

26. Apart, that is, from the case of coordination of subordinate clauses, where the second member is treated, in some varieties only, as a main assertive clause (if the verb is initial, clitics are enclitic; see note 19).

27. A natural consequence is that there cannot be any prosodic reason for the position of clitics with respect to an inflected verb, that is, for the choice between enclisis and proclisis. The generalizations we have seen render this kind of explanation even weaker than it already appeared to the contemporaries of A. Mussafia, who cast some doubts on it (see the discussion in Mussafia [1886/1983, 298]). If enclisis were a way to avoid clitics in sentence-initial position, we would not expect enclitic pronouns in sentence-internal position. This is instead possible, as pointed out here, but only in specific syntactic contexts, when what precedes the verb is not in FocusP.

28. Raposo (2000) develops this idea for what concerns the very similar case of modern Portuguese.

29. I am referring to phenomena reported and analysed by Tortora (2002), for the Piedmontese variety of Borgomanero, and Shlonsky (2002) for some Franco-Provençal dialects, which seem to suggest the existence of a layer for clitics in the functional area of VP in addition to the clitic area in IP. Cinque (2001) also makes this hypothesis on the basis of Standard Italian data. A location for clitics in CP has been proposed for some northern Italian dialects by Poletto (2000), for the so-called vocalic

subject clitics, and by Munaro, Poletto, and Pollock (2001) and Penello (2003) for enclitic subjects in questions. It seems a natural possibility to have a functional structure of a pronominal nature in the three main layers of the structure of the clause.

30. Kayne (1984, 221–22), commenting on the syntactic status of subject clitics in northern Italian dialects (which, in contrast with French, are part of agreement), suggested that "this would appear to be related to Italian being a 'pro-drop' language." At the time, it seemed to me that this idea did not make any sense, as the dialects of Italy each have their own history, independent and parallel to Italian. Today, it still does not make much sense, but seems to be supported by the common characteristics of medieval Italian varieties.

TEXTS AND SOURCES

Old Florentine (OFlor.):

(i) *Novellino* (1300): Favati, G. 1970. *Il Novellino.* Genoa: Bozzi. (The number cited in the text refers to the number of the tale).

(ii) *Testi fiorentini:* Schiaffini, A. 1954. *Testi fiorentini del Dugento e dei primi del Trecento.* Florence: Sansoni.

(iii) *Lettera di messer Consiglio de' Cerchi,* (1291): Castellani, A. 1952. *Nuovi testi fiorentini del Dugento.* Florence: Sansoni.

(iv) *Bono Giamboni* (1292): Segre, C. 1968. *Bono Giamboni. Il Trattato di Virtú e di Vizî.* Torino, Einaudi.

Old Italian data also come from the database of the *Opera del Vocabolario Italiano* (OVI) (Florence-Chicago) http://www.lib.uchicago.edu/.

Old French (OFr.):

(i) *Artu* (circa 1230): Frappier, J. 1954. *La mort le roi Artu.* Geneva: Droz.

(ii) Béroul (circa 1180): Muret, E. 1947. *Béroul. Le roman de Tristan.* 4th ed. Paris: Champion.

(iii) Chrétien (1181): Kunstmann, P. *Chrétien de Troyes. Conte du graal.* Paris, B.N. fr. 794 (ms. A).

(iv) Pierre de Saint-Cloud (circa 1175): Roques, M. 1955. *Le roman de Renart, Branche 7.* Paris: Champion.

(v) *Enéas* (Twelfth century): Petit, A. 1997. *Le roman d'Enéas.* Paris: Librairie générale française.

Old French data also come from the database of the *Laboratoire de français ancien,* Université d'Ottawa-Chicago, http://www.lib.uchicago.edu.

Old Milanese (OMil.):

(i) Bonvesin (1280): Contini, G. 1941. *Le opere volgari di Bonvesin da la Riva.* Rome: Società Filologica Romana.

(ii) *Elucidario* (1310): Degli Innocenti, M. 1984. *Volgarizzamento in antico milanese dell' "Elucidarium" di Onorio Augustodunense.* Padua: Editrice Antenore.

Old Piedmontese (OPied.) :

Sermoni subalpini (Thirteenth century): Babilas, W. 1968. *Untersuchungen zu den Sermoni subalpini.* Munich: Hueber.

Old Portuguese (OPort.):

(i) Huber, J. 1933. *Altportugiesisches Elementarbuch.* Heidelberg: Winter.

(ii) Ribeiro, I. 1995. Evidence for a verb-second phase in Old Portuguese. *In Language Change and Verbal Systems,* ed. A. Battye and I. Roberts, 110–39. Oxford: Oxford University Press.

Old Provencal (OProv.) :

(i) Gaucelm Faudit (1202) : Mouzat, J. 1965. *Les poèmes de Gaucelm Faidit, troubadour du XIIe siècle.* Paris: Les Classiques d'Oc.

(ii) *Venjansa de la mort de Nostre Senhor:* Appel, C. 1930. *Provenzalische Chrestomathie mit Abriss der Formenlehre und Glossar.* Leipzig: O. R. Reisland.

(iii) Bertran Carbonel (1300): Jeanroy, A. 1913. *Les coblas de Bertran Carbonel,* Annales du Midi 25, 137–88 and Contini, G. (1937) Annales du Midi 49, 5–41, 113–52, and 225–40.

Old Sicilian (OSic.) :

    Scremin, M.F. 1984–5. *La struttura della frase nella lingua poetica siciliana.* Laurea thesis, University of Padua.

Old Spanish (OSp.)

    Fontana, J. 1993. Phrase structure and the syntax of clitics in the history of Spanish. PhD diss., University of Pennsylvania.

Old Tuscan (OTusc.)

    Fr. da Barberino (1314): Egidi, F. 1905–27. Francesco da Barberino, Documenti d'Amore, Rome: Società Filologica Romana.

Old Umbrian (OUmbr.)

    Jacopone (1300): Ageno, F. 1953. *Jacopone da Todi, Laudi Trattato e Detti.* Florence: Le Monnier.

Old Venetian (OVen.):

    (i) *Lio Mazor:* Levi, U. 1904. *I monumenti del dialetto di Lio Mazor.* Venice: Visentini.

    (ii) *Rainaldo* (1300): Lomazzi, A. 1972. *Rainaldo e Lesengrino,* 156–82. Florence: Olschki.

REFERENCES

Adams, M. 1987. Old French, null subjects and verb second phenomena. PhD diss., University of California, Los Angeles.

Barbosa, P. 2000. Clitics: A window into the Null Subject property. In *Portuguese syntax,* ed. J. Costa, 31–93. Oxford: Oxford University Press.

Belletti, A., ed. 2004. *Structures and beyond. The cartography of syntactic structures,* vol. 3. Oxford: Oxford University Press.

Benincà, P. 1983/1984. Un'ipotesi sulla sintassi delle lingue romanze medievali. *Quaderni Patavini di Linguistica* 4: 3–19. Repr. in Benincà, P. 1994. *La variazione sintattica. Studi di dialettologia romanza,* 177–194. Bologna: Il Mulino.

———. 1989. Le lingue romanze medievali. Paper presented at the XIX Congreso Internacional de Lingüística e Filoloxía Románicas, Round Table on Word Order in Romance, Universidade de Santiago de Compostela, Spain.

———. 1995. Complement clitics in medieval Romance: The Tobler-Mussafia law. In *Clause structure and language change,* ed. A. Battye and I. Roberts, 325–44. Oxford: Oxford University Press.

———. 2001. The position of Topic and Focus in the left periphery. In *Current studies in Italian syntax. Essays offered to Lorenzo Renzi,* ed. G. Cinque and G. Salvi, 39–64. Amsterdam: Elsevier-North Holland.

Benincà, P. and C. Poletto. 2004a. A case of do-support in Romance. *Natural Language and Linguistic Theory* 22 (1), 51–94.

———. 2004b. Topic, Focus and V2: Defining the CP sublayers. In *The structure of CP and IP.* Vol. 2 of *The cartography of syntactic structures,* ed. L. Rizzi, 52–75. Oxford: Oxford University Press.

Bocci, G. Forthcoming. Some remarks on the cartography of the left periphery of the clause in Italian. *Rivista di Grammatica Generativa.*

Cecchetto, C. 1999. A comparative analysis of Left and Right Dislocation in Romance. *Studia Linguistica* 53, (2): 40–67.

Chomsky, N. 1995. *The minimalist program.* Cambridge, MA: MIT Press.

Cinque, G. 1990. *Types of A´-dependencies.* Cambridge, MA: MIT Press.

———. 1996. On the relative order of certain "lower" adverbs in Italian and French. In *Linguistique comparée et langues au Maroc,* ed. A. Fassi Fehri, 11–24. Rabat, Morocco: Université Mohammed V.

———. 1999. *Adverbs and functional heads. A cross-linguistic perspective.* Oxford: Oxford University Press.

———. 2001. "Restructuring" and functional structure. Unpublished manuscript, University of Venice.

———, ed. 2002. *Functional structure in DP and IP. The cartography of syntactic structures,* vol.1. Oxford: Oxford University Press

———. 2003. Issues in adverbial syntax. Unpublished manuscript. University of Venice.

Cinque, G., and G. Salvi, eds. 2001. *Current studies in Italian syntax. Essays offered to Lorenzo Renzi.* Amsterdam: Elsevier-North Holland.

Costa, J., ed. 2000. *Portuguese syntax.* Oxford: Oxford University Press.

Dryer, M. S. 2003. Three types of Noun Phrase preposing in English. University at Buffalo, New York. http://wings.buffalo.edu/soc-sci/linguistics/people/faculty/dryer/ dryer/papers.

Duarte, I. and G. Matos. 2000. Romance clitics and the minimalist program. In *Portuguese syntax,* ed. J. Costa, 116–42. Oxford: Oxford University Press.

Fontana, J. 1993. Phrase structure and the syntax of clitics in the history of Spanish. PhD diss., University of Pennsylvania.

Hirschbühler, P. and M.-O. Junker. 1988. Remarques sur les sujets nuls en subordonnées en ancien et en moyen français, *Revue québécoise de linguistique théorique et appliquée* 7, (3): 63–84.

Kayne, R. 1984. *Connectedness and binary branching.* Dordrecht : Foris.

———. 2005. Some notes on comparative syntax, with special reference to English and French. In *The Oxford handbook of comparative syntax,* ed. G. Cinque and R. Kayne, 3–69. Oxford: Oxford University Press.

Krapova, I. 2002. On the left periphery of the Bulgarian sentence. *University of Venice Working Papers in Linguistics* 12: 107–28.

Ledgeway, A., and A. Lombardi. 2002. Verb movement, adverbs, and clitic positions in Romance. Unpublished manuscript, University of Manchester, UK.

Lonzi, L. 2005. Contrastive intonation and its disguises of syntactic structure in Italian. *Rivista di Grammatica Generativa.*

Martins, A.M. 1994. Clíticos na história do português. PhD diss., University of Lisbon, Portugal.

Munaro, N., C. Poletto, and J.-Y. Pollock. 2001. *Eppur si muove!* On comparing French and Bellunese *wh*-movement. *Linguistic Variation Yearbook* 1: 147–80.

Mussafia, A. 1886/[1983]. Una particolarità sintattica della lingua italiana dei primi secoli. In *Adolfo Mussafia. Scritti di filologia e linguistica,* ed. A. Daniele and L. Renzi, 291–301. Padua: Antenore.

Penello, N. 2003. Capitoli di morfologia e sintassi del dialetto di Carmignano di Brenta. PhD diss., University of Padua, Italy.

Poletto, C. 2000. *The higher functional field. Evidence from Northern Italian dialects.* Oxford: Oxford University Press.

Raposo, E. 2000. Clitic positions and verb movement. In *Portuguese syntax,* ed. J. Costa, 266–98. Oxford: Oxford University Press.

Renzi, L., and G. Salvi. Forthcoming. *Grammatica dell'Italiano antico.* Bologna: Il Mulino.

Ribeiro, I. 1995. Evidence for a verb-second phase in Old Portuguese. In *Language change and verbal systems,* ed. A. Battye and I. Roberts, 110–39. Oxford: Oxford University Press.

Rivero, M.-L. 1986. Parameters in the typology of clitics in Romance and Old Spanish. *Language* 62: 774–807.

Rizzi, L. 1997. The fine structure of the left periphery. In *Elements of grammar. Handbook of generative syntax,* ed. L. Haegeman, 281–337. Dordrecht: Kluwer.

———. 2001. On the position "Int(errogative)" in the left periphery of the clause. In *Current studies in Italian syntax. Essays offered to Lorenzo Renzi,* ed. G. Cinque and G. Salvi, 286–96. Amsterdam: Elsevier-North Holland.

———. 2002. Locality and left periphery. Unpublished manuscript, University of Siena, Italy.

———, ed. 2004. *The Structure of CP and IP. The cartography of syntactic structures,* Vol. 2. Oxford: Oxford University Press.

Rouveret, A. 2002. How are resumptive pronouns linked to the periphery? *Linguistic Variation Yearbook* 2: 123–84.

Salvi, G. 1990. La sopravvivenza della legge di Wackernagel nei dialetti occidentali della Penisola Iberica. *Medioevo Romanzo* 15: 177–210.

Schiaffini, A. 1954. *Testi fiorentini del Dugento e dei primi del Trecento.* Firenze: Sansoni.

Shlonsky, U. 2002. Notes on the syntax of the so called euphonic [l] in some Romance dialects. Paper presented at the Incontro di Grammatica Generativa, University of Lecce, Italy.

Tobler, A. 1875/[1912]. Review of J. Le Coultre, De l'ordre des mots dans Chrétien de Troyes. In *Vermischte Beiträge zur Französische Grammatik.* Leipzig: S. Hirzel.

Tortora, C. 2002. Romance enclisis, prepositions, and aspect. *Natural Language and Linguistic Theory* 20: 725–58.

Vance, B. 1989. Null subjects and syntactic change in medieval French. PhD diss., Cornell University, New York.

Vanelli, L., L. Renzi, and P. Benincà. 1985. Typologie des pronoms sujets dans les langues romanes. In *Actes du 17ème Congrès International de Linguistique et Philologie Romanes* (Aix-en-Provence, 1983), vol. 3, 164–76. Aix-en-Provence, France: Université de Provence.

Vikner, S. 1995. *Verb movement and expletive subjects in the Germanic languages.* Oxford: Oxford University Press.

4

Questions and Questioning in a Local English

JAMES MCCLOSKEY
University of California, Santa Cruz

1. Introduction

In this chapter, I investigate a small question—why the examples in (1) and (2) are possible:

(1) a. I wondered would I be offered the same plate for the whole holiday.
   Roddy Doyle, *The Woman Who Walked into Doors,* 154

   b. I wondered would the place always look like an abandoned building site.
   Ibid., 192

   c. I wondered was he illiterate.
   Ibid., 96

   d. I asked Jack was she in his class.
   Ibid., 96

   e. I'm sure she wasn't far from the truth when she asked was he thinking of throwing her in.
   John McGahern, *That They May Face the Rising Sun,* 40

   f. He paused briefly and we wondered was he going to list more names and would the then Minister for Defence Jim Gibbons be among them.
   The Irish Emigrant, April 29, 2001

   g. When asked directly by counsel for the families, Michael Lavery QC, did he believe those shot dead on Bloody Sunday had been armed he replied, "Oh yes, I believe that, yes and still do."
   The Irish Emigrant, March 17, 2002

   h. She asked the stewards was any member of the committee in the hall.
   James Joyce, *Dubliners,* 170

(2) a. I asked him from what source could the reprisals come.
   Irish Times, April 24, 2001

   b. The baritone was asked what did he think of Mrs Kearney's conduct.
   James Joyce, *Dubliners,* 176

   c. Joe was nearly getting cross over it and asked how did they expect Maria to crack nuts without a nutcracker. James Joyce, *Dubliners,* 126

   d. I wonder what is he like at all.
   Filppula (1999, 168)

   e. You'd be better off asking why did he marry me.
   Frank McGuinness, *Dolly West's Kitchen,* 55

The crucial property of (1) and (2) is the application of Subject-Aux(iliary) Inversion (understood here as raising of the content of the functional head T to C) in a complement clause—in polar questions in (1) and in *wh*-questions in (2).

The question of what makes such structures possible is a small one but is worth asking. First, it is important to set the empirical record straight. It is routinely claimed that examples like (1) and (2) are impossible in English. There do seem to be kinds of English of which this claim is true, but structures such as (1) and (2) are extremely common in formal and informal Englishes in many different places around the world. The discussion of this paper is based on detailed investigation of (mostly middle class) Irish varieties of English, but the crucial patterns seem to be very widespread.[1] In Irish English, at least, the sentence types in (1) and (2) are widely attested both in speech and in published sources.[2]

Second, while the question of why (1) and (2) are possible is a small one, the effort of answering it thoroughly leads quickly into difficult and interesting theoretical territory. This is true initially because there are theoretical principles which would lead one to expect the general impossibility of (1) and (2). These principles were not proposed lightly and they do useful work. What becomes of those principles in the face of the many varieties of English in which (1) and (2) are in fact possible? This question is related to a second, in that understanding why (1) and (2) are possible entails understanding why examples such as (3) are impossible:

(3) a. *I found out how did they get into the building.

   b. *The police discovered who had they beaten up.

   c. *How many people should you invite depends on how big is your place.

   d. *I usually know who might they hire.

   e. *I remember clearly how many people did they arrest.

This pattern of lexical restrictedness is partly familiar (from work on the formal semantics of questions), and, as we shall see, more complicated than it at first seems to be.

Trying to explain this contrast will therefore be a core concern of the chapter. The question of what makes standard English different and special will also be addressed. It is as well to admit now, though, that the proposal will not be thrilling—the difference between the two sets of varieties will not follow from anything interesting or deep. Boring as it may seem, this is correct, I think, since the relevant difference seems in fact to be fairly superficial.

The contrast between (1) and (2) on the one hand and (3) on the other seems, however, to be very general and to reflect something more interesting about the syntax, semantics, and pragmatics of interrogative complements. Even speakers for whom (1) and (2) are in some sense impossible detect a strong difference in acceptability between those examples on the one hand, and the ones in (3) on the other. Explicating that contrast, therefore, will be a core concern of the chapter.

These questions have been worked on before. To the best of my knowledge, the basic facts were first observed in the literature of generative grammar by Lee Baker

(Baker 1968, 66), who cites examples from literary texts from the turn of the last century. The matter is further discussed in McCloskey (1992) (the ancestor of the present paper) and subsequently in Henry (1995), Grimshaw (1997), Harris (1993, 168), Corrigan (1997), and especially in Filppula (1999, 167–183), all of whom correct, extend, and add to the discussion found in McCloskey (1992). The present discussion will in turn draw on all of these contributions.

2. Parenthesis or Parataxis?

A suggestion often made when people first encounter examples such as (1) or (2) is that they do not in fact represent cases of genuine complementation at all but involve rather parenthesis or a species of parataxis. On this view, the clause in which T-to-C applies is actually a root clause (as expected) to which a parenthetical tag has been added. What makes the general idea plausible is that a case like (4a), a parenthetical structure by many criteria, can be regarded as in some sense a minor stylistic variant of (4b):

    (4) a. What should we do, I wonder?

       b. I wonder what should we do.

As we will see at a later point, there is something fundamentally right about the intuition behind this analysis. But it cannot be literally correct.

    Examples of deeper embedding, such as (5), are hard to reconcile with parenthesis:

    (5) a. I don't think I was ever asked did I see any Provos, Stickies or anyone.
                          Irish Times, May 1, 2001

       b. They would have been rebuffed if they had inquired was there anything they could do.
                John McGahern, *That They May Face the Rising Sun,* 174

It stretches plausibility to take examples such as (5) as root questions decorated with a parenthetical tag. Rather, they mean exactly what we would expect them to mean if they involved routine patterns of complementation. That is, they are exactly paraphrasable in standard English as in (6):

    (6) a. I don't think I was ever asked if I saw any Provos, Stickies or anyone.

       b. They would have been rebuffed if they had inquired if there was anything they could do.

In fact, it turns out that all of the standard properties of complementation hold of the embedded inversion cases—sequence-of-tense phenomena, for instance, as in (7), and pronominal binding, as in (8):

    (7) a. Miss Beirne expected them at any minute and asked could she do anything.
                      James Joyce, *Dubliners,* 171

       b. *Miss Beirne expected them at any minute and asked can she do anything.

    (8) Every male physicist wonders will he be awarded a Nobel Prize.

Probably the clearest way, though, to see the inadequacy of this family of (potential) proposals is to consider cases like (9):

(9) a. ?She's the kind of person that you wonder will your parents like t .

b. ?That's the job that I asked her would she apply for t .

In (9), the clause in which T-to-C has applied is a subpart of a relative clause. Such examples are very mildly deviant in a way that is typical of examples involving extraction of a complement (or of a referential argument) from a *wh*-island. Corresponding examples involving subject extraction (10) and adjunct extraction (11) are, by contrast, severely degraded (see McCloskey 1991):

(10) a. *She's the kind of person that you wonder will t like your parents.

b. *That's the job that I asked her would t be right for her.

(11) a. *How well were you wondering would your parents like them t?

b. *How did you ask them would they tackle this problem t?

The pattern in (9) through (11) is the very familiar pattern of extraction out of a *wh*-island (Huang 1982 and much subsequent work). It is the expected pattern if the clauses in which T-to-C has applied are true interrogative complements—*wh*-islands. The data have no coherent interpretation, as far as I can tell, if all apparent instances of complement T-to-C are understood in terms of parenthesis.

It will be useful to make a final observation. Declaratives with a rising intonation pattern are absolutely impossible in this context. That is, although (12a) and (12b) might seem to be at least roughly equivalent in their semantic import, (13) is utterly impossible (I use a final *?* to indicate rising intonation):

(12) a. Is it raining?

b. It's raining?

(13) *I wonder it's raining?

Such "rising declaratives," however, are at least marginally compatible with true quotative parentheticals:

(14) It's raining?, she mused.

The impossibility of (13) constitutes a puzzle given the conjunction of two positions—first, that the distinctive intonation pattern of (12b) is an alternative (suprasegmental) realization of the question marker, and second, that examples such as (1) involve root, or at any rate unsubordinated, questions. Given this pairing of assumptions, we would expect (13) to be possible, counter to fact. We will return to this issue.

We will see at a later point in the discussion that there is something fundamentally right about the intuition that complement T-to-C always marks a direct question. For now, though, I take forward from this discussion the conclusion that the syntax of parenthesis or parataxis (whatever that turns out to be) will not provide a complete understanding of the well-formedness of (1) and (2).

How then should we understand it? To help resolve the puzzle, we can deepen it a little. To do that, I want to begin an excursus on adjunction possibilities whose relevance to the current problem will probably not be immediately evident.

3. The Adjunction Prohibition

Jackendoff (1972) established the basic outlines of the distributional typology of adverbs in English. One of the adverb types whose existence and properties were established in that work is a class of adverbs which have as one of their canonical positions a left peripheral position in TP. This class in English includes (among others) a group of temporal modifiers at the sentential level such as *in general, most of the time, half the time, next Christmas, usually, every day, tomorrow, yesterday, in a few days,* and so on:

(15) $\begin{Bmatrix} \text{Usually} \\ \text{Most of the time} \end{Bmatrix}$ I understand what he's talking about.

Some, but not all, of these adverbs may also appear at the left edge of VP—that is, to the right of T.

(16) a. I would usually go to Bundoran for my holidays.

    b. *I will next Christmas go to Bundoran for my holidays.

The adverbs that make up this class were for long conventionally taken to be left adjoined to TP, and I will adopt that proposal here. This decision flies in the face of some recent and justly influential work, by Guglielmo Cinque especially (see in particular Cinque 1999). It will become clearer as the discussion proceeds why it will be useful to understand (15) in terms of adjunction, but let us first see why the traditional analysis seems plausible (see also Ernst 1999; Ernst 2001; Potsdam 1998).[3] The adjunction proposal accounts immediately for the fact that in embedded clauses, adverbs of this type may appear between a lexical complementizer and a subject, and be construed as modifying material in the embedded clause:

(17) a. It's probable that $\begin{Bmatrix} \text{in general} \\ \text{most of the time} \end{Bmatrix}$ he understands what is going on.

    b. That in general he understands what is going on seems fairly clear.

The assumption that the adverbs in question are adjoined also correctly allows for multiple attachment (in any order) of adverbs of the same distributional class:

(18) a. [$_{TP}$ In general [$_{TP}$ around Christmas time [$_{TP}$ I go to my parents' house.]]]

    b. [$_{TP}$ Around Christmas time [$_{TP}$ in general [$_{TP}$ I go to my parents' house.]]]

A particularly salient subgroup is the class of adverbial clauses:

(19) a. When he got home, he cooked dinner for the children.

    b. After she finished her thesis, she moved to Paris.

    c. While washing the dishes, he cut his thumb.

Such complex clausal adverbs mix freely with the adverbs we have already considered, once again suggesting adjunction to TP:

(20) a. In general, after people finish their theses, they don't know what to do
with themselves.

b. After people finish their theses, in general, they don't know what to do
with themselves.

c. Usually, around Christmas time, before it gets too cold, we spend a
week by the sea.

Adverbial clauses too, as is well known, may appear between complementizer and subject in embedded clauses, again suggesting adjunction to TP:

(21) a. He promised that when he got home, he would cook dinner for the
children.

b. She swore that after she finished her thesis, she would move to Paris.

c. It seems that while washing the dishes, he cut his thumb.

d. He asked us if after we arrived home, we would cook dinner for
the kids.

Adverbs of this class, however, may not appear to the left of a complementizer when construed with material in the clause headed by that complementizer. Thus (22) and (23) are ungrammatical if the adverbials are construed with the lower clause:

(22) a. *It's probable in general (most of the time) that he understands what is
going on.

b. *In general that he understands what is going on is fairly clear.

(23) a. *He promised when he got home that he would cook dinner for the
children.

b. *She swore after she finished her thesis that she would move to Paris.

c. *It seems while washing the dishes that he cut his thumb.

d. *The police worked out after they got back from Reno what their
movements had been.

It should be recognized at once that the uncompromising * in the examples of (22) and (23) overstates the matter for many speakers. Such examples are not completely ruled out. There will be something to say on this point later, after more of the analytical groundwork has been laid. For now, I persist in the assumption that such examples are categorically ungrammatical. This is an expositional fiction to be repaired later.

The patterns observed so far are those schematized in (24) through (26):

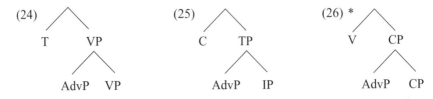

That is, adjunction to the VP complement of T, and to the TP complement of C are possible, but adjunction to the CP complement of a lexical head is impossible.

Similar observations can be made in the case of nonfinite clauses. Here things are complicated a little by the fact that left adjunction of an adverbial phrase to nonfinite TP is impossible:

(27) a. *I want very much for by the time I get home her to have left.

    b. *For by the time I get home her to have left would be great.

The standard assumption (going back to Stowell 1981) is that in such cases, the adjoined adverbial interferes with the Case-licensing of the complement subject, a process in which the complementizer *for* must be implicated, probably in concert with nonfinite Tense (Stowell 1981; Watanabe 1996; Rizzi 1997). But attachment of the adverb to nonfinite CP (for which Case considerations are presumably irrelevant) is also impossible:

(28) a. *I want very much by the time I get home for her to have left.

    b. *By the time I get home for her to have left would be great.

The only remaining possibility is right adjunction to VP or TP:

(29) a. I want very much for her to have left by the time I get home.

    b. For her to have left by the time I get home would be great.

The general pattern that emerges so far, then, is that adjunction of an adverbial phrase to VP or to TP is freely available, but that adjunction to CP is impossible.

What will account for this?

I take it, to begin with, that whatever theory is constructed over this domain must be based on an appeal to general principle rather than on an appeal to parochial or language-particular statements. The kinds of patterns which we have just documented for English can be replicated for many other languages.[4]

There already exists, in fact, a proposed constraint which will have the required effect. Chomsky (1986, 6) proposes that there is a general prohibition against adjunction to argument categories (a proposal which we will refine slightly in a moment). Adjunction to VP and to TP is possible, since these are not argument categories in the relevant sense; adjunction to CP in the cases that we have seen so far is impossible since in each case, CP occupies an argument position (complement or subject). I will call this condition the Adjunction Prohibition, and interpret it as in (30):

(30) Adjunction to a phrase which is s-selected by a lexical (open class) head is ungrammatical.

As in the Aspects theory (Chomsky 1965), we take the domain of s-selection (the domain in which selectional restrictions are imposed, as opposed to the domain in which subcategorization requirements are checked) to include both complement positions and subject positions.

The Adjunction Prohibition as formulated by Chomsky is intended only (as far as I know) as a condition on movement-derived adjunctions. To provide a full account of the kind of data we have been considering here, the prohibition must be interpreted as a condition on all adjunctions. This extension is very natural, if not forced, in the context of the Minimalist Program (Chomsky 1995) since, within that conception, adjunction by movement will subsume the adjunction subcase of the operation MERGE as a suboperation. We will return to the theoretical status of the Adjunction Prohibition at a later point in the discussion. For now let us investigate the empirical ramifications of the formulation in (30).

First, it is clear that adjunction of an adverbial phrase to CP will be permitted just in case the CP in question is not an argument. One case against which we can test this prediction is the case of root CPs, which are nonarguments virtually by definition. The class of adverbs we have been dealing with do in fact attach to root CP.[5] The examples in (31) through (33) illustrate this possibility, on the assumption that interrogative and affective operators appear in the specifier of CP, and that Subject-Aux Inversion involves movement of finite T to C:[6]

(31) a. When you get home, what do you want to do?

    b. When you get home, will you cook dinner for the kids?

(32) a. Next Christmas, whose parents should we go to?

    b. Most of the time, do you understand what's going on?

(33) a. Next Christmas, under no circumstances will I be willing to cook dinner.

    b. Most of the time, when she is working on a paper, only rarely does she leave her office.

We will consider a number of other instances of adjunction to CP in section 4 below.

The approach developed here also accounts for an observation made by Pullum (1991) having to do with the distribution of adverbial phrases within gerunds. Pullum observes that left adjunction of an adverbial phrase to a gerund is impossible:

(34) a. *They resent last Christmas your having been here.

    b. *They resent while you were at home your having visited us.

    c. *During the winter your having been here astonished many.

This is true despite the fact that adverbials appear freely at the right edge of a gerund phrase.

(35) a. They resent your having been here last Christmas.

    b. They resent your having visited us while you were at home.

    c. Your having been here during the winter astonished many.

Moreover, those adverbs which can in general appear left adjoined to VP may also appear left adjoined to VP within gerunds:

(36) a. They resent our having so often rejected their applications.

    b. Our always saying no makes us look bad.

The picture that emerges, then, is that the pattern of adverb distribution within gerunds is exactly the same as in clauses, except that the possibility of left adjunction to the entire phrase is missing.

Gerund phrases, whether analyzed as NP (Pullum 1991), as DP (Abney 1987), or as clausal (Reuland 1983) are always arguments to lexical categories, being either subjects, objects or objects of prepositions. That being so, the ungrammaticality of (34) fits without adjustment into the framework of assumptions developed so far. The acceptable examples in (35) and (36) are instances of adjunction to the VP predicate of the gerund, not to an argument of an open class category, and therefore involve a legitimate adjunction site according to (30).

We can see what are arguably the same principles at work in the case of small clauses. Adjunction to a complement small clause itself is, of course, impossible:

(37) a. He needed her by his side always.

b. He needed her always by his side.

c. *He needed always her by his side.

The ungrammaticality of (37c) is consistent with the Adjunction Prohibition but might be explained in terms of the Case requirements of the subject of the small clause. We can factor out the contribution of this effect, though, by considering subject small clauses, whose subjects, for reasons that are poorly understood, are licensed independently of any external Case-assigner (Safir 1983):

(38) a. Adam on the roof last summer was a wonderful sight.

b. Adam last summer on the roof was a wonderful sight.

c. *Last summer Adam on the roof was a wonderful sight.

The thorough ungrammaticality of (38c) (on the relevant interpretation) is expected on our terms, since it must involve adjunction to the small clause, which, being a subject, is an s-selected argument. For small clauses then also, the facts can be schematized as in (39) through (41):

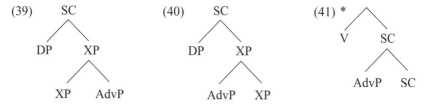

Once again, these patterns are understandable in terms of the Adjunction Prohibition. Finally, consider nominal phrases, such as (42):

(42) The lecture last night (that Erica gave) is mentioned in this morning's paper.

Cases such as these we take to involve adjunction of the modifying phrase (adverbial or adjectival) to the complement of D. Not being an argument of a lexical head, this is a legal adjunction site. Kyle Johnson (1991; 1992) points to the contrast in (43):

(43) a. The review in the Times of Chomsky's book was very favorable.

b. *Of Chomsky's book the review in the Times was very favorable.

Here too, we can take (43a) to involve adjunction to the complement of D (legal in terms of the Adjunction Prohibition). Example (43b), by contrast, would involve illegal adjunction to the subject DP. The ungrammaticality of (44) can be understood in similar terms:[7]

> (44) a. *Last night the lecture (that Erica gave) is mentioned in this morning's paper.
>
>   b. *I really didn't like last night the lecture (that Erica gave).

Finally, the hypothesis that we are exploring suggests that there is no absolute right of adjunction to TP. If there are cases in which TP is the argument of a lexical (open class) head, then adjunction to TP in that circumstance should be impossible. Finding clear instances of this configuration is not easy.[8] However, one plausible case is that of adverbial clauses built around prepositions such as *before, after,* or *since:*

> (45) After we got home, we cleaned up after the cats.

There would seem to be two plausible analyses of such structures available. One is that they are (adverbial) PPs in which a preposition directly selects a TP complement:

> (46) [$_{PP}$ [$_P$ after] [$_{TP}$ we got home]]

This proposal is perhaps supported by the observation that the elements which standardly appear in the specifier position of PP also occur with these adverbial clauses:

> (47) $\begin{cases} \text{Right} \\ \text{Just} \\ \text{Immediately} \end{cases}$ after we left home . . .

A second possibility is that *after, before,* and *since* are actually prepositional complementizers (finite counterparts to *for*), so that the structure of the adverbial clause in (45) would be (48):

> (48) [$_{CP}$ [$_C$ after] [$_{TP}$ we got home]]

The analysis in (48) is argued for by Huang (1982) and by Lasnik and Saito (1992, 91, 113–15). If the analysis schematized in (46) is right, then it is clear that the TP is lexically selected. But, even if (48) is right, there is evidence, as shown by Lasnik and Saito (1992, 91), that the prepositional complementizer L-marks (in the sense of Chomsky 1986) its TP complement in these cases. That is, these are lexically selected TPs under both available analyses. The crucial observation now is that adjunction of an adverbial phrase to TP is impossible in just this circumstance. Compare the (a) and (b) examples of (49) through (51). As throughout, I take it that adverbials which appear at the right edge of TP may be analyzed as instances of right adjunction to VP and are therefore compatible with the Adjunction Prohibition.[9]

> (49) a. *After while washing the dishes he cut his thumb . . .
>
>   b. After he cut his thumb while washing the dishes . . .
>
> (50) a. *Before last year she retired . . .
>
>   b. Before she retired last year . . .

(51) a. *Since a year ago she went away . . .

     b. Since she went away a year ago . . .

These observations suggest strongly that TP, too, is unavailable as an adjunction site when selected by a lexical head. That is, the patterns we have seen so far can be organized as in (52), suggesting again that the Adjunction Prohibition is in play:

(52)   * PP

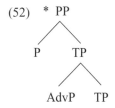

Certain complications arise at this point, however, since *because, while, although,* and *when* work differently:

(53) a. Because most of the time I understand what's going on

     b. Although at the time I thought he was sincere

     c. When a year ago I decided I was going to resign

Causal (but not temporal) *since* behaves similarly:

(54) Since most of the time/usually I understand what's going on, I think I should pass this course.

The "subordinating conjunctions" which exhibit the pattern in (53) seem to be those which forbid the structure [P DP]:

before	*[TP AdvP [TP	before Christmas
after	*[TP AdvP [TP	after Christmas
since (temporal)	*[TP AdvP [TP	since Christmas
because	[TP AdvP [TP	*because this
although	[TP AdvP [TP	*although that
since (causal)	[TP AdvP [TP	*since your incompetence

A plausible interpretation is that the elements which allow adjunction to their complement TP are members of the category C (suggested by their inability to take DP complements), and that the elements which forbid adjunction to their TP complements are members of the category P (suggested by their ability to take DP complements). If this interpretation is roughly correct, then the Adjunction Prohibition will once again be seen to lie behind the ungrammaticality of (49) through (51).[10]

The Adjunction Prohibition, as we understand it so far, is clearly not a complete theory of adjunction possibilities. Adjunction of adverbial phrases to relative clauses and to adjunct clauses in general, for instance, must also be ruled out:

(55) *The people [CP when you get home [CP who want to talk to you right away . . .

(56) *I graduated [while at college [without having really learned anything]].

Neither of these possibilities is ruled out by the Adjunction Prohibition as formulated in (30) or by any obvious extension of it. Grimshaw (1997), responding in part to an earlier version of the present chapter, suggests a way in which these cases (and some cases we have still to consider) can be unified.

We will return to these issues shortly in a slightly different context. For present purposes, I will assume either that the Adjunction Prohibition as formulated in (30) will be among the statements that make up a general theory of adjunction possibilities, or else that its empirical effects will follow as a consequence of some more general system of principles, when the theory of adjunction possibilities is complete. If that is so, then we can use the Adjunction Prohibition as a useful diagnostic probe.

4. A Connection Made—Adjunction and Inversion

At this point, the discussion of adjunction possibilities can be linked back to the announced topic of the chapter. The connection is that apparent problems for the Adjunction Prohibition arise when we observe the (relative) well-formedness of (57):

(57) a. ?He asked me when I got home if I would cook dinner.

b. ?I wonder when we get home what we should do.

How can (57) be possible if the Adjunction Prohibition reflects a true generalization? To answer this question, we must first note that the pattern in (57) is possible only in the complements of certain predicates. The examples in (58) are all completely impossible (with, as always, the lower construal of the adverbial):

(58) a. *It was amazing while they were out who had got in to their house.

b. *The police established while we were out who had broken in to our apartment.

c. *While you're out how many people break in to your apartment depends on where you live.

d. *Who your friends are depends on while you were growing up where you lived.

e. *In the course of a single year how much he had grown really astonished me.

The contrast between (57) and (58) mirrors exactly the contrast already observed between the predicates which allow embedded T-to-C and those which do not. That is, my claim is that the class of predicates which allow inversion in their complements is exactly the class which allows the initially unexpected adjunction pattern in (57).

Corresponding to the instances of embedded T-to-C in (1) and (2), we have the following instances of adjunction of adverbials to CP. For this class of matrix predicates, the results are either good or only marginally unacceptable:[11]

(59) a. ?Ask your father when he gets home if he wants his dinner.

b. ?I was wondering next Christmas if he would come home.

c. ?Ask them when they were in Derry if they lived in Rosemount.

    d. ?He never asked me when he went to England if I wanted to go with him.

    e. ?He inquired when we were young how we used to get about.

And for varieties which allow embedded T-to-C, the corresponding examples are perfect:

(60) a. I wonder this time will he make a move.

                      Frank McGuinness, *Dolly West's Kitchen,* 12

    b. Ask your father when he gets home does he want his dinner.

    c. I was wondering next Christmas would he come home.

    d. I'll ask them when they get home do they want a cup of tea.

    e. I wonder if a baby was presented with equal exposure to several different languages would they retain their "universal phonetician" status.   Student Essay, June 2003, California

But those predicates which completely disallow the option of adjunction of an adverbial phrase to their CP complement also completely disallow the option of embedded T-to-C:

(61) a. *It was amazing who did they invite.

    b. *The police established who had they beaten up.

    c. *Who are your friends depends on where did you live while you were growing up.

    d. *How much had he grown really astonished me.

The contrast between this class of verbs and those in (59) is very robust for those speakers who allow embedded T-to-C. It is also, I believe, clearly detectable for speakers of the "standard" variety.

    The correlation is, in fact, closer even than this would suggest. One important complication in the distributional pattern investigated so far has been passed over. It turns out that the possibility or impossibility of embedded T-to-C depends not only on the governing verb but also on certain other properties of the matrix clause. Specifically, the verbs which forbid T-to-C in their complements in (3) and in (61) will permit it to varying degrees of acceptability if the clauses they head are negative or interrogative. This is seen in the illustrative paradigm of (62) and is illustrated with attested examples in (63).

(62) a. *I remember who did they hire.

    b. ?Do you remember who did they hire?

    c. ?I don't remember who did they hire.

(63) a. 'Ah, he's a nice young fellow.' 'I don't know is he.'

                 William Trevor, *The Story of Lucy Gault,* 98

    b. Do you think will he ever be able to get them right?

                 John McGahern, *That They May Face the Rising Sun,* 331

c. Do you think will Herself get married again?

John McGahern, *That They May Face the Rising Sun,* 11

The examples in (64) are cited in Filppula (1999, 168, 171). Example (64d) is from Hebridean English and is cited originally in Sabban (1982). The other examples are all from varieties of Irish English.

(64) a. I don' know was it a priest or who went in there one time with a horse collar put over his neck.

b. I don' know what is it at all?

c. Do you think is it done?

d. But he was telling me he didn't know how did he manage it.

And in just this circumstance, the unexpected adjunction pattern of (59) and (60) turns up again, with the same elaboration that adjunction is most clearly acceptable when in combination with overt T-to-C, as in (66):

(65) a. ?Do you remember when they were in Derry if they lived in Rosemount?

b. ?I was never sure when he went to England if I should go with him.

c. ?I've never found out if I'd asked him if he really would have come with me.

d. ?Did he tell you when he was young how he did it?

(66) a. Do you remember when they were in Derry did they live in Rosemount?

b. I was never sure when he went to England should I go with him.

c. I've never found out if I'd asked him would he really have come with me.

d. Did he tell you when he was young how did he do it?

We will be in a position at a later point in the discussion to say something about why negation and interrogation should have this licensing effect (both for adjunction and for allowing T-to-C). For now, we use the observations only to further confirm the pattern with which we are most closely concerned at present, namely that there is a very exact correlation indeed between the possibility of adjunction to CP and the possibility of T-to-C in complement CP.

5. An Initial Proposal

At this point we have a cluster of related puzzles, and the challenge is to construct an understanding of those puzzles that will do the following:

▪ It must allow for the possibility of T-to-C in embedded interrogatives, while preserving whatever was right about the principles that suggested that that possibility should not exist.

▪ It must provide an understanding of why that possibility is restricted in the ways just documented (determined by the governing verb, in interaction with the presence of negation and interrogation in the matrix clause).

- It must provide an understanding of why the possibility of T-to-C correlates so precisely with the adjunction possibilities in the way just documented.
- It must provide an understanding of why rising declaratives are impossible in the contexts in which complement T-to-C is possible.

The chief puzzle concerning the possibility of embedded T-to-C in the varieties which allow it is that it seems to violate certain well-established general conditions on T-to-C movement. The consensus view that has emerged in studies of the Verb-Second pattern is that T-to-C fronting is possible if and only if the target C-position is not lexically selected (see especially Rizzi and Roberts 1989, developing earlier ideas of Kayne's 1982, 1983; and den Besten 1983). T-to-C substitution will be possible on this conception in a CP which is not selected at all (in a matrix clause, for instance, or in an adjunct clause such as a conditional) or in a CP which is selected by a functional rather than by a lexical head. Call this the KRR-effect (the Kayne/Rizzi/Roberts effect).

Apparent exceptions to the KRR-effect occur in many of the Germanic languages—cases in which declarative Verb-Second clauses (and hence clauses which exhibit T-to-C movement) appear in what seem to be lexically selected contexts. A number of close studies of this phenomenon came to the conclusion that the syntax which underlies the possibility of embedded Verb Second is the availability of a C which itself takes a CP complement—a line of analysis sometimes referred to informally (and a little misleadingly) as the CP-recursion analysis. Such analyses have been most commonly deployed for declarative complements.[12] However, similar analyses have been developed for interrogative complements in Dutch (see especially van Craenenbroeck 2004, building in part on earlier work by Erik Hoekstra, Jan-Wouter Zwart, and Hans Bennis), and in Spanish (Rivero 1978, 1980; Plann 1982; Suñer 1991, 1993; Lahiri 2002, 263–284). We can easily adapt such proposals for our purposes here, proposing something like (68) for (67):

(67) I wonder what should we do.

(68)

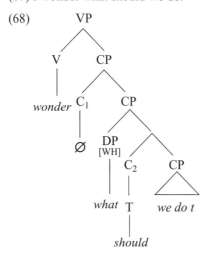

If (68) is on the right track, then we have an understanding of the observations made so far. The possibility of T-to-C movement to the lower C-position of a structure like (68) is expected since that position is not lexically selected. The possibility of adjunction to the lower CP is expected for exactly the same reason. Since that CP is not selected by a lexical head, adjunction to it will not lead to a violation of the Adjunction Prohibition. The structure in (68) allows us, then, to tie together the patterns observed so far and to relate them in turn to a well-established array of syntactic patterns in other languages.

Two remarks are in order about this proposal and about its place in larger theoretical context. First, one might well interpret the structure of (68) in terms of recent work deriving from Rizzi (1997) which develops the idea that rather than a single C-projection there is an elaborated series of functional projections devoted to the expression of information-structural notions like Focus and Topic and also to illocutionary and clause-typing information (see especially Rizzi 2004). C_1 and C_2 of (68) would on this view be distinct but related heads—members of the family of categories which jointly define the C-field. In particular, within the framework presented by Benincà (this volume), one might identify C_1 of (68) with the Force projection (the projection devoted to the expression of illocutionary force and clause typing) and the lower C_2 with the Focus projection.[13]

The second remark has to do with what we have called the KRR-effect and how it should be understood. As we have seen, what requires explanation here is this: why might it be that a head position which is the target of lexical selection would resist head movement? Rizzi and Roberts (1989) suggest that the forbidden head movement gives rise to what are, in effect, selectional violations. A verb which subcategorizes for a particular complementizer requires that the head of its complement be that complementizer. But if that head position hosts an application of head movement, the complex object so created is distinct from the complementizer, and a violation of selectional requirements results.

This account has great intuitive appeal and considerable explanatory force, but it made little sense in the theoretical context in which it was originally proposed—the framework of Principles and Parameters theory. A core commitment of that framework is the idea that the level of D-structure is the level which is relevant for satisfaction of lexical requirements. In this context, it is hard to see why an application of head movement into the selected position should pose any difficulty, since it will apply, by definition, subsequent to the level of D-structure.

Within the terms of the Minimalist Program, though, the larger context is very different. In the absence of a level of D-structure, heads are introduced and their selectional requirements satisfied as the derivation proceeds. In this context, a C-head will host a head movement from within its complement before the CP which it projects is in turn merged with its selecting head. Head movement, then (as long as it is a syntactic operation), will be expected to interfere with, or interact with, selectional requirements which target heads.[14]

To be more specific, we can follow Pesetsky (1982) and Pesetsky (1991, ch. 1) in maintaining that a central aspect of the selectional system is l-selection—that is, that a lexical item may require that the head of its complement be a particular lexical item. In terms of the theory of Bare Phrase Structure, we can understand this as follows: what it means for a lexical item to bear an l-selectional feature [__ H] is that its complement must be a syntactic object whose label is the lexical item H. Head movement from a lower to a higher head position modifies the properties of the element that it targets (by adding information), creating a modified lexical item—an object that is not part of the syntactic lexicon. From this, and from the understanding of l-selection just outlined, it follows that any head which hosts a head movement may not enter into legal l-selectional relations with a subsequently merged lexical item. The KRR-effect can be understood in this way. If particular verbs, adjectives, or nouns l-select particular complementizers, then head movement into those C-positions will give rise to violations of l-selectional requirements.

For this to be maintainable, it must be the case that the selectional relations which hold among functional heads are not instances of l-selection (otherwise, head movement would everywhere be impossible). There is, however, a large body of work (see, for instance, Abney 1987; Grimshaw 1992) which develops exactly this position. If this is right, then we can understand both the KRR-effect and the possibility of T-to-C into the lower C-position of (68).[15]

This account will extend to the Adjunction Prohibition, given certain assumptions (admittedly outdated) about how the adjunction relation is encoded in syntactic structures. In earlier versions of the theory of Bare Phrase Structure (Chomsky 1995, ch. 4), the difference between adjunction and other structures was encoded on the label of the complex syntactic object formed by adjunction. Specifically, adjunction of α to β, where β has label K, creates a syntactic object whose label consists of the ordered pair <K, K>:

$$\{<K, K>, \{ \alpha, \beta\}\}$$

Adjunction of PP to CP headed by *that,* for instance, will, on this view, create the syntactic object below:

$$\{<that, that>, \{ PP, CP \}\}$$

The label in such cases is not a lexical item. Therefore, no syntactic object so formed could legitimately satisfy an l-selectional feature borne by a subsequently introduced lexical item. If this is maintainable, then the Adjunction Prohibition and the KRR-effect would both be reflections of a more general requirement on modes of satisfaction of l-selectional features.

Taking stock, then, we can say that the double-CP syntax of (68) makes the right distinctions and correlations, while letting us preserve (and arguably improve on) essential insights concerning the KRR-effect. Two important analytical tasks remain. The first and most important is that we need the right theory of context sensitivity. That is, the structure in (68) and its associated syntactic effects may appear only in a restricted range of environments. We need an understanding of why this is so. The second is that we need to discharge the worry about the emptiness of the higher

C-head (C_1 of [68]). Discharging the worry involves two tasks. One is that of providing evidence for the existence of two heads where there seems, in the general case, to be only one (or none). The second task is that of providing an account of why one of those heads is typically empty. Section 6 deals with the second of these issues; section 7 deals with the first.

6. Double-Headed Clauses

In this section, I want to present some evidence that the structure in (68) is a reasonable one and also to be a little more precise about the mechanisms that it implies.[16]

A central element of our proposals is that the lower CP of a double-CP structure becomes a legal adjunction site in virtue of being selected by a functional rather than a lexical head. As pointed out to me by Richard Kayne, there is direct evidence that the double-CP structure does in fact serve this function. Examples such as (69) are extremely common in both written and spoken English:[17]

(69) a. But the simple analysis which suggests that because American
       investment takes place here that we should be a lapdog for their efforts
       in the war is one that I think is quite objectionable and quite offensive.
                                                    Irish Times, February 7, 2003

   b. He thinks that if you are in a bilingual classroom that you will not be
      encouraged to learn English.   Student Essay, California

   c. My fervent prayer is that for the sake of the president and the sake of
      this nation that this matter is resolved soon.
                                                     AP wire report, Jan 29, 1999

   d. He invited people to remember that whatever their station in life that
      there was a merciful God who cared about them.
              Morning Edition; National Public Radio; Sunday, December 22, 2002

   e. They know that in general that a jury is not going to be financially
      savvy.
                                        BBC World Service News; Monday, April 5, 2004

The basic shape of such examples is that in (70), with the analysis in (71):

(70) . . . that AdvP that [$_{TP}$ . . .]   (71)

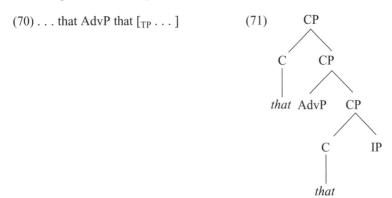

There is much that is mysterious about (69). In the first place, the two instances of *that* may occur if and only if an adverbial intervenes between them. Secondly, that adverbial must be substantial, though not necessarily clausal, as shown by (69c–e).[18]

The crucial property of these structures for our immediate purposes, though, is that adjunction of the adverbial phrase is clearly made possible by the "protecting" higher C-projection, whose existence is unambiguously signaled by the presence of two instances of *that*. It is hard, in fact, to avoid the suspicion that that higher layer of structure is projected exactly so as to allow the lower adjunction (that is, to use a crude metaphor, the extra structure is projected as a way of "getting around" the Adjunction Prohibition).

The net of correlations can be extended in one remaining important way. For Irish varieties at least, we also have interrogative examples such as (72), which are in an important sense exact interrogative counterparts to the declarative (69):[19]

(72) a. Patsy asked him if, when he was sent to college, was it for a clergyman or a solicitor.

b. John Fleetwood . . . asks if in the event that a member of Portmarnock Golf Club had a sex change operation, would he/she still be eligible for membership?

c. John was asking me if, when the house was sold, would they move back to Derry.

Just as the examples of (69) exhibit two instances of the declarative complementizer *that,* separated by an adverbial phrase, so (72) exhibits two instances of the interrogative complementizer separated by an adverbial phrase. The higher of the two is realized as *if;* the lower of the two hosts raising of the inflectional head:

(73)
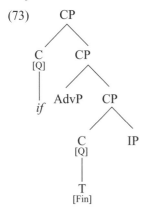

Beside the grammatically parallel examples (69) and (72) we have the paired ungrammaticalities of (74) (impossible in all varieties, as far as I have been able to discover).

(74) a. *They claimed that that they wouldn't harm us.

b. *I asked them if would they like a cup of tea.

c. *I asked them if if they would like a cup of tea.

Many important questions about (72) and (73) remain (some of which will be addressed in section 7). Their very existence, however, provides support for two key elements of the proposals we have developed so far. First, they provide direct evidence for the existence of double-CP structures in certain interrogative contexts (complements of the *wonder/ask/inquire* class specifically). Second, they provide evidence for the interpretation of adverbial adjunction possibilities suggested earlier (adjunction to the lower CP is possible, because it is not lexically selected).

But the pattern in (72) is also important because it lets us glimpse and therefore identify the higher head of the interrogative double-CP structure (68)—it is *if,* an interrogative complementizer. But the lower head is also interrogative *if.* We know this because of the (relative) well-formedness of the examples in (65) from section 4 above, some of which are repeated here as (75):

(75) a. ?Ask your father when he gets home if he wants his dinner.

b. ?I was wondering next Christmas if he would come home.

c. ?Ask them when they were in Derry if they lived in Rosemount.

By the logic of our proposals, the adverbial clause here must be adjoined to the lower CP of (68) (to escape the effect of the Adjunction Prohibition), and the higher C must be null. It follows that the lower C of (68) must also be *if.*[20] If no material intervenes, then, between the higher and lower C, we will have a sequence of two interrogative complementizers, as in (74c).

To construct an account of these observations, let us assume that the lexicon of English makes available two variants of the interrogative complementizer, one with and one without an uninterpretable T-feature.

$$(76)\ \underset{[Q]}{C} \qquad (77)\ C\begin{bmatrix} Q \\ uT \end{bmatrix}$$

The C in (76) is realized as *if* ; the C in (77) forces an application of raising of T, to ensure the elimination of its uninterpretable feature.

All interrogative taking predicates l-select C bearing [Q]. Because of the KRR, however, the C in (77) may not appear in a position exposed to selection by a higher lexical head. T-to-C is therefore impossible in the complement of *discover,* since (for reasons which will be clarified in section 7 below) that verb generally forbids the double-CP interrogative structure in its complement position. The C in (77) may, however, appear in the lower C-position of the complement of *wonder* (selected by the higher C, not by the verb) and T-to-C therefore may (and in fact must) target that lower position.

All varieties of English (as far as I know) require that a root interrogative complementizer must be (77). What makes "standard" English special is that it in addition imposes a restriction that (77) may occur only in the root, a requirement which obscures almost all of the patterns that we have been concerned with here.[21]

This set of assumptions yields directly the pattern seen in (72). Some additional mechanism must ensure that, in conditions other than those of (72), one at least of the heads goes unpronounced. Let us assume, then, that interrogative C is deletable, but that the filter below constrains possible outcomes:

The Complementizer Haplology Filter:

$$* \quad C \quad C \quad \text{If both instances of C have phonological content.}$$
$$[\alpha Q] \, [\alpha Q]$$

This will forbid all of (74) but allow (69) as well as (72).

I assume that recoverability requirements guarantee that a raised auxiliary will never delete, and further that such requirements also guarantee that both complementizers may not simultaneously delete. These are embarrassingly large promissory notes, but I am not in a position to make good on them here.

Summarizing to this point, however, it has been argued that the CP complements of *wonder, ask,* and similar predicates must contain at least two distinct projections of the C-type—their presence indicated by facts concerning adjunction and head movement. Such structures must exist in all varieties of English (so that we can understand the adjunction facts). While the presence of the two heads and their associated projections is revealed clearly in the local and informal varieties studied here, it is obscured in more "standard" varieties by the kinds of morphosyntactic factors dealt with in this section.

Of the analytical goals set out at the beginning of the chapter, then, the principal one that remains is that of constructing an understanding of the context sensitivity of the phenomena we have been concerned with. That task now reduces to the task of understanding why the double-CP syntax of (68) (with its associated syntactic effects) is restricted to its characteristic set of environments. To a first approximation, we must ensure that these structures may occur in the complement of *wonder, ask,* and *inquire* but not in the complement of *discover, find out,* or *remember.* We will have to, in addition, construct an understanding of how it is that the presence of negation or interrogation in the matrix clause can influence these distributional possibilities.

Trying to address these issues brings us into the most difficult territory we have had to explore so far.

7. Semantics, Pragmatics, and Selection

As an important preliminary, we can observe that the crucial distributional patterns are not specific to English. In Italian, for instance, Clitic Left Dislocation may place a topic (resumed by a pronoun internal to the clause) to the left of an interrogative phrase, as in the examples in (78) (see especially Cresti 1995):

(78) a. Mi domando Mario chi l'   ha visto.
     me I-ask   who him has seen
     'I wonder who has seen Mario.'

    b. Mi domando Mario chi l'   abbia   visto
       me I-ask   who him has-SUBJ seen
       'I wonder who has seen Mario.'

The verb governing this structure in (78) is (the Italian version of) *wonder,* the same verb which in English licenses both the unexpected adjunction pattern and the unexpected application of T-to-C in its complement. Changing the verb in question to one which forbids these two patterns in English produces corresponding ungrammaticality in Italian (data from Paolo Acquaviva, Luigi Burzio, Anna Cardinaletti, Giulia Centineo, Michela Ippolito, Cecilia Poletto, and Luigi Rizzi, to all of whom I am very grateful):

(79) a. *Ricordo   Mario chi l'   ha visto.
           I-remember   who him has seen
           'I remember who saw Mario.'

    b. *Ti   ho   detto Mario chi l'   ha visto.
        you I-have told   who him has seen
        'I told you who saw Mario.'

    c. *Ho   scoperto Mario chi l'   ha visto.
        I-have found-out   who him has seen
        'I found out who saw Mario.'

And the correlation is again closer, since, as reported by one of the consultants:

> . . . but your examples with *stabilito* 'establish', *detto* 'say',
> *scoperto* 'discover' sound degraded; they seem to become
> fine again if the main clause is a question, though: *ti hanno*
> *detto, Mario, chi lo ha visto? Hai poi scoperto, Mario,*
> *chi lo ha visto?*

In addition, it seems that negating the matrix verb has a similar, but weaker, ameliorating effect:

(80) a. *Ricordo Mario chi l'ha visto.
    b. ?Non ricordo Mario chi l'ha visto.

(81) a. Non so   Mario chi l'   abbia   visto.
       NEG I-know   who him have-SUBJ seen
       'I don't know who saw Mario.'

    b. Non ricordo   Mario chi l'   abbia   visto.
       NEG I-remember   who him have-SUBJ seen
       'I don't remember who saw Mario.'

In such cases, we are dealing with movement of an argument from a clause-internal position rather than with merge of an adverbial phrase as in our discussion of English. The logical structure of the puzzle, however, is the same in the two cases: the Adjunction Prohibition correctly predicts the ungrammaticality of (79) if we assume (counter to fashion) that these cases, too, involve adjunction to CP. The puzzle—in Italian as in English—is to understand why certain governing predicates (and the influence of negation and interrogation in the matrix structure) can license structures in which the effects of the Adjunction Prohibition are amnestied. Given the analysis we have developed so far, we must assume that the complement of *domandarsi* is (at least) a double-CP structure, while the complement of *ricordare* is the simpler single-CP structure. And, as in English, the subtler challenge is to allow for the effect of negation and questioning in the matrix.

It can hardly be an accident that the lexical partition documented here (in English and in Italian) corresponds exactly to a distinction that has been central in work on the formal semantics of questions. One of the core issues in that body of work has been what Ginzburg and Sag (2000, 65) call the Interrogative Uniformity Thesis—the thesis that all syntactic constituents corresponding to the pretheoretical category *interrogative* have a uniform denotational type. Karttunen's influential (1977) discussion accepted the thesis, assigning to the complement of *wonder* and *ask* the same semantic type as that assigned to the complement of *know, remember, tell,* and so on. Almost from the beginning, however (see for instance Boër 1978), skepticism was expressed about the thesis, in particular because it requires the postulation of numerous lexical doublets so that alternations like those in (82) will be allowed for:

(82) a. They told me/discovered/knew/forgot who had been nominated.

    b. They told me/discovered/knew/forgot that Susan had been nominated

The alternation illustrated in (82) seems systematic rather than idiosyncratic. Verbs like *wonder* and *ask* of course do not permit the option of (82b):

(83) a. They wondered/asked who had been nominated.

    b. *They wondered/asked that Susan had been nominated.

Partly as a consequence, there is a conviction running through much of the relevant literature that the contrast between (82) and (83) reflects some fundamental difference between the two classes of verbs and the complement types that they take. For this and for other reasons (see especially Szabolcsi 1997), a large body of work argues that the complement of *wonder* is semantically very different from the complement of *discover* (Groenendijk and Stokhof 1984a, 1984b, 1989, 1997; Munsat 1986; Berman 1991; Lahiri 1991, 2000, 2002; Ginzburg 1992; Suñer 1993; Szabolcsi 1997; Krifka 1999, 2001; Ginzburg and Sag 2000).

No single terminological system has so far established itself in this discussion, but I will follow Ginzburg and Sag (2000) in distinguishing between the two classes by using *question predicates* as a name for the class that includes *wonder, ask,* or *inquire,* and the term *resolutive predicates* for verbs such as *find out, discover, remember,* and so on.

The common thread running through the work cited above is that question predicates embed complements whose semantic type is the same as that of a root question, while resolutive predicates embed complements which are more akin to propositions (hence their occurrence with predicates which also select propositions). This central intuition has been worked out in a variety of different ways. In one influential strand (Groenendijk and Stokhof 1984a, 1984b, 1989), complements to resolutive predicates are taken to be extensional (propositions which express true and complete answers to a question) while root questions and the complements of question predicates denote the corresponding intensions (functions from possible worlds to propositions, which divide the set of possible worlds into partitions defining the space of possible answers to a given question). For Ginzburg and Sag (2000), working in the context of Situation Semantics, *wonder* selects a "question," while *find out* selects a "fact"—a model-theoretic construct which constitutes an answer to the question expressed by the interrogative clause. An important subsidiary claim for them is that the *that*-complement of (82b) also denotes a fact, and they thus succeed in making a natural connection between the possibility of (82a) and the possibility of (82b).

For much of what I want to argue here, it does not matter which theory of interrogative types turns out to be right; what is important is that there be a difference between two types. At a later point in the discussion, I would like to follow down a particular one of these paths, but for immediate purposes, I will circumvent the issue by speaking of the semantic type assigned to the complement of *wonder* as the *higher* interrogative type, and speaking of the type assigned to the complement of *find out* as the *lower* interrogative type. The initial analytical strategy should then be fairly clear; we will say that question predicates select complements in the higher interrogative type and that resolutive predicates select complements in the lower interrogative type, and we will hold that the larger structure of (68) is the syntactic correlative of the higher interrogative type and that the smaller, single-CP structure is the syntactic correlative of the lower interrogative type.

More must be said, of course, but we can make two observations even at this preliminary point. First, we can now redeem a promissory note issued in section 2 above, where it was observed that embedded inversion routinely brings with it the intuition that the complement clause is in some sense a direct question. Since the complement of a question predicate and a root question are assigned to the same semantic type (the higher interrogative type), this intuition has a real basis in the analysis sketched so far.

Second, the debate on the Interrogative Uniformity Thesis has largely proceeded on the assumption that there is no syntactic difference between the two types of interrogative complement. The inability to detect syntactic differences between the two complement types has, in fact, been the source of some skepticism about whether the type differentiation is real (see, for instance, Lahiri 2000 and especially Lahiri 2002, ch. 6). If our argumentation here is correct, the proposed difference in semantic type is mirrored closely by a difference in syntactic structure, and a source of skepticism about the type differentiation is eliminated.

Pushing further, though, we can ask some additional questions. One of the conclusions we have been brought to on syntactic grounds is that the complement of a question predicate is "larger" than the complement of a resolutive predicate, in a very particular sense: the former includes a layer of structure not present in the latter (this is the "protective" layer of higher structure which crucially allows raising to the lower head and adjunction to the lower CP). Put another way, the syntax corresponding to the higher interrogative type properly contains the syntax of the lower interrogative type. One can ask why this should be so.

In thinking about this, I will follow the account of Krifka (1999), which develops a set of proposals that dovetail particularly well with the syntactic conclusions argued for here. Krifka's theory of the higher interrogative type is that it is the type of question acts. Root questions and the complements to verbs of the *wonder/ask/inquire* class are taken to denote speech acts (question speech acts, more specifically). It is proposed that the denotational semantics for speech acts is properly modeled by a semilattice—more limited than a full Boolean algebra in that the operation of conjunction is defined but the operations of disjunction and negation are not. This proposal yields an appropriate semantics for pair-list readings of multiple questions, as well as a solution to a puzzle which has bedeviled work on the formal semantics of questions since the beginning: the puzzle of why apparent wide scope readings are available for universal quantifiers (but supposedly only for universal quantifiers) inside *wh*-questions:

(84) Which dish did every student make?

Krifka's resolution of this puzzle is grounded in the observation that universal quantification (but not other kinds of quantification) can be understood in terms of the conjunction operation alone. In addition, the proposal also yields a good understanding of conjunctions of questions.

Resolutive predicates, by contrast, do not select a question act but rather an interrogative sentence radical (which denotes a set of propositions; Hamblin 1976; Karttunen 1977). From this difference is derived the well-known differences in quantificational behavior between the two classes of complement (Berman 1991; Lahiri 1991; Szabolcsi 1997; Lahiri 2002). Interrogative radicals (the lower interrogative type) stand in a systematic relation to question acts (the higher interrogative type), in that there is an operator QUEST, which is a function taking sets of propositions and yielding a corresponding interrogative speech act. The application of this function to the denotation of an interrogative sentence radical (the denotation type for the complement of a resolutive predicate) yields an object (a speech act) which is of the right type to be the complement of a question predicate. That is, the semantics of the complement of *wonder* involves an extra compositional step (application of the QUEST operator) deriving it from the semantics of the complement of a verb such as *discover*.

The connection to the concerns of the present chapter should by now be apparent. Our core syntactic proposal is that there exists a layer of syntactic structure in the complement of a question predicate which is absent in the interrogative complement of a resolutive predicate. The natural move to make at this point is to assume that that additional layer of phrase structure is the syntactic correlate of the extra compositional step proposed by Krifka, the step in which the QUEST operator is introduced and applied to the interrogative radical (realized by the lower CP). Put another way, the double-CP structure is the canonical structural realization (in Grimshaw's sense) of the semantic type of speech acts, the projection of the higher CP rationalized since it is the locus of the introduction of the QUEST operator. Such a proposal links the syntactic effects which have been at the center of the present discussion with the semantic differences between the two classes of interrogative complement, and links both with the distributional differences that have been documented here throughout.

In addition, the connection between those complement clauses in which inversion applies and direct questions is very directly made (both denote question acts).[22]

It has been routine in descriptive work in syntax and in pragmatics to assume that illocutionary force indicators may be embedded; witness the line of work extending from Hooper and Thompson (1973) on embedded assertions, through discussions of embedded Verb Second in Germanic languages (dominated by the effort to make sense of the notion *embedded assertoric force*), to recent work in the "cartographic project" (Rizzi 1997, 2004; Benincà, this volume; among many others). In the proposal just sketched here, combining our syntactic conclusions with the semantic proposals of Krifka (1999), the higher C-projection of (68) is exactly an embedded illocutionary force indicator. In a different intellectual tradition, however (in the philosophy of language and in work in formal semantics informed by logic and philosophy of language), there is a well-established and widely held view that there can be no such thing as an embedded illocutionary force indicator and that analyses which make appeal to such notions are incoherent. This is one of the reasons why Krifka's proposals about the semantics of questions have been controversial. The issues, then, are of fundamental importance.[23]

Partly for that reason, I want to end by suggesting that Krifka's proposals may provide the basis for understanding the nonlexical effects on the distribution of the higher interrogative type that we have documented here for English and for Italian— the contribution of matrix negation and interrogation to the licensing of embedded questions.[24]

The starting point for the discussion is the kind of paradigm seen in (85):

(85) a. *I remember was Henry a Communist.

b. ?I don't remember was Henry a Communist.

c. Do you remember was Henry a Communist?

That is, predicates which normally reject inversion in their complements (resolutive predicates) are more tolerant of such complements when they are themselves negated or head an interrogative clause. In the framework developed here, this must mean that negated and questioned verbs will accept the double-CP structure of (68), even when their nonnegated or nonquestioned counterparts will not. And it must follow in turn, then, that matrix verbs which will not normally tolerate the higher interrogative type in their complements will tolerate it when the matrix is negative or interrogative. This is so because the logic of our analysis implies that embedded inversion is always the surface sign of a complement of the higher interrogative type (a true question), a consequence whose plausibility is enhanced by the observations we are dealing with here.

In the context of Krifka's idea that the higher interrogative type is a question act, a natural solution to this puzzle presents itself.[25] Speech acts can be viewed as having a particular kind of context change potential—they induce transitions from one commitment state to another, where commitments may be shared or not by participants in the conversation and may be private or public (Gunlogson 2001; Krifka 2001). Each such act will be subject to a characteristic set of felicity conditions, defined, in part, on the basis of the commitments which hold at the point in the conversation at which it is made. For a question, one of the conditions that must be met is that the semantic content it puts forth must be at issue (unresolved, or controversial) in the initial state of the transition. A direct question such as (86) is felicitous only in the context of a commitment state which does not include either the proposition that Bush will win the election or the proposition that he will not.

(86) Will Bush win the November election?

If we take seriously the idea that speech acts may be embedded as complements to certain predicates (that *wonder,* for instance, denotes a relation between an individual and a certain type of context change potential), then we will expect that the effect of their characteristic felicity conditions will be felt in the embedded context and not at the root. So in a case like (87):

(87) I wonder will Bush win the November election.

the complement to *wonder* will be felicitous only if the issue of Bush's electoral success is unresolved for the referent of the experiencer argument of *wonder* at the present time. In the particular case of (87), because of the accident of identity of reference between the speaker and the experiencer argument of *wonder,* and because what is relevant is the commitment state at the present time (the time of speaking), the effect of uttering (87) (which is, strictly speaking, an assertion) is barely distinguishable from the effect of performing a question act—barely distinguishable, that is, from (86). In the case of (88), however, the appropriateness of the complement will depend on the commitment state of the speaker at some point in the past (not the commitment state at the time of the conversation), and the effect is clearly distinguishable from the asking of a direct question.

(88) I wondered would Bush win the November election.

Finally, for (89), the calculation to be made is whether or not the issue of Bush's electoral success was resolved for Mary, at the time in the past which functions as reference time:

(89) Mary wondered would Bush win the November election.

The commitment state of the speaker is crucial for calculating the felicity of the matrix assertion, but is irrelevant for judging the felicity of the embedded question (a term now understood literally).

Ginzburg and Sag (2000, 65, 111, 352–57) introduce the term *resolutive predicates* for the class of predicates which do not embed true questions, and their characterization of these predicates (*tell, discover, remember,* and so on) is that they carry "a presupposition that the embedded question is resolved" (65n10). Given that characterization, we understand why (85a) fails. The embedded inversion means that this is, in our terms, a double-CP structure. It follows (on the assumptions that we are currently exploring) that the complement must denote a question act, understood as a certain kind of context change potential. The question act is appropriate in this context only if the issue it raises is unresolved for the individual denoted by the experiencer argument of the embedding verb (in this case, as it happens, the speaker). But lexical properties of the predicate entail that this condition cannot be met. A way of understanding this would be to hold that the syntactic and semantic computation proceeds to an outcome in a case like (85a) but that that outcome incorporates a contradiction. It simultaneously entails or presupposes that the issue defined by the embedded question is resolved for the experiencer (the rememberer) and entails or presupposes that it is not.

But we also understand why (85b) becomes possible. The effect of negation here is exactly to entail or assert that the issue defined by the complement is not resolved (for the referent of the experiencer argument). As a consequence, the question act is felicitous in its context.

We can also understand why (85c) is possible. It is a direct question, which in its turn brings with it a felicity condition, namely, that the issue it raises is not resolved (for the participants in the conversation). Assume that the addressee in (85c) is Sandy Chung. It is then appropriate to use (85c) only if it is an open issue at that point in the conversational game whether or not Sandy Chung remembers whether or not Henry was a communist. But if it is an open issue for Sandy Chung whether or not she remembers if Henry was a communist, the issue of whether or not Henry was a communist cannot be resolved for Sandy Chung (the individual referred to by the experiencer argument of *remember*). It follows in turn that the felicity condition on the embedded question is met and that (85c) should be possible.

The fact that the matrix subject of (85c) is second person plays a crucial role in the chain of inference just laid out. That is the accident which ensures that issues unresolved for the participants in the conversation are also unresolved for the referent of the experiencer argument of the embedding verb. In this way, we understand an observation that has been made to me many times in the course of the years during which I have been presenting this material to audiences in various parts of the English-speaking world, namely, that the person of the matrix subject is crucial in licensing the embedded inversion. There is an enormous contrast between (90) and (91):

(90) a. Do you remember was he a communist?

    b. Do you think will he be reelected?

    c. Do you know will he accept the offer?

(91) a. *Does Sally remember was he a communist?

    b. *Does Sally think will he be reelected?

    c. *Does Sally know will he accept the offer?

The examples in (91) fail because the fact that it is an open issue for participants in the conversation what Sally remembers or thinks or knows implies nothing whatever about what is an open issue for Sally. But it is this last circumstance which is crucial for licensing of the embedded inversion (via the mechanisms discussed earlier).[26]

Negation and questioning are not the only devices which can expand the licensing capabilities of resolutive predicates. Any of a number of devices which determine nonveridical contexts (in the sense of Giannakidou 1997) have the same effect.

Consider the examples in (92), the first noted in conversation, the other two from literary texts.

(92) a. Everybody wants to know did I succeed in buying chocolate for
Winifred.

b. Aunt Kate wants to know won't you carve the goose as usual.

James Joyce, *Dubliners,* 223

c. I was dying to find out was he circumcised.

James Joyce, *Ulysses,* 615

In (92a), licensing of the higher interrogative type in the complement of *know* depends on the epistemic state of the individuals denoted by the experiencer argument of *know;* that state is in turn evaluated with respect to the parameters defined in the matrix clause (realistic and finite, therefore at the present time in the actual world).[27] Evaluated in this way, the issue raised by the embedded question is unresolved for the wanters and the knowers (the same individuals in this case because of the Control configuration). For those individuals, at the present time in the actual world, the issue raised in the question is unresolved. As a matter of historical fact, in the conversation of which (92a) was a part, the issue raised in the embedded question was completely resolved for both participants, but that is not a relevant consideration for licensing of the embedded question. What matters for that is the commitment state for the individuals referred to by the experiencer argument of *know.*

Unsurprisingly, the same effect can be achieved by use of an imperative:

(93) Find out does he take sugar in his tea.

For (93), what is relevant is whether or not the issue raised by the question is resolved or open for the addressee. Clearly it is open.[28]

Why are rising declaratives impossible (see [13] of section 2 above and its associated promissory note), despite their apparent similarity to polar interrogatives? This fact, too, is understandable given the present proposals and those of Gunlogson (2001, 2002), where it is demonstrated that in their syntax and in their semantics, rising declaratives simply are what they appear to be—declarative CPs which have propositions as their denotation type. Their particularity (what is signaled by their distinctive intonation) is that they withhold commitment to the truth of their propositional content on the part of the speaker but attribute such commitment to the addressee. The proposition introduced is thus rendered controversial (in a sense formally defined in her system), and the overall effect of uttering such a sentence is as a consequence very close to (but not identical to) that of introducing a question. On this view (developed, of course, without reference to the present set of puzzles), the impossibility of rising declaratives in the complement of any question embedding verb (see [13]) reflects an irreparable violation of selectional requirements.[29]

This is amateur semantics, and the discussion skates blithely over some formidably difficult issues. Many questions remain open, and the proposals may or may not survive incorporation into a serious formal framework. Nevertheless, the general approach holds out enough preliminary promise, it seems to me, at the explanatory and descriptive levels, that it is worth asking where we will be, theoretically, if it turns out to be roughly on the right track.

Where we end up, it seems, is with a version of the Interrogative Uniformity Thesis. That is, there is no deep divide between the question predicates and the resolutive predicates with respect to their selectional properties. Rather, there are two related semantic types systematically associated with interrogative clauses: a lower type and a higher type. Whatever the correct understanding of these types turns out to be, all interrogative selecting predicates may, in principle, combine with complements of either type. Some of the resultant meanings are filtered out by a clash between felicity conditions associated with the higher type (true questions) and entailments (or presuppositions) associated with one subclass of embedding predicates (the resolutive predicates).

This general conclusion is close in spirit to that of Ginzburg and Sag (2000) and also to that of Lahiri (2002), both of whom argue for a uniform type assignment for interrogative complements but also propose that there exists a repair mechanism for the type clash which results when a resolutive predicate finds an object of inappropriate type (a question) in its complement position. Lahiri's idea is that the complement of *know* differs from the complement of *wonder* neither in syntactic category nor in semantic type. Rather, the CP complement of *wonder* is interpreted in situ, but the CP complement of *know* undergoes obligatory Quantifier Raising forced by a type mismatch between the complement and the verb with which it must combine. For Ginzburg and Sag (2000), the repair mechanism is a kind of coercion which is stated as a constraint on the lexical entries of resolutive predicates.

If the suggestions made here are on the right track, though, there is no deep incompatibility between question meanings and resolutive predicates. For the effects discussed here, at least, the necessary discriminatory work is done by ultimately pragmatic conditions on the use of true questions, and we do not want to hardwire into the lexical entry of a resolutive predicate a constraint which forbids it to combine with a complement of the higher interrogative type.

8. Declarative Complements

There is no reason to believe that the effects just considered should be exclusive to interrogative complements and question speech acts. Indeed, Krifka's (1999) analysis is explicitly designed to be a general theory of embedded speech acts and their relation to the sentence radicals (sets of propositions in the case of questions, propositions in the case of assertions and orders) upon which they are based. Given the ideas developed earlier, then, it is natural for us to expect double-CP structures in declarative contexts also, with the associated syntactic effects, conveying embedded assertions rather than embedded questions.

These expectations are entirely in harmony with the numerous studies of embedded Verb-Second phenomena in a range of Germanic languages and of "embedded root" phenomena more generally. It was in this context, as noted earlier, that the recursive-CP hypothesis first emerged. Further, an intuition that runs through this line of work (see especially Hooper and Thompson 1973; Wechsler 1991; Reis 1997;

Gärtner 2000, 2001; among many others) is that embedded Verb-Second structures have assertoric force.

However these important issues are ultimately resolved (and the corresponding issues for interrogative clauses and question speech acts), we can with reasonable confidence adopt the idea that double-CP structures are attested in declarative contexts as well as in interrogative contexts, that they have *assertoric protoforce* as their semantic content, or else that (as in Krifka's 1999 system) they directly denote assertoric speech acts.[30]

This much granted, it becomes possible to clear up some loose ends and to indulge in some larger speculations. We can, in the first place, redeem a promissory note made earlier and better understand the intermediate status of (22) and (23), repeated here as (94):

(94) a. *It's probable in general (most of the time) that he understands what is going on.

b. *He thought when he got home that he would cook dinner for the children.

c. *She believed after she finished her thesis that she would move to Paris.

d. *It seems while washing the dishes that he cut his thumb.

It was pointed out when this phenomenon was introduced that such examples are not uncompromisingly ungrammatical for all speakers. Given the idea that a certain class of verbs (the "weak assertives" of Hooper and Thompson 1973; the "bridge verbs" of Erteschik-Shir 1973; and much of the literature on embedded Verb-Second phenomena) take, as one option, double-CP complements with assertoric force, we now expect examples such as (94) to be grammatical or ungrammatical depending on whether or not they are construed as having single-CP or double-CP structures (with the associated semantics). The judgment task is thus a rather subtle one, and the variation attested is as a consequence expected.

Furthermore, the distribution of such double-CP structures is known to be limited in a very mysterious way (Vikner 1991, 1995; Iatridou and Kroch 1992). Iatridou and Kroch (1992) is especially useful as a survey and an integration of much of the relevant observations and literature. Their statement of the restriction is as in (95):

(95) Embedded verb second . . . is found only in clauses governed by an L-marking non-negative, non-irrealis bridge verb.

Iatridou and Kroch (1992, 7)

It follows from (95) that the judgments about adverbial adjunction to CP should sharpen in contexts in which the double-CP structure is ruled out by (95). This is clearly the case, as is shown in (96):[31]

(96) a. That in the course of the day the weather would worsen was very clear.

b. *In the course of the day that the weather would worsen was very clear.

c. That after graduating she would move to Paris was widely predicted.

d. *After graduating that she would move to Paris was widely predicted.

e. They expressly denied that while coming home they had been delayed.

f. *They expressly denied while coming home that they had been delayed.

Analogous considerations apply in the case of interrogatives. It was noted earlier (see [65], section 4 and [75], section 6) that examples such as (97) are marginal in a way that the corresponding examples in which inversion has applied in the complement clause, as in (98), are not (see also [60]):

(97) ?Ask them when they were in Derry if they lived in Rosemount.

(98) Ask them when they were in Derry did they live in Rosemount.

This subtle effect we can now understand in the same terms as (95) (earlier [22], [23]). In asking a consultant to provide a judgment on (97), the task we are asking them to perform is this: First decide if the complement is a true question. If it is, then a double-CP structure must be postulated. Given that, there is a structural ambiguity to resolve—(97) could reflect either a structure in which the adverbial is adjoined to the higher CP layer (in which case, *if* could appear either in the higher or the lower head position) or else a structure in which the adverbial is attached to the lower CP layer, in which case *if* must appear in the lower C-position. The latter parse should yield a judgment of acceptability; the former should yield a judgment of unacceptability. No wonder judgments are tentative. Example (98), by contrast, involves one less level of uncertainty. The appearance of the fronted modal identifies that position unambiguously as the lower C-position (since raising to the higher C-position is impossible by the KRR-effect).

There are other phenomena for which these considerations are relevant. Alison Henry has documented a variety of English in which one finds T-to-C in the complement to a bridge verb, triggered by successive-cyclic movement of a *wh*-phrase (Henry 1995):

(99) a. They wouldn't say which candidate they thought should we hire.

b. I'm not sure which one I think should we buy.

If these structures also involve the licensing of assertoric double-CP structures and raising of T to the lower of the two C-positions, these observations also fall into line with theoretical expectation.[32]   ∎

ACKNOWLEDGMENTS

This chapter has an overlong history. It derives from a working paper first circulated in 1992. I am grateful for advice and help from Sandy Chung, Bill Ladusaw, Jane Grimshaw, Richie Kayne, Cathal Doherty, Sten Vikner, Hubert Haider, Kyle Johnson, Armin Mester, Hans den Besten, Alison Henry, John Frampton, Chris Potts, Magui Suñer, Bruce Hayes, Pete Alrenga, Héctor Campos, and Raffaella Zanuttini. Discussions with Hans-Martin Gärtner were particularly helpful at an important point. Much of the research reported on here was done while I was a visitor in the School of Celtic Studies of the Dublin Institute for Advanced Studies, and I am grateful for the ideal working conditions that I enjoyed there. The work was supported in part by National Science Foundation grants no. BNS-9021398 and no. BCS00131767 and in part by research funds made available by the Academic Senate of the University of California, Santa Cruz. The chapter has benefited a great deal from presentations at the University of California, Santa Cruz

(October 1999); Massachusetts Institute of Technology (November 1999); Rutgers University (April 2000); University of California, Los Angeles (June 2000); the University of Konstanz, Germany (February 2003); the University of Christchurch, New Zealand (August 2003); the Georgetown University Round Table on Syntax and Semantics (March 2004); and ZAS (the Center for General Linguistics, Typology and Universals Research) in Berlin (April 2004).

NOTES

1. See, for instance, Miller (1993, 126), Filppula (1999, 170–173), Edwards and Weltens (1985), Beal (1993, 204). Examples from current usage in the United States will be cited from time to time below. In addition, all of the patterns and generalizations considered in the present paper seem to hold of New Zealand English. Thanks to Jen Hay, Kate Kearns, and Kon Kuiper for discussion.

2. The term "standard English," used for the varieties in which (1) and (2) are ungrammatical, is not a good one, since it implies that the varieties in which they are grammatical are nonstandard in some way. But there is no clear sense in which (1) and (2) are nonstandard in, for instance, the Irish context, since there seems to be little or no normative pressure directed against them. I have no good alternative to offer, though, and so I will continue to use the term to make the needed distinctions.

3. It is perfectly possible, of course, that the relevant class of adverbs might originate in the specifier of a designated functional head, as in Cinque's theory, and subsequently raise to the adjoined position that the discussion here assumes.

4. See Vikner and Schwarz (1991, 3–4) on various Germanic languages, for instance. Cinque (1990, 94–95) discusses some Italian facts that seem initially problematical for the idea that adjunction of sentential adverbs to argument CP is in general impossible.
His examples include (i):

   (i) Mi ha promesso, domani, che verrà
       me has promised tomorrow that will-come
       'He promised me that he will come tomorrow.'

   In (i), the adverb *domani* is construed with the embedded clause although it appears to the left of the complementizer *che*. These examples however, do not in fact seem to involve adjunction to CP. In the examples cited (his [106a–c]), Cinque is careful to demarcate the adverb with commas, and in fact the adverb in this kind of example is set off prosodically from the rest of the clause. The prosodic features involved suggest parenthesis and the pre-COMP positioning of the adverb is probably the result of the kind of freedom of positioning often granted to parenthetical elements. As Cinque notes, all such examples have a less marked variant in which the adverb appears in the post-COMP position we would expect given our general set of assumptions, as seen in (ii):

   (ii) Mi ha promesso che domani verrà

   Of course a question remains as to why parenthetical placement of the adverb in the pre-COMP position is available in Italian but unavailable in general in English (although the considerations of section 8 below may well be relevant here). Thanks to Guglielmo Cinque and to Giulia Centineo for discussion of this issue.

5. Reinhart (1983, ch. 3) takes such cases as (31) to involve attachment of the adverbial phrase to the E(xpression) node of Banfield (1973), but, as she points out, it is not crucial for her discussion whether the adjunction is to E or to some higher clausal projection (CP in our terms). The consequences for Condition-C effects follow equally well on the assumption that the adverbials in question adjoin to CP. Anticipating later discussion, it would be natural to identify E with the higher C-projection of a double-CP structure.

6. Examples analogous to those in (31) through (33) but involving declarative V2 clauses seem to be ungrammatical in some of the V2 Germanic languages but grammatical in others. For German, the relevant structures seem to be uniformly bad in declarative V2 clauses. Example (i) is cited in Vikner and Schwarz (1991, 4):

   (i) *Gestern   Peter hat tatsächlich dieses Buch gelesen.
       yesterday   has actually   this   book read
       'Yesterday Peter actually read this book.'

The situation, however, is complicated by the fact that corresponding structures for interrogative V2 clauses are grammatical for many (but not for all) speakers:

(ii) Wenn wir nach Hause kommen, was   sollen wir kochen?
    when we to   house come   what should we cook
    'When we get home, what should we cook?'

This difference between declaratives and interrogatives seems to be systematic; it holds in many of the Scandinavian languages. The Swedish examples below are from Vikner and Schwarz (1991, 4) and from Wechsler (1991, 187) respectively:

(iii) *Trots allt Johan vill inte läsa de   här bökerna
    despite all   will not read these here books
    'In spite of everything, John will not read these books.'
(iv) I en stad som Fremont vem skulle inte vara uttråkad
    in a town like   who would not be   bored
    'In a town like Fremont, who wouldn't be bored?'

I have no suggestion to make about what explains these differences.

7. Tom Ernst raises the difficulty of examples like (i) and (ii):

(i) Probably our strongest argument is summarized on page two.
(ii) Arguably the best solution to this problem is illustrated in Figure 3.

If these adverbs—*probably* in (i) or *arguably* in (ii)—are adjoined to the subject, we have a difficulty for the Adjunction Prohibition as formulated in (30). It is very unclear to me what the syntax of such examples is, but it seems far from obvious that they involve simple adjunction of *probably* or *arguably* to the subject. Semantically, the adverb seems to modify the superlative adjective. Note, in fact, that such cases are grammatical only if there is a superlative (or marginally a comparative) adjective in the NP:

(iii) *Probably a sound argument against this proposal is presented in Chapter 3.
(iv) ??Probably a stronger argument against this proposal is presented in Chapter 3.

What we have instead is the more expected (v):

(v) A(n) arguably/probably/possibly sound argument against this proposal

Cases such as (v) are entirely consistent with the Adjunction Prohibition, of course, since here the adverb has adjoined to an AP modifier of NP.

    Possibly the adverbs in cases such as these occupy the position also occupied by *all* or *both* in phrases such as *all God's children* or *both Susan's parents.* In any event, in the absence of an understanding of the phenomenon, it seems premature to conclude that the preferred analysis will involve a violation of the Adjunction Prohibition.

    Similar questions arise about *only* and *even,* which seem to attach to essentially any maximal projection, regardless of its status as argument, predicate, or modifier. For an early proposal about how to understand such elements, see Hornstein (1977, 158). For more recent discussion, see Iatridou and Kroch (1992, 21–23), Bayer (1995).

8. In addition to those discussed in the text, there are two obvious cases to consider: ECM complements and complements to Raising predicates. In both cases, however, there are complicating factors which make it hard to assess the issue.

    Examples such as (i) are certainly ungrammatical, as predicted by the Adjunction Prohibition, if *consider* selects a TP complement:

(i) *I consider [$_{TP}$ in general [$_{TP}$ this kind of issue difficult to resolve]].

The ill formedness of such examples is often attributed to a disruption of the Case-licensing relationship between the governing verb and the infinitival subject, as, for instance, in the adjacency requirement explored initially in Stowell (1981). The status of the adjacency condition is unclear in current contexts, though, and the Adjunction Prohibition might provide an alternative account of some of the observations that originally motivated it, such as (i). The account would extend to (27) if the kinship of the complementizer *for* with preposition *for* were sufficient to cause the Adjunction Prohibition to be invoked.

Similarly, (ii) is not perfect:

(ii) ?*Tom tends at Christmas to visit his parents.

But there are a number of confounding factors—the absence of an audible subject and the possibility of extraposition—which make it difficult to be sure what the attachment point for the adverbial is.

9. The grammaticality of (i) suggests that the classical complementizer deletion analysis of such examples is correct.

(i) He said when he got home he would do the dishes.

If (i) involved selection of TP, then the contrast between it on the one hand and (49a) through (51a) on the other would be unexplained. For further discussion, see Stowell (1981), Doherty (1993), Grimshaw (1997).

10. A difficulty with this interpretation is *until,* which allows a DP complement (suggesting that it is a preposition) but which still allows at least some cases of adverbial adjunction to its apparent complement:

(i) until next year/tomorrow/the next time we meet/Easter
(ii) until finally/at last/in 1996 she was forced to resign

Given the proposal in the text, such dual possibilities would have to reflect a lexical ambiguity: *until* would have to belong to two word classes, C and P.

11. We will be in a position to say something about the marginality of these examples when more of the analysis has been developed. See section 8.

12. For detailed discussion, see Haan and Weerman (1985), Vikner (1991, 1995), Rizzi and Roberts (1989, 21–22), Cardinaletti and Roberts (1991, 5–6), Iatridou and Kroch (1992). All the Germanic languages but Dutch permit embedded Verb-Second structures in declarative clauses. German is exceptional in this group in forbidding embedded Verb Second under an overt complementizer.

T-to-C is impossible in complement interrogative clauses in most Germanic Verb-Second languages but possible in recent varieties of Afrikaans (Diesing 1990, 54n10; Biberaur 2001). It occurs, however, only in *wh*-interrogatives, not in polar interrogatives. Biberaur reports that T-to-C occurs in Modern Spoken Afrikaans in 70 percent of embedded *wh*-questions in her corpora. The examples she cites are consistent with the lexical restrictions documented in the present chapter (embedded under *wonder* and not *know)* but no ungrammatical examples are presented.

Embedded T-to-C in complement interrogatives seems also to occur in certain varieties of nonstandard French, judging by Rizzi and Roberts (1989, 28n22).

13. Benincà's idea is that interrogative *wh*-movement targets first the specifier of the Focus projection and subsequently the specifier of the Force projection. The latter idea, though, is not consistent with some of the observations made here, since in cases in which an adjoined element appears to the left of a *wh*-phrase, the logic of the analysis to be developed implies that the *wh*-phrase is in the lower specifier position (specifier of C_2 in [68]).

14. See Matushansky (2000) for arguments that head movement is not exclusively on the PF side of the derivation.

15. Head movement of D to N, as in Longobardi (1994), will be permitted in direct object position as long as the D-head is not a target of l-selection. This seems right: verbs do not select particular determiners. See also Pesetsky (1982, 1991).

16. Interrogative structures which seem to have the structure in (68), as well as many of the distributional and interpretive properties we associate with (68), are well known from Spanish and have been well studied (Rivero 1978, 1980), Plann (1982), Suñer (1991, 1993), Lahiri (2002, 263–284).

17. The pattern seen in (69) seems to be fully productive in Galician, judging by the discussion in Iatridou and Kroch (1992, 16–17), which draws on observations made by Juan Uriagereka. Fontana (1993) observes that the same pattern was productive in literary Spanish up until the sixteenth century. See also Rizzi (1997, 330).

18. An initial reaction that many have to examples such as (69) is that they represent performance errors rather than aspects of the grammar. One reason for resisting this skepticism is that the structures in

question are commonly found even in the most carefully monitored and closely edited prose. Other considerations will come up below when the general problem of the licensing of double-CP structures is considered.

19. Example (72a) is from *Gort Broc—Scéalta agus Seanchas Ó Bhéarra,* Máirtín Verling, Coiscéim, Dublin, 1996, p. xxxix. It represents a contemporary rural West Cork variety. Example (72b) is from a letter to the editor, *Irish Times,* December 11, 2002. Example (72c) is due to Cathal Doherty. Thanks to Cathal Doherty, Maryrose Bourke, and Angela Bourke for discussion of these facts. Similar facts seem to hold in New Zealand English and for many speakers of American English.

20. I postpone until section 8 the issue of why the examples in (75) are marginal and why the cases in which inversion applies (i.e., [60] of section 4 above) are not similarly marginal.

21. As pointed out by Héctor Campos and Raffaella Zanuttini, this assumption leaves unresolved the difficult question of why T-to-C apparently fails in subject *wh*-questions. If (77) occurs in every root question, and if subject *wh*-questions involve the CP-layer, then we expect T-to-C in such questions, counter to fact. The alternatives open seem to be: (i) to claim that subject *wh*-questions do not involve the CP-layer, (ii) to claim that the restriction on (77) is that it may only occur (but need not occur) in the root C-position, or (iii) to follow Pesetsky and Torrego (2001) in holding that the uninterpretable tense feature of (77) in such cases is satisfied by means other than head movement (i.e., in interaction with the nominative subject). I have nothing to add here to the debate on these questions.

22. It should be recognized, however, that Krifka (2001) revises the proposals in ways that are less clearly compatible with the syntactic framework developed in the present paper. In that later work, the complement of a resolutive predicate is also taken to denote a speech act (an answer) and no predicate directly selects an interrogative radical. These proposals mesh less well with the syntactic proposals developed here, in that the correlation between syntactic category and semantic type is less harmonious. As far as I know, Krifka (2001) presents only one reason for abandoning the proposal of Krifka (1999). This has to do with examples like (i):

(i) Molly announced how many cakes three/most/several visitors had eaten.

The observation is that we seem to have to allow for wide scope for the subject of the *wh*-complement (i.e., for three/most/several visitors, Molly announced how many cakes they had eaten). This creates a dilemma for the earlier proposal, according to which the complement of a resolutive predicate denotes an interrogative radical (a set of propositions). If the subject takes wide scope only in the lower clause, that clause is not of the appropriate logical type (it denotes a set of propositions) for the quantificational structure to be interpretable. But the other obvious alternative (raising the embedded subject so that it takes scope in the matrix clause) is also problematical, in that it will violate widely accepted constraints on quantifier raising. To implement the idea, one must tolerate raising out of the subject position of a *wh*-island. The response of Krifka (2001) is to rethink the nature of the "lower" interrogative type (which, on this view, is not in fact lower at all), maintain that it too corresponds to a speech act (an answer), and argue that the denotational algebra for this type is such that it will support the needed quantification.

I have no serious response to offer in the face of this dilemma, but I would like to make two remarks. The first is that the observation here is a very delicate one. The second is that there is in fact independent reason to believe that a scope-extending operation of the type needed in (i) (one which would raise the embedded subject of a *wh*-complement to a matrix scope position) is needed. Although it has not been much discussed in the formal literature on reciprocals, it is very well known that reciprocals in the position of the embedded subject of (i) can have antecedents in the matrix clause:

(ii) The linguists and the philosophers had no idea what each other were doing.

Examples like (ii) are extremely common in informal English. If the binding of reciprocals subsumes a covert scope extending mechanism (as in Heim, Lasnik, and May 1991), it must be possible for the embedded subject of a *wh*-complement to take matrix scope in at least some circumstances.

23. For a recent survey and for extensive discussion, see Green (2000), who argues that the traditional ban is too strong and that what is justified and required is a weaker condition which he calls Illocutionary Tolerance of Force Indicators (Green 2000, 441). This principle holds that if a sentence S contains a substructure ψ, which in turn contains an illocutionary force indicator *f,* then ψ cannot

constrain the variety of forces with which S (or its semantic value) may be put forth. This is consistent with Krifka's proposals, and with the syntactic extension of those proposals developed here. The force indicator is the higher C of (68), and ψ is the CP complement projected from it. But of course, the embedded force indicator has no effect whatever on the force with which the root structure is put forth (it can be used as an assertion, a question, an order, a threat, a promise, or whatever else).

24. For negation, this discussion is at one level just a generalization of Groenendijk and Stockof's (1984b) decision to treat *not-know* as a question-embedding predicate of the same type as *wonder*.

25. The discussion that follows has been deeply influenced, in ways that might not be fully obvious, by Gunlogson (2001) and by Groenendijk (1999), as well as by discussions with Bill Ladusaw and Sandy Chung.

26. There is, in fact, a similar effect for the negation cases. That is, (i) is more natural than (ii):

   (i) I don't know will she get married again.
   (ii) Fred doesn't know will she get married again.

This contrast in naturalness is reflected, I believe, in the fact that the majority of attested examples of this type that I have seen have first person subjects. The contrast between (i) and (ii) seems to depend on the following difference: in (i) the issue defined in the embedded question is unresolved both for the referent of the experiencer argument of *know* and for at least one of the participants in the conversation (the speaker). In (ii), by contrast, the issue is unresolved only in the embedded context. I do not understand why this should make a difference, but the effect is probably related to that of (87).

27. Presumably, evaluation takes place with respect to parameters defined in the matrix clause because this is a context of Control and/or because *want* is a restructuring predicate. The licensing effect in question is otherwise more local:

   (i) *Do you think that Freddy knows what will he do?

As Bill Ladusaw points out, the interpretation in terms of restructuring is close to the observation that *want-to-know* is a near synonym for *wonder*.

28. An intriguingly similar set of observations and proposals can be found in work by Paul Portner and Raffaella Zanuttini on exclamatives (Zanuttini and Portner 2003). Portner and Zanuttini observe that the felicity of an exclamative complement under a predicate like *amazing* is sensitive to many of the same factors considered here—presence or absence of negation in the embedding context, presence or absence of interrogation in the embedding context. Their account is that the exclamative complement introduces an implicature that the semantic content put forth is noteworthy in some way, an implicature which can be in harmony with, or at odds with, the effect of negating or questioning the matrix factive.

29. Suggesting that Ginzburg and Sag (2000) are right in their claim that interrogative embedding verbs never select propositions.

30. It might be that the examples of (69) reflect this possibility directly—that is, that such structures are only possible as embedded assertions. If this is the correct interpretation, examples of the type in (69) should appear only in the restricted range of contexts allowed by (95) (see discussion below). Unfortunately, my investigation of this prediction yielded results which were too inconclusive to be worth presenting here.

   The other view of these structures that one might take is that the higher layer of CP structure exists only to facilitate the adjunction. By a requirement of economy of representation, it is absent when there is no adjunction, because in this circumstance, the higher layer would serve no grammatical function. Example (74a) is ungrammatical because it violates this economy requirement. Bury (2003) develops a set of proposals in which this intuition can be fleshed out in a particularly interesting way.

31. The distribution of interrogative double-CP structures is also subject to this strange restriction, in that they may appear only in complement position:

   (i) *What did he think was never asked.

Compare (2b) above.

32. More specifically, what would characterize these dialects is the existence in the lexicon of C bearing an Operator feature (facilitating successive-cyclic movement) as well as the uninterpretable T-feature which forces T-to-C. More familiar varieties restrict the appearance of this lexical item to the root C-position.

REFERENCES

Abney, S. 1987. The English noun phrase in its sentential aspect. PhD diss., Massachusetts Institute of Technology.

Baker, C. L. 1968. Indirect questions in English. PhD diss., University of Illinois, Urbana-Champaign.

Banfield, A. 1973. Grammar of quotation, free indirect style, and implications for a theory of narrative. *Foundations of Language* 10 (1): 1–39.

Bayer, J. 1995. *Directionality and logical form.* Studies in Natural Language and Linguistic Theory, vol. 34. Dordrecht: Kluwer.

Beal, J. 1993. The grammar of Tyneside and Northumbrian English. In *Real English: The grammar of English dialects in the British Isles,* ed. J. Milroy and L. Milroy, 187–213. London: Longman.

Benincà, P. A detailed map of the left periphery in medieval Romance, this volume.

Berman, S. 1991. On the semantics and logical form of WH-clauses. PhD diss., University of Massachusetts, Amherst.

Besten, H. den. 1983. On the interaction of root transformations and lexical deletive rules. In *On the formal syntax of the west Germania,* ed. W. Abraham, 47–131. Amsterdam: Benjamins.

Biberaur, T. 2001. How real is embedded V2? Evidence from Afrikaans variation and change. Paper presented at the Seventh Germanic Linguistics Annual Conference, Banff, Canada, April 21–23, 2001.

Boër, S. 1978. Towards a theory of indirect question clauses. *Linguistics and Philosophy* 2: 307–46.

Bury, D. 2003. Phrase structure and derived heads. PhD diss., University College London.

Cardinaletti, A. and I. Roberts. 1991. Clause structure and X-second. Unpublished manuscript, University of Venice and University of Geneva.

Chomsky, N. 1965. *Aspects of the theory of syntax.* Cambridge, MA: MIT Press.

———. 1986. *Barriers.* Cambridge, MA: MIT Press.

———. 1995. *The minimalist program.* Cambridge, MA: MIT Press.

Cinque, G. 1990. *Types of A'-dependencies.* Cambridge, MA: MIT Press.

———. 1999. *Adverbs and functional heads: A crosslinguistic perspective.* Oxford: Oxford University Press.

Corrigan, K. 1997. The syntax of South Armagh English in its socio-historical perspective. PhD diss., University College Dublin.

Cresti, D. 1995. Extraction and reconstruction. *Natural Language Semantics* 3:79–122.

Diesing, M. 1990. Verb movement and the subject position in Yiddish. *Natural Language and Linguistic Theory* 8:41–79.

Doherty, C. 1993. Clauses without 'that': The case for bare sentential complementation in English. PhD diss., University of California, Santa Cruz.

Edwards, V., and B. Weltens. 1985. Research on non-standard dialects of British English: Progress and prospects (1). In *Focus on England and Wales,* ed. W. Viereck, 97–139. Amsterdam: John Benjamins.

Ernst, T. 1999. Adjuncts, the universal base, and word order typology. In *NELS 29,* ed. P. Tamanji, M. Hirotani, and N. Hall, 209–23. Amherst: GLSA, University of Massachusetts,.

———. 2001. *The syntax of adjuncts.* Cambridge Studies in Linguistics 96. Cambridge: Cambridge University Press.

Erteschik-Shir, N. 1973. On the nature of island constraints. PhD diss., Massachusetts Institute of Technology.

Filppula, M. 1999. *The grammar of Irish English: Language in Hibernian style.* Routledge Studies in Germanic Linguistics 5. London: Routledge.

Fontana, J. 1993. Phrase structure and the syntax of clitics in the history of Spanish. PhD diss., University of Pennsylvania.

Gärtner, H.-M. 2000. Are there V2 relative clauses in German? *The Journal of Comparative Germanic Linguistics* 3 (2): 97–141.

———. 2001. On the force of V2 declaratives. Unpublished manuscript, Zentrum für Allgemeine Sprachwissenschaft, Berlin, Germany.

Giannakidou, A. 1997. *The landscape of polarity items.* Groningen Dissertations in Linguistics 18. Groningen: Rijksuniversiteit Groningen.

Ginzburg, J. 1992. Questions, theories and facts: A semantics and pragmatics for interrogatives. PhD diss., Stanford University.

Ginzburg, J., and I. A. Sag. 2000. *Interrogative investigations.* Stanford, CA: CSLI.

Green, M. 2000. Illocutionary force and semantic content. *Linguistics and Philosophy* 23: 435–73.

Grimshaw, J. 1992. Extended projection. Unpublished manuscript, Rutgers University.

———. 1997. Projection, heads and optimality. *Linguistic Inquiry* 28: 373–422.

Groenendijk, J. 1999. The logic of interrogation, classical version. In *SALT IX,* ed. T. Mathews and D. Strolovitch, 109–26. Ithaca, NY: CLC Publications, Cornell University..

Groenendijk, J., and M. Stokhof. 1984a. Semantic analysis of *wh*-complements. *Linguistics and Philosophy* 5:77–164.

———. 1984b. Studies on the semantics of questions and the pragmatics of answers. Amsterdam: Akademisch Proefschrift, University of Amsterdam.

———. 1989. Type-shifting rules and the semantics of interrogatives. In *Properties, types, and meanings.* vol. 2, *Semantic issues,* ed. G. Chierchia, B. Partee, and R. Turner, 21–68. Kluwer. Repr. in *Formal Semantics, The Essential Readings,* ed. P. Portner and B. H. Partee, 421–56. Oxford: Blackwell, 2002.

———. 1997. Questions. In *Handbook of logic and language,* ed. J. vanBenthem and A. terMeulen, 1055–1124. Amsterdam: Elsevier; Cambridge, MA: MIT Press.

Gunlogson, C. 2001. True to form. PhD diss., University of California, Santa Cruz.

———. 2002. Declarative questions. In *SALT XII,* ed. B. Jackson, 355–426. Ithaca, NY: CLC Publications, Cornell University.

Haan, G. de and F. Weerman. 1985. Finiteness and verb fronting in Frisian. In *Verb second phenomena in Germanic languages,* ed. H. Haider and M. Prinzhorn. Dordrecht: Foris.

Hamblin, C. L. 1976. Questions in Montague English. In *Montague grammar,* ed. B. Partee, 247–59. New York: Academic Press. Also in *Foundations of Language* 10: 41–53.

Harris, J. 1993. The grammar of Irish English. In *Real English: The grammar of English dialects in the British Isles,* ed. J. Milroy and L. Milroy, 139–86. London: Longman.

Heim, I., H. Lasnik, and R. May. 1991. Reciprocity and plurality. *Linguistic Inquiry* 22: 63–101.

Henry, A. 1995. *Belfast English and Standard English: Dialect variation and parameter setting.* Oxford: Oxford University Press.

Hooper, J., and S. A. Thompson. 1973. On the applicability of root transformations. *Linguistic Inquiry* 4: 465–97.

Hornstein, N. 1977. S and X' convention. *Linguistic Analysis* 3: 137–76.

Huang, J. 1982. Logical relations in Chinese and the theory of grammar. PhD diss., Massachusetts Institute of Technology.

Iatridou, S., and A. Kroch. 1992. The licensing of CP-recursion and its relevance to the Germanic verb second phenomenon. *Working Papers in Scandinavian Syntax* 50:1–24.

Jackendoff, R. 1972. *Semantic interpretation in generative grammar.* Cambridge, MA: MIT Press.

Johnson, K. 1991. On the v < adverb < np word order. Paper presented to The Seventh Workshop on Comparative Germanic Syntax, University of Stuttgart, November 22–24, 1991.

———. 1992. Head movement, word order and inflection. Unpublished manuscript, University of Massachusetts, Amherst.

Karttunen, L. 1977. Syntax and semantics of questions. *Linguistics and Philosophy* 1: 3–44.

Kayne, R. 1982. Predicates and arguments, verbs and nouns. *GLOW Newsletter* 8: 24.

———. 1983. Chains, categories external to S, and French Complex inversion. *Natural Language and Linguistic Theory* 1:109–37.

Krifka, M. 1999. Quantifying into question acts. In *SALT IX,* ed. T. Matthews and D. Strolovitch. Ithaca, NY: CLC Publications, Cornell University.

———. 2001. Quantifying into question acts. *Natural Language Semantics* 9 (1): 1–40.

Lahiri, U. 1991. Embedded interrogatives and predicates that embed them. PhD diss., Massachusetts Institute of Technology.

———. 2000. Lexical selection and quantificational variability in embedded interrogatives. *Linguistics and Philosophy* 23: 325–89.

———. 2002. *Questions and answers in embedded contexts.* Oxford Studies in Theoretical Linguistics 1. Oxford: Oxford University Press.

Lasnik, H., and M. Saito. 1992. *Move α: Conditions on its application and output.* Cambridge, MA: MIT Press.

Longobardi, G. 1994. Reference and proper names. *Linguistic Inquiry* 25 (4): 609–65.

Matushansky, O. 2000. Movement of degree/degree of movement. PhD diss., Massachusetts Institute of Technology.

McCloskey, J. 1991. Clause structure, ellipsis and proper government in Irish. *Lingua* 85: 259–302.

———. 1992. Adjunction, selection, and embedded verb second. Unpublished manuscript, University of California, Santa Cruz.

Miller, J. 1993. The grammar of Scottish English. In *Real English: The grammar of English dialects in the British Isles,* ed. J. Milroy and L. Milroy, 99–138. London: Longman.

Munsat, S. 1986. WH-complementizers. *Linguistics and Philosophy* 9: 191–217.

Pesetsky, D. 1982. Paths and categories. PhD diss., Massachusetts Institute of Technology.

———. 1991. Infinitives. Unpublished manuscript, Massachusetts Institute of Technology.

Pesetsky, D. and E. Torrego. 2001. T-to-C movement: Causes and consequences. In *Ken Hale: A life in language,* ed. M. Kenstowicz, 355–426. Cambridge, MA: MIT Press.

Plann, S. 1982. Indirect questions in Spanish. *Linguistic Inquiry* 13: 297–312.

Potsdam, Eric. 1998. A syntax for adverbs. In *WECOL 98, Proceedings of the Western Conference on Linguistics 1998,* ed. E. Van Gelderen. Tempe, Arizona: Arizona State University.

Pullum, G. K. 1991. English nominal gerund phrases as noun phrases with verb phrase heads. *Linguistics* 29: 763–99.

Reinhart, T. 1983. *Anaphora and semantic interpretation.* Cambridge: Cambridge University Press.

Reis, M. 1997. Zum syntaktischen Status unselbständiger Verbzweit-Sätze. In *Sprache im Fokus,* ed. C. Dürscheid, 121–44. Tübingen: Niemeyer.

Reuland, E. 1983. Governing -*ing. Linguistic Inquiry* 14: 101–36.

Rivero, M.-L. 1978. Topicalization and wh-movement in Spanish. *Linguistic Inquiry* 9: 513–17.

———. 1980. On left-dislocation and topicalization in Spanish. *Linguistic Inquiry* 11: 363–93.

Rizzi, L. 1997. The fine structure of the left periphery. In *Elements of grammar: Handbook of generative syntax,* ed. L. Haegeman, 281–337. Dordrecht: Kluwer.

———, ed. 2004. *The structure of CP and IP.* Vol. 2 of *The cartography of syntactic structures.* Oxford: Oxford University Press.

Rizzi, L., and I. Roberts. 1989. Complex inversion in French. *Probus* 1: 1–30.

Sabban, A. 1982. *Gälisch-englischer sprachkontakt.* Heidelberg: Julius Groos.

Safir, K. 1983. On small clauses as constituents. *Linguistic Inquiry* 14: 730–35.

Stowell, T. 1981. Origins of phrase structure. PhD diss., Massachusetts Institute of Technology.

Suñer, M. 1991. Indirect questions and the structure of CP. In *Current issues in Spanish linguistics,* ed. H. Campos and F. Martínez-Gil. Washington, D.C.: Georgetown University Press.

———. 1993. About indirect questions and semiquestions. *Linguistics and Philosophy* 16: 45–77.

Szabolcsi, A. 1997. Quantifiers in pairlist readings. In *Ways of scope taking,* ed. A. Szabolcsi, 311–47. Dordrecht: Kluwer.

van Craenenbroeck, J. 2004. *Ellipsis in Dutch dialects.* Utrecht: Netherlands Graduate School of Linguistics.

Vikner, S. 1991. Verb movement and the licensing of NP-positions in the Germanic languages. PhD diss., University of Geneva.

———. 1995. *Verb movement and expletive subjects in the Germanic languages.* Oxford: Oxford University Press.

Vikner, S., and B. Schwarz. 1991. The verb always leaves IP in V2 clauses. Unpublished manuscript, Boston University and University of Stuttgart.

Watanabe, A. 1996. *Case absorption and wh-agreement.* Studies in Natural Language and Linguistic Theory 37. Dordrecht: Kluwer.

Wechsler, S. 1991. Verb second and illocutionary force. In *Views on phrase structure,* ed. K. Leffel and D. Bouchard, 177–91. Dordrecht: Kluwer.

Zanuttini, R., and P. Portner. 2003. Exclamative clauses at the syntax semantics interface. *Language* 79: 39–81.

5

■ VP-, D°-Movement Languages

LISA DEMENA TRAVIS
McGill University

1. Introduction

In the Minimalist Program (Chomsky 1995), syntactic movement is triggered by a requirement that the computational system eliminate features that are uninterpretable at the relevant interface. Once we understand which elements move, it is just an exercise to determine which features might be responsible for the movement for which we have independent evidence. Looking at the system that is eventually created, however, in a system of features, one is led to ask certain questions about the typology of movement. In this paper, I examine asymmetries that arise in the system as it stands and ask whether the asymmetries are derivable or whether they are an artifact of the languages that are commonly studied. In this context, I argue that there are languages that show an asymmetry that is the opposite of the one we find in English and suggest that, in fact, these asymmetries should be built into the larger view of movement, thereby creating a language typology. Further, through an investigation of both types of asymmetry we can learn more about the details of movement.

2. Features and Movement Asymmetries

In order to set up a context in which to study movement asymmetries, I review briefly an early view of feature-triggered movement. As we can see in the structures below, a functional category such as T is merged into the structure with uninterpretable features, such as D and V, which must be eliminated before the derivation is sent to either interface. These features probe the structure to which they have been merged. The D-feature seeks an element with an interpretable D-feature and the V-feature seeks an element with an interpretable V-feature. In the first step, (1a), the features probe the structure; in the second step (if, perhaps, a further feature such as EPP forces movement), (1b), a DP will move to Spec, TP, and a V will undergo head movement and adjoin to T.

(1) a.

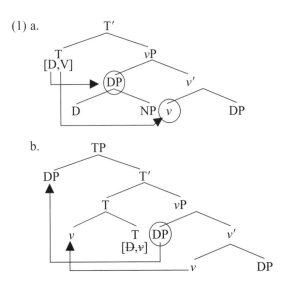

b.

Observationally we know that DPs move and Vs move. However, it is not clear, given the features, why this is so—why the D-feature targets a maximal projection and the V-feature targets a head. Chomsky (2001, 38) notes this asymmetry.

> It has always been taken for granted that the strong V-feature is satisfied by V-raising to T (French vs. English), not VP raising to SPEC-T; and the strong NOMINAL-feature by raising of the nominal to SPEC-T (EPP), not raising of its head to T. But the theoretical apparatus provides no obvious basis for this choice. The same is true of raising to C and D. In standard cases, T adjoins to C, and an XP (say, a WH-phrase) raises to SPEC-C, instead of the WH-head adjoining to C while TP raises to SPEC-C. And N raises to D, not NP to Spec-D.

Before investigating this asymmetry further, I point out two other asymmetries that exist between XP movement and X-movement.

2.1 Head Movement and Maximal Projection Movement

We have seen above that different features target different types of categories—heads versus maximal projections. There are other asymmetries that also show up with respect to head versus maximal projection movement. One is that head movement is typically seen to move a lexical (as opposed to functional) head up through the heads of its extended projection (Grimshaw 2000). Maximal projection movement, on the other hand, usually moves elements that are in specifier positions along this extended projection. We can see this distinction in (2) below. A head V will move through the functional heads in its extended projection (shown in [2] *within* the box), while XP movement would normally target the DPs which appear in satellite positions along the extended projections (shown in [2] *outside* the box).

(2)

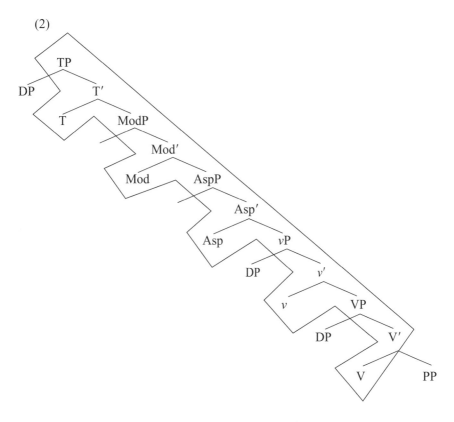

Another asymmetry that we find relates not so much to what moves or where it moves to, but rather how it moves. XP movement typically moves cyclically from Spec position to Spec position, but the form of the element that moves does not change.[1] No material is accumulated through the movement. This is very different for head movement, which typically picks up material through its cyclic movement through other heads. This is shown below, where a DP will typically move up a tree without changing its shape, while a V will pick up inflectional morphology. For want of better terminology, I call the effect of the first type of movement, illustrated in (3), *rolling stone,* since no material is gathered, and the effect of the second type of movement, illustrated in (4), *snowball.*

(3)

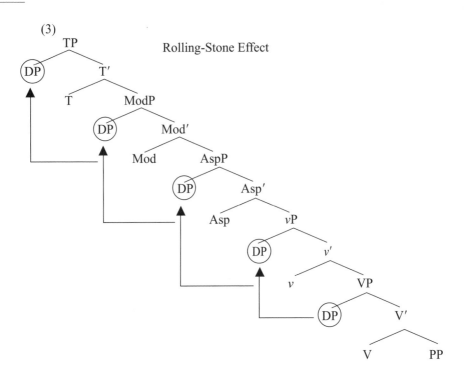

(4)

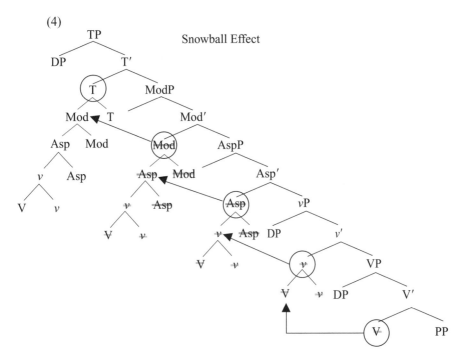

Just like the asymmetry that appears with features, we can ask about the nature of these two asymmetries. Is there something about the nature of head movement that ensures that it occurs along the extended projection of a lexical head and that it picks up material? Or is there something about the nature of XP movement that ensures that only satellites off the extended projection move and that no material is picked up? Chomsky (2001, 38), after noting the asymmetry in what type of constituent each feature targets, writes:

> These conclusions . . . follow naturally if overt V-to-T raising, T-to-C raising, and N-to-D raising are phonological properties, conditioned by the phonetically affixal character of the inflectional categories.

This seems to be correct. We could say that the purpose of head movement is to collect the relevant inflectional morphemes for a lexical root. Head movement could then be placed outside of the main syntactic computational component. Now, with only one type of movement, XP movement, no asymmetries would exist and that would be the end of the story. However, before being content with this conclusion, we should at least try to imagine what sort of movements we would be ruling out. In other words, what would the opposite side of the asymmetry look like? I will call the type of language exemplified in the structure sketched in (1) above an A-type language. I will call the type of language exemplified by the opposite side of the asymmetry (in other words, a VP-, D°-movement language) a B-type language.

3. VP-, D°-Movement Languages

Let us start by first imagining what a B-type language would look like where the D-feature would attract a head while the V-feature attracted a maximal projection. In its simplest form, we might get a structure like that given in (5).

(5)

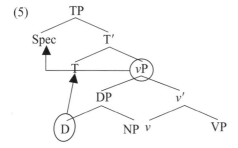

In this sketch, the closest verbal projection, the vP, would move to the Spec, TP to check the V-feature in T. The D-feature would attract the closest D-head, which would be found in the external argument DP. Filling this structure in with English words, we might expect to find a string such as the one given in (6) below.

(6) $[_{TP}\ [_{vP}\ [_{DP}\ t_k\ \ [_{NP}$ children $]\ ]$ come home $]_i\ [_{T'}$ the$_k$.PST t_i $]]$

Here, we see where a vP, which contains the external argument minus its determiner, has fronted. The determiner, which has moved to T (where presumably it will adjoin to a tense marker), is stranded sentence-finally. This word order has an unnatural feel to it, suggesting again that we want to rule out such a derivation. But often language data are not as simple as a first approximation. Before concluding that B-type languages do not exist, therefore, we should see whether proposals for either VP-fronting or D°-movement have been made independently. We will see below that Malagasy arguably has both predicate movement and D°-movement.

3.1 Predicate Fronting in Malagasy

Malagasy is a Western Malayo-Polynesian (WMP) language spoken in Madagascar. It is a VOS language with fairly rigid word order.[2] WMP languages are known for their complex voice system which can designate a particular DP as the subject. In Malagasy, there are basically three types of voices—Actor Topic (AT), Theme Topic (TT), and Circumstantial Topic (CT).[3] An example of the paradigm is given below. The root *sasa* 'wash' appears in three different forms—*manasa* when the Agent is the subject as in (7a), *sasana* when the Theme is the subject as in (7b), and *anasana* when the Instrumental is the subject as in (7c).

(7) a. [Manasa   ny lamba amin'ny savony] ny lehilahy
       PRES-AT.wash DET clothes with-DET soap   DET man
       'The man washes the clothes with the soap.'

   b. [Sasan'ny   lehilahy amin'ny savony] ny lamba
       TT.wash-DET man   with-DET soap   DET clothes
       'The clothes are washed with the soap by the man.'

   c. [Anasan'ny lehilahy ny lamba] ny savony
       CT.wash-DET man   DET clothes DET soap
       Lit.: 'The soap is washed-with the clothes by the man.'
       'The man washes the clothes with the soap.'

There have been several proposals made for a predicate-fronting account for Malagasy.[4] These accounts were meant to explain not only the VOS order of the language (assuming Kayne's 1994 proposal that languages are basically SVO), but also to explain adverb orders and the ordering of arguments within the VP. These are discussed in turn.

In order to look at the word order more closely, we will take an instance of the Circumstantial Topic where the instrumental *ny savony* is the subject of the sentence. This means that the Theme *lamba* 'clothes' has remained within the VP. Within this construction, we notice two things in the examples below. First, the order of the adverbs (underlined) is the opposite of the order we find in the English translation. Second, while the indefinite object (in bold) must appear to the left of the adverb *tsara* 'good/well,' the definite object may appear to its right.

(8) a. [Anasan-dRakoto   **lamba** <u>tsara</u> <u>foana</u>] ny savony
       PRES.CT.wash-Rakoto **clothes** well always DET soap
       Lit.: 'The soap is always washed-with clothes well by Rakoto.'
       'Rakoto always washes clothes well with the soap.'

   a'. *Anasan-dRakoto <u>tsara</u> **lamba** <u>foana</u> ny savony.

    b. [Anasan-dRakoto   <u>tsara</u> **ny**   **lamba** <u>foana</u>] ny savony
    PRES.CT.wash-Rakoto well **DET clothes** always DET soap
    Lit.: 'The soap is always washed-with the clothes well by Rakoto.'
    'Rakoto always washes the clothes well with the soap.'

The basic outline for the word order in Malagasy would be as in (9) below.

   (9) [V Agent Theme$_{indef/def}$ <u>Adverb2</u> Theme$_{def}$ <u>Adverb1</u>] Subject/Topic

Rackowski (1998) tackles the problem of the adverb ordering. She starts with Cinque's (1999) phrase structure account for the ordering of adverbs and proposes the account sketched below. First, she assumes that adverbs are functional heads along the extended projection of V.[5] As we see in the tree, adverbs are arranged so that they have the same hierarchical order as proposed by Cinque. Rackowski also proposes that AgrPs are not visible for movement. With this in place, we see below that definite Theme movement to Spec, AgrOP and iterative predicate fronting of maximal projections along the extended projection of the V will lead to the appropriate word order. However, we can already note two movements that depart from our simplest version of VP-, D°-fronting languages. We do have V-movement to F, and we still seem to have DP movement, since the object moves to Spec, AgrOP and the subject to Spec, AgrSP.[6] I set these two issues aside until later.

(10)

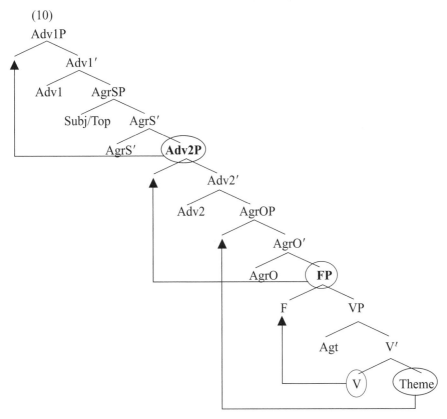

(11)

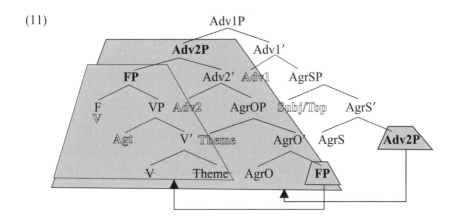

Note that Rackowski's account of Malagasy seeks to explain not only the predicate-initial property of the language but also VP-internal word orders. Pearson (1998) continues in this direction and proposes a language typology based on VP-internal word orders. He divides VO languages into two types—*direct* and *inverse* languages. Direct languages (like English, French, Indonesian, Icelandic) have the two characteristics already mentioned. Adverbs with higher scope precede adverbs with lower scope, and definite objects can appear in positions to the left of where indefinite objects must appear. We have seen examples of the adverb ordering in the English translation of (8a) above. An instance of leftward movement of a definite object in a direct language is given below in the Icelandic Object Shift example. This example can be compared with the Malagasy example in (8) above.

(12) Icelandic (Holmberg 1986, 166)[7]

    a. Hvers vegna lasu stúdentarnir ekki allir <u>greinina</u>

       why   read the.students not all the article

       'Why didn't all the students read the article?'

    b. Hvers vegna lasu stúdentarnir <u>greinina</u> ekki allir

As a last distinction between direct and inverse VO-languages, Pearson gives examples of the relative ordering of direct objects and indirect objects. In direct languages, indirect objects precede direct objects, while in inverse languages indirect objects follow direct objects in Double-Object constructions. An example from Malagasy is given below. The word order in Malagasy should be compared with the word order of the English translation.

(13) Nanolotra <u>ny</u> <u>dite</u> ny vahiny ny zazavavy   (Pearson's [3])

      PST.AT.offer DET tea DET guest   DET girl

      'The girl offered the guests <u>the tea</u>.'

Pearson sums up his findings in the following table.

(14) Direct: English, French, Indonesian, Dutch, Turkish . . .
     Indirect: Malagasy, Tzotzil, Quiavini Zapotec, Palauan . . .

	Direct		Inverse
	OV	VO	VO
Double Object	IO DO V	V IO DO	V DO IO
Adverb order	Adv2 Adv1 V	V Adv2 Adv1	V Adv1 Adv2
Object Shift	DP_i Adv t_i V	V DP_i Adv t_i	V t_i Adv DP_i

Once this typology is set up, two further observations can be made. Pearson gives examples of both VO and OV languages that are direct. We have mentioned some of the VO languages above (English, French, Indonesian, and Icelandic), and two examples of the OV languages are Dutch and Turkish. However, inverse languages are all VO (Malagasy, Tzotzil, Quiavini Zapotec, and Palauan). Pearson accounts for direct versus inverse orders through VP-internal predicate fronting. I believe that the account can be extended beyond the VP. While not mentioned by Pearson, none of these languages are SVO, they are all V-initial. This stronger generalization—that all inverse languages are predicate initial—will become important to the discussion later when this generalization is combined with other generalizations about V-initial languages. What I will argue eventually is that these languages all move the closest verbal projection into Spec, TP.

Let us now return to Malagasy and evidence that this language has the other part of the movement asymmetry—D°-movement.

3.2 D°-Movement in Malagasy
We saw above in our simple version of a B-type language that a D-feature in T would attract the D of the closest DP, which would be the external argument in the Spec, vP. While many languages do not allow Agents to remain in Spec, vP while another DP is in the Spec, TP position, Malagasy and related languages make use of both positions (see Guilfoyle, Hung, and Travis 1992). In fact, many of the examples we have seen have exactly this characteristic. One of these, (7c), is repeated in (15) below.

(15) Anasan'ny   lehilahy lamba ny savony
     CT.wash-DET man   clothes DET soap
     Lit.: 'The soap is washed-with the clothes by the man.'
     'The man washes clothes with the soap.'

Note that the Agent follows the verb directly and appears between the verb and the indefinite object. We have already seen that adverbs may not appear between verb and an indefinite object. Therefore, we will assume that the object is in its merged position and that the verb has moved across the Agent in Spec, vP to a higher functional category.[8] The conclusion that we need here is that the Agent is in the Spec, vP. Following the orthographic conventions of Malagasy, the determiner of this Agent is joined with the preceding verb. In fact, this convention reflects a morphophonological process that Keenan (2000) has discussed under the label of N-bonding (see also Paul 1996). I refer the reader to these articles for details, but what is important to the issue at hand is that three elements can undergo N-bonding—determiners (16a), pronouns (16b), and proper names (16c).[9]

(16) a. [Hitan'ny lehilahy] ny   trano
      TT.see-DET man   DET house
      'The house was seen by the man.'

    b. [Hitanao] ny   trano.
      TT.see-2SG DET house
      'The house was seen by you.'

    c. [Hitan-dRabe] ny   trano.
      TT.see-Rabe   DET house
      'The house was seen by Rabe.'

N-bonding is obligatory in these positions and has the phonological characteristics of other processes in Malagasy such as compounding, as shown below.[10]

(17) a. híta   + Rabé   → hitandrabé
      seen   + Rabe   seen by Rabe

    b. tráno + rázana   → tranondrázana
      house + ancestor   tomb

The syntactic account of N-bonding is, I argue, the surface effect of $D°$-movement.[11] The three elements that undergo this process—determiners, pronouns, and proper names—are the three elements that Postal (1969) argued are determiners, which in current phrase structure would be contained in D.

    In sum, in one language, Malagasy, we have found evidence for both of the kinds of movement we expect to find in a B-type language: the closest predicate projection moving to Spec, TP and the closest $D°$ adjoining to a higher functional head. Let us, then, look at the details of the structure of Malagasy and see how it differs from the simple system that was outlined in (5) above.

3.3 Structure of Simultaneous VP-, D°-movement

We saw above what we expected from a B-type language. The whole vP was fronted, including at least a remnant of the external argument. The sentence began with the N of the external argument and ended with the D of the external argument, which had moved to a tense marker. This is shown in bracketing in (18a) below. A similar (though simplified) bracketing structure of Malagasy is given for comparison in (18b), with the associated phrase structure in (19).

(18) a. $[_{TP} [_{vP} [_{DP} \ t_i \ NP] \ v \ VP \ ]_k \ D_i\text{-}T \ t_k \ ]$
    b. $[_{XP} [_{TP} T\text{-}v_m\text{-}D_i \ [_{vP} [_{DP} t_i \ NP] t_m \ VP \ ] \ ]_k \ X \ [_{YP} DP \ Y \ t_k \ ]]$

(19)

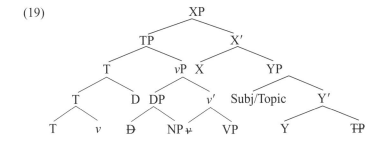

The picture we have seen for Malagasy is different from the simple structure in three ways. First, the D°-movement is contained within the predicate phrase that is fronted. Because of this, the D is not stranded sentence-finally. In the structure given in (18b) above, we can see that the D° has moved to T and the whole TP has moved to the specifier position of another functional projection, which I have labeled XP, along the extended projection line of the verb. Another difference between Malagasy and the simple structure is that, in Malagasy, there is, in addition to the external argument that has remained within the *v*P, another DP which acts as the subject and which appears sentence-finally. I have placed this DP in the specifier position of another maximal projection labeled YP. Finally, there is evidence of V°-movement accounting for the sentence-initial position of the verb.

Because of space considerations, I do not discuss the details of the departure from the simplest version of a B-type language. In Travis (forthcoming) I deal with these issues directly. I argue that the verb movement in Malagasy is contained within the heads that are event related, as opposed to A-type languages where verb movement enters the inflectional domain of the clause. I also argue that there is no XP movement in Malagasy outside of predicate fronting. Subjects are base generated in the Spec, YP position and related to their predicates via a form of Clitic Left Dislocation. *Wh*-questions are formed through a pseudocleft construction (see Paul 2001) which contains these predication structures rather than through *wh*-movement.[12] What is necessary for the the point being made here is that a slightly more complicated side of the asymmetry under investigation is appearing. Further, the existence of a language like Malagasy suggests that there may be a language typology that is circumscribed by the feature system used to trigger movement. We turn to an investigation of this possibility next.

4. Language Typology

Above, in our discussion of Malagasy, we made use of a language generalization that is brought to light in Pearson's discussion of direct versus inverse languages. My revision of his generalization was that only predicate-initial languages show inverse order within the VP. Now we will look at two other generalizations that have been made about predicate-initial languages. Again, I will change the original formulation of these generalizations slightly, but I believe that with these changes, a consistent picture emerges.

4.1 Baker and Hale's Generalization: Breton and D°-Movement

Baker and Hale (1990) propose that some cases of subject agreement are best accounted for through movement of a D to the head which contains the verb. They point out that this analysis would explain the complementary distribution of overt subjects and subject agreement on the verb. Breton is a language which displays such complementarity, as shown in their example given below. In (20a), there is an overt subject and the verb shows no agreement. In (20b), where there is agreement morphology on the verb, the subject is nonovert. Finally, (20c) shows that co-occurrence of an overt subject and subject agreement is not possible.

(20) a. Bemdez   e   lenn ar vugale eul levr
        every.day PRT read the kids   DET book
        'The kids read a book every day.'

     b. Bemdez   e   lenn-*ont* __ eul levr
        every.day PRT read-3PS   DET book
        'They read a book every day.'

     c. *Bemdez   e   lenn-*ont ar vugale* eul levr
        every.day PRT read-3PS the kids   DET book

Structurally, the D°-movement may be represented as in (21) below.

(21)

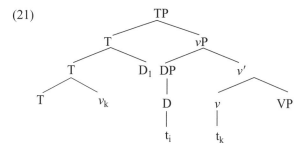

As we can see, this is very similar to the structure we have proposed for D°-movement in B-type languages. What is particularly intriguing in this context, then, is the generalization Baker and Hale make. They argue, for reasons closely tied to the goals of their paper, that only V-initial languages can have this sort of D-movement.[13] Interestingly, the other example of a language that they give with this characteristic is Yatee Zapotec, another VSO language. I will come back to the importance of this observation below. Now we turn to another generalization that has been made about V-initial languages.

4.2 Oda's Generalization: Irish and VP Fronting

Oda (2002) notes that V-initial languages fall into two types with respect to how *wh*-questions are formed. He argues that those that use *wh*-cleft constructions are predicate-fronting languages, while those that use *wh*-fronting are V-movement languages.[14] His work is important since, as Massam's (1998) investigation of Niuean has shown, some VSO languages are best analyzed as having remnant-VP movement.

Oda's work adds another probe into what is otherwise a very subtle phenomenon. Much of his research centers on Irish, which he argues is, like Niuean, a VSO language with remnant-VP movement. First, he notes that Irish forms *wh*-constructions with a cleft construction. As we see below, the same marker is used for relative clause formation (22b) as is used for *wh*-constructions (22a) (from Oda 2002, 75; taken from McCloskey 1979, 52). Oda argues that this marker indicates the nominal characteristics of the material following the *wh*-element.

(22) a. Cé a^L   dhíol an domhan
        who COMP sold the world
        'Who sold the world?'

     b. an fear a^L   dhíol an domhan
        the man COMP sold the world
        'the man who sold the world'

He backs up his claim that Irish is a predicate XP-fronting language with the observation that nonverbal predicates clearly appear before the subject in an XP form. Below we see an example where a nominal XP predicate appears sentence-initially.

(23) Is [amhrán a^L   bhuailfidh an píobaire] "Yellow Submarine"
     COP [song   COMP be.FUT   the piper   "Yellow Submarine"
     'Yellow Submarine is a song which the bagpiper is going to play.'

Oda presents the generalization as a one-way implication—predicate-initial languages utilize *wh*-cleft constructions. If we hypothesize that this is a two-way implication, however, the use of *wh*-cleft constructions can be another indication of the predicate-fronting status of a language.[15] In my terms, languages that use *wh*-clefting strategies to form *wh*-constructions are B-type languages. In a B-type language, XP movement will target only predicate projections. If this is so, apparent *wh*-movement must be a case of predicate fronting. Through my revision of Oda's generalization, we gain another way to distinguish B-type languages. In the next section I argue that this hypothesis leads us to the right analysis of Malay.

4.3 Problem

My hypothesis above is that languages whose main *wh*-strategy is clefting are predicate-fronting languages, but we immediately run into a problem with Malay. This language is quite clearly an SVO language, as shown in (24) below.

(24) Ali/Saya/Lelaki itu membaca buku itu dengan teliti.
     Ali/I   /boy   the AT-read book the with   care
     'Ali/I/the boy read the book carefully.'

However, unexpectedly, given my hypothesis, *wh*-constructions use a clefting strategy. The complementizer *yang* marks the following material as being nominal.

(25) Siapa yang membaca buku itu
     who   COMP AT-read   book the
     'Who read the book?'

As the verbal morphology may have signaled to the reader (even if the language name did not), Malay is another WMP language. Like other WMP languages, it uses a *wh*-cleft construction. However, unlike most other WMP languages, it is SVO rather than predicate initial. But before deciding that Malay must be an A-type language, we can turn to the other main characteristic of B-type languages, D°-movement. In fact, another case of D°-movement can be found in the literature. In Guilfoyle, Hung, and Travis (1992) (GHT), I argued with my coauthors that the word order facts of a certain passivelike construction in Malay was best accounted for through D°-movement. The relevant data are given below. We have seen that Malay is generally SVO. However, as we can see in (26), when we get a bare verb form, certain elements may appear in a position between the subject and the verb. In particular, pronouns and proper names may appear in this position (26a) but not common nouns (26b).

(26) a. Buku itu Ali/kamu baca dengan teliti.

       book the Ali/you   read with   care

       'The book was read by Ali/you carefully.'

   b. *Buku itu lelaki itu baca dengan teliti.

       book the man the read with   care

       'The book was read by the man carefully.'

This is similar to the N-bonding of Malagasy that we saw above.[16] It appears, then, that in the bare verb form constructions in Malay, where the Theme appears in the subject position, the Agent may appear preverbally if it is exhaustively dominated by D°. In GHT, we accounted for this by proposing a D°-movement to a preverbal position. The relevant tree structure is given below.[17]

(27)

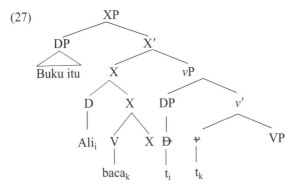

We see now that Malay has two of the hallmarks of a B-type language—D°-movement and *wh*-clefts. What Malay is missing, then, is the predicate fronting. This is true not only at the level of the sentence (it is SVO rather than V-initial), but also VP-internally. Pearson mentions Indonesian as a direct (rather than inverse) language. Given the close links between Bahasa Indonesia and Malay, one can assume that Malay is also a direct language. This means that there is no predicate fronting internal to the VP, either, in Malay. This might seem problematic. Within the Minimalist Program, however, lack of overt (phonological) effects of movement has been one of the main ways that languages may vary. Just as we have cases of languages with covert *wh*-movement (Japanese, Chinese) and covert V-movement (English), we might expect languages with covert predicate movement. In fact, we must resort to covert D°-movement in many cases of B-type languages as this process appears to be quite rare crosslinguistically. Malay, then, would be a B-type language with overt D°-movement and covert predicate movement. We are now ready to look at our language typology.

4.4 The Typology

Below we see a table which gives examples of different types of languages in terms of what type of projection (X° vs. XP) is targeted by a particular feature and whether or not the movement is overt.[18] It is interesting that in the discussion of the language generalizations above, the same languages or language families reappear. Malagasy (WMP) has been used to argue for predicate fronting. Malay (WMP) has been used to illustrate D°-movement. Oda argues that Irish (Celtic) is a predicate-fronting language and therefore a *wh*-cleft language. Baker and Hale argue that Breton (Celtic) has D°-movement and therefore must be predicate initial. The other example of a D°-movement language given by Baker and Hale is Yatee Zapotec. Pearson gives Quiavini Zapotec as an example of an inverse language, and Lee (2000) has argued that Quiavini Zapotec is a VP-fronting language. I claim that the clustering of these properties falls out from the typology of V°-, DP-movement languages versus D°-, VP-movement languages. Some possible language variations are given below.

(28) Features	V	D
A. French	X	XP
Greek	X	—
English	—	XP
B. Malagasy	XP	X
Niuean	XP	—
Malay	—	X

Other characteristics of B-type languages that fall out from this typology are the use of *wh*-clefts for *wh*-constructions and evidence that there is no A-movement of subjects and objects.[19] These are empirical issues that need more data to support them and are left for future research.

5. Movement Typology

There is another result of this line of research. By looking at familiar movements in unfamiliar surroundings, we can learn more about what is central to their nature. Two additional movement asymmetries were sketched above. It appears that head movement moves something along a maximal projection picking up affixal matter, while XP movement moves satellite elements that do not change content during the derivation. In B-type languages, we can examine whether the behavior of head versus XP-movement is truly related to the bar level of the item being moved. We will see that it is not the level, but rather the category type, that is crucial to the behavior of movement. On one hand, this is what we expect in a movement theory that relies on categorial features. However, it does not support Chomsky's (2001) observations about the nature of head movement. Let us look at this in more detail.

5.1 V(P)-Movement

In looking at VP fronting, the question we can ask is whether it will behave more like DP movement (because it is an XP) or V-movement (because it is verbal).[20] We have two reasons below to argue that VP fronting is similar to V-movement. By definition, it moves something from the extended projection rather than from a satellite. More interesting, perhaps, is that it shows the snowball effect. Schematically, it works as in the tree in (29) below. Once the WP moves into the Spec, ZP position, it no longer moves on its own. Rather, it is the ZP that dominates it that is targeted for the next movement.

(29)

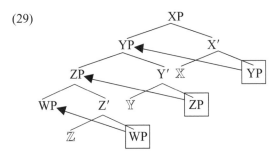

This snowball effect introduced in (11) is clearly shown in the structure above. Correlations, then, go along categorial distinctions rather than level distinctions. This result is supported by the D°-movement facts discussed in the next section.

5.2 D°-Movement

The behavior of D°-movement is harder to investigate. It happens rarely, and when it does happen, it seems to be frozen after one move. However, it does provide us with one observation. It is clear that a D can move outside of its extended projection. In this way, it is very different from what we have seen in the most common cases of V°-movement and suggests that it has more in common with DP movement. It is hard to argue, as Chomsky (2001, 38) did, that the function of this movement is "conditioned by the phonetically affixal character of the inflectional categories."[21] No affixal material can be used to explain the position of the external argument in Malay.

The second characteristic of movement is not reflected. Because there is only one link of the chain, we cannot determine whether the effect is snowball or rolling stone. It is interesting to note, however, that its movement to V seems to block further movement of either the V or the D. I speculate at the end of this chapter why this might be. Now we turn to an account of the details of movement that relies crucially on features.

5.3 An Account

Chomsky (2001) suggests that the snowball effect of head movement is due to the affixal nature of the landing sites. This is clearly not the case when predicate movement forces a snowball effect. Let us go through a derivation step by step, but let us assume (i) that features target the largest X(P) category with the relevant feature and (ii) that every head and projection along an extended projection line of V carries a V-feature. Now we turn to the relevant phrase structures. In (30a) below we see a derivation at the point where a functional head (say T) with an uninterpretable V-feature is merged into the structure. In the case of a B-type language, this feature will target a VP, and in the case of an A-type language, the feature will target a V°.[22] Now the derivations diverge. In an A-type language, the V will adjoin to F1, as in (30b), and in a B-type language, the VP will move to Spec, F1P, as in (30c). Now we ask the question what will happen when another functional category with the V-feature is merged into the structure. In the A-type language, this new V-feature will target the largest X° carrying the feature.[23] This will be the F1 which contains V and F1. In the B-type language, the largest XP carrying the V feature will be F1P.

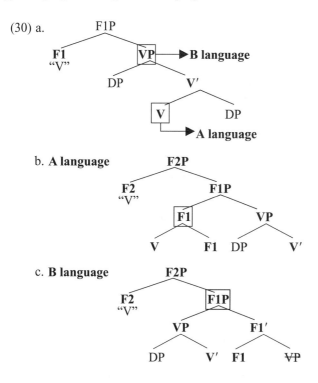

(30) a.

b. **A language**

c. **B language**

Now we can see that the snowball effect has nothing to do with affixes and everything to do with features. DP movement will never show this effect within the extended projection of a verb because the features will never be the same.[24] A DP in the Spec, TP, for example, will be chosen over TP for movement because it alone will have the relevant D-feature.

I end with a speculation about the oddities of D°-movement (as compared with V°-movement). We have seen that D°-movement is frozen after one move. There is no further movement of the D° or the V° to which it has adjoined. It should come as no surprise that the V° does not move any further, since, by hypothesis, there is no head movement of the V into the inflectional domain of a B-type language. However, we might expect the D° to move higher. It may be, however, that there is one constant in the behavior of feature attraction in head movement. We can imagine that a feature probe cannot locate a feature that is attached to a subpart of an X°. If we look at the tree in (27) below, in order to have the D move further, a higher D-feature would have to see the D inside the verbal head X. It is plausible that the V-specification of X would block access to the D-feature below.[25] Note that this does not mean that there are two reasons for the snowball effect of head movement—one due to the largest X(P) requirement and one due to the invisibility of a feature. In the first case, an alternative target is sought, while in the second, movement is simply not an option. In any case, this explanation for the freezing of D°-movement requires more data and more thought.

6. Conclusion

The aim of this chapter was to argue for accepting both sides of an asymmetry that is set up by a system where movement is triggered by the features V and D. While Chomsky (2001) suggests that VP-, D°-movement languages are not expected to occur, there are fairly robust arguments that they do. In fact, by using movement of VP and D° versus V° and DP to divide languages into two types, we find interesting correlations with other language phenomena such as *wh*-clefts and base-generated predication structures (i.e., lack of DP movement). Further, we can better understand the nature of movement by first accepting that there are two types—X°-movement and XP movement—and examining both types within the context of the two types of language. It is only at this point that we can move beyond how we feel the two types of movement should behave to truly understanding their nature.   ■

ACKNOWLEDGMENTS

The first step of this material was presented at the Theoretical and Applied Linguistics Laboratory at the University of Western Ontario. I appreciate feedback from that audience as well as from audiences at the University of California-Santa Cruz, AFLA XI, GURT, TEAL, Academia Sinica, and the University of Arizona. I am also grateful for the financial support of SSHRCC grant 410-2004-0966 and the patience of my native language consultants.

NOTES

1. Many cases of remnant movement often work differently with respect to these asymmetries. At this point, I leave aside a discussion of work such as Koopman and Szabolcsi (2000), but this will certainly become relevant in the next stage of this research.
2. There is an ongoing debate within the WMP literature on the status of the DP that I call the subject. It has been analyzed as a Topic (e.g., Richards 2000; Pearson 2001), an absolutive DP in an ergative system (Aldridge 2004; de Guzman 1988; Gerdts 1988), and a nominative adjunct (Sells 1998). I, like Kroeger (1993), Paul (2000), and Keenan (2000), call it a subject but in fact believe that it is

base generated externally and is related to the predicate through the verbal morphology in a construction which is similar to Clitic Left Dislocated structures in Italian (Cinque 1990).

3. There are a variety of Actor Topic and Theme Topic forms and a variety of Circumstantial Topic uses. See Rajemisa-Raolison (1971) for a description of some of these and Paul (2000) for an account.

4. These proposals were triggered by similar proposals made by Massam (1998) and Massam and Smallwood (1997) for Niuean, a language on the Polynesian side of the Austronesian language family.

5. In this respect, the adverbs in Malagasy would behave syntactically like the functional particles described in Cinque (1999, 58).

6. I haven't specified where the subject moves from in this case since the merged position of instrumentals raises further questions that I do not intend to address.

7. I have glossed (12a) as Holmberg has done. Presumably *hvers vegna* together mean 'why.'

8. This is also shown on Rackowski's tree given in (10), though she uses the notation *VP* rather than *vP*.

9. This form of the 2SG pronoun is listed in grammars as -*nao* since it is always a suffix. Other forms of the pronoun are *ianao* (nominative) and *anao* (accusative).

10. There are some important differences between the two outlined in Paul (1996) that are, I would argue, due to the fact that N-bonding is movement triggered by a feature while compounding is not.

11. A remaining question or problem in this analysis of N-bonding is the apparent right adjunction of the movement. At this point, I have no alternative but to allow right adjunction. Below, in the discussion of Malay, we will see an example of D°-movement that is done with left adjunction.

12. Object placement and apparent movement also have to be done through base generation. This clearly needs to be researched more.

13. The point of their paper is to show that D-incorporation from subjects behaves differently from N-incorporation from subjects and that the languages that allow the former will never have the latter. For my purposes, their correlation with the V-initial status is what is crucial.

14. As pointed out by Oda, more accurately, the *wh*-structure is that of a pseudocleft of the form *The one who sold the world is who?*

15. A-type languages can create *wh*-clefts and *wh*-pseudoclefts, but this would not be their primary strategy for creating *wh*-constructions. A-type languages can also front predicates for discourse reasons (*Do their homework they will*), but again these constructions are marked in discourse.

16. For some reason, if the head movement of the D is string vacuous as in Malagasy, the determiner of a common noun can be included in the process. When the movement is not string vacuous as in Malay, only Ds that do not take a complement NP can undergo movement. This is a concern and I leave it for further study.

17. Again, I have labeled the projection above VP *XP* to be deliberately vague.

18. Note that I am assuming that no language utilizes head movement in both cases or XP movement in both cases. I have doubts that such languages exist, and we would like this to be for principled reasons. This is one of the next steps of this project.

19. Guilfoyle (1990) argues that Irish has no A-movement, though see McCloskey (2001) for a differing viewpoint. In Travis (2001), I argue that Malagasy does not have derived objects.

20. Oda (2002), Massam (1998), and Massam and Smallwood (1997) treat it more like DP movement in that it moves to Spec, TP to satisfy EPP-type features. Pearson (2001), on the other hand, correlates predicate fronting in Malagasy with V-movement in V2 languages.

21. Note that the examples that Chomsky gives are, indeed, of this nature. The point here is that not all head movement is of this type.

22. I haven't said how the relevant parameter is encoded and this requires more work. Somehow, features "know" whether they are seeking X°s or XPs.

23. Obviously, it also has to meet any locality conditions on movement.

24. This snowball effect would be expected to appear within the extended projection of an N, however. And, as pointed out to me by Liliane Haegeman, this is, in fact, attested.

25. Obviously this would only happen within X°s, since DPs are visible for further movement from Spec, TP.

REFERENCES

Aldridge, E. 2004. Ergativity and word order in Austronesian languages. PhD diss., Cornell University.

Baker, M., and K. Hale. 1990. Relativized minimality and pronoun incorporation. *Linguistic Inquiry* 21: 289–97.

Chomsky, N. 1995. *The minimalist program*. Current Studies in Linguistics, vol. 28. Cambridge, MA: MIT Press.

———. 2001. Derivation by phase. In *Ken Hale: A life in language,* ed. M. Kenstowicz, 1–52. Cambridge, MA: MIT Press.

Cinque, G. 1990. *Types of A'-dependencies*. Linguistic Inquiry Monograph, vol. 17. Cambridge, MA: MIT Press.

———. 1999. *Adverbs and functional heads: A cross-linguistic perspective*. Oxford Studies in Comparative Syntax. Oxford: Oxford University Press.

De Guzman, V. 1988. Ergative analysis for Philippine languages: An analysis. In *Studies in Austronesian linguistics,* ed. R. McGinn, 323–45. Athens, OH: Ohio University Center for International Studies.

Gerdts, D. 1988. Antipassives and causatives in Ilokano: Evidence for an ergative analysis. In *Studies in Austronesian linguistics,* ed. R. McGinn, 323–45. Athens, OH: Ohio University Center for International Studies.

Grimshaw, J. 2000. Locality and extended projection. In *Lexical specification and insertion,* ed. P. Coopmans, M. Everaert, and J. Grimshaw, 115–34. Amsterdam: John Benjamins.

Guilfoyle, E. 1990. Functional categories and phrase structure parameters. PhD diss., McGill University.

Guilfoyle, E., H. Hung, and L. Travis. 1992. Spec of IP and Spec of VP: Two subjects in Austronesian languages. *Natural Language and Linguistic Theory* 10: 375–414.

Holmberg, A. 1986. *Word order and syntactic features in the Scandinavian languages and English.* Stockholm: University of Stockholm.

Kayne, R. 1994. *The antisymmetry of syntax*. Linguistic Inquiry Monographs, vol. 25. Cambridge, MA: MIT Press.

Keenan, E. 2000. Morphology is structure: A Malagasy test case. In *Formal issues in Austronesian linguistics,* ed. I. Paul, V. Phillips, and L. Travis, 27–47. Dordrecht: Kluwer.

Koopman, H., and A. Szabolcsi. 2000. *Verbal complexes.* Cambridge, MA: MIT Press.

Kroeger, P. 1993. *Phrase structure and grammatical relations in Tagalog.* Stanford, CA: CSLI.

Lee, F. 2000. VP remnant movement and VSO in Quiavini Zapotec. In *The syntax of verb initial languages,* ed. A. Carnie and E. Guilfoyle, 143–62. Oxford: Oxford University Press.

Massam, D. 1998. VSO is VOS: Aspects of Niuean Order. In *The syntax of verb initial languages,* ed. A. Carnie and E. Guilfoyle, 97–116. Oxford: Oxford University Press.

Massam, D., and C. Smallwood. 1997. Essential features of predication in English and Niuean. In *Proceedings of North East Linguistics Society 27,* ed. K. Kusumoto, 363–72.

McCloskey, J. 1979. *Transformational syntax and model theoretic semantics.* Synthese Language Library, vol. 9. Dordrecht: D. Reidel.

———. 2001. On the distribution of subject properties in Irish. In *Objects and other subjects: Grammatical functions, functional categories, and configurationality,* ed. W. D. Davies and S. Dubinsky, 157–92. Dordrecht: Kluwer.

Oda, K. 2002. Wh-questions in V-initial languages. MA Forum Paper, University of Toronto.

Paul, I. 1996. The Malagasy genitive. In *The Structure of Malagasy,* ed. M. Pearson and I. Paul, 76–91. Los Angeles: Department of Linguistics, UCLA.

———. 2000. Malagasy clause structure. PhD diss., McGill University.

———. 2001. Concealed pseudo-clefts. *Lingua* 111: 707–27.

Pearson, M. 1998. Two types of VO languages. In *The derivation of VO and OV,* ed. P. Svenonius, 327–63. Amsterdam: John Benjamins.

———. 2001. The clause structure of Malagasy: A minimalist approach. PhD diss., University of California, Los Angeles.

Postal, P. 1969. On so-called pronouns in English. In *Modern Studies in English,* ed. D. Reibel and S. Schane, 201–24. Englewood Cliffs, NJ: Prentice-Hall.

Rackowski, A. 1998. Malagasy adverbs. In *The structure of Malagasy,* vol. 2, ed. I. Paul, 11–33. Los Angeles: UCLA Occasional Papers in Linguistics.

Rajemisa-Raolison, R. 1971. *Grammaire malgache.* Fianarantsoa: Centre de Formation Pédogogique.

Richards, N. 2000. Another look at Tagalog subjects. In *Formal issues in Austronesian linguistics,* ed. I. Paul, V. Phillips, and L. Travis, 105–16. Dordrecht: Kluwer.

Sells, P. 1998. The functions of voice markers in Philippine languages. In *Morphology and its relation to phonology and syntax,* ed. S. G. Lapointe, D. K. Brentari, and P. M. Farrell, 111–37. Stanford, CA: CSLI.

Travis, L. 2001. Derived objects in Malagasy. In *Objects and other subjects: Grammatical functions, functional categories, and configurationality,* ed. W. D. Davies and S. Dubinsky, 123–55. Dordrecht: Kluwer.

———. Forthcoming. Through the looking glass: Malagasy in Wonderland. In *Clause structure and adjuncts in Austronesian languages,* ed. H.-M. Gärtner, P. Law, and J. Sabel. Berlin: Mouton de Gruyter.

Negation

6

Parasitism, Secondary Triggering, and Depth of Embedding

MARCEL DEN DIKKEN
CUNY Graduate Center

1. Introduction

In den Dikken (2002), I present what is to my knowledge the first detailed discussion in the literature of the peculiar properties of a Dutch polarity item (PI), the word *heel,* a cognate of English *whole,* illustrated in (1a).

(1) a. ik ken   die *hele*   vent *(niet)
       I   know that whole bloke not
       'I don't know that bloke at all.'

     b. die (*hele*) vent   kent   me niet
       that whole   bloke knows me not

I argue there that "polar *heel*" is dependent for its direct licensing on a sentential negation that does not have scope over it, as becomes evident from a comparison of the triplets in (2) and (3). In this respect, polar *heel* fits in the same slot in the typology of polarity-sensitive expressions that is also occupied by a particular subspecies of "n-words"—specifically, those that, as Giannakidou (2000) has shown in detail, behave "as polarity sensitive universal quantifiers which need negation in order to be licensed, but must raise above negation in order to yield the scoping ∀¬" (Giannakidou 2000, 457).

(2) a. ik wil   met die hele   vent   nie praten
       I   want with that whole bloke not talk

     b. *ik wil   niet met die hele   vent   praten
       I   want not with that whole bloke talk

     c. ?ik wil   niet praten met die hele   vent
       I   want not talk   with that whole bloke
       'I don't want to talk to that bloke at all.'

(3) a. ik wil   met al die   mensen niet praten   ∀>¬
       I   want with all those people   not talk

     b. ik wil   niet met al die   mensen praten   ¬>∀
       I   want not with all those people   talk

      c. ik wil   niet praten met al die   mensen $\neg > \forall$ / $\forall > \neg$
         I want not talk   with all those people
         'I don't want to talk to all those people.'

Den Dikken (2002) shows furthermore that polar *heel* must not be separated from its licensing negation by a clause boundary and that it cannot be inserted in noun phrases which are prevented from undergoing A′-movement. Arguing that these restrictions follow from an analysis of the direct licensing of polar *heel* that involves A′-movement of the noun phrase containing polar *heel* into Spec, NegP in overt syntax, I provide a straightforward explanation for the fact that polar *heel* cannot be directly licensed in the subject of the negated clause (1b), for the clausemate restriction on the direct licensing of polar *heel* (4), and for the ban on embedding polar *heel* in the indirect object (5b).

(4) a. *ik geloof niet dat ik die *hele*   vent ken
       I believe not that I that whole bloke know
       'I don't believe I know that bloke at all.'

    b. *ik geloof niet dat die *hele*   vent me kent
       I believe not that that whole bloke me knows

(5) a. hij wil   die student die (*hele*) constructie niet uitleggen
       he wants that student that whole construction not explain
       'He doesn't want to explain that construction to that student at all.'

    b. hij wil   die (?**hele*) student die constructie niet uitleggen
       he wants that   whole student that construction not explain

The ill-formedness of (1b) is a reflex of the illegitimacy of downgrading movement from Spec, TP into Spec, NegP (with NegP being below TP in Dutch; see Haegeman and Zanuttini 1991 and subsequent work).[1] The ungrammaticality of (4) follows from the fact that both conceivable derivations of these sentences fail: fell-swoop movement of polar *heel*'s container across CP into the matrix Spec, NegP violates subjacency, and successive-cyclic movement through the embedded Spec, CP, while in accordance with subjacency, violates Müller and Sternefeld's (1993) Principle of Unambiguous Binding, constituting an improper-movement effect of sorts.[2] And the fact that polar *heel* cannot be embedded in the indirect object (5b) is a consequence of the general ban on A′-movement of indirect objects.[3]

    Interestingly, however, the ungrammaticality of sentences that violate the conditions on direct licensing of polar *heel* can often be lifted if an additional polarity item is included in the structure, with the otherwise offending token of polar *heel* piggybacking on that additional polarity item. Thus, while (5b) is ungrammatical, (5c) is perfectly well formed. The difference between (5b) and (5c) is precisely the fact that (5c) contains an additional token of polar *heel* (underscored in the example) inside the direct object, where, as we know from (5a), polar *heel* is legitimately licensed. Apparently the presence of this additional polar *heel* helps out the otherwise illegitimate polar *heel* in the indirect object. This effect is part and parcel of a more general phenomenon which, in den Dikken (2002), I dubbed *parasitic licensing* of polar *heel*. Some more examples of this are provided in (6), where systematically the result is grammatical only if the additional polarity item (once again underscored) is included in the sentence. Parasitic polar *heel* can be embedded in an indirect object, as in (5c), or in a subject, as in (6b), and it does not depend on a clausemate negation: in (6a, b), polar *heel* is separated from the negation in the matrix clause by a CP boundary, but it does not seem to care. In fact, parasitically licensed polar *heel* does not even depend on a negative morpheme: though conditionals and downward-entailing verbs like *betwijfelen* 'doubt' do not license polar *heel* directly, (6c, d) are grammatical if they include an additional PI (*ooit* 'ever') that *is* legitimately licensed in these contexts.

(5) c. hij wil   die *hele*   student die <u>hele</u>   constructie   niet uitleggen
      he wants that whole student that whole construction not explain
      'He doesn't want to explain that construction to that student at all.'

(6) a. ik geloof niet dat ik die *hele*   vent *(<u>ooit</u>) gezien heb
      I believe not that I that whole bloke ever seen   have

   b. ik geloof niet dat die *hele*   vent *(<u>ook maar iets</u>)   tegen me
      I believe not that that whole bloke also but   anything to   me
      gezegd heeft
      said   has

   c. als je   die *hele*   vent *(<u>ooit</u>) bezoekt, kijk ik je   nooit meer   aan
      if you that whole bloke ever visit   look I you never anymore PRT

   d. ik betwijfel of ik die *hele*   vent *(<u>ooit</u>) gezien heb
      I doubt   if I that whole bloke ever seen   have

Parasitic licensing of polar *heel* is severely restricted, in ways that mimic the restrictions on the more familiar instance of parasitism in syntax, the licensing of parasitic gaps: both obey an anti-c-command condition (the parasite must not be c-commanded by what it aims to piggyback on) and an S-structure licensing condition.[4]

The preceding paragraphs summarize the key ingredients of the analysis of direct and parasitic polarity item licensing laid out in den Dikken (2002). In the present chapter, I will take a closer look at the restrictions on parasitic licensing of polar *heel*. On the basis of an investigation of novel data that show that depth of embedding is an important restrictor of parasitic licensing, I will argue for a distinction between *parasitic licensing* and *secondary triggering* (see Horn 1996). In the course of that discussion, I will invoke and support a key ingredient of Postal's (2000) recent perspective on the syntax of polarity: the idea that negation can originate within the projection of the PI.

2. Two Depth-of-Embedding Restrictions on Parasitism

The analysis of polar *heel* licensing outlined in den Dikken (2002) predicts that as long as there is some other PI that is licensed and to which polar *heel* can legitimately link up (in conformity with the anti-c-command condition and the S-structure licensing condition), parasitic licensing should make all restrictions on the licensing of polar *heel* disappear. But there are at least two contexts in which parasitic licensing of polar *heel* is unsuccessful: (i) it is impossible for polar *heel* to be parasitically licensed by another PI if the two are in a clause that is more than one clause boundary removed from the licensing negation, and (ii) it is also impossible for polar *heel* and the additional PI themselves to be separated by a clause boundary: that is, polar *heel* can only piggyback on a clausemate "helper," even if that helper is further down the tree than *heel* (so that anti-c-command is ensured) and is itself perfectly legitimate in this deeply embedded position. These are two contexts in which depth of embedding plays a key role in the licensing of polar *heel*—unexpectedly, on the analysis presented in den Dikken (2002).

2.1 Restriction I: The Licensing Negation Must Not Be More Than One Clause Boundary Away

Let me start by addressing the first problem: the fact that it is impossible for polar *heel* to piggyback on another PI if the two are in a clause that is more than one clause boundary removed from the licensing negation.

2.1.1 The Facts   That this is the case is shown by a comparison of the examples in (7), (8), and (9). In the monoclausal examples in (7), we find the familiar split between polar *heel* in the direct object, on the one hand, and polar *heel* embedded in the indirect object or the subject on the other: while (7a) is perfect, (7b, c) are degraded.

(7) a. ik heb   [die (*hele*) vent]$_{DO}$ nooit gemogen   [MONOCLAUSAL]
       I have that whole bloke   never liked
       'I have never liked that bloke at all.'

   b. ik zal   [die (?*hele) vent]$_{IO}$ die constructie   niet uitleggen
       I will that   whole bloke   that construction not explain
       'I won't explain that construction to that bloke at all.'

   c. [die (*hele) vent]$_{SU}$ heeft nooit met me gesproken
       that   whole bloke   has   never with me spoken
       'That bloke has never spoken to me at all.'

This follows straightforwardly from the fact that in (7), only direct licensing is possible, where *direct licensing,* on den Dikken's (2002) analysis, means overt syntactic A'-movement of the container of polar *heel* to Spec, NegP. The ungrammaticality of (7b) follows from the general ban on A'-movement of indirect objects (recall note 3), and (7c) is bad because movement to Spec, NegP starting from the subject position would involve downgrading movement.

The well-formedness of all three examples in (8) shows, once again, that these restrictions on the licensing of polar *heel* are lifted in parasitic licensing contexts: in all examples, polar *heel* can link up to the licensing dependency of the other PI, *ooit,* which is legitimately licensed by a nonclausemate negation.

(8) ik denk niet dat . . .   [BICLAUSAL]
       I think not that
       'I don't think that . . .'

    a. . . . ik [die (*hele*) vent]$_{DO}$ <u>ooit</u> heb gemogen
        I that whole bloke   ever have liked

    b. . . . ik [die (*hele*) vent]$_{IO}$ <u>ooit</u> die constructie zal uitleggen
        I that whole bloke ever that construction will explain

    c. . . . [die (*hele*) vent]$_{SU}$ <u>ooit</u> met me gesproken heeft
        that whole bloke ever with me spoken   has

When we now look at (9), we see that, in triclausal constructions where both polarity items are two clause boundaries removed from the licensing negation, we get back the single-clause asymmetry between direct objects on the one hand and indirect objects and subjects on the other.[5]

(9) ik denk niet dat ze   zullen geloven dat . . .   [TRICLAUSAL]
   I think not that they will   believe that
   'I don't think that they will believe that . . .'

    a. . . . ik [die (*?hele*) vent]$_{DO}$ <u>ooit</u> heb gemogen
        I that   whole bloke ever have liked

    b. . . . ik [die (*?*hele*) vent]$_{IO}$ <u>ooit</u> die constructie zal uitleggen
        I that   whole bloke ever that construction will explain

    c. . . . [die (**hele*) vent]$_{SU}$ <u>ooit</u> met me gesproken heeft
        that   whole bloke ever with me spoken   has

The facts in (9) pose two immediate questions:

▪ Why does parasitic licensing of polar *heel* fail here while it succeeded perfectly well in (8)?

▪ How does the polar *heel* inside the direct object of the most deeply embedded clause in (9a) still manage to get licensed, while (9b) and (9c) are ungrammatical?

The most deeply embedded clause in (9) gives us precisely the same asymmetry that we see in monoclausal (7)—the most deeply embedded clause in (9) behaves as though it were the only clause in the structure, and, moreover, as though it were negative.

2.1.2 Two Types of Negative Polarity Items: Negative NPIs and Nonnegative NPIs   I would like to argue that the constellation of facts seen in (7) through (9) can be made to follow if we make a distinction between two types of negative polarity items (NPIs), following the essence of Postal's (2000) work on the syntax of polarity.[6] Postal's work is motivated by the desire to uphold "[t]he maximum and boldest generalization," namely, "that negative polarity items are licensed *only* by negations as tradition, the terminology and a few previous researchers including Linebarger (1980, 1987) would have it, but that this is obscured by the invisibility of many negations of relevance" (Postal 2000, 15). He accomplishes this by assuming, contrary to Klima (1964), that "all so-called negative polarity *any* forms underlyingly occur with Determiner-internal negations.

Any forms occur when the negation in closest combination with the non-negative part of the determiner raises out of it" (p. 17). Specifically, he proposes that *any*-NPIs come in two varieties, represented as (10a) and (10b). Of the two structures, (10a) is formally negative, downward entailing, and antiadditive;[7] (10b), on the other hand, is nonnegative (the two negations on D cancel each other out in the semantics) and upward entailing.[8]

(10) a. [$_{DP}$ [$_D$ NEG1 [$_D$ *some*]] [$_{NP}$ . . . N . . .]]

b. [$_{DP}$ [$_D$ NEG2 [$_D$ NEG1 [$_D$ *some*]]] [$_{NP}$ . . . N . . .]]

This two-way typology of NPIs is motivated by contrasts of the type seen in (11a', b'), presented in Postal (2000, 22). NPIs of type (10a) are licensed only in antiadditive contexts, and, in virtue of being formally negative, can trigger negative inversion in embedded contexts; nonnegative, upward-entailing NPIs of type (10b), on the other hand, cannot bring about negative inversion. The fact that *not every juror,* the licenser of *any* in (11b, b'), is not antiadditive, unlike *no juror* in (11a, a'), ensures that in the (b) examples only the nonnegative, upward-entailing NPI can be chosen, which in turn guarantees that negative inversion is unsuccessful.

(11) a. No jurors believed that she had described any detail correctly.

a'. No jurors believed that any detail had she described correctly.

b. Not every juror believed that she had described any detail correctly.

b'. *Not every juror believed that any detail had she described correctly.

In this chapter, I adopt Postal's insight that some NPIs are formally negative. But I deviate from Postal's assumptions reflected in (10) in a number of ways, bringing them more in line with a minimalist syntax and allowing them to transparently accommodate the polar *heel* facts. My most significant departure from Postal (2000) is that I do not assume that *any* is the suppletive lexicalization of an indefinite D that has lost a negative morpheme (i.e., the Spell Out of the "leftover" of *not (not) some*); instead, I take *any,* in its negative incarnation, to be a D specified for the abstract feature [NEG]—an uninterpretable formal feature that needs to be checked by a matching [NEG] feature in some DP-external Neg° in the course of the syntactic derivation.[9]

With (10a) recast in terms of an abstract [NEG] feature, as in (12a), and with the negation originating DP-externally, there is no place in the analysis for a representation of the type in (10b): viewed as abstract, uninterpretable [NEG] features, the two negations in D in Postal's (10b) would check against each other and delete within DP; as a result, this would be indistinguishable from a representation that has zero negations in D. I therefore analyze nonnegative, upward-entailing NPIs as simple indefinites that depend on a local licenser (a downward-entailing [Ladusaw 1979] or nonveridical [Giannakidou 1998] element; the choice between these two will be immaterial here), with no negation raising out of them, as in (12b). This chapter thus adopts what could be characterized as a blend of the classic Klima (1964) approach to NPIs, appropriately updated and instantiated here by (12b), and Postal's (2000) alternative analysis represented by (12a).

(12) a. Formally negative PIs, with a [NEG] feature in D launched to a higher
        [NEG] head

     b. Indefinite PIs, dependent on a clausemate, downward-entailing/
        nonveridical licenser

The typology in (12) predicts that PIs of the type in (12b) can be embedded no
deeper than a CP directly embedded under a negative. For the C-head of a CP immediately embedded below a negative, Laka (1990) and Progovac (1988) have argued
that it possesses a [NEG] feature (a licenser in the sense of [12b]) assigned under selection from the matrix negation. They base this claim on the contrast between examples such as (13a) and (13b) (the former ill formed on a polarity reading of *anything,*
though not on a free-choice interpretation, irrelevant here): for Laka and Progovac,
the [NEG] feature on the C-head of the clause embedded under *doubt* (imposed on that
C-head by the matrix verb) licenses the *any*-NPI in (13b). But the C-head of a more
deeply embedded CP cannot be assigned a [NEG] feature because it is not itself selected by a negation. Since a CP that is twice removed from a negation does not have
its C-head specified for the feature [NEG], it follows that any PI that is successfully licensed within such a CP (as in [13c], or Uribe-Etxebarria's 1994 Spanish examples
of the same type, featuring n-words) must itself be a negative constituent, of type
(12a). That is to say, such PIs must themselves possess a [NEG]-specified head and
launch that head up the tree (in line with the analysis that Postal gives for [NEG]-spec-
ified PIs), into the clause that harbors the negation.

(13) a. *I doubt anything/any claims.

     b. I doubt that anything will happen.

     c. I doubt that he thinks that anything will happen.

2.1.3 The Triclausal Cases   With this as background, let me return to the Dutch facts in (8)
and (9), on which the typology in (12) affords us an interesting perspective. If we assume that Dutch PIs like *ooit* 'ever' are themselves lexically ambiguous between PIs
of types (12a) and (12b), this means that *ooit* has the option but not the obligation to
be marked for the feature [NEG]. Its [NEG]-specified incarnation is perfectly allowed
to be embedded two clauses down from the negation that will license its abstract
[NEG] feature: the [NEG] feature can make its way up to its licenser (the Neg head in
the matrix clause) via successive-cyclic head movement (see below for more details,
and also Troseth 2004), thereby circumventing any phase boundaries in between.
And given that an *ooit* that is two clauses removed from the negation must be a negative constituent of type (12a), since local licensing in keeping with (12b) would fail
in such a context, it comes to play an instrumental role in helping out polar *heel* in the
most deeply embedded clause of the triclausal examples in (9). The polar *heel* in the
direct object in (9a) will in fact end up being legitimate as a result of direct licensing
by a secondary Neg head—whence the label *secondary triggering* (borrowed from
Horn 1996).[10] Let me spell this out in more detail.

The *ooit* in the most deeply embedded clause in (9) is a negatively specified PI
of type (12a). Its abstract, uninterpretable [NEG] feature is in need of checking

against the [NEG] feature borne by the matrix Neg°, but a direct Agree relationship between the matrix Neg° and the NPI in the embedded clause is unestablishable: at least two strong phase boundaries (the embedded CP and the matrix vP) are in between. The bearer of the uninterpretable [NEG] feature of the polarity item (its D-head) hence has to be launched up the tree, first to the C-head of the embedded clause. But fell-swoop movement to the embedded C is prohibited: it would violate the locality conditions on head movement. Movement therefore has to proceed via a succession of smaller steps. First, the abstract [NEG]-specified head of the PI raises to the Neg head of the most deeply embedded clause;[11] that Neg head will subsequently raise to the C-head of the most deeply embedded CP, and so forth.[12] The thing to note here is that in order to reach the root Neg head, the [NEG] feature of the PI in the most deeply embedded clause must minimally be able to reach the Neg head of its own clause. Once it is there, it will enable that secondary Neg head to directly license polar *heel* by attracting the container of polar *heel* to its specifier, as in the single-clause examples in (7).[13] The relevant part of the structure of the sentences in (9) is shown in (14).

(14)

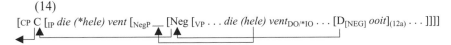

[CP C [IP *die (*hele) vent* [NegP __ [Neg [VP ... *die (hele) vent*DO/*IO ... [D[NEG] *ooit*](12a) ...]]]]

The successful licensing of polar *heel* in (9a) now falls out as a case of secondary triggering similar in its essentials to what we find in something like (15) (see Horn 1996; Postal 2000), where *in weeks* is licensed by the presence of a secondary negation—the [NEG] feature of (12a)-type *anybody*.

(15) I'm surprised {*John/✓anybody} has been here *in weeks.*

With (9a) being a case of secondary direct licensing of polar *heel,* we expect the distribution of polar *heel* in this doubly embedded context to match that of a polar *heel* licensed directly by a clausemate negation. And this is precisely what we find: the sentences in (9b) and (9c) are ill formed, exactly on a par with those in (7b, c). The deviance of these examples follows from the fact that direct licensing of polar *heel* involves pied-piping A′-movement into the clausemate Spec, NegP, which is impossible here. That parasitic licensing fails here as well will become clear after we have analyzed the examples in (8), to which I now turn.

2.1.4 The Biclausal Cases   The single-embedding paradigm in (8) suspends the asymmetries found in (7) and (9) because, in that particular context but not in (7) and (9), parasitic licensing is successful. That parasitic licensing is available in (8) follows from the fact that the *ooit* 'ever' in the single-embedding, biclausal examples in (8) does not have to be a negative constituent but can also be a PI of type (12b)—that is, a nonnegative indefinite establishing a local dependency relationship with a clausemate, downward-entailing/nonveridical element (here C[NEG]), as shown in (16). It is this dependency relationship between C[NEG] and *ooit* that polar *heel* successfully parasitizes on in all of the sentences in (8). Since parasitic licensing does not involve A′-movement of the container of polar *heel,* and since polar *heel* can legitimately link up to the dependency between the structurally higher $C_{[NEG]}$-head and *ooit,* we do not expect to find any asymmetries between direct objects on the one hand and indirect objects and subjects on the other—and indeed, no such asymmetries are found in (8).

(16)

[CP $C_{[NEG]}$ [IP *die (*hele) vent . . .* [VP *. . . die (hele) vent*DO/IO *. . .* [*ooit*](12b) *. . .*]]]

Parasitic licensing fails in (9). Even though the C-head in (14) above comes to harbor a [NEG] feature in the course of successive-cyclic raising of $D_{[NEG]}$, the fact that this [NEG] feature entertains a movement dependency with the D-head of *ooit* 'ever', not a licensing dependency of the type referred to in (12b), makes it impossible for polar *heel* to link up with this dependency and be licensed parasitically as a result. Parasitism is highly sensitive to the kind of dependency that the parasite is to piggyback on. From the domain of parasitic gaps, we are familiar with the fact that these link up with A'-movement dependencies, not A'-binding dependencies (cf. the contrast in *this article*$_i$*, I filed t*$_i$*/*it*$_i$ *without reading pg*$_i$). But parasitic polar *heel* is not a gap and does not move; as a consequence, it cannot parasitize on a movement dependency but instead requires, for its parasitic licensing to be successful, that there be a local head (Neg or C) with its own [NEG] feature engaging in a licensing dependency with a (12b)-type PI in its c-command domain. Since there is no such head in (14), parasitic licensing of polar *heel* is not possible there.

To summarize the discussion of (7) through (9), what we have seen is that parasitic licensing of polar *heel* succeeds only in contexts in which the C-head of the clause containing polar *heel* and the additional PI that it seeks to piggyback on is specified for the feature [NEG], thanks to being the head of the CP complement immediately embedded under a negated clause. In other contexts, polar *heel* can only survive if it can be licensed directly, via movement of its container to Spec, NegP. Such direct licensing itself comes in two types: primary direct licensing by the Neg head of a clause that is itself negated by a physical negation and secondary direct licensing by a Neg head (or Σ-head; see note 11) that has the [NEG]-specified head of a (12a)-type NPI raise through it and thus receives an abstract [NEG] feature.

2.1.5 Licensing Polar Heel under Negative Verbs   Before moving on to the second depth-of-embedding restriction on parasitic licensing of polar *heel,* let me briefly examine two further issues that come up under the rubric of secondary triggering versus parasitic licensing. Recall first of all that the fact that in (8) parasitic licensing is successful is thanks to the presence of a [NEG] feature on the C-head of the clause embedded under the matrix negation. Recall also that Laka (1990) and Progovac (1988) motivated this $C_{[NEG]}$ on the basis of the distribution of PIs in the complement of verbs such as *doubt,* as shown in (13). A natural question to ask at this point, therefore, is what happens with polar *heel* in the complement of such verbs. What we predict is that it should not be licensed via primary direct licensing (since there is no NegP in the complement CP) and that it should be able to be licensed parasitically in the CP immediately embedded under the *doubt*-type verb but not in a CP embedded within *doubt*'s own complement. We have already seen that the former prediction is correct: (6d) is ungrammatical without *ooit*. The fact that it becomes perfect with *ooit* inserted tells us that parasitic licensing does indeed work here. The examples in (17a, b) reproduce this effect. To probe what happens under further embedding, we need to compare biclausal (17b) and triclausal (17c). The contrast between these sentences confirms that parasitic licensing of polar *heel* under verbs like *doubt* is indeed restricted in the expected way.

(17) a. ik betwijfel of ik die (**hele*) vent   ken   (see [6d])

     I doubt   if I that   whole bloke know

     'I doubt that I know that bloke at all.'

  b. ik betwijfel of die (*hele*) vent   <u>ook maar iemand</u> zal   groeten

     I doubt   if that whole bloke also but   anyone will greet

     'I doubt that that bloke will greet anyone at all.'

  c. ik betwijfel of ze   zullen geloven dat die (**hele*)   vent   <u>ook maar</u>

     I doubt   if they will   believe that that   whole bloke also but

     <u>iemand</u> zal   groeten

     anyone will greet

     'I doubt that they will believe that that bloke will greet anyone at all.'

  d. ik betwijfel of ze   zullen geloven dat ik die (?*hele*)   vent   <u>ooit</u>

     I doubt   if they will   believe that I   that   whole bloke ever

     gemogen heb

     liked   have

     'I doubt that they will believe that I have ever liked that bloke at all.'

In (17b, c), I chose subjects as containers of polar *heel* to make sure that only parasitic licensing could ever help *heel* out. These examples, therefore, do not allow us to check whether secondary direct licensing could succeed two clauses down. To verify this, I added (17d), which predictably fails as an instance of parasitic licensing (because the local C-head in the most deeply embedded CP is not [NEG] specified) but which, in view of the fact that it is acceptable with polar *heel* included, does converge as an instance of secondary triggering: (12a)-type *ooit* 'ever' launches its [NEG] feature up to its ultimate licenser, via successive-cyclic movement, stopping by at the Neg head (or Σ-head) of its own clause, which can then take care of direct licensing of polar *heel*.[14]

2.1.6 Licensing Polar *Heel* in Conditional Clauses
Finally, let us ask what happens in nonnegative environments such as conditional clauses. In (6c), we saw that parasitic licensing of polar *heel* is successful in a conditional. But it should break down once an additional clause is inserted between *als* 'if' and polar *heel*'s container. And indeed, it does: while (18a, b) are both fine with *heel* included, we find a contrast between (19a) and (19b), the latter being ungrammatical due to the fact that parasitic licensing fails in the context at hand because (12b)-type *ooit* cannot establish a local dependency with a clausemate, downward-entailing/nonveridical element in this context.

(18) (see [6c])

  a. als je   die *(hele)* vent <u>ooit</u> zou   bezoeken, kijk ik je   nooit meer aan
  if you that whole bloke ever would visit   look I you never more PRT
  'If you ever were to visit that bloke at all, I would never look you in
  the eye again.'

  b. als die *(hele)* vent me <u>ooit</u> zou   bezoeken, zou   ik hem direct
  if that whole bloke me ever would visit   would I him directly
  de deur uitgooien
  the door out-throw
  'If that bloke were to ever visit me at all, I would throw him out the
  door immediately.'

(19) a. als je   denkt dat ik die (?*hele*) vent <u>ooit</u> zou   bezoeken, heb
  if you think that I that whole bloke ever would visit   have
  je   het mis
  you it   wrong
  'If you think that I would ever visit that bloke at all, you're wrong.'

  b. als je   denkt dat die (**hele*) vent me <u>ooit</u> zou   bezoeken, heb
  if you think that that whole bloke me ever would visit   have
  je   het mis
  you it   wrong
  'If you think that that bloke would ever visit me at all, you're wrong.'

Example (19a) is acceptable because direct-object contained polar *heel* can be licensed via secondary triggering here: the [NEG] feature launched successive cyclically from (12a)-type *ooit* enables polar *heel* to be licensed directly by a secondary
NegP in its own clause.[15] The analysis thus makes the right predictions in the context
of negative matrix verbs and conditional clauses as well.

2.2 Restriction II: The Parasite and Its Helper
Must Be Clausemates

The division of labor between primary direct licensing, secondary direct licensing,
and parasitic licensing gives polarity items like polar *heel* an abundance of opportu-
nities to survive in all sorts of syntactic contexts. But it is plain that there are plenty
of contexts in which polar *heel* can be licensed neither through secondary triggering
nor through parasitic licensing. We have already come across several such contexts.
In this subsection, I would like to address another context, illustrated by the example
in (20), first noted in Hoeksema (2003).[16]

(20) ik denk niet dat die *hele*   vent (*<u>geloofde dat ze</u>) hem <u>ooit</u>
  I think not that that whole bloke believed that she him ever
  gemogen heeft
  liked   has
  'I don't think that that bloke (believed that she) ever liked him at all.'

Hoeksema's example shows that in order for parasitic licensing of polar *heel* to be successful, the additional PI that polar *heel* is to piggyback on must be a clausemate of polar *heel:* (20) is well formed if the doubly underscored middle clause is absent, which tells us that it is apparently impossible for polar *heel* and the additional PI *ooit* 'ever' to be constituents of different clauses. The ungrammaticality of the triclausal version of (20) follows from the fact that polar *heel* in this example can be licensed neither through secondary triggering nor through parasitic licensing, as I will now show.

It should be immediately clear that, regardless of whether the doubly underscored portion is included or not, direct licensing of subject-contained polar *heel* in (20) will always fail. All direct licensing, whether primary or secondary, involves pied-piping movement of the container of polar *heel* into Spec, NegP, and such movement would of necessity be downgrading movement if launched from the clausemate Spec, TP. So there is no hope of direct licensing of polar *heel* in (20), no matter whether polar *heel* and *ooit* are clausemates or not.[17] But now notice that the question of whether polar *heel* and its helper *ooit* are clausemates or not does become highly relevant when it comes to the alternative licensing strategy for polar *heel:* parasitic licensing. In successful cases of parasitic licensing, polar *heel* piggybacks on the licensing of another PI—an *ooit* of type (12b) in the case at hand. Now, *ooit* in (20) can only be legitimately of type (12b) in the biclausal version of the sentence, where it can locally depend on a [NEG]-specified C-head. In the triclausal variant, the lowest CP is not [NEG] specified since it neither contains an overt negation nor serves as a complement clause immediately embedded below a negation. As a result, (12b)-type *ooit* is not licensable in (20) if the doubly underscored part is included, and with (12b)-type *ooit* ruled out in triclausal (20), it follows (since secondary direct licensing had already been eliminated independently) that there is no chance of survival for polar *heel* in the version of (20) that has the doubly underscored part included.

3. The S-Structure Condition on Parasitism Revisited

Finally, I would like to return to something I noted in passing in the introduction (recall the text below [6]): the fact that parasitic licensing of polar *heel* has to be established at S-structure. This was demonstrated and discussed in den Dikken (2002) on the basis of the examples in (21).

(21) a. [dat ze die (*hele) vent <u>ook maar een cent</u> meer salaris zouden
       that they that whole bloke also but   a   cent more salary would

       geven] was tijdens de vergadering niet besproken
       give   was during the meeting   not discussed

       'That they would give that bloke a penny more in salary at all wasn't
       discussed in the meeting.'

    b. [een dokter die die (*hele) vent <u>ook maar enigszins</u>   kon   helpen]
       a   doctor who that whole bloke also but   in.any.way could help

       was niet te vinden
       was not to find

       'A doctor who could help that bloke in any way at all was nowhere to
       be found.'

In these sentences, licensing of the underlined *ook maar* NPIs inside the bracketed constituents is successful, under reconstruction at LF (à la Uribe-Etxebarria 1994; see also Linebarger 1980). But LF licensing of the *ook maar* NPIs apparently does not help out polar *heel* in these examples: it comes too late, parasitism being an S-structure affair (see the familiar ungrammaticality of [22b]).

(22) a. *which article* did you file *t* without reading *pg*?

b. *who filed *which article* without reading *pg*?

3.1 Raising to Subject Versus Topicalization and the Role of $C_{[NEG]}$

With this as background (and see den Dikken 2002 for more detailed discussion), consider the fact that the sentences in (23b, c) are perfectly grammatical and contrast markedly with the ungrammatical variant of (21a) with *hele* included.[18] The example in (23c) is particularly instructive: the fact that polar *heel* here is subject contained tells us unequivocally that we are dealing with parasitic licensing, not secondary triggering.

(23) a. [dat we die (*hele*) vent   toen hebben uitgenodigd] kan ik nu

that we that   whole bloke then have   invited   can I now

niet meer begrijpen

not more understand

'That we invited that bloke at all back then, I can no longer understand.'

b. [dat we die (*hele*) vent   <u>ooit</u> hebben uitgenodigd] kan ik nu   niet

that we that whole bloke ever have   invited   can I   now not

meer begrijpen

more understand

'That we ever invited that bloke at all, I can no longer understand.'

c. [dat die (*hele*) vent   ons <u>ooit</u> heeft uitgenodigd] kan ik nu   niet

that that whole bloke us   ever has   invited   can I   now not

meer begrijpen

more understand

'That that bloke ever invited us at all, I can no longer understand.'

The key difference between (21a) on the one hand and (23b, c) on the other seems to be that (23b, c) are cases of topicalization while (21a) has the bracketed clause function as a subject. But while subject versus topic is indeed an important distinction, it cannot be the whole story, for (21b) cannot be similarly "rescued": (24a) through (24c) are bad if *heel* is included.

(24) a. [dokters die die   (*hele*) vent <u>ook maar enigszins</u>   kunnen helpen]

doctors who that   whole bloke also but in.any.way can   help

vind je   nergens

find you nowhere

'Doctors who can help that bloke in any way, you can't find anywhere.'

b. [dokters die die (*hele) vent <u>ook maar iets</u>   kunnen toedienen]
doctors who that   whole bloke also but   anything can   serve
vind je   nergens
find you nowhere
'Doctors who can serve that bloke anything at all, you can't find
anywhere.'

c. [dokters die   die (*hele) vent <u>ook maar enigszins</u>   vertrouwt] vind
doctors who that   whole bloke also but   in.any.way trusts   find
je   nergens
you nowhere
'Doctors whom that bloke trusts in any way, you can't find
anywhere.'

Regardless of whether *die hele vent* 'that bloke' is the direct object, as in (24a), the indirect object (24b), or the subject (24c) within the relative clause, the output of topicalization of the relativized noun phrase crashes.[19] The facts in (23) and (24) and their relationship with (21) raise important questions that need to be addressed. If (21a, b) are bad because licensing of the *ook maar* NPIs under reconstruction comes too late to rescue polar *heel,* then how can (23b, c) be grammatical while (24a) through (24c) continue to crash?

Let me start with the contrast between (21a) and (23b, c). These examples involve a CP embedded in a negative clause. For such CPs, the foregoing discussion had adopted (from Progovac 1988 and Laka 1990) the idea that its C-head is equipped with a [NEG] feature that can license clausemate NPIs of type (12b) under c-command. Let us assume, plausibly, that the [NEG] feature of a C-head embedded under a matrix negation is uninterpretable and needs to be checked against a matching [NEG] feature of Neg°, and let us further assume that in order for a dependency between a [NEG]-specified head and a (12b)-type PI to be able to parasitically license polar *heel,* that dependency itself must have been fully established, with all uninterpretable features erased. For a CP that serves as the complement of a transitive verb, which is separated from Neg by a *v*P phase boundary, this means that CP must minimally raise to a position on the edge of the *v*P phase within which it is embedded to allow parasitic licensing of polar *heel* to happen. Such licensing must, moreover, happen in overt syntax, since parasitic licensing in general never happens covertly. Now, in (23) we are dealing with topicalization. As an instance of A′-movement, this should be allowed to proceed via intermediate A′-positions, including an adjunction position to *v*P. With CP adjoined to *v*P, an Agree relationship between Neg° and the [NEG] feature of the C-head is established, as a result of which C's [NEG] feature is checked against the matching [NEG] feature in the matrix Neg°, and the dependency between (12b)-type *ooit* and the interpretable [NEG] feature of the matrix clause is fully established. On this dependency, polar *heel* then parasitizes in (23b, c). Notice, crucially, that the parasitic licensing of polar *heel* in this example is thus effectuated already at S-structure, thanks to overt raising of the CP to a *v*P adjoined position on its way up to the topic position.[20]

In the example in (21a), a [NEG] feature on the C-head of the left-peripheral CP cannot be overtly checked, however. In line with Koster's (1978) argument to the effect that subject sentences do not exist, I will take the "subject CP" in (21a) to be base generated in a position in the left periphery, linked to a pronoun (optionally spelled out in Dutch as a so-called *d*-word, as shown in [25]) originating in the θ-position and making its way up to Spec, TP. Since the CP's overt syntactic position, high up in the left periphery, is not one from which an Agree relationship can be established with Neg, it follows that this CP's head cannot be equipped with an uninterpretable [NEG] feature: if it had possessed such a feature, the failure of getting it checked would have resulted in a Full Interpretation violation. No NPIs of any kind can be licensed inside the physical CP in (21a), therefore. That (12b)-type NPIs nonetheless do survive in this context is due to the fact that the base copy of the (null) *d*-word to which the physical CP is associated gets replaced at LF by a full (though silent) copy of its associate CP.[21] Unlike the physical CP in the left periphery, this VP-internal copy can be equipped with a [NEG] specification: this feature can be checked at LF as a result of feature movement to Neg. At LF, therefore, the [NEG] feature of the C-head of the silent VP-internal copy of the "subject CP" can license a (12b)-type PI, as desired: (21a) and (25) are grammatical so long as polar *heel* is not included. That polar *heel* cannot be included in these examples follows from the fact that the licensing of the (12b)-type NPIs in examples of the type in (21a) and (25) cannot be established prior to LF and as a result cannot facilitate parasitic licensing of polar *heel,* which (like all parasitism) has to be accomplished in overt syntax.

(25) [dat ze   die (**hele*) vent   <u>ook maar een cent</u> meer salaris zouden
     that they that   whole bloke also but   a   cent more salary would
     geven], **dat**   was tijdens de vergadering niet besproken
     give   that (*d*-word) was during the meeting   not discussed
     'That they would give that bloke a penny more in salary at all wasn't
     discussed in the meeting.'

That the examples in (21b) and (24) are all ungrammatical with polar *heel* included can now be understood as well. Parasitic licensing in these examples is dependent on the establishment of a licensing relationship between a (12b)-type NPI and a local [NEG] feature. The [NEG] feature local to the *ook maar* NPIs inside the relative clauses in (21b) and (24) would have to be hosted by the C-head of the relative clause.[22] Suppose, therefore, that this C° has a [NEG] specification—how would that uninterpretable [NEG] feature be checked? The fact that it is separated from the Neg head of the matrix clause by a DP node, combined with the fact that DP is arguably a phase,[23] tells us that C's [NEG] feature could only be checked if this feature first made its way up to the head of the relativized DP. In other words, the licensing of (12b)-type NPIs within a relativized noun phrase is dependent on LF feature movement. That is fine as far as these NPIs themselves are concerned, but of course it wreaks havoc for their chances of facilitating the parasitic licensing of polar *heel* in the examples in (21b) and (24): since they themselves are not licensed until LF, they cannot help polar *heel* out because parasitism must be established by spell out.

Notice that the account of (21b) and (24) outlined in the previous paragraph predicts that even with the relativized noun phrase in object position, it should be impossible to get polar *heel* licensed parasitically by a (12b)-type NPI that depends for its licensing on the $C_{[NEG]}$ of the relative clause. This is correct: (26a) is ungrammatical with *heel* included.

(26) a. ik kon   nergens [een dokter [die die (*hele) vent   ook maar
       I could nowhere a   doctor who that whole bloke also but
       enigszins   kon   helpen]] vinden
       in.any.way could help   find
   b. ik kon   nergens een dokter vinden [die die (hele) vent   ook maar
      I could nowhere a   doctor find   who that whole bloke also but
      enigszins   kon   helpen]
      in.any.way could help
      'Nowhere could I find a doctor who could help that bloke in any way at all.'

Interestingly, however, (26b) is well formed with polar *heel*. And this, too, is as predicted. What has happened here is that the relative clause has been extraposed from its containing noun phrase, which, basically regardless of one's assumptions concerning the details of relative clause extraposition, means that CP is not dominated by a DP or vP phase boundary in this example.[24] That, in turn, means that an uninterpretable [NEG] feature on the C-head of the relative clause, licensing the (12b)-type NPI *ook maar enigszins,* can in fact be checked in overt syntax under an Agree relationship with Neg°. And with the licensing of *ook maar enigszins* fully established in overt syntax, parasitic licensing of polar *heel* is successful in (26b), as desired.

3.2 Negatively Polar Hoeven, Verb Second, and S-Structure Parasitism

In the context of the S-structure licensing condition on parasitism, the behavior of the negatively polar verb *hoeven* 'need' (see van der Wouden 2001 and references cited there) is also of great interest. This verb, similar to English auxiliary *need* in key respects, is dependent on a negation (or a nonveridical context; note, though, that *hoeven* is legitimate only in a subset of nonveridical contexts and is more restrictive than English auxiliary *need,* as van der Wouden notes explicitly). The licensing negation can but does not have to be a clausemate of *hoeven:* in Neg-raising contexts such as (27a), *niet* 'not' can be placed either in the matrix or in the embedded clause. And surprisingly, the negation does not have to c-command *hoeven* at S-structure: in (27b, c), *hoef(t)* has raised to the highest functional head in the clause (to which I will refer as the C-head), producing a Verb-Second construction; despite the fact that *hoeft* has raised past both the negation *niet* and the abstract functional head Neg°, (27b, c) come out perfectly grammatical.

(27) a. ik denk <niet> dat je   dat <niet> hoeft te doen
       I think not   that you that not   need to do
       'I don't think you need to do that.'

b. je hoeft dat niet te doen
you need that not to do
'You needn't do that.'

c. dat hoef je niet te doen
that need you not to do
'That you needn't do.'

One could conceivably argue that in Verb-Second constructions of the type in (27b, c), *hoeven* is licensed under reconstruction, at LF. But the facts of parasitic licensing of polar *heel* in sentences featuring negatively polar *hoeven* show that the dependency between *hoeven* in C and the negation further down is in fact syntactically real already at S-structure, despite its apparent "backwardness" at that point. The key fact here is that the examples in (28) are grammatical.[25] These involve polar *heel* embedded in the indirect object and the subject, respectively—positions in which, for reasons laid out in den Dikken (2002) and briefly recapitulated above, direct licensing of polar *heel* is systematically impossible. That polar *heel* is not being licensed directly in these examples is evident also from the fact that its legitimacy is dependent on the presence of negatively polar *hoeven* 'need.' It thus appears that it is *hoeven* that helps out polar *heel* in these examples, the latter somehow parasitizing on the former's dependency on the sentential negation.

(28) a. je <u>hoeft</u> die (*hele*) vent die constructie niet uit te leggen
you need that whole bloke that construction not PRT to explain
'You needn't explain that bloke that construction at all.'

b. die constructie <u>hoeft</u> die (*hele*) vent me niet uit te leggen
that construction need that whole bloke me not PRT to explain
'That construction, that bloke needn't explain to me at all.'

But that dependency seems to be backwards at S-structure, with the dependent higher up than the negation. It does not have to be backwards: in the Neg-raising examples in (29), the matrix negation c-commands *hoeft* perfectly straightforwardly, and parasitic licensing of polar *heel* is as expected. But interestingly, if the negation is a clausemate of *hoeven* and the negatively polar verb does not raise to C, as in (30), polar *heel* fails to be licensed parasitically: polar *heel* cannot parasitize on the licensing relationship between *niet* and the in situ verb *hoeven*.

(29) a. ik denk niet dat je die (*hele*) vent die constructie <u>hoeft</u> uit
I think not that you that whole bloke that construction need PRT
te leggen
to explain

b. ik denk niet dat die (*hele*) vent me die constructie <u>hoeft</u> uit
I think not that that whole bloke me that construction need PRT
te leggen
to explain

(30) a. ik denk dat je die (*hele) vent die constructie niet <u>hoeft</u> uit
        I think that you that whole bloke that construction not need PRT
        te leggen
        to explain

   b. ik denk dat die (*hele) vent me die constructie niet <u>hoeft</u> uit
        I think that that whole bloke me that construction not need PRT
        te leggen
        to explain

The grammaticality of (29) and the ill-formedness of (30) with *heel* included are
both straightforward from the point of view of the analysis of parasitic licensing of polar *heel* outlined in den Dikken (2002) and summarized above. In (29), the licensing relationship between *niet* in the matrix clause and *hoeven* in the embedded clause is such
that polar *heel* can legitimately "latch on" to it in keeping with connectedness—(31a)
attempts to bring this out graphically, with the larger box indicating the structure covered by the licensing relationship between *niet* and *hoeven* and the smaller box identifying the parasite: the latter is contained in the former, and parasitism is successful. In
(30), on the other hand, the two boxes do not connect, as (31b) tries to show.

(31) a. | *niet* . . . [$_{CP}$ . . . | *die hele vent* | . . . *hoeft* | . . .] |

   b. [$_{CP}$ . . . | *die hele vent* | . . . | *niet hoeft* | . . .]

When we now look back at (28) and graphically represent these examples as in (32),
we see that it is in a real sense analogous to (31a), with the polar *heel* box once again
fully contained in the box indicating the licensing dependency between *hoeven* and
the negation. The fact that (28) patterns with (29) is thus unsurprising in that respect:
these facts fit in perfectly with the connectedness account of parasitic licensing es-
poused in den Dikken (2002).

(32) [$_{CP}$ XP | *hoeft*$_i$ . . . | *die hele vent* | . . . *niet* t_i | . . .]

What *is* surprising, however, is that the dependency marked by the large box in (32)
is the reverse, both linearly and hierarchically, of the corresponding dependency in
(31a). Polar *heel* really does not care whether the dependent, *hoeven,* is structurally
lower or higher than the negation that licenses it: all that it cares about is that there be
an S-structure dependency relationship involving polarity item licensing that it can
structurally connect to.

   For our purposes in this chapter, this conclusion is sufficient. It lends support to
the connectedness approach to parasitism, and it shows that despite the fact that there
is no S-structure c-command between *hoeven* and its licensing negation in Verb-Second constructions of the type in (28), the dependency between the two has already
been established prior to verb fronting and is extended, as a result of V-to-C raising,
all the way up to the CP.[26] On this extended dependency, polar *heel* manages to parasitize in (28) at S-structure, as desired.

Much more could be said about *hoeven* 'need,' its role in the parasitic licensing of polar *heel,* and the structures sketched in (31) and (32). But for the purposes of this chapter, the remarks in the previous paragraphs will suffice. I will leave questions raised by these remarks for some future occasion.

4. Theoretical Results

Let me conclude by listing the main theoretical results of the foregoing discussion. I have argued that parasitic licensing and secondary triggering are independent and fundamentally different phenomena: the former is of the same type as the parasitic licensing of gaps, a finding which shows that parasitism in syntax is not confined to parasitic gap phenomena; the latter involves direct licensing by a secondary negation, which remains abstract. Confirming one of Postal's (2000) central claims, the analysis of parasitic licensing and secondary triggering of polar *heel* outlined here has made a distinction within the class of PIs between formally negative (12a)-type PIs, dependent on a local Neg° (which itself may raise out of the clause, thus creating apparent long-distance dependencies), and (12b)-type PIs, dependent on a clausemate $C_{[NEG]}$ (and thus supporting the Laka/Progovac approach to polarity item licensing in CPs immediately embedded under negation). Both (12a)-type and (12b)-type PIs are licensed locally on my account. Thus, if the analysis of primary and secondary direct licensing and parasitic licensing of PIs presented in this paper stands up to scrutiny, it leads to the general (and desirable) conclusion that all PI licensing is syntactically local.

ACKNOWLEDGMENTS

Most of the material for this chapter was first developed as part of a seminar on the syntax of negation and polarity items that I taught at the CUNY Graduate Center in the fall of 2003. An earlier version of this paper (not containing section 3.2 and featuring a rudimentary precursor of the discussion in section 3.1) was presented at the Georgetown University Round Table on Comparative and Crosslinguistic Research in Syntax, Semantics and Computational Linguistics on March 26, 2004, in Washington, D.C. I thank the participants of the seminar and the GURT conference for their invaluable feedback. Special thanks are due to Bob Frank, Elena Herburger, Paul Postal, Erika Troseth, and Raffaella Zanuttini for their written comments on an earlier version of this chapter. Mine alone is the responsibility for the final product.

NOTES

1. For those assuming an AgrSP/TP split (contra Chomsky 1995, ch. 4 et passim), NegP (the higher NegP of Haegeman 2002; van Craenenbroeck 2004) is between AgrS and TP, again below the licensing position of the subject. The problem posed by (1b) cannot be avoided by launching the subject to Spec, NegP from its *v*P/VP-internal base position. Though that would not be an instance of downgrading movement, it would ultimately lead to improper movement: after landing in Spec, NegP, the subject would still need to raise on to Spec, TP to satisfy the EPP (which I assume is in effect in Dutch; this is particularly evident if subject-initial root clauses in Dutch are TPs, as argued forcefully in Zwart 1997); but movement from an A-position to a higher A-position via a touchdown in an intermediate A'-position is illicit.

2. To be specific, raising the container of polar *heel* to a position in the C-domain (the embedded Spec, CP) will henceforth destine this phrase uniquely for positions in the C-domain; movement from a position in the C-domain into a position that is not in the C-domain is improper, regardless of whether the latter position is an A- or A'-position.

3. See Baker's (1988) Non-Oblique Trace Filter for the ban on A'-movement of the indirect object; see also den Dikken (1995, ch. 4). While literal A'-extraction of the indirect object under overt-syntactic category movement is ungrammatical, construal of an indirect object in a surface A'-position with a *pro* in the corresponding θ-position (à la Cinque 1990) is possible. It is via this strategy, irrelevant

here, that apparent counterevidence to the ban on A′-extraction of indirect objects (such as Dutch *wie heb je dat boek gegeven?* 'who have you that book given') can be accommodated. See den Dikken (2002, sec. 1.6).

4. I refer the reader to den Dikken (2002) for detailed illustration and discussion of these two constraints on parasitic licensing. On the requirement that parasitic licensing of polar *heel* be established at S-structure, see also section 3 below.

5. I should note that in (9), even the (a) example, featuring direct-object contained polar *heel,* is less than perfect, whence the question mark on *hele* in (9a). There seems to be a general negative effect of distance on the felicity of polar *heel,* which may be rooted in extrasyntactic restrictions on the parser. For some speakers this distance effect is so strong that none of the examples in (9) sound acceptable to them. I will be concentrating the discussion on those speakers for whom (9a) is relatively acceptable, but who still reject (9b, c) for reasons discussed in the text.

6. Szabolcsi (2004) has recently extended Postal's (2000) analysis to cover positive polarity items, too.

7. A functor is antiadditive iff $f(\text{X or Y}) \rightarrow f(\text{X})$ and $f(\text{Y})$.

8. It is important to realize that the semantic nonnegativity/upward-entailingness of NPIs of type (10b) themselves leaves unaffected the well-known fact that their licensing is dependent on a negative/downward-entailing context. Just as in (10a), in (10b) the NEG-D raises out of the DP on Postal's analysis, and is realized DP-externally as the negation on which, on the standard dependency-based approach to NPI licensing, the NPI depends.

9. Paul Postal (pers. comm.) asks how the language learner/user can recognize the abstract [NEG] feature of negative, downward-entailing NPIs. Since [NEG] is not morphophonologically instantiated, the only way the language user can diagnose it is on the basis of the syntactic behavior of the NPI in question—in particular, by its licensing environments. I will illustrate this for Dutch in the remainder of this chapter. While I realize that the learnability questions raised by my variant of the "two *any*s" story are potentially more serious than those raised by Postal's (2000), it should be said that very similar questions arise for Szabolcsi's (2004) extension of Postal's analysis to positive PIs, where there are multiple ways in which *some* can be represented: the two ways listed in Szabolcsi (2004, 441), which both involve the structure in (10b), plus a simple indefinite structure in which *some* is in D all by itself.

10. Horn (1996) points out that the discovery of secondary triggering dates back at least to unpublished work by himself, John Lawler, and Paul Neubauer from the early 1970s.

11. If one should have reservations about the inclusion of a NegP in the structure of the most deeply embedded clause in (9), one should feel free to read *NegP* here as Laka's (1990) *ΣP;* the net result will be identical: a Σ-head that receives a [NEG] feature will become syntactically equivalent to a Neg head.

12. The details of the derivation do not particularly concern me here, though they are not necessarily trivial. I will assume that successive-cyclic head movement of the type circumscribed in the text is legal, as it clearly must be if Postal's (2000) analysis is on the right track. It may well be significant that the matrix verbs in the Dutch examples are Neg-raising verbs; an analysis of Neg-raising along the lines of the text discussion would be straightforward. Whether the [NEG]-specified head of a (12a)-type NPI ultimately raises all the way up to the Neg head that checks its uninterpretable [NEG] feature or stops in the head of the first phase below that Neg head (which will be sufficient when it comes to establishment of an Agree relationship) is a question I cannot settle on the basis of the empirical evidence available at this time; I will leave the matter open for now.

13. The fact that the [NEG] feature of the (12a)-type NPI is itself uninterpretable does not mean that it cannot be multiply checked; on the lifespan of uninterpretable features marked for deletion, see in particular Pesetsky and Torrego (2001).

14. The ultimate licenser of this [NEG] feature is either the $C_{[NEG]}$ of the clause embedded under *betwijfelen* 'doubt' or, if negative verbs project a NegP in their own clause (see den Dikken 2002, 43–45), an (abstract) Neg head in the root clause.

15. The licenser of (12a)-type *ooit*'s [NEG] feature in the conditional matrix clause is the conditional complementizer *als* 'if' itself, which is apparently endowed with a [NEG] feature of its own. I have no insights to offer with respect to the question of why Dutch *als* apparently does, but English conditional *if* evidently does not, possess a [NEG] feature. The latter can be deduced from Paul

Postal's (pers. comm.) observation that when it comes to the behavior of polar *heel* and the ways in which it can be licensed, there are echoes in the domain of English taboo NPIs such as *squat* (see Postal 2000 for detailed discussion), but only to a certain extent. Thus, *squat* is like polar *heel* in being unable to appear as a finite subject or indirect object (ia, b) (these are ungrammatical on an NPI reading for *squat*), and it can also be licensed via secondary triggering, once again like polar *heel* (ic). But unlike polar *heel,* parasitic licensing in, for instance, a conditional *if*-clause fails completely: (id) is impossible, unlike (18).

(i) a. *I don't think that *squat* happened at the meeting.
   b. *He never gives *squat* his undivided attention.
   c. I did not testify that he *(ever) said *squat.*
   d. *If you (ever) learn *squat,* I will never make fun of you anymore.

This is interesting in light of Postal's (2000) conclusion that NPI *squat* is always of his type (10a), never of type (10b). This conclusion is based on the fact that in contexts in which *any* NPIs of type (10b) are impossible, and hence exceptives are blocked, NPI *squat* is impossible as well; see (ii). Updated from the point of view of (12), this means that NPI *squat* always has an uninterpretable [NEG] feature that must be checked against a matching [NEG] feature higher up in the structure. This is arguably responsible for the failure of (id): if *if* lacks a [NEG] feature, it does manage to license (12b)-type NPIs (*ever* in [id]) thanks to being downward entailing/nonveridical, but it cannot license *squat* directly, nor can the dependency relationship between *if* and *ever* be piggybacked on by *squat* in the hopes of getting its [NEG] feature checked; as a result, (id) crashes as a Full Interpretation violation.

(ii) a. She never said anything (but nonsense)/squat.
    b. Nobody said anything (but nonsense)/squat at the meeting.
    c. Not every professor said anything (*but nonsense)/*squat at the meeting.
    d. It is evil to say anything (*but nonsense)/*squat about this during a cabinet meeting.
    e. Did she say anything (*but nonsense)/*squat?
    f. Who did she say anything (*but nonsense)/*squat to?
    g. Who would say anything (*but nonsense)/*squat to him?

16. Hoeksema in fact notes solely that triclausal (20) is ungrammatical. He does not explicitly contrast it with its biclausal counterpart, which is well formed as a garden variety case of parasitic licensing: polar *heel* in that case can piggyback effortlessly on the dependency relationship between *ooit* and the [NEG]-specified C-head of the clause embedded under the matrix negation.

17. Unfortunately, there does not appear to be a way of embedding a polar *heel* in the middle clause of a triclausal construction inside a container that could, on independent grounds, legitimately move into Spec, NegP, thereby effecting direct licensing of polar *heel:* in the middle clause, the only two positions available for polar *heel*'s container would be the subject and indirect object positions, and we know independently (recall section 1 above) that direct licensing of polar *heel* contained in subjects and indirect objects fails. The fact, then, that (i) below is ungrammatical is entirely on a par with the fact that (ii) is as well. Therefore, there does not seem to be a way of testing whether secondary direct licensing could ever take place in the middle clause of a triclausal construction facilitated by the presence of a (12a)-type PI in the most deeply embedded clause. [Of course, (i) contrasts minimally with (iii), which is perfectly well formed thanks to the fact that parasitic licensing of polar *heel* by the dependency relationship between the C[NEG] of the middle clause and the clausemate *ooit* of type (12b) is successful here, as it is in biclausal (20).]

   (i) *ik denk niet [dat ik die *hele* vent verteld heb [dat ik hem ooit gemogen heb]]
       I think not that I that whole bloke told have that I him ever liked have
   (ii) ?*ik heb die *hele* vent niet verteld dat ik hem verafschuw
       I have that whole bloke not told that I him despise
   (iii) ik denk niet [dat ik die *hele* vent ooit verteld heb [dat ik hem verafschuw]]
       I think not that I that whole bloke ever told have that I him despise

18. A variant of (23b) was originally pointed out to me by Jack Hoeksema (pers. comm.), who started me thinking about the difference between subject sentences and topicalized clauses.

19. At the end of this subsection, I will turn to the question of what happens to (24) if one forgoes topicalization of the relativized noun phrase.

20. In an earlier version of this paper, I assumed that CP transits through Spec, NegP and has its [NEG] feature checked at that point, under Spec-head agreement. An Agree-based analysis makes movement through Spec, NegP superfluous, so in keeping with Occam's Razor, I will assume here that it does not take place. It is ultimately an empirical question, of course, whether CP does or does not transit through Spec, NegP when it topicalizes. One thing that potentially bears on this question is the fact that CP topicalization does not result in direct licensing of polar *heel:* (23a) is bad with *heel.* This is straightforwardly guaranteed by the text analysis. If, on the other hand, CP were to transit through Spec, NegP, the deviance of (23a) with *heel* would seem to be unexpected. It could be blamed, though, on the general fact (addressed in detail in den Dikken 2002, sec. 2.2) that polar *heel* must not be too deeply embedded within the container phrase that raises to Spec, NegP. This, combined with the fact that direct licensing fails within the bracketed clause as well (because this clause lacks a NegP into whose specifier position polar *heel*'s container could raise) and the fact that there is no additional PI on which polar *heel* might piggyback either, may ensure that (23a) bars *heel* even if CP does transit through Spec, NegP on its way up to the topic position. The ban on *heel* in (23a) thus does not appear to be fatal for the raising-through-Spec, NegP analysis. I cannot at this time think of any empirical evidence that would allow one to settle the question of whether a touchdown in Spec, NegP is made.

21. The same operation will take care of the binding facts catalogued in Grohmann (2003, 149–51) as well as the fact that the left-peripheral topic in *d*-word left dislocations can form an idiom together with material in the matrix clause (Grohmann 2003, 151–52), given that idiomatic fixing is an LF affair (see Chomsky 1995, ch. 3). See de Vries (2001), Grohmann (2003, ch. 4), Van Craenenbroeck (2004, ch. 3), and references cited there for detailed discussion of *d*-word and other topicalization and left-dislocation strategies in the West-Germanic languages. Van Craenenbroeck opts for a base-generation approach similar to the one adopted in the main text (though he does not address the NPI-connectivity effect and leaves open precisely how reconstruction would come about). De Vries has the left dislocate and the *d*-word form a constituent (an asyndetic coordination: [&P [XP] [& (=Ø) *dat/die*]]) that moves as a unit, from the θ-position to the topic position. Grohmann's analysis takes the *d*-word to be a reduced copy of the left-dislocated constituent itself. For *d*-word left-dislocation constructions not involving a subject sentence, movement analyses à la de Vries or Grohmann are in principle available alongside the text base-generation approach (though see van Craenenbroeck 2004, 48–49 for an interesting nonsubject case for which movement accounts would be difficult to uphold). The fact that the examples in (23b, c) can be adorned with a *d*-word (i) while still allowing polar *heel* to be parasitically licensed indicates that in these examples, the (12b)-type NPI (*ooit* 'ever') can be licensed in overt syntax even in the presence of a *d*-word. A Grohmann- or de Vries-style movement analysis can ensure this; the text approach in terms of base generation will not extend to (i). For *d*-word left dislocations featuring a subject sentence in left-peripheral position, however, Grohmann's analysis would conflict with the general ban on CPs in subject positions (Koster 1978), and though De Vries's analysis does not strictly speaking violate that ban (because it postulates a coordination structure of which CP is merely the first conjunct), it, too, should be ruled out for the derivation of *d*-word left dislocations featuring a subject sentence—the failure of polar *heel* parasitism in (21a) shows clearly that there can be no point in the overt syntactic derivation at which the (12b)-type NPI could be licensed. For *d*-word left dislocations with a subject sentence in left-peripheral position, therefore, only a base-generation analysis (cum LF replacement of the *d*-word by its associate) of the type presented in the main text is available.

    (i) a. [dat we die (*hele*) vent <u>ooit</u> hebben uitgenodigd] **dat** kan ik nu niet meer begrijpen
            that we that whole bloke ever have invited   that can I now not more understand
       b. [dat die (*hele*) vent ons <u>ooit</u> heeft uitgenodigd] **dat** kan ik nu niet meer begrijpen
           that that whole bloke us ever has invited   that can I now not more understand

22. Even if one were to extend the local domain up to the relativized DP, this would not help out: it can independently be shown to be impossible to select for a [NEG] feature in D; see the ungrammaticality of **I doubt (the) claims about anything,* alongside (13b): if the D-head of *claims about anything*

could host a [NEG] feature, it ought to be possible to license (12b)-type *anything* in this environment, which is not the case. That morphologically and semantically nonnegative D, unlike C, cannot host an uninterpretable [NEG] presumably has something to do with the fact that there exist morphologically and semantically negative Ds (e.g., English *no*) while morphologically and semantically negative Cs are much less common (English *lest* might be a candidate).

23. The question of whether DP is a phase is complex, but both general and specific considerations lead one to assume that DP, like CP, is indeed a strong phase. The general considerations that suggest that DP is a phase include the fact that DP is arguably propositional and the fact that there are systematic syntactic parallels between DP and CP, as shown by Abney (1987) and especially Szabolcsi (1994); more specific considerations supporting the status of DP as a phase are the fact that Spec, DP, like Spec, CP, is employed as an escape hatch for extraction (see for example Szabolcsi's 1994 discussion of "runaway" possessors in Hungarian) and, concomitantly, the fact that a DP with a filled specifier is an island for extraction, on a par with a CP whose specifier is occupied. See Chomsky (2001, 14) for brief remarks that go in the same direction: "the general typology should include among phases nominal categories . . . Phases are then (close to) functionally headed XPs. Like TP, NP cannot be extracted, stranding its functional head." Matushansky (2003) denies that DP is a phase, however, and does so precisely by attacking the above considerations. Several of her claims in this connection are open to debate (consider, for instance, the assertion that *propositional* in Chomsky's 2000 sense should translate as 'having the semantic type <*t*>;' this seems straightforwardly false in view of the phasehood of *v*P), but this is not the place to enter into a discussion of the pros and cons of DP as a phase. The text discussion will simply assume that DP is a phase and will, if the account based on it is successful, lend support to this assumption.

24. That is, regardless of whether one assumes a movement or base-generation account, and if the former, whether movement is rightward or leftward. The only thing that has to be crucially assumed is that the extraposed CP is not dominated by DP or *v*P.

25. These sentences contrast with those in (i), which crash with *heel* included, though they may improve with heavy stress on *probeert*. The stressed variants of (i) then mimic the pattern in (28) in two ways: (a) in (28) as well, *hoeft* is typically heavily stressed, and (b) when stressed in this way, *probeert* in (i) becomes dependent on the presence of a negation: *je PROBEERT die vent die constructie *(niet eens) uit te leggen!* 'you're *(not even) TRYING to explain that bloke that construction.' Assuming that heavily stressed *probeert* does indeed pattern with negatively polar *hoeven* 'need' in its syntactic behavior, the text account of (26) will carry over to the stressed variants of (i).

   (i) a. je   probeert die (*hele) vent die constructie niet uit te leggen
        you try   that whole bloke that construction not PRT to explain
     b. die constructie probeert die (*hele) vent me niet uit te leggen
        that construction tries   that whole bloke me not PRT to explain

26. This will obviate the need for an analysis that seeks to undo the backwardness of the relationship between *hoeven* and *niet* in (28) by reconstructing *hoeven* into a position c-commanded by the negation at LF. Note also that it is only verbs that do actually depend on negation for their licensing that will create an extended dependency when raising to C; for verbs that do not need a licensing negation, V-to-C does not create a negation-based dependency on which polar *heel* can then piggyback. That this is as desired is shown by the ungrammaticality, with *heel* included, of the examples in (i) in note 25.

REFERENCES

Abney, S. 1987. The English noun phrase in its sentential aspect. PhD diss., Massachusetts Institute of Technology.

Baker, M. 1988. *Incorporation.* Chicago: University of Chicago Press.

Chomsky, N. 1995. *The minimalist program.* Cambridge, MA: MIT Press.

———. 2000. Minimalist inquiries: The framework. In *Step by step: Essays on minimalist syntax in honor of Howard Lasnik,* ed. R. Martin, D. Michaels, and J. Uriagereka, 89–155. Cambridge, MA: MIT Press.

———. 2001. Derivation by phase. In *Ken Hale: A life in language,* ed. M. Kenstowicz, 1–52. Cambridge, MA: MIT Press.

Cinque, G. 1990. *Types of A'-dependencies*. Cambridge, MA: MIT Press.

Craenenbroeck, J. van. 2004. Ellipsis in Dutch dialects. PhD diss., University of Leiden/ULCL.

Dikken, M. den. 1995. *Particles: On the syntax of verb-particle, triadic and causative constructions*. Oxford Studies in Comparative Syntax. Oxford: Oxford University Press.

———. 2002. Direct and parasitic polarity item licensing. *Journal of Comparative Germanic Linguistics* 5: 35–66.

Giannakidou, A. 1998. *Polarity sensitivity as (non)veridical dependency*. Amsterdam: John Benjamins.

———. 2000. Negative . . . concord? *Natural Language and Linguistic Theory* 18: 457–523.

Grohmann, K. 2003. *Prolific domains: On the anti-locality of movement dependencies*. Amsterdam: John Benjamins.

Haegeman, L. 2002. West Flemish negation and the derivation of SOV-order in West Germanic. *Nordic Journal of Linguistics* 25: 154–89.

Haegeman, L., and R. Zanuttini. 1991. Negative heads and the Neg Criterion. *The Linguistic Review* 8: 233–51.

Hoeksema, J. 2003. Parasitic licensing of negative polarity items. Unpublished manuscript, University of Groningen.

Horn, L. 1996. Flaubert triggers, squatitive negation, and other quirks of grammar. *Tabu* 26. Repr. in *Perspectives on negation and polarity items*, ed. J. Hoeksema, H. Rullman, V. Sanchez-Valencia, and T. van der Wouden, 173–200. Amsterdam: John Benjamins, 2001.

Klima, E. 1964. Negation in English. In *The structure of language*, ed. J. Fodor and J. Katz. Englewood Cliffs, NJ: Prentice-Hall.

Koster, J. 1978. Why subject sentences don't exist. In *Recent transformational studies in European languages*, ed. S. J. Keyser, 53–65. Cambridge, MA: MIT Press.

Ladusaw, W. 1979. Polarity sensitivity as inherent scope relations. PhD diss., University of Texas at Austin.

Laka, I. 1990. Negation in syntax: On the nature of functional categories. PhD diss., Massachusetts Institute of Technology.

Linebarger, M. 1980. The grammar of negative polarity. PhD diss., Massachusetts Institute of Technology.

———. 1987. Negative polarity and grammatical representation. *Linguistics and Philosophy* 10: 325–87.

Matushansky, O. 2003. DPs and phase theory. Unpublished manuscript, CNRS/University of Paris VIII.

Müller, G., and W. Sternefeld. 1993. Improper movement and unambiguous binding. *Linguistic Inquiry* 24: 461–507.

Pesetsky, D., and E. Torrego. 2001. T-to-C movement: Causes and consequences. In *Ken Hale: A life in language*, ed. M. Kenstowicz, 355–426. Cambridge, MA: MIT Press.

Postal, P. 2000. An introduction to the grammar of *squat*. Unpublished manuscript, New York University.

Progovac, L. 1988. A binding approach to polarity sensitivity. PhD diss., University of Southern California.

Szabolcsi, A. 1994. The noun phrase. In *Syntax and Semantics* 27: *The syntactic structure of Hungarian*, ed. F. Kiefer and K. É. Kiss. New York: Academic Press.

———. 2004. Positive polarity—Negative polarity. *Natural Language and Linguistic Theory* 22: 409–52.

Troseth, E. 2004. Negative inversion and degree inversion in the English DP. *Linguistics in the Big Apple*. New York: CUNY/NYU. Available from http://web.gc.cuny.edu/Linguistics/liba/papers/troseth_LIBA.pdf.

Uribe-Etxebarria, M. 1994. Interface licensing conditions on negative polarity items: A theory of polarity and tense interactions. PhD diss., University of Connecticut, Storrs.

Vries, M. de. 2001. The syntax of relativization. PhD diss., University of Amsterdam/LOT.

Wouden, T. van der. 2001. Three modal verbs. In *Zur Verbmorphologie germanischer Sprachen*, ed. S. Watts, J. West, and H.-J. Solms, 189–210. Tübingen linguistische Arbeiten. Tübingen: Niemeyer.

Zwart, J-W. 1997. *Morphosyntax of verb movement. A minimalist approach to the syntax of Dutch*. Dordrecht: Kluwer.

7

■ Light Negation and Polarity

BERNHARD SCHWARZ AND RAJESH BHATT

McGill University and University of Massachusetts at Amherst

1. Introduction

Baker (1970a) observed that in certain linguistic environments, positive polarity items like *some* and *already* can be interpreted in the immediate scope of sentential negation, from which they would normally be prohibited. This phenomenon has since come to be known as *rescuing* (Szabolcsi 2004, Schwarz 2004). Ladusaw (1979) analyzed rescuing as involving a special negation morpheme homophonous with regular sentential negation, which, unlike regular negation, permits positive polarity items to appear in its immediate scope. This chapter provides empirical support for the special negation morpheme that Ladusaw posited, which we dub *light negation,* and thus for Ladusaw's view of rescuing.[1] We show that in German, light negation can be distinguished from regular negation on independent grounds. We introduce diagnostics for light negation (section 3) and study its distribution (section 3.1), scopal properties (section 3.2), and semantic contribution (section 4). We conclude with the discussion of the implications of the theory of light negation for the theory of rescuing (section 5).

2. Antilicensing and Rescuing of Positive Polarity Items

This section presents some basic observations concerning so-called antilicensing of positive polarity items and so-called rescuing of positive polarity items by higher operators.

2.1 Antilicensing

Positive polarity items are so called because they often cannot be interpreted in the scope of sentential negation. In sentence (1a) below, for example, the existential indefinite introduced by the positive polarity item *some* can only be interpreted with wide scope relative to negation. That is, the sentence can mean that among these typos, there were some they did not find, but not that they found none of them. And example (1b) is unacceptable, as surface word order prevents the positive polarity item *sometimes* from taking semantic scope over the preceding negation.

(1) a. They didn't find some of these typos.

   b. *They didn't sometimes complain.

Adopting standard terminology, we will say in the following that sentential negation in such cases *antilicenses* the positive polarity item. Apart from sentential negation, many positive polarity items can also be antilicensed by other negative expressions, such as quantifiers introduced by *no*. Sentence (2a) below, for example,
can mean that some of these typos were found by no one, but not that no one found
any of them. And example (2b) is unacceptable, as the surface position of the adverb
prevents it from taking semantic scope over the subject.

(2) a. No one found some of these typos.

b. *No one sometimes complained.

As Ladusaw (1979) noted, positive polarity items can often be interpreted in the
scope of a potential antilicenser as long as they are not interpreted in its immediate
scope: positive polarity items can be shielded from negation by clause boundaries or
intervening operators. For example, all the operators in (3a) below, that is, negation,
the quantificational adverb *always,* and the indefinite, can be interpreted with surface
scope. Thus the sentence can be read as denying that they always found typos. And in
(3b), the indefinite can be interpreted within the embedded clause, that is, the embedded clause can be understood as expressing the proposition that they found typos.

(3) a. They didn't always find some typos.

b. I didn't say they found some typos.

2.2 Rescuing

Not only can positive polarity items be shielded from a potential antilicenser by an intervening operator or clause boundary, in a class of cases discussed in Baker (1970a),
they can also be rescued by a higher operator that has both the potential antilicenser
and the positive polarity item in its semantic scope. For example, sentential negation
can be immediately followed by *sometimes* if negation and the adverb appear in the
restrictor of the determiner *no* or in the scope of the adversative predicate *surprised.*
In contrast to (1), the sentences in (4) allow for the *some* indefinite to be interpreted
with narrowest scope. Thus (4a) and (4b) can mean that there is no one here who
didn't find typos, and that I am surprised they didn't find typos, respectively. Also, in
contrast to (1), the sentences in (5) are acceptable.

(4) a. There is no one here who didn't find some typos.

b. I am surprised they didn't find some typos.

(5) a. There is no one here who this didn't sometimes annoy.

b. I am surprised this didn't sometimes annoy you.

But not every operator can rescue a positive polarity item from its antilicenser.
As shown in (6), for example, the sentences in (5) become as unacceptable as (1) if
no and *surprised* are replaced with *some* and *certain,* respectively.

(6) a. *There is someone here who this didn't sometimes annoy.

b. *I am certain this didn't sometimes annoy you.

The question that arises, then, is how one might characterize in general the contexts where positive polarity items can be rescued in this way, that is, the contexts where positive polarity items can exceptionally be interpreted in the immediate scope of an antilicenser. Krifka (1992) and Szabolcsi (2004) offer an interesting answer, proposing that rescuing contexts are exactly those contexts where negative polarity items such as *any* and *ever* are licensed. This view is certainly consistent with the data presented so far, as negative polarity items are known to be licensed in the restrictor of *no* and in the scope of *surprised* but not in the restrictor of *some* or in the scope of *certain*.

Szabolcsi (2004) demonstrates that positive polarity items can be rescued from their antilicensers in a variety of other familiar negative polarity licensing contexts, including the scope of the adversative predicate *regret,* the scope of various downward-entailing noun phrases, the restrictor of *every,* and antecedents of indicative conditionals. In addition, Szabolcsi finds that positive polarity rescuing is subject to much the same locality and intervention effects that negative polarity licensing has been known to be subject to since Linebarger (1987).

2.3 Two Accounts of Rescuing

These observations point to the natural conclusion that rescuing of positive polarity items is a special case of negative polarity licensing. Krifka (1992) and Szabolcsi (2004) more specifically propose that an antilicenser always composes with a positive polarity item in its immediate logical scope into a derived negative polarity item, which is then subject to the same licensing conditions as lexical negative polarity items such as *any* or *ever.* Krifka and Szabolcsi implement this proposal in different ways. For the present purposes, the details of these implementations are not important. What is important is that both accounts equate antilicensing of a positive polarity item with the formation of a derived negative polarity item.

An alternative way of looking at the rescuing phenomenon is suggested in Ladusaw (1979, 180). Ladusaw denies the existence of a process by which an antilicensed positive polarity item is rescued by the larger linguistic context. He takes antilicensing to always result in irreparable ill-formedness. Accordingly, he proposes that in cases of rescuing, the antilicensing of the positive polarity item is only apparent. Ladusaw posits two homophonous negation morphemes *not:* ordinary sentential negation and a special negation morpheme which is stipulated not to be an antilicenser. In this view, then, it is the existence of this non-antilicensing negation that gives rise to the rescuing phenomenon. And so the distribution of rescuing reflects the distribution of non-antilicensing negation. Specifically, if rescuing has the distribution of negative polarity licensing, then this is indicative of the fact that non-antilicensing negation itself is a negative polarity item.[2]

In support of his view of rescuing, Ladusaw notes that not all antilicensers are alike with respect to rescuing. Specifically, Ladusaw reports that rescuing positive polarity items from negative quantifiers is hard or impossible. For example, the cases in (7) below are much less acceptable than their counterparts in (5) above.

(7) a. ??There is no one here who nothing sometimes annoys.

    b. ??I am surprised that nothing sometimes annoys you.

This finding is evidently inconsistent with an analysis that equates antilicensing with the formation of a derived negative polarity item. In Ladusaw's lexical account, in contrast, it merely indicates that negative quantifiers differ from sentential negation in that they do not have non-antilicensing homophones.

Note, however, that Ladusaw's proposal is not the only possible analysis consistent with the data presented above. In an amended version of the type of analysis proposed in Krifka (1992) and Szabolcsi (2004), all occurrences of sentential negation are antilicensers. The contrast between (5) and (7) is not taken to be indicative of two different types of sentential negation but of two different types of antilicensing. Antilicensing by sentential negation is indeed to be analyzed as the formation of a derived polarity item, whereas antilicensing by negative quantifiers results in irreparable ill-formedness.

In summary, then, there are two conceivable views of why a negative polarity licenser can come to the rescue of a positive polarity item in the immediate scope of sentential negation. In one view, the negative polarity licenser licenses the derived negative polarity item formed by negation and the positive polarity item. In the other view, the negative polarity licenser licenses a non-antilicensing negation which is itself a lexical negative polarity item.

Naturally, to sustain the second view, one needs to have independent evidence for the existence of a special negation with the relevant properties. Schwarz (2004) presents evidence from German for the existence of such a negation, which he calls *light negation*. He shows that light negation appears in almost exactly those environments which support rescuing of positive polarity items in English. The remainder of this chapter examines the syntactic and semantic properties of light negation.

3. Light Negation

What Schwarz (2004) calls light negation differs from regular sentential negation in German in that its position in the clause is less tightly regulated than the position of ordinary sentential negation. The negation of a German affirmative sentence can often be expressed by inserting the morpheme *nicht* 'not' in the appropriate position. For example, the negation of sentence (8a) can be expressed as in (8b).

(8) a. Fritz ist nach Luckenbach gefahren.

     Fritz is to   Luckenbach gone

     'Fritz went to Luckenbach.'

  b. Fritz ist nicht nach Luckenbach gefahren.

     Fritz is not to   Luckenbach gone

     'Fritz did not go to Luckenbach.'

In this particular case, *nicht* sits at the left edge of what might be analyzed as the verb phrase. This is not a position, however, that can be occupied by *nicht* in all cases. Specifically, examples where *nicht* immediately precedes a definite or indefinite noun phrase or a disjunction of noun phrases are typically judged to be ungrammatical. For example, the negations of the grammatical affirmative sentences in (9) cannot normally be worded as in (10).[3]

(9) a. Fritz hat Frage   3 beantwortet.
     Fritz has question 3 answered
     'Fritz answered question 3.'
  b. Fritz kann   eine Fremdsprache.
     Fritz knows a   foreign language
     'Fritz knows a foreign language.'
  c. Fritz hat Frage   3 oder Frage   4 beantwortet.
     Fritz has question 3 or   question 4 answered
     'Fritz answered question 3 or question 4.'

(10) a. *Fritz hat nicht Frage   3 beantwortet.
      Fritz has not   question 3 answered
  b. *Fritz kann   nicht eine Fremdsprache.
      Fritz knows not   a   foreign language
  c. *Fritz hat nicht Frage   3 oder Frage   4 beantwortet.
      Fritz has not   question 3 or   question 4 answered

Instead, they are most naturally expressed through the sentences in (11). In (11a), *nicht* is sandwiched between the definite object noun phrase and the verb, whereas in (11b) and (11c), negation is conveyed through different morphological means. Sentence (11b) features the negative determiner *keine* 'no' and (11c) the negative disjunction *weder . . . noch* 'neither . . . nor.'

(11) a. Fritz hat Frage   3 nicht beantwortet.
     Fritz has question 3 not   answered
     'Fritz didn't answer question 3.'
  b. Fritz kann   keine Fremdsprache.
     Fritz knows no   foreign language
     'Fritz doesn't know a foreign language.'
  c. Fritz hat weder Frage   3 noch Frage   4 beantwortet.
     Fritz has neither question 3 nor   question 4 answered
     'Fritz answered neither question 3 nor question 4.'

However, in certain environments these positional constraints on sentential negation are lifted. Meibauer (1990), Büring and Gunlogson (2000), and Romero and Han (2004) observe that in negative polar questions, negation can immediately precede an indefinite. The same is true for definites and disjunctions. This is illustrated in (12) below.

(12) a. Hat Fritz nicht Frage   3 beantwortet?
     has Fritz not   question 3 answered
     'Didn't Fritz answer question 3?'
  b. Kann   Fritz nicht eine Fremdsprache?
     knows Fritz not   a   foreign language
     'Doesn't Fritz know a foreign language?'

c. Hat Fritz nicht Frage   3 oder Frage   4 beantwortet?
has Fritz not   question 3 or   question 4 answered
'Didn't Fritz answer question 3 or question 4?'

Also, Meibauer (1990, 449) notes that negation can immediately precede a definite in the antecedent of a subjunctive conditional. The same is true for indefinites and disjunctions. The examples in (13) illustrate.

(13) a. Wenn Fritz nicht Frage   3 beantwortet hätte,   wäre
if   Fritz not   question 3 answered   have.SUBJ be.SUBJ
er durchgefallen.
he failed
'If Fritz hadn't answered question 3, he would have failed.'

b. Wenn Fritz nicht eine Fremdsprache   könnte,   wäre
if   Fritz not   a   foreign language know.SUBJ be.SUBJ
er durchgefallen.
he failed
'If Fritz didn't know a foreign language, he would have failed.'

c. Wenn Fritz nicht Frage   3 oder Frage   4 beantworte hätte,
if   Fritz not   question 3 or   question 4 answered   have.SUBJ
wäre   er durchgefallen.
be.SUBJ he failed
'If Fritz hadn't answered question 3 or question 4, he would have failed.'

Throughout this chapter we will use the lifting of positional constraints on the placement of negation as a diagnostic for the presence of light negation. With this diagnostic in hand, we now turn to a systematic examination of the syntactic environments that permit light negation.

3.1 The Distribution of Light Negation

As noted earlier, the class of environments in which light negation appears is essentially coextensive with positive polarity rescuing environments. In this section, we first show that, just like rescuing, light negation can appear in the classic negative polarity environments. We then demonstrate that light negation and rescuing also pattern together in subjunctive clauses, with the correlation with negative polarity licensing replaced by a correlation with counterfactuality. Finally, we introduce a new set of environments involving expletive negation, showing that here, too, rescuing and light negation go hand in hand.

As mentioned in the discussion of rescuing above, Krifka (1992) and Szabolcsi (2004) suggest that positive polarity items are rescued in exactly those environments where negative polarity items are licensed. For example, we saw that positive polarity *some* is rescued in the restrictor of the determiner *no* and the scope of adversative *surprised.* It is shown in (14) and (15) that light negation is permitted in the same environments in German.

(14) a. Wir haben keinen angenommen, der nicht Frage   3 beantwortet hat.
     we have no one admitted   who not question 3 answered   has
     'We admitted no one who did not answer question 3.'

  b. Wir haben keinen angenommen, der nicht eine Fremdsprache   kann.
     we have no one admitted   who not a   foreign language knows
     'We admitted no one who doesn't know a foreign language.'

  c. Wir haben keinen angenommen, der nicht Frage   3 oder Frage   4
     we have no one admitted   who not question 3 or   question 4
     beantwortet hat.
     answered   has
     'We admitted no one who did not answer question 3 or question 4.'

(15) a. Wir waren überrascht, dass Fritz nicht Frage   3 beantwortet hat.
     we were surprised   that Fritz not   question 3 answered   has
     'We were surprised that Fritz didn't answer question 3.'

  b. Wir waren überrascht, dass Fritz nicht eine Fremdsprache   kann.
     we were surprised   that Fritz not   a   foreign language knows
     'We were surprised that Fritz doesn't know a foreign language.'

  c. Wir waren überrascht, dass Fritz nicht Frage   3 oder Frage   4
     we were surprised   that Fritz not   question 3 or   question 4
     beantwortet hat.
     answered   has
     'We were surprised that Fritz didn't answer question 3 or question 4.'

And just like the illegitimate cases of rescuing that we saw in (6) above, light negation is not permitted in the cases in (16) and (17), where the negative polarity licensers *kein* 'no' and *überrascht* 'surprised' are replaced with the nonlicensers *ein* 'a' and *überzeugt* 'convinced,' respectively.

(16) a. *Wir haben einen   angenommen, der nicht eine Fremdsprache
       we have someone admitted   who not a   foreign language
       kann.
       knows

  b. *Wir haben einen   angenommen, der nicht Frage   3 beantwortet hat.
       we have someone admitted   who not question 3 answered   has

  c. *Wir haben einen   angenommen, der nicht Frage   3 oder
       we have someone admitted   who not question 3 or
       Frage   4 beantwortet hat.
       question 4 answered   has

(17) a. *Wir waren überzeugt, dass Fritz nicht Frage   3 beantwortet hat.
        we   were   convinced that Fritz not   question 3 answered   has
     b. *Wir waren überzeugt, dass Fritz nicht eine Fremdsprache   kann.
        we   were   convinced that Fritz not   a   foreign language knows
     c. *Wir waren überzeugt, dass Fritz nicht Frage   3 oder Frage   4
        we   were   convinced that Fritz not   question 3 or   question 4
        beantwortet hat.
        answered   has

More generally, it seems that light negation is permitted in all negative polarity licensing environments (with a few exceptions that are discussed later). In particular, as noted in Schwarz (2004), light negation can appear in the restrictor of the universal determiner *jeder* 'every,' in the antecedents of indicative conditionals, and as we have already seen in (12), in polar questions.

However, Schwarz (2004) notes that the set of environments permitting light negation is both wider and narrower than the set of environments which permit negative polarity items. On the one hand, light negation is permitted in counterfactually interpreted subjunctive clauses which do not license negative polarity items. For example, light negation is acceptable in a counterfactually interpreted main clause of a subjunctive conditional. Negative polarity items are not permitted in this environment. So being in a negative polarity context is not always required for light negation.

(18) a. Wenn Fritz dumm wäre, hätte   er nicht Frage   3 beantwortet.
        if   Fritz stupid be.SUBJ have.SUBJ he not   question 3 answered
        'If Fritz were stupid, he wouldn't have answered question 3.'
     b. Wenn Fritz dumm wäre,   könnte   er nicht eine Fremdsprache.
        if   Fritz stupid be.SUBJ know.SUBJ he not   a   foreign language
        'If Fritz were stupid, he wouldn't know a foreign language.'
     c. Wenn Fritz dumm wäre, hätte   er nicht Frage   3 oder
        if   Fritz stupid be.SUBJ have.SUBJ he not   question 3 or
        Frage   4 beantwortet.
        question 4 answered
        'If Fritz were stupid, he wouldn't have answered question 3 or question 4.'

On the other hand, we also find that being in a negative polarity context is sometimes not enough for light negation. While negative polarity items are always licensed in the antecedent of a conditional, be it indicative or subjunctive, light negation in subjunctive antecedents is acceptable only if this antecedent is interpreted counterfactually. We saw in (13) above that light negation is permitted in the antecedents of subjunctive conditionals. However, these sentences do not have the full range of readings which are available in the absence of light negation. To see this, consider the examples in (19) below, which differ from those in (13) merely in that negation in the antecedent is not light.

(19) a. Wenn Fritz Frage   3 nicht beantwortet hätte,   wäre
      if   Fritz question 3 not   answered   had.SUBJ be.SUBJ
      er durchgefallen.
      he failed
      'If Fritz hadn't answered question 3, he would have failed.'

    b. Wenn Fritz keine Fremdsprache   könnte,   wäre   er durchgefallen.
      if   Fritz no   foreign language know.SUBJ be.SUBJ he failed
      'If Fritz didn't know a foreign language, he would have failed.'

    c. Wenn Fritz weder Frage   3 noch Frage   4 beantworte hätte,
      if   Fritz neither question 3 nor   question 4 answered   had.SUBJ
      wäre   er durchgefallen.
      be.SUBJ he failed
      'If Fritz had answered neither question 3 nor question 4, he would have
      failed.'

The examples in (19) allow for an interpretation in which the antecedent is not taken to be counterfactual. In particular, they can be used as part of an explanation for the truth of the consequent. For example, each of the examples in (19) can be used as continuations of the following discourse, which assumes the truth of the consequent, that is, that Fritz indeed failed.

(20) A: Was glaubst du warum Fritz durchgefallen ist?
      what think   you why   Fritz failed   is
      'Why do you think Fritz failed?'

    B: Ich bin mir nicht sicher, aber . . .
      I   am self not   certain but
      'I'm not sure, but . . .'

In these contexts, speaker B presents the proposition expressed by the relevant antecedent as a possible reason for Fritz's failing. The speaker therefore is not committed to the falsehood of the antecedent. In other words, the falsehood of the antecedent is clearly not implied in this context.

That the antecedents of subjunctive conditionals do not need to be interpreted counterfactually has been known at least since Anderson (1951), who discusses cases analogous to the ones presented above. What is interesting, however, is that a noncounterfactual interpretation is not available if the antecedent of the subjunctive conditionals contains light negation. That is, none of the examples in (13) can function as a continuation of the discourse in (20).

So in subjunctive clauses, negative polarity licensing and the distribution of light negation are independent of each other. In this environment, the distribution of light negation instead correlates with the presence of a counterfactual interpretation. Given the generalization on rescuing proposed by Krifka (1992) and Szabolcsi (2004), it might seem, therefore, that rescuing and light negation come apart in subjunctive environments. However, this is not actually the case. Observations reported in Baker (1970b), Karttunen (1971), and Schwarz (2004) indicate that rescuing in subjunctives also correlates with counterfactuality rather than with negative polarity licensing.[4]

So far we have seen two environments where light negation appears, namely negative polarity contexts and counterfactually interpreted subjunctive clauses. In both environments, light negation is semantically contentful. There are also certain instances of light negation which do not seem to make any truth-conditional contribution. These instances fall under the rubric of what has been referred to in the literature as *expletive negation*. Some instances of expletive negation are shown in (21).[5] As the English translations suggest, the negation in the embedded clauses in (21) is not actually interpreted as logical negation. In fact, the meanings of these sentences do not change perceptibly if the embedded negation is omitted.

(21) a. Ich gehe nicht, bevor du   nicht aufgeräumt hast.

      I   leave not   before you not   cleaned-up have

      'I won't leave before you've cleaned up.'

   b. Man kann ihm   nicht absprechen, dass er nicht singen kann.

      one can he.DAT not deny   that he not   sing   can

      'One cannot deny that he can sing.'

The phenomenon of expletive negation is familiar from the literature (e.g., van der Wouden 1994; Portner and Zanuttini 1996, 2000). What does not seem to have been noted, however, is that expletive negation in German is always light. The examples in (22) show that expletive negation can be light, as in both cases negation immediately precedes an indefinite, which cannot normally follow sentential negation.

(22) a. Ich gehe nicht, bevor du   nicht einen Apfel gegessen hast.

      I   leave not   before you not   an   apple eaten   have

      'I won't leave before you've eaten an apple.'

   b. Man kann ihm   nicht absprechen, dass er nicht was   getan hat.

      one can he.DAT not deny   that he not   something done has

      'One cannot deny that he did something.'

Furthermore, negation which is not light cannot be expletive. This can be seen by contrasting the light negation examples in (22) with their regular negation variants in (23). In sentence (23a), the presence of a semantically active negation in the subordinate clause leads to semantic anomaly. While sentence (23b) is felicitous, the embedded negation is semantically interpreted, as indicated in the English translation.[6]

(23) a. #Ich gehe nicht bevor du   keinen Apfel gegessen hast.

       I   leave not   before you no   apple eaten   have

       'I won't leave before you've eaten no apple.'

   b. Man kann ihm   nicht absprechen, dass er nichts getan hat.

      one can he.DAT not deny   that he nothing done has

      'One cannot deny that he did nothing.'

Given that the negation in (22) is expletive, one would naturally expect it not to antilicense a positive polarity item in its immediate scope. That this is indeed the case is demonstrated in (24), where the embedded negation immediately precedes the positive polarity item *einige* 'some.' Once again, therefore, the distribution of light negation patterns with rescuing.[7]

(24) a. Ich gehe nicht bevor du   nicht einige Äpfel gegessen hast.

      I   leave not   before you not   some apples eaten   have

      'I won't leave before you've eaten some apples.'

    b. Man kann ihm   nicht absprechen, dass er nicht einiges   getan hat.

      one can he.DAT not   deny   that he not   something done has

      'One cannot deny that he did something.'

3.2 The Scope of Light Negation

In this section, we establish the generalization that light negation in German must always be interpreted in the immediate scope of its licenser. We discuss a possible way of deriving this requirement from the assumption that light negation is a strong negative polarity item, concluding that such a derivation is only partially successful.

3.2.1 Light Negation Takes Widest Scope   Light negation is more restricted in its scope potential than ordinary negation in that it often takes wider semantic scope than a corresponding regular negation. The contrast between (25a), where the relative clause hosts ordinary negation, and (25b), where negation in the relative clause is light, provides a first illustration of this observation.

(25) a. Wir haben keinen zugelassen, der keine Fremdsprache   kann   und

      we have no one admitted   who no   foreign language knows and

      in Mathe schlecht ist.

      at math   bad   is

      'We admitted no one who does not know a foreign language and is bad at math.'

    b. !Wir haben keinen zugelassen, der nicht eine Fremdsprache   kann

      we have no one admitted   who not a   foreign language knows

      und in Mathe schlecht ist.

      and at math   bad   is

      'We admitted no one such that it is not the case that he knows a foreign language and is bad at math.' (= such that he knows no foreign language or he is good at math)

In (25a), the scope of negation in the relative clause is confined to the first conjunct. In (25b), in contrast, light negation in the relative clause can only be interpreted as taking scope over the conjunction. This results in an unlikely interpretation according to which being good at math prevents one from being admitted.

A similar contrast is found in (26). Regular negation in (26a) can be interpreted as taking scope within the complement of *wagt* 'dare.' This results in a plausible reading, according to which not wearing a shirt is a daring thing to do and can be grounds enough for not being let in. In contrast, light negation in (26b) can only be interpreted as taking scope over *wagt* 'dare.' This leads to an unlikely reading which implies that wearing a shirt is a daring thing to do.

(26) a. Wir lassen keinen rein, der   kein Hemd zu tragen wagt.

       we let   no one in   who no   shirt   to wear   dares

       'We let no one in who dares not to wear a shirt.'

    b. !Wir lassen keinen rein, der   nicht ein Hemd zu tragen wagt.

       we let   no one in   who not   a   shirt   to wear   dares

       'We let no one in who does not dare to wear a shirt.'

Assuming that the semantic scope of sentential negation is determined by its surface-structural location, the observations in (25) and (26) indicate that the structures of the relative clauses in (25) and (26) are the ones shown in (27), where light negation is in the immediate scope of its licenser, and not those in (28). Assuming the structures in (27), our observations on the semantic interpretation of (25) and (26) follow straightforwardly.

(27) a. . . . der   nicht [[eine Fremdsprache   kann]   und [in Mathe schlecht ist]]

       who not   a   foreign language knows and at math bad   is

    b. . . . der   nicht [[ein Hemd zu tragen] wagt]

       who not   a   shirt   to wear   dares

(28) a. . . . der [nicht eine Fremdsprache   kann]   und [in Mathe schlecht ist]

       who not   a   foreign language knows and at math bad   is

    b. . . . der [nicht ein Hemd zu tragen] wagt

       who not   a   shirt   to wear   dares

If light negation must be in the immediate scope of its licenser, we expect that word order variants of (25) and (26) that force a parse like (28) are unacceptable. This expectation is borne out. Consider (29a), where word order forces negation to be within the second conjunct, and (29b), where the negation can only be part of the extraposed infinitival complement of *wagt* 'dare.' Since in these cases, negation cannot be in the immediate scope of its licenser, the sentences are correctly expected to be ungrammatical.

(29) a. *Wir haben keinen zugelassen, der   in Mathe schlecht ist und nicht

       we   have no one admitted   who at math   bad   is and not

       eine Fremdsprache   kann.

       a   foreign language knows

    b. *Wir lassen keinen rein, der   wagt, nicht ein Hemd zu tragen.

       we let   no one in   who dares not   a   shirt   to wear

The preceding examples have illustrated that light negation needs to take scope over conjunctions and intensional operators. The examples in (30) below show that the same holds for quantificational phrases such as *jemand* 'someone.' In (30a), light negation precedes both the quantifier phrases in its clause and is accordingly interpreted as taking scope over them. In (30b), in contrast, light negation follows *jemand*. Given that semantic scope in German is usually determined by linear precedence, one expects that *jemand* has to take scope over negation. The oddness of (30b), therefore, can be interpreted as another illustration of the wide-scope requirement of light negation.[8]

(30) a. Wir haben keinen zugelassen, den   nicht jemand   einem
        we have no one admitted   who.ACC not   someone.NOM one.DAT
        von uns empfohlen   hatte.
        of us   recommended had
        'We admitted no one who someone didn't recommend to one of us.'

    b. ??Wir haben keinen zugelassen, den   jemand   nicht einem
        we have no one admitted   who.ACC someone.NOM not   one.DAT
        von uns empfohlen   hatte.
        of us   recommended had

The generalization that seems to emerge from the above examples is that light negation is always interpreted as taking wider scope than any other operator within the scope of its licenser. In other words, light negation is always in the immediate scope of its licenser. This generalization seems to apply to all instances of light negation. Consider the case of polar questions. In (31a), light negation takes widest scope in the question that contains it and (31b) is bad because the indefinite quantifier *jemand* 'someone' takes wider scope than light negation.

(31) a. Hat nicht jemand   Fritz einem   von uns empfohlen?
        has not   someone.NOM Fritz one.DAT of us   recommended
        'Didn't someone recommend Fritz to us?'

    b. *Hat jemand   nicht Fritz einem   von uns empfohlen?
        has someone.NOM not   Fritz one.DAT of us   recommended

Next, we turn to expletive negation. Since in (32a), negation precedes the existential indefinite *einen Lehrer* 'a teacher' and therefore can be in the immediate scope of *bevor* 'before,' an expletive reading is available. In (32b), in contrast, the indefinite intervenes between *bevor* 'before' and negation. Therefore, the negation cannot be light in this case and hence cannot be expletive. The negation must be interpreted as semantically contentful, and the resulting reading is incoherent.

(32) a. Ich gehe nicht bevor du nicht einen Lehrer begrüßt hast.
        I   leave not   before you not   a   teacher greeted have
        'I won't leave before you have greeted a teacher.'

b. #Ich gehe nicht bevor du   einen Lehrer   nicht begrüßt hast.
   I   leave not   before you a   teacher not   greeted have
   'I won't leave before you haven't greeted some teacher.'

Finally, we examine a case where light negation does not behave like a negative polarity item. This is the case of light negation in counterfactually interpreted subjunctive clauses. We find that in these cases, too, light negation takes widest scope. This is exemplified by the contrast in (33). In (33a), light negation takes widest scope in the subjunctive embedded clause in which it is licensed. The sentence in (33b) is bad because the operator *gewagt* 'dared' must be interpreted as taking scope above the light negation within the extraposed complement clause.

(33) a. Wenn Fritz schüchtern wäre,   hätte   er nicht eine Perücke zu
        if   Fritz shy   be.SUBJ have.SUBJ he not   a   wig   to
        tragen gewagt.
        wear   dared
        'If Fritz were shy, he wouldn't have dared to wear a wig.'
     b. *Wenn Fritz mutig   wäre,   hätte er gewagt, nicht eine Perücke
        if   Fritz courageous be.SUBJ had   he dared   not   a   wig
        zu tragen.
        to wear

3.2.2 Deriving the Scopal Properties of Light Negation   The widest-scope properties of light negation are not completely surprising given the fact that their distribution patterns to a considerable extent with well-known negative polarity items such as English *any* or *ever*.[9] Since Linebarger (1987), it has been known that the licensing of negative polarity items is subject to intervention effects. For example, even though *any* is in the scope of negation in both (34a) and (34b), only in (34a) is it licensed. In (34b), the presence of the scopal intervener *always* between the licensing negation and the negative polarity item *any* blocks licensing.

(34) a. Few people ate any potatoes.
     b. *Few people always ate any potatoes.

Some of the light negation examples in the preceding section can be interpreted in the same way if we think of light negation as a negative polarity item. This is illustrated in (35) and (36). In (35), the intervener is a conjunction, while in (36), the intervener is a quantificational noun phrase.

(35) a. *Few people ate rice and any potatoes.
     b. *Wir haben keinen zugelassen, der   in Mathe schlecht ist und nicht
        we   have no one admitted   who at math bad   is and not
        eine Fremdsprache   kann.
        a   foreign language knows

(36) a. *Few people offered all of their guests any potatoes.

    b. ??Wir haben keinen zugelassen, den jemand nicht einem   von uns
           we have no one admitted   who someone not   one.DAT of us
       empfohlen   hatte.
       recommended had

Of course, from the discussion of the distribution of light negation, we know that light negation in subjunctive clauses does not behave like a negative polarity item. And yet, as illustrated in (33) above, the immediate scope constraint is operative in subjunctive clauses as much as it is in nonsubjunctives.

But even confining attention to those instances of light negation which are plausibly analyzed as negative polarity items, we find that the scopal properties of light negation cannot be completely derived from its negative polarity behavior. Negative polarity items like *any* or *ever* are known to be licensed across clause-embedding verbs. For example, the acceptability of *I didn't say that he ever called* shows that a matrix negation can license negative polarity *ever* across the clause-embedding verb *say.* The German version of this example is acceptable as well. That licensing across clause-embedding verbs is possible in German is further illustrated in (37), where the negative polarity item *jemals* 'ever' can be licensed across *wagt* 'dares.' That is, in (37a), *jemals* can be understood as being part of the clause embedded under *wagt.* Moreover, in (37b) this is the only way to interpret *jemals,* which is expected, given that the adverb is included in the extraposed embedded clause, a domain known to be an island for operator scope.

(37) a. Wir lassen keinen rein, der [jemals ein Hemd zu tragen] wagt.
       we let   no one in   who ever   a   shirt to wear   dares
       'We let no one in who dares to ever wear a shirt.'

    b. Wir lassen keinen rein, der   wagt, [jemals ein Hemd zu tragen].
       we let   no one in   who dares ever   a   shirt to wear
       'We let no one in who dares to ever wear a shirt.'

But as we have already seen in (26) and (29) above, repeated below in (38), *wagen* 'dare' cannot intervene between light negation and its licenser. While (38a) is grammatical, it has only the unlikely interpretation which results from negation outscoping the embedding verb. And given that negation is part of the extraposed infinitive in (38b), it cannot scope over *wagt,* and so ungrammaticality ensues.

(38) a. !Wir lassen keinen rein, der nicht ein Hemd zu tragen wagt.
        we let   no one in   who not a   shirt to wear   dares
        'We let no one in who does not dare to wear a shirt.'

    b. *Wir lassen keinen rein, der   wagt, nicht ein Hemd zu tragen.
       we let   no one in   who dares not a   shirt to wear

To recast the preceding discussion in terms of intervention, one could say that *wagen* and other clause-embedding predicates function as interveners for the licensing of light negation but not for the licensing of negative polarity items. More generally, the licensing of light negation seems to be subject to a strict immediate-scope constraint. Known exceptions to the immediate-scope constraint for the licensing of negative polarity items like *any* and *ever* do not seem to apply to the licensing of light negation. The discussion of (non)licensing across clause-embedding predicates provides one example of this contrast. The contrast is further illustrated by examining negative polarity items and light negation in disjunctions. Example (39a) shows that the negative polarity item *jemals* can be licensed across a disjunction, whereas (39b) shows that light negation is impossible in this configuration.

(39) a. Wir haben keinen zugelassen, der   in Mathe schlecht ist oder jemals
      we   have   no one admitted   who at math   bad   is or   ever
      abgeschrieben hat.
      copied   has
      'We admitted no one who is bad at math or has ever copied.'

    b. *Wir haben keinen zugelassen, der   in Mathe schlecht ist oder nicht
      we   have   no one admitted   who at math   bad   is or   not
      eine Fremdsprache   kann.
      a   foreign language knows

The strict immediate-scope constraint found with light negation is reminiscent of facts about the licensing of certain strong negative polarity items noted by Szabolcsi (2004). Szabolcsi notes that some negative polarity items that need an antiadditive licenser require the licenser to be a clausemate. In English, *squat* and, for some speakers, *yet* need a clausemate licenser. For example, *I didn't say that he knew squat* cannot mean that I didn't say that he knew anything. Similarly, for the relevant speakers, *I didn't say that he had been here yet* is unacceptable. In these cases, the presence of a clause-embedding predicate such as *say* blocks the matrix negation from licensing the strong negative polarity item in the embedded clause. This is analogous to what happens with light negation. Hence, it might seem attractive to assimilate light negation to the class of negative polarity items that contains *yet* and *squat*.

But one important difference remains. Unlike *squat* and *yet,* which require antiadditive licensers, such as sentential negation or a negative quantifier, light negation is licensed by a larger class of negative polarity licensers, not all of which are antiadditive. For example, in sentence (40), light negation is licensed in the restrictor of *wenige* 'few,' an operator which is known not to be antiadditive. In contrast, *squat* is not licensed in the restrictor of *few,* as shown by the unacceptability of *Few people who knew squat about this issue were present.*

(40) Wir haben wenige angenommen, die   nicht eine Fremdsprache   können.
     we have   no one admitted   who not   a   foreign language know
     'We admitted few who don't know a foreign language.'

To sum up, we have found that light negation of all kinds obeys a strict immediate-scope constraint according to which no operator can scopally intervene between it and its licenser, but that it permits a larger class of licensers than so-called strong polarity items. Descriptively, then, we can think of light negation as a negative polarity item with strict locality conditions on licensing (like *yet* and *squat*) but liberal conditions on its licensers (like *any* and *ever*).

We conclude this section by pointing to another difference between light negation and more familiar negative polarity items: Light negation in German does not permit a licenser in its own clause. This is illustrated in (41) below.

(41) a. ??Wenige haben nicht Frage   3 beantwortet.

      few   have not question 3 answered

   b. ??Wenige können nicht eine Fremdsprache.

      few   know not a   foreign language

   c. ??Wenige haben nicht Frage   3 oder Frage   4 beantwortet.

      few   have not question 3 or   question 4 answered

We do not have a definite explanation for this fact. It would follow from the assumption that light negation, unlike ordinary negative polarity items, always takes widest scope in its clause. This requirement would prevent it from falling under the scope of a potential clausemate licenser.[10]

4. Semantic Contribution of Light Negation

In this section, we discuss the lexical semantic properties of light negation. We note that apart from not antilicensing positive polarity items, light negation also fails to license negative polarity items. We also speculate that the distribution of light negation in subjunctive conditionals can be derived in part from the assumption that it triggers a factive presupposition.

4.1 Nonlicensing and Non-antilicensing

Our discussion of light negation began with Schwarz's (2004) observation that light negation appears in almost exactly those environments that support rescuing of positive polarity items in English. In the spirit of Ladusaw (1979), Schwarz notes that light negation, in contrast to regular negation, is not an antilicenser for positive polarity items. Some examples that illustrate this are provided in (42), where in each case, light negation is followed by the positive polarity item *einige* 'some.'

(42) a. Hat er nicht das Bild   einigen   von uns gezeigt?

      has he not   the picture some.DAT of   us   shown

      'Didn't he show the picture to some of us?'

   b. Ich kenne keinen, der nicht das Bild   einigen   von uns gezeigt hat.

      I   know no one who not   the picture some.DAT of   us   shown has

      'I know no one who didn't show the picture to some of us.'

   c. Ich bin überrascht, dass er nicht das Bild   einigen   von uns gezeigt hat.

      I   am surprised   that he not   the picture some.DAT of   us   shown has

      'I'm surprised that he didn't show the picture to some of us.'

It can be shown further that light negation, in contrast to regular negation, does not license negative polarity items. This is illustrated in (43), where in each case, light negation precedes the negative polarity item *jemals* 'ever.'[11]

(43) a. *Hat er uns   nicht das Bild   jemals gezeigt?
        has he us.DAT not   the picture ever   shown

     b. *Ich kenne keinen, der uns   nicht das Bild   jemals gezeigt hat.
        I   know no one who us.DAT not   the picture ever   shown has

     c. *Ich bin überrascht, dass er uns   nicht das Bild   jemals gezeigt hat.
        I   am surprised   that he us.DAT not   the picture ever   shown has

4.2 The Content of Light Negation

We have seen that light negation differs from regular negation in both distribution and licensing potential. It should therefore not come as a surprise that light negation differs from regular negation in its semantic content as well. The first thing to note is that it does not seem possible to assign the same semantic content to all instances of light negation. This is apparent from the existence of expletive light negation, which does not seem to have any semantic content at all. Setting aside expletive negation, we are left with instances of counterfactual light negation and negative polarity light negation.

Turning to counterfactual light negation, consider the examples in (44) below. We note that example (44a), where negation is light, is very close in meaning to (44b), which contains regular negation. Further, omission of light negation in (44a) leads to an obvious change in meaning.

(44) a. Wenn Fritz nicht eine Fremdsprache   könnte, wäre er durchgefallen.
        if   Fritz not a   foreign language knew   be.SUBJ he failed
        'If Fritz didn't know a foreign language, he would have failed.'

     b. Wenn Fritz keine Fremdsprache   könnte, wäre er durchgefallen.
        if   Fritz no   foreign language knew   be.SUBJ he failed
        'If Fritz didn't know a foreign language, he would have failed.'

These facts indicate that counterfactual light negation is semantically contentful and reverses truth values just like regular negation. But as the discussion in section 3.1 pointed out, these two examples are not entirely synonymous. The sentence in (44b) has uses in which the antecedent is not counterfactual, whereas the presence of light negation enforces a counterfactual reading in (44a). We do not know for sure how light negation comes to enforce counterfactuality. But one possibility that comes to mind is that counterfactual light negation triggers a factive presupposition, that is, the presupposition that its scope is true. In this view, the light negation in (44a) introduces the presupposition that Fritz knows a foreign language. This presupposition will project to the top level and so will rule out a noncounterfactual interpretation of the conditional.[12]

Finally, we turn to instances of semantically contentful negative polarity light negation. At first glance, the semantic contribution of this kind of light negation seems to be identical to that of regular negation. For example, there is no obvious difference in meaning between the two sentences in (45).

(45) a. Wir haben jeden   abgelehnt, der nicht eine Fremdsprache   kann.
        we have everyone rejected   who not a   foreign language knows
        'We rejected everyone who doesn't know a foreign language.'

  b. Wir haben jeden   abgelehnt, der keine Fremdsprache   kann.
        we have everyone rejected   who no   foreign language knows
        'We rejected everyone who doesn't know a foreign language.'

However, a closer examination reveals that this kind of light negation and regular negation are not always interchangeable. Regular negation can be felicitous in contexts where light negation cannot be used. One such context is the inference schema in (46). Light negation is not felicitous here, but regular negation is.

(46) a. #Wir haben jeden   abgelehnt.
          we have everyone rejected
   ∴ Wir haben jeden   abgelehnt, der nicht eine Fremdsprache   kann.
        we have everyone rejected   who not   a   foreign language knows

  b. Wir haben jeden   abgelehnt.
        we have everyone rejected
   ∴ Wir haben jeden   abgelehnt, der keine Fremdsprache   kann.
        we have everyone rejected   who no   foreign language knows

Another indication that negative polarity light negation makes a different semantic contribution than regular negation comes from the contrast in (47). Note that the oddness of (47a) is not due to a failure of licensing of light negation, as the acceptability of the structurally parallel (45a) shows.

(47) a. !!Wir haben jeden,   der nicht eine Fremdsprache   kann,
           we have everyone who not a   foreign language knows
        zugelassen oder abgelehnt.
        admitted   or   rejected

  b. Wir haben jeden,   der keine Fremdsprache   kann, zugelassen
        we have everyone who no   foreign language knows admitted
        oder abgelehnt.
        or   rejected
        'We rejected or admitted everyone who does not know a foreign language.'

We speculate that light negation must always introduce a new nonaccidental generalization. In this view, light negation is infelicitous in (46a) because the sentence containing it is presented as a mere entailment of the premise. It does not constitute an independent nonaccidental generalization. Similarly, by virtue of its quasitautologous nature, sentence (47a) also does not introduce a new nonaccidental generalization. It should be noted that our observations about the semantics of light negation are preliminary and barely scratch the surface. They are intended to invite more work on this topic.[13]

5. Conclusion

Having explored the syntactic distribution and semantic properties of light negation, we now return to the relationship between light negation and the theory of rescuing. We have seen intriguing parallels between the distribution of light negation and rescuing. Could a theory of light negation be a complete theory of rescuing? We have seen that rescuing is possible from under negation and that, as Ladusaw (1979) had already shown, rescuing is not always available from under negative quantifiers like *no one*.

(48) a. There is no one here who this didn't sometimes annoy.

   b. I am surprised this didn't sometimes annoy you.

(49) a. ??There is no one here who nothing sometimes annoys.

   b. ??I am surprised that nothing sometimes annoys you.

The contrast between (5) and (7), repeated above as (48) and (49), follows from a light negation theory of rescuing. In this theory, rescuing reduces to non-antilicensing by a light negation, and assuming that only sentential negation has a light variant, the impossibility of rescuing from *no one* in (49) follows. In contrast, a theory that equates antilicensing with the formation of a derived negative polarity item and rescuing with the licensing of such a derived polarity item is unable to account for the contrast between (48) and (49).

However, it turns out that not all instances of rescuing are rescuing from sentential negation. Rescuing also seems to be possible from under *without* (Schwarz 2004) and *never* (Anna Szabolcsi, pers. comm.), as illustrated in (50) and (51).

(50) a. She doesn't make her cakes without adding some butter.

   b. There's no baker in this town that makes her cakes without adding some butter.

   c. I'm surprised that she makes her cakes without adding some butter.

   d. Let's suppose she made her cakes without adding some butter.

(51) a. There was no one there who they never offered some cookies.

   b. I was surprised that they never had some cookies.

   c. If they had never brought some cookies, we would not have had dessert.

   d. Suppose they had never brought some cookies.

To handle these facts within a light-negation style theory of rescuing, we would need to postulate the existence of light versions of *without* and *never*, which on an analogy with light negation would be non-antilicensers. But unlike in the case of light negation, there seems to be no independent evidence for the existence of light variants of *without* and *never*. A derived polarity item view of antilicensing, in contrast, automatically covers these cases. And yet, as the unacceptability of (49a) and (49b) indicates, without further restrictions, a derived polarity item approach to rescuing overgenerates. A proper division of labor between a light-negation analysis of rescuing and a derived polarity item approach might succeed in handling all the relevant observations. We have shown that a theory of light negation is needed on grounds independent of the rescuing phenomenon. The proper characterization of the division of labor between the two approaches to rescuing, we leave to future work. ▪

ACKNOWLEDGMENTS

For comments and helpful discussion, we thank Junko Shimoyama, Carlota Smith, the participants of our Spring 20/04 polarity seminar at the University of Texas at Austin, and the audience at GURT 2004, in particular Paul Portner and Peggy Speas.

NOTES

1. In his study of negative polar questions, Ladd (1981) distinguishes between two kinds of sentential negation in English: an *inner* negation, which corresponds to what we call regular negation, and an *outer* negation, which corresponds to our light negation. Büring and Gunlogson (2000) and Romero and Han (2004) adopt Ladd's distinction between inner and outer negation in their discussion of German polar questions. They note that these two negations in German can be distinguished on syntactic grounds.

2. It should be noted that the generalization about rescuing reached by Ladusaw was different from the one assumed in the main text. Ladusaw related the special negation to denial contexts (as in SOME men aren't chauvinists—ALL men are chauvinists). We side with Baker (1970a) and Szabolcsi (2004), who argue that rescuing contexts cannot be reduced to denial contexts.

3. As shown in Kratzer (1995) and Schwarz (2004), a potential explanation of the ungrammaticality of the cases in (10) according to which definites, indefinites, and disjunctions in German are themselves positive polarity items can be ruled out. The positional constraints are surface constraints. All the cases in (10) became acceptable if the object noun phrase is topicalized as in (i), where the object can be interpreted in the scope of negation.

   (i) Eine Fremdsprache   kann   Fritz nicht.
       a   foreign language knows Fritz not
       'Fritz doesn't know a foreign language.'

   In this, the object noun phrases are unlike positive polarity items, which can never be interpreted in the immediate scope of negation.

4. For example, positive polarity *some* can be rescued in the antecedent of a subjunctive conditional, as in *If John didn't know some foreign language, he would have failed.* But this is only possible if the antecedent is interpreted counterrfactually. Thus the preceding example cannot be used as a continuation of the following discourse, where the antecedent is not presupposed to be false: A: *Why do you think that John failed?* B: *I'm not sure, but . . .* For further details, see Baker (1970b), Karttunen (1971), and Schwarz (2004).

5. We owe examples like (21) to Sigrid Beck (pers. comm. to Bernhard Schwarz, January 30, 1996).

6. This is in contrast to the other two types of light negation, that is, light negation in negative polarity contexts and light negation in counterfactually interpreted subjunctive clauses. It seems that in these environments, light negation can always be replaced without loss of acceptability. The choice between light and regular negation does have an effect on semantic interpretation in these environments; see the main text of this section and section 4 for discussion.

7. That *einige* is a positive polarity item is illustrated by the unacceptability of example (i).

   (i) ??Keiner hat einige Birnen gegessen.
       no one   has some   pears   eaten
       'No one ate some pears.'

8. We know that negation is light in (30), as it precedes an indefinite in each case. Also, note that the contrast found in (30) disappears if the subject *jemand* 'someone' is replaced with a referential noun phrase such as the proper name *Fritz*. Both resulting sentences are perfectly acceptable.

9. In an influential view of negative polarity licensing, going back at least to Kadmon and Landman (1993), the licensing needs of negative polarity items stem from their particular semantic properties. In this approach, unlicensed negative polarity items yield a semantic anomaly. The fact that expletive light negation needs to be licensed, too, suggests that this approach to negative polarity licensing cannot be applied to all instances of light negation unless an analysis of expletive negation can be given in which it is semantically contentful (see Portner and Zanuttini 1996, 2000 for such an analysis of expletive negation in Paduan).

10. Since light negation cannot have a clausemate licenser in German, we predict that a downward-entailing operator cannot rescue a clausemate positive polarity item from an intervening antilicenser. This prediction seems to be borne out, as shown in (i) below.

    (i) ??Wenige haben nicht mit einigen Studenten gesprochen.
        few   have   not with some   students   talked

    But in contrast to German, the English counterpart of (i), *Few people didn't talk to some students,* does seem to allow for rescuing of the positive polarity item. Szabolcsi (2004), for example, reports that rescuing is possible in such cases. Within the terms of our analysis, this would indicate the availability of light negation in the English counterpart of (i) and hence indicate that light negation can have a clausemate licenser in English. It is possible that the nonclausemate licenser requirement on the licensing of light negation is subject to crosslinguistic variation.

11. Apparently, not only does light negation not license the negative polarity item *jemals* in these cases, it also blocks licensing of *jemals* by the higher licenser.

12. One property of this proposal is that there is no semantic/pragmatic licensing condition on the distribution of light negation in subjunctive clauses. Instead, light negation is licensed by subjunctive morphology alone. Restrictions on the distribution of light negation in subjunctive clauses are imposed by the lexical meaning of light negation in that environment. In an alternative view (Paul Portner, pers. comm.), the light negation is licensed by subjunctive morphology in conjunction with a counterfactual presuppostion. This counterfactual presupposition would have to be a pragmatic presupposition, given that subjunctive morphology in conditionals does not trigger a semantic presupposition (see the discussion of example [20] in section 3.1).

13. One important aspect of the meaning of light negation that we did not discuss is its impact on the interpretation of polar questions. It has been noted in Büring and Gunlogson (2000) and Romero and Han (2004), following observations by Ladd (1981), that light negation in polar questions introduces what they call a *positive bias*. For details, we refer the reader to the references cited.

REFERENCES

Anderson, A. R. 1951. A note on subjunctive and counterfactual conditionals. *Analysis* 11: 35–38.

Baker, C. L. 1970a. Double negatives. *Linguistic Inquiry* 1: 169–86.

———. 1970b. *Problems of polarity in counterfactuals.* In *Studies presented to Robert B. Lees by his students,* ed. J. Sadock and A. Vanek, 1–15. Edmonton, Canada: Linguistics Research Inc.

Büring, D., and C. Gunlogson. 2000. Aren't positive and negative polar questions the same? Unpublished manuscript, University of California, Santa Cruz.

Kadmon, N., and F. Landman. 1993. *Any. Linguistics and Philosophy* 16: 353–422.

Karttunen, L. 1971. Subjunctive conditionals and polarity reversal. *Papers in Linguistics* 4: 279–98.

Kratzer, A. 1995. Stage-level and individual-level predicates. In *The generic book,* ed, G. N. Carlson and F. J. Pelletier, 125–75. Chicago: Universtiy of Chicago Press.

Krifka, M. 1992. Some remarks on polarity items. In *Semantic universals in universal semantics,* ed. D. Zäfferer, 150–89. Dordrecht: Foris.

Ladusaw, W. A. 1979. Polarity sensitivity as inherent scope relations. PhD diss., University of Texas at Austin.

Ladd, R. D. 1981. A first look at the semantics and pragmatics of negative questions and tag questions. In *Papers from the seventeenth regional meeting of the Chicago Linguistic Society,* 164–71. Chicago: Chicago Linguistics Society, University of Chicago.

Linebarger, M. 1987. Negative polarity and grammatical representation. *Linguistics and Philosophy* 10: 387–437.

Meibauer, J. 1990. Sentence mood, lexical categorial filling, and non-propositional *nicht* in German. *Linguistische Berichte* 130: 441–65.

Portner, P., and R. Zanuttini. 1996. The syntax and semantics of scalar negation: Evidence from Paduan. In *The proceedings of NELS 26,* ed. K. Kusumoto, 257–71. Amherst: GLSA, University of Massachusetts.

———. 2000. The Force of Negation in Wh Exclamatives and Interrogatives. In *Studies in Negation and Polarity,* ed. L. Horn and Y. Kato, 193–231. Oxford: Oxford University Press.

Romero, M., and C. Han. 2004. On Negative Yes/No Questions. *Linguistics and Philosophy* 27: 609–58.

Schwarz, B. 2004. How to rescue negative polarity items. Unpublished manuscript, University of Texas at Austin.

Szabolcsi, A. 2004. Negative polarity—positive polarity. *Natural Language and Linguistic Theory* 22: 409–52.

van der Wouden, T. 1994. Polarity and illogical negation. In *Dynamics, polarity, and quantification,* ed. M. Kanazawa and C.J. Piñón, 17–45. Stanford, CA: CSLI.

8

Marking and Interpretation of Negation
A Bidirectional Optimality Theory Approach

HENRIËTTE DE SWART
Universiteit Utrecht

1. Introduction

Languages generally have ways to express negation, that is, something that corresponds to the first-order logic connective ¬. In English, this would be *not*. Many languages also have nominal expressions negating the existence of individuals having a certain property, that is, something that corresponds to $\neg \exists x$. In English, this would be *nobody, nothing*. If we assume that knowledge of first-order logic is part of human cognition, we would seem to predict that negation and negative quantifiers behave alike across languages. From empirical research by typologists and theoretical linguists, we know that this is not the case. The key insight is that languages make use of the same underlying mechanisms but exploit the relation between form and meaning in different ways. Optimality Theory (OT) can capture this kind of generalization. I adopt a bidirectional version of OT that calculates the optimal form for a given meaning, and the optimal meaning for a given form, on the basis of a ranking of violable constraints. The constraints are universal but the ranking of the constraints is language specific, which accounts for typological variation.

The organization of the chapter is as follows. Propositional negation is discussed in section 2. Section 3 gives an overview of indefinites under negation and introduces the analysis of double negation and negative concord proposed by de Swart and Sag (2002). Section 4 develops a typology of double-negation and negative-concord languages in bidirectional OT. Section 5 extends the analysis to the occurrence, position, and interpretation of markers of sentential negation. Section 6 concludes the chapter.

2. Propositional Negation

The expression of propositional negation ($\neg p$) and negative quantifiers ($\neg \exists x$) takes various forms across languages (see Jespersen 1917/1962, 1933/1964; Dahl 1979; Payne 1985; Horn 1989; Ladusaw 1996; Bernini and Ramat 1996; and Haspelmath 1997 for overviews of the facts). This chapter does not aim at typological completeness, but it is in line with what typologists have observed. The aim of this section is to determine how languages express a meaning that could be written in first-order logic as ¬p and how they interpret sentential negation. We treat this question in an OT syntax where the input is a meaning (a first-order formula), the set of candidates generated by GEN is a set of possible forms, and a ranked set of violable constraints selects the optimal form for the given meaning. Furthermore, we set up an interpretation mechanism in OT semantics, where the input is a form (a well-formed sentence), the set of candidates is a set of possible meanings (first-order formulae), and a ranked set of violable constraints selects the optimal interpretation for the given form.

Negative sentences are formally and interpretationally marked with respect to affirmative sentences. Now, negation is not a sentential force in the sense of Portner and Zanuttini (2003), because it is compatible with different clause types (declaratives, interrogatives, exclamatives). However, there are certain similarities. According to Portner and Zanuttini (2003), all exclamatives share the need to represent in the syntax two semantic properties, namely, that exclamatives are factive and that they denote a set of alternative propositions. Similarly, we require that the syntax reflect, in some way, the fact that negative sentences are not affirmative by means of the constraint that we call FaithNeg (Faith negation):

■ FaithNeg
Reflect the nonaffirmative nature of the input in the output.

FaithNeg is a faithfulness constraint, that is, a constraint that aims at a faithful reflection of input features in the output. Within a generation perspective (OT syntax), FaithNeg means that we reflect negation in the meaning (input) in the output (form). In OT, faithfulness constraints are usually balanced by markedness constraints, which are output oriented and aim at the reduction of structure in the output. The markedness constraint that plays a role in negative statements is *Neg:

■ *Neg
Avoid negation in the output.

*Neg is in conflict with FaithNeg, which requires a reflection in the output of negative features we find in the input. Such conflicting constraints are characteristic of OT-style analyses. The conflict is resolved by the ranking of constraints in terms of strength. If we rank FaithNeg higher than *Neg, making it a stronger, more important constraint, we can derive the fact that negative meanings are formally expressed:

Tableau 1: Generation of negative sentences

Meaning	Form	FaithNeg	*Neg
¬p	S	*	
☞	not S		*

Note that the input in tableau 1 is a meaning, and the output candidates evaluated by the grammar are forms. All our generation tableaux will have this setup. The ranking FaithNeg >> *Neg reflects the generally accepted view that negative statements are crosslinguistically more marked in form than their affirmative counterparts (Payne 1985; Horn 1989; Haspelmath 1997). All the sentences in (1) express a negative proposition and contain a linguistic marker expressing negation (in italics):

(1) a. John is *not* sick. English

    b. *Ou* petetai Sokrates   Ancient Greek

       not flies   Sokrates.

       'Socrates doesn't fly.'

    c. Dokumenty *ne* obnaružilis. Russian

       documents not were-found

       'Documents were not found.'

    d. *No* vino Pedro. Spanish

       not came Pedro

       'Pedro did not come.'

We assume that there are no languages in which *Neg outranks FaithNeg. So negation is, in some sense, claimed to be a universal category (Dahl 1979).

The interpretation of negative sentences is a mirror image of their generation:

Tableau 2: Interpretation of negative sentences

Form		Meaning	FaithNeg	*Neg
not S		p	*	
	☞	¬p		*

Note that the input in tableau 2 is a form, and the output candidates evaluated by the grammar are meanings. All our interpretation tableaux will have this setup. For lack of time and space, we restrict ourselves in this paper to monoclausal examples, setting aside the problems of negation, Neg-raising, and NC in multiclausal constructions. For the expression of indefinites under negation, we need additional constraints.

3. Indefinites under Negation

Section 3.1 develops an empirical classification of the expression of indefinites under negation ($\neg\exists x_1 \exists x_2 \ldots \exists x_n$ in first-order logic). We base our analysis of negative concord on de Swart and Sag (2002), which we discuss in section 3.2.

3.1 Empirical Classification

Haspelmath (1997, 193–4) and Corblin and Tovena (2003) describe how natural languages express the meaning $\neg\exists x_1 \exists x_2 \ldots \exists x_n$. We roughly follow their classification and distinguish three main cases: indefinites, negative polarity items, and n-words.

Case 1: indefinites under negation

The simplest possible forms that express the meaning $\neg\exists x_1 \exists x_2 \ldots \exists x_n$ are markers of sentential negation or negative quantifiers with n/n-1 indefinites in its scope.

(2) a. Ik heb daar toen *niet iets*   van durven zeggen.   Dutch

    I have there then *not something* dare   say.

    'I didn't dare to say anything about that at that time.'

b. *Niemand* heeft *iets*   gezien.

    nobody   has *something* seen.

    'Nobody saw anything.'

Haspelmath (1997, 193) gives an example from Turkish:

(3) Birşey   duy-ma-dı-m.

    something hear-NEG-past-1.SG

    'I didn't hear anything.'

So what seems to be the simplest possible formal combination from a (first-order) logical point of view is actually realized in several natural languages. However, not all languages allow this straightforward expression of indefinites under negation.

Case 2: negative polarity items

The simplest possible forms as in case 1 are blocked because indefinites are positive polarity items (PPIs) that are allergic to negative contexts. Instead, negative polarity items (NPIs) are used to express existential quantification in the scope of negation.

(4) a. #I did *not* buy *something*.   English

b. I did *not* buy *anything*.

(5) a. #*Nobody* saw *something*.

b. Nobody saw *anything*.

c. Nobody said *anything* to *anyone*.

Negative polarity items occur in a wider range of contexts than just negation:

(6) a. If you saw *anything*, please tell the police.

b. Did *anyone* notice *anything* unusual?

c. Few people wrote down *anything*.

The examples in (6) illustrate that NPIs such as *anything* do not inherently carry a negative meaning. Rather, they correspond to existential quantifiers with some additional meaning component (characterized as "widening" of alternatives by Kadmon and Landman 1993; or as indicating the bottom of a scale by Fauconnier 1975, 1979; Krifka 1995; Israel 1996; de Swart 1998).

Haspelmath (1997) gives the following example from Basque:

(7) Ez dut   inor   ikusi.

    NEG I.have.him anybody seen.

    'I haven't seen anybody.'

Case 3: n-words

The simplest forms as in case 1 are blocked because indefinite pronouns are PPIs. Instead, existential quantification in the scope of negation is expressed by means of "n-words." N-words behave as negative quantifiers in isolation (8a) or in sentences in which they are the only expression of negation (8b), but they express a single negative statement in combination with sentential negation or other n-words (8c, d).

(8) a. A: Qué viste?   B: Nada   Spanish
     A: What did you see?   B: Nothing

   b. Nessuno mangia.   Italian
     nobody ate
     'Nobody ate.'

   c. No vino nadie.   Spanish
     not came nobody.
     'Nobody came.'

   d. Nadie miraba a nadie.
     nobody looked at nobody.
     'Nobody looked at anybody.'

N-words differ from negative polarity items in three ways, according to Ladusaw (1992), Vallduví (1994), Bernini and Ramat (1996), and Haspelmath (1997). First, they behave as negative quantifiers in isolation (8a, b), whereas negative polarity items behave as indefinites and contribute an existential quantifier $\exists$ rather than a negative existential quantifier $\neg\exists$ (6). NPIs like *anything* do not mean 'nothing' as the elliptical answer to a question and do not occur in subject position, because they must be licensed by an operator with the right semantic properties (downward entailing, nonveridical or whatever; see Fauconnier 1975, 1979; Ladusaw 1979; Zwarts 1986; van der Wouden 1997; Giannakidou 1998; etc.).[1] N-words can occur in the context of another antiadditive operator, but they don't need a licenser; they are "self-licensing" (Ladusaw 1992). As a result, n-words can be used in sentences in which no other expression conveys a negative meaning (8b).[2] This chapter concentrates on n-words and does not provide an OT analysis of the generation and interpretation of NPIs.

    Languages that use n-words express what is known as *negative concord:* a sequence of seemingly negative expressions gets a single negation reading. Negative concord (NC) raises major questions for semantics, because it seems to violate the principle of compositionality of meaning. Many existing proposals try to answer this question, for example, Zanuttini (1991), Ladusaw (1992), van der Wouden and Zwarts (1993), Corblin (1996), Déprez (1997, 2000), Giannakidou (2000), Herburger (2001), de Swart and Sag (2002), among others. For lack of space, I will not compare the different theories but refer the reader to Corblin et al. (2004) for a review. This paper builds on the proposals made by de Swart and Sag (2002), so we will only discuss this analysis.

3.2 An HPSG Analysis of Double Negation and Negative Concord

The main semantic claims made by de Swart and Sag (2002) are that n-words are inherently negative and that both double negation (DN) and NC involve polyadic quantification. DN involves iteration (function application) and is first-order definable. Negative concord is interpreted in terms of resumption.

- Resumption of a k-ary quantifier (Keenan and Westerståhl 1997). $Q'_E{}^{A_1, A_2, \ldots A_k}(R) = Q_{E^k}{}^{A_1 \times A_2 \times \ldots A_k}(R)$.

To put this in words, we have a sequence of k monadic quantifiers Q' binding just one variable each, interpreted on the universe of discourse E, with a one-place predicate A as their restrictor, and taking a k-ary relation R as their scope. This sequence is interpreted as one polyadic quantifier Q binding k variables, interpreted in the universe of discourse E^k, taking the subset $A_1 \times A_2 \times \ldots A_k$ of E^k as its restrictor and the k-ary predicate R as its scope. So, a sequence of pronominal quantifiers *No x, No y, No z R(x, y, z)* is interpreted as $No_{x, y, z} R(x, y, z)$, indicating that there is no triple $<x, y, z>$ satisfying the three-place relation R. At the first-order level, the resumptive quantifier is equivalent to $\neg \exists x \exists y \exists z R(x, y, z)$, so we obtain the NC reading as desired.

The syntax-semantics interface defines how we obtain the DN and NC readings from the syntax. HPSG uses a notion of Cooper storage in which all quantifiers are collected into a store and interpreted upon retrieval from the store (see Manning, Sag, and Iida 1999). This mechanism is generally used to account for scope ambiguities, but de Swart and Sag (2002) extend it to polyadic quantification. All negative (antiadditive) quantifiers are collected into a so-called N-store. Interpretation upon retrieval from the store is by means of iteration of monadic quantifiers (leading to DN) or by resumption, building a polyadic quantifier (leading to NC). We will not spell out the retrieval mechanism here but refer to de Swart and Sag (2002) for formal details. What is crucial for us here is that the grammar does not decide between DN and NC. This is what we need for a language like French, in which both readings are available. Consider the ambiguity of the following sentence in the HPSG analysis of de Swart and Sag (2002):

(9) Personne n'aime personne. French
a. Arg-St<[Store $\{NO_{\{x\}}{}^{\{Person(x)\}}\}$], [Store $\{NO_{\{y\}}{}^{\{Person(y)\}}\}$]>
Content Quants <$NO_{\{x\}}{}^{\{Person(x)\}}$, $NO_{\{y\}}{}^{\{Person(y)\}}$>
Nucleus *Love(x, y)*
Semantic interpretation: NO(HUM, {x|NO(HUM, {y|x loves y})})
In first-order logic: $\neg \exists x \neg \exists x$ Love(x,y) DN
b. Arg-St<[Store $\{NO_{\{x\}}{}^{\{Person(x)\}}\}$], [Store $\{NO_{\{y\}}{}^{\{Person(y)\}}\}$]>
Content Quants <$NO_{\{x, y\}}{}^{\{Person(x), Person(y)\}}$>
Nucleus *Love(x,y)*
Semantic interpretation: $NO_{E2}{}^{HUM \times HUM}(LOVE)$
In first-order logic: $\neg \exists x \exists y$ Love(x, y) NC

Note that (9a) and (9b) are identical as far as the argument structure, the storing mechanism, and the interpretation of the *love* relation is concerned. The difference resides in the interpretation of the polyadic quantifier: iteration in (9a), resumption in (9b). The main insights of this analysis are the following. The HPSG grammar assumes no lexical difference between negative quantifiers and n-words, so in the rest of this paper we use the term *neg expression* to generalize over both. The analysis works for n-words in argument and adjunct position alike (so *nobody, nothing* as well as *never, nowhere*). Finally, it does not involve empty elements or "hidden" negations in the syntactic structure. These are major advantages of this proposal.

The OT analysis comes in when we try to relate the HPSG analysis to languages that do not allow DN and NC as freely as French does. In general, the combination of two negative quantifiers in English leads to a DN reading, and resumption is only marginally available as an interpretive strategy. On the other hand, Spanish, Greek, Polish, and many other languages are typically NC languages, which hardly ever realize the iteration version of the polyadic quantifier analysis. In other words, the analysis proposed by de Swart and Sag (2002) does not predict crosslinguistic variation where it arises (Spanish vs. English, for example). The aim of this chapter is to extend the earlier analysis with a bidirectional OT component in order to define a typology of negation.

4. Marking and Interpretation of Negation in Bidirectional OT

In this section, we develop a bidirectional OT analysis of negation. We will do so in two steps, giving first the OT syntax (section 4.1) and then the combination with an interpretive mechanism (section 4.2). Section 4.3 discusses DN readings in NC languages. For now, we focus on indefinites and neg expressions. The interaction with sentential negation is taken up in section 5 below.

4.1 Generation of Double Negation and Negative Concord in OT

According to Corblin and Tovena (2003, 326), natural languages frequently have linguistic means to indicate that an argument must be interpreted within the scope of negation. They refer to this as marking of "negative variables." Similarly, Haspelmath (1997, 231), building on Tanaka (1994), claims that the use of n-words is functionally motivated by the desire to mark the focus of negation, that is, the participants that are affected by the negation. In terms of OT syntax, the use of n-words constitutes a case of marking an input feature in the output: the negative variable is formally marked as such. In our OT setup, we express this by means of a Max constraint:

▪ MaxNeg
  Mark all negative variables.
  (i.e., mark all arguments that are interpreted in the scope of negation)

The functional approach explains why the use of n-words is widespread among natural languages. However, we know from section 3.1 above that the use of n-words is not universal: languages like Dutch, English, Basque, and so on do not use n-words. This suggests that MaxNeg is not a hard constraint and that its position in the constraint ranking is not the same for every language. We can account for the difference between languages with and without n-words by changing the position of MaxNeg relative to *Neg. MaxNeg and *Neg are conflicting constraints: MaxNeg wants to reflect an input feature concerning negation in the form, whereas *Neg wants to avoid negation in the form. If *Neg is ranked higher than MaxNeg, the optimal way to express the meaning $\neg\exists x_1\exists x_2\ldots\exists x_n$ is by means of indefinite pronouns. If MaxNeg is ranked higher than *Neg, n-words are used to express indefinites under negation. The following tableaux reflect this for the binding of two variables:

Tableau 3: Generation of indefinite

Meaning	Form	FaithNeg	*Neg	MaxNeg
$\neg\exists x_1\exists x_2$	indef + indef	*		**
☞	neg + indef		*	*
	neg + neg		**	

Tableau 4: Generation of n-word

Meaning	Form	FaithNeg	MaxNeg	*Neg
$\neg\exists x_1\exists x_2$	indef + indef	*	**	
	neg + indef		*	*
☞	neg + neg			**

The high ranking of FaithNeg (recall section 1) makes it impossible to express indefinites under negation by indefinites exclusively (in the absence of a marker of sentential negation). In tableaux 3 and 4, the candidates that we need to compare are those that somehow mark negation in the output. This invariably leads to a violation of *Neg. Two neg expressions are worse than one, so the combination of two neg expressions incurs two violations of *Neg.

As far as generation is concerned, we conclude that languages that allow indefinites under negation (e.g., Dutch), and languages that use n-words (e.g., Romance) differ in their ranking of the two constraints MaxNeg and *Neg. The question that immediately arises at this point concerns the interpretation of the expressions involved. A combination of a neg expression with a sequence of indefinites allows us to recover the meaning $\neg\exists x_1\exists x_2\ldots\exists x_n$ by application of the standard rules of first-order logic. However, for languages that mark negative variables by means of n-words, the issue of the interpretation of these structures is less trivial. We address this question in section 4.2.

4.2 Interpretation of Neg-Expressions

In isolation, we cannot determine whether a particular expression is a negative quantifier or an n-word, because they both contribute the meaning $\neg\exists$ (8a, b). Following de Swart and Sag (2002), I assume that this question is decided in the grammar, not in the lexicon. This is why I use the term *neg expression* to generalize over expressions that are formally marked for negation but are interpreted either as negative quantifiers or as n-words. The use of neg expressions in a generative OT system means that we run into the recoverability problem: from the expressions generated, we can derive multiple interpretations, not only the intended one.

Recoverability is assured by the way the generation of negative sentences hangs together with their interpretation. In this section, we extend the OT syntax with an OT semantics. We need the familiar constraints FaithNeg and *Neg. These are double-edged constraints in the sense that they work in the generation as well as in the interpretation perspective. In the OT semantics, FaithNeg requires a reflection of the negative form in a nonaffirmative meaning. *Neg avoids a proliferation of negations in the semantics, preferring resumption over iteration. The third constraint we need is IntNeg:

- IntNeg
  Force iteration (i.e., interpret every neg expression in the input form as contributing a semantic negation at the first-order level in the output).

MaxNeg and IntNeg both maximize the reflection of input features in the output, MaxNeg in the syntactic form, IntNeg in the semantic interpretation. As semantic constraints, both FaithNeg and IntNeg are instantiations of the general constraint FaithInt proposed by Zeevat (2000) and are defined as a principle that forces the hearer to interpret all that the speaker has said. The three constraints together account for DN and NC languages.

FaithNeg outranks all the other constraints, as usual. MaxNeg is a purely syntactic constraint that does not play a role in interpretation. So the constraints that need to be ordered are *Neg and IntNeg. If *Neg is ranked higher than IntNeg in the OT semantics, a sequence of multiple neg expressions leads to a single negation meaning by resumption. If IntNeg is ranked higher than *Neg, a series of neg expressions is interpreted as multiple negation by forcing iteration. The following tableaux illustrate the two possible rankings and their optimal output:

Tableau 5: Double negation (interpretation)

Form	Meaning	FaithNeg	IntNeg	*Neg
neg + neg	$\exists x_1 \exists x_2$	*	**	
	$\neg \exists x_1 \exists x_2$		*	*
☞	$\neg \exists x_1 \neg \exists x_2$			**

Tableau 6: Negative concord (interpretation)

Form	Meaning	FaithNeg	*Neg	IntNeg
neg + neg	$\exists x_1 \exists x_2$	*		**
☞	$\neg \exists x_1 \exists x_2$		*	*
	$\neg \exists x_1 \neg \exists x_2$		**	

We cannot interpret a statement involving two neg expressions without a reflection of the nonaffirmative meaning because of the top ranking of FaithNeg. As a result, the relevant candidates we compare have at least one negation in the output and always incur a violation of *Neg. The combination of two neg expressions leads to a double negation reading in languages like Dutch and English, for the constraint IntNeg is ranked higher than *Neg in tableau 5. Because *Neg outranks IntNeg in tableau 6, single negation readings win over double negation readings in such languages as Spanish, Italian, Greek, Polish, and so forth.

Collapsing the generation and interpretation perspective, we derive the following two rankings for NC and DN languages:

Bidirectional grammar
- Negative concord languages: FaithNeg >> MaxNeg >> *Neg >> IntNeg
- Double negation languages: FaithNeg >> IntNeg >> *Neg >> MaxNeg

Even if we assume that FaithNeg outranks the other constraints across all languages under consideration, we need to consider more rankings than the two orders given above. Aside from FaithNeg, we are working with three constraints, and obviously, three constraints permit six rankings, at least in principle:

MaxNeg >> *Neg >> IntNeg	NC
MaxNeg >> IntNeg >> *Neg	unstable
*Neg >> MaxNeg >> IntNeg	unstable
*Neg >> IntNeg >> MaxNeg	unstable
IntNeg >> MaxNeg >> *Neg	unstable
IntNeg >> *Neg >> MaxNeg	DN

So far, we have established the top ranking and the bottom one as reflections of a particular family of languages. What about the other four possibilities? I claim that the other four rankings cannot represent stable linguistic systems because generation and production are not well balanced. Consider the following examples:

Tableau 7: MaxNeg >> IntNeg >> *Neg (original meaning not recovered)

Meaning	Form	MaxNeg	IntNeg	*Neg
$\neg\exists x_1 \exists x_2$	neg + indef	*		*
☞	neg + neg			**
Form	Meaning	MaxNeg	IntNeg	*Neg
neg + neg ☞	$\neg\exists x_1 \neg\exists x_2$			**
	$\neg\exists x_1 \exists x_2$		*	*

This ranking generates two neg expressions as the optimal output for the single negation input. But the interpretation of two neg expressions leads to double, rather than single, negation. This means that the original meaning is not recovered. The ranking IntNeg >> MaxNeg >> *Neg is equally unstable. Given that there is no direct interaction between IntNeg and MaxNeg, the argumentation is the same. We conclude that MaxNeg and IntNeg cannot both be higher than *Neg.

Tableau 8: *Neg >> IntNeg >> MaxNeg (form not motivated)

Meaning	Form	*Neg	IntNeg	MaxNeg
$\neg\exists x_1 \exists x_2$ ☞	neg + indef	*		*
	neg + neg	**		
Form	Meaning	*Neg	IntNeg	MaxNeg
neg + neg	$\neg\exists x_1 \neg\exists x_2$	**		
☞	$\neg\exists x_1 \exists x_2$	*	*	

Here we get the reverse problem. Indefinites are the optimal form for expressing indefinites under negation, but a neg expression also leads to an NC reading. However, the use of the n-word is not functionally motivated by the low ranking of MaxNeg. The same problems arise with the ranking *Neg >> MaxNeg >> IntNeg, because MaxNeg and IntNeg do not interact directly. This shows that MaxNeg and IntNeg cannot both be lower than *Neg either.

The conclusion must be that only rankings where MaxNeg and IntNeg are distributed on either side of *Neg reflect viable options for a linguistic system that balances generation and interpretation of negative statements. In sum:

- Negative Concord: if you mark negative variables (MaxNeg >> *Neg in syntax), then make sure you do not force iteration (*Neg >> IntNeg in semantics).

- Double Negation: if you force iteration, (IntNeg >> *Neg in semantics), then make sure you do not mark negative variables (*Neg >> MaxNeg in syntax).

4.3 Double Negation in Concord Languages

Although most languages clearly belong to either the DN class or the NC class, there are some intermediate cases. Corblin (1996), Corblin and Tovena (2003), and Corblin et al. (2004) argue that the French sentences in (10) and (11) are truly ambiguous:

(10) Personne n'a   rien   payé.
   nobody   ne has *nothing* paid
   'No one has paid anything.'   NC
   'Everyone has paid something.'   DN
(11) Personne n' est le   fils de personne.
   nobody   ne is the son of *nobody*
   'No one is the son of anyone.'   NC
   'Everyone is the son of someone.'   DN

For (10), the two readings are equally available. The DN reading of (11) conforms to our world knowledge in ways that the NC reading of this sentence does not. Corblin argues that pragmatic factors may block the NC reading of examples like (11).

We can account for this situation by moving the constraints *Neg and IntNeg more closely together in a stochastic version of OT (see Boersma 1998; Boersma and

Hayes 2001). In stochastic OT, constraints are ranked on a continuous scale. If adjacent constraints have an overlapping range, their order can be reversed in certain outputs. In modern French, we may assume that there is overlap between the range of *Neg and IntNeg in the interpretive system, so that in some contexts, the ranking can be reversed. Context plays an important role in disambiguation in general (de Hoop 2004), so cases like (10) and (11) would not be that unusual.

The stochastic view suggests that French occasionally switches to an unbalanced system in which both MaxNeg and IntNeg are ranked higher than *Neg. It is therefore quite likely that the ambiguities will be fairly restricted, unless the whole system is shifting towards a DN language in which n-words are reinterpreted as negative quantifiers (and MaxNeg is reranked below *Neg). This would obviously be the next step in terms of the Jespersen cycle (see Jespersen 1917/1962; de Swart and Sag 2002). French is assumed to be more advanced than other Romance languages in its stage of development in the Jespersen cycle (e.g., Haspelmath 1997), but there are some reports on similar ambiguities in Italian and Spanish. Zanuttini (1991, 144–45) claims that (12) exemplifies DN in Italian:

(12) *Nessuno* è rimasto con *niente* in mano.

    no one   is left   with *nothing* in hand

    'No one was left with nothing.'

And Herburger (2001) reports that the Spanish example in (13) is ambiguous:

(13) *Nadie*   *nunca* volvió   a   Cuba.

    nobody never returned to Cuba

    'Nobody ever returned to Cuba.'   NC

    'Nobody never returned to Cuba.'   DN

MaxNeg is currently still high in the ranking of Spanish, Italian, and even French, and there are no clear signs of it being demoted, so we are more on the side of a concord language than on the side of a DN language as far as generation is concerned. Because of the tension between the functional motivation for MaxNeg and the desire to respect IntNeg, it is impossible to predict if and when a complete rebalancing between form and meaning will take place in Romance. Possibly the system as it is (with just occasional outranking of *Neg by IntNeg in the interpretive system) is sufficiently stable to last.

5. Neg Expressions and Sentential Negation

Haspelmath (1997) distinguishes three subtypes of negative indefinites, depending on their relation to the marker of sentential negation. His classification is presented in section 5.1. Sections 5.2 and 5.3 implement the two main classes of NC languages in our bidirectional OT analysis. Section 5.4 treats Catalan as a mixed type.

5.1 Empirical Classification of
Co-Occurrence Restrictions

Haspelmath's classification serves as the starting point of our investigation, but see also the discussions in den Besten (1986), Hoeksema (1997), van der Wouden

(1997), and Giannakidou (1998). Haspelmath (1997, 201) distinguishes three types of co-occurrence restrictions between neg expressions and markers of sentential negation.

Type I: SNV-NEG

Negative indefinites (NEG) always co-occur with verbal negation (SN), for example, the Polish *ni*-series (*nikt* 'nobody', *nic* 'nothing', etc.). Similar examples are found in other Slavic languages, Greek, Hungarian, Rumanian, and so forth. The examples in (14) are from Haspelmath (1997, 201); the examples in (15) from Corblin and Tovena (2003):

(14) a. Nikt   nie przyszedł.   Polish
        nobody SN came.
        'Nobody came.'
     b. Nie widziałam nikogo.
        SN saw   nobody.
        'I saw nobody.'
(15) a. Nimeni *(nu) a   venit.   Rumanian
        nobody *(SN) has come.
        'Nobody came'
     b. *(Nu) a   venit nimeni.
        *(SN) has come nobody.
        'Nobody came'

The type SNV-NEG is the most frequent type in Haspelmath's (1997) language sample. He refers to Tanaka (1994) for evidence that this type is functionally motivated, because both the scope and the focus of negation are marked. The close connection between the verb and sentence negation is expected if Aristotle's and Jespersen's view of negation as predicate denial is adopted, as argued extensively in Horn (1989). Den Besten (1986), Hoeksema (1997), van der Wouden (1997), and Giannakidou (1998) refer to this type as *negative doubling, proper* or *strict* NC.

Type II: V-NEG

In this type, negative indefinites never co-occur with verbal negation, for example, the English *no*-series.

(16) a. Nobody came.
     b. I saw nobody.

According to Haspelmath (1997, 202), type II (V-NEG) is rare in crosslinguistic distribution. In his language sample, only European languages represent this type. He explains the relative rarity of type V-NEG as the result of a discrepancy between the semantics (which requires clausal scope of negation) and the surface expression of negation (which is on a participant, rather than on the verb in this type.)

Type III: (sn)V-neg

This type includes negative indefinites (neg) that sometimes co-occur with verbal negation (sn) and sometimes do not, for example, the Italian, Spanish, and Portuguese *n*-series.

(17) a. *Ninguém* veio.   European Portuguese
         nobody came
         'Nobody came.'
    b. *Não* veio *ninguém.*
         sn came nobody.
         'Nobody came.'

Type III ((sn)V-neg) is strong in Romance, but rare elsewhere (Haspelmath 1997). According to Zanuttini (1991, 152–3) and Ladusaw (1992), the functional motivation for this type is that postverbal n-words are unable to take sentential scope. A preverbal expression of negation (n-word or sn) is thus motivated by the desire to express negation at the clausal (propositional) level.

In our terminology, type I and type III neg expressions are n-words, and type II neg expressions are negative quantifiers in DN languages. DN languages are captured by the bidirectional analysis of section 4 above and will not be discussed here. I propose two additional constraints for the class I and class III languages. These constraints are relevant for production only (OT syntax): the interpretation process is that of a concord language.

5.2 Class III Languages: Preverbal/
Postverbal Asymmetry
Class III languages are characterized by the general constraint ranking of NC languages in combination with the additional constraint NegFirst:

■ NegFirst
   Negation is preverbal.

Variants of NegFirst are discussed in the literature, for example, Jespersen (1917/ 1962, 1933/1964), Dahl (1979), Horn (1989), Haspelmath (1997), Corblin and Tovena (2003), Corblin et al. (2004). NegFirst is functionally motivated by the desire "to put the negative word or element as early as possible, so as to leave no doubt in the mind of the hearer as to the purport of what is said" (Jespersen 1933/1964, 297 as quoted by Horn 1989, 293, who dubs this principle *NegFirst*). Although NegFirst is found in many languages, Horn points out that it is not absolute. In OT, it works well as a violable constraint.

NegFirst is operative in several Romance languages, including Spanish, Italian, and Sardinian Portugese (compare Posner 1984), but also in New Testament Greek and older varieties of several Slavic languages (which are class I languages in their modern varieties, see Haspelmath 1997, 212). Since Zanuttini (1991) and Ladusaw

(1992), it is well known that n-words in these languages can occur without negation in preverbal position but need the support of a marker of sentential negation to mark clausal scope when they occur in postverbal position and there is no preverbal n-word:

(18) a. Mario *(*non*) ha parlato di   *niente* con *nessuno*.   Italian

Mario *(SN)   has talked   about *nothing* to   *nobody*.

'Mario didn't talk about anything to anyone.'

b. *Nessuno* (*?*non*) ha   parlato con   *nessuno*.

Nobody (*?SN)   has talked   with *nobody*.

'Nobody talked to anybody.'

As these examples indicate, negation must be preverbal, but it does not matter whether it is expressed by a marker of sentential negation (18a), or by an n-word (18b). When the preverbal negation is expressed by a neg expression, a marker of sentential negation is excluded. Insertion of a preverbal marker of sentential negation in combination with a preverbal n-word generally leads to ungrammaticality and marginally to DN readings (in certain dialects only; see Zanuttini 1991).

In the OT analysis, we need to establish a distinction between preverbal and postverbal n-words as the correlation of clausal/VP scope. If we complement the usual constraint ranking for concord languages with a highly ranked constraint NegFirst, we obtain as a result that the sentence without preverbal sentential negation is an optimal output in the production direction when the indefinite under negation is postverbal (18a, tableau 9). This ranking also leads to the desired (concord) interpretation.

Tableau 9: Generation/interpretation of class III with postverbal n-word

Meaning	Form	MaxNeg	NegFirst	*Neg	IntNeg
$\neg\forall\exists x$	V neg		*	*	
☞	sn V neg			**	
Form	Meaning				
sn V neg	$\neg V\neg\exists x$			**	
☞	$\neg V\exists x$			*	*

These tableaux do not include candidates that violate MaxNeg, so we only consider neg expressions. Note further that NegFirst and MaxNeg are not in direct competition, so their mutual order is irrelevant, as long as they are both ranked above *Neg. In all potential constraint rankings in which NegFirst is ranked below *Neg, the constraint is inactive. The interpretation doesn't care how many negations there are in the form: the ranking *Neg >> IntNeg implies that resumption applies. In the resumption process, the marker of sentential negation is simply absorbed. Given that it does not contribute a binding variable, it does not affect the resumptive quantifier (see de Swart and Sag 2002 for discussion). Accordingly, it is relevant to add constraints like NegFirst to the OT syntax, but they do not affect the OT semantics. So from now on, we don't need to spell out the NC interpretation anymore.

For sentences in which the postverbal indefinite is in the scope of a preverbal neg expression (18b), the optimal output on the production side is a sentence with a preverbal and a postverbal n-word but without a preverbal sentential negation. An additional preverbal SN incurs an extra violation of *Neg, which is not economical. In the semantics, there is no gain from an extra marker of sentential negation, either, because the meanings of the sentences with and without a marker of sentential negation are the same under the ranking *Neg >> IntNeg.

Tableau 10: Generation of class III with preverbal n-word

Meaning		Form	MaxNeg	NegFirst	*Neg	IntNeg
$\neg\exists x_1 \lor \exists x_2$	☞	neg V neg			**	
		neg SN V neg			***	

The constraint ranking in tableau 10 accounts for the fact that class III languages do not insert a marker of sentential negation with preverbal n-words. The relevance of NegFirst is not restricted to NC languages. Horn (1989, 456–7) relates English *do*-support to the preference for preverbal negation.

5.3 Class I Languages: Obligatory Marker of Sentential Negation

Just like class III languages, class I languages require a marker of sentential negation with a postverbal n-word (14b, 15b). Unlike type III language, type I languages also require such a marker when the sentence contains a preverbal n-word (14a, 15a). NegFirst does not account for such a situation; the constraint that applies is MaxSN:

■ MaxSN
A negative clause must bear a marker of sentential negation.

Tableau 11: Generation of type I languages with preverbal n-word

Meaning		Form	MaxNeg	MaxSN	*Neg	IntNeg
$\neg\exists x_1 \lor \exists x_2$		neg V neg		*	**	
	☞	neg SN V neg			***	

MaxSN and MaxNeg are not in direct competition, so their mutual ranking is irrelevant. It suffices that they are both ranked higher than *Neg. The meaning of the sentence is not affected, for all n-words are absorbed into one resumptive negative quantifier. This meaning effect is guaranteed by the ranking of IntNeg below *Neg.

In class I languages that contain a preverbal marker of negation (e.g., Slavic, Greek), NegFirst is "harmonically bound" by MaxSN. This means that NegFirst is automatically satisfied when MaxSN is, so it cannot be evaluated independently. However, the constraints can be shown to be independent in NC languages that satisfy the constraint MaxSN with a postverbal marker of SN. Afrikaans *nie* provides an example:

(19) a. Jan het gehoop dat *niks*   met hom sou   gebeur *nie.*

      Jan has hoped that nothing with him would happen not

      'Jan hoped that nothing would happen to him.'

    b. Sy hou   *nooit* op met werk *nie.*

      she holds never up with work not

      'She never stops working.'

Type I and type III languages thus support the view put forward by de Swart and Sag (2002) that sentential negation does not affect the semantics of NC. Whether or not we find a (pre)verbal marker of sentential negation in concord languages depends on syntactic constraints like NegFirst or MaxSN.

5.4 Catalan: A Mixed Case

The constraints NegFirst and MaxSN interact in a language like Catalan, which exemplifies a mix of class I and class III properties (Ladusaw 1992; Vallduví 1994):

(20) a. En Pere *(no)* ha fet *res.*

      the Peter *(not)* has done *nothing*

      'Peter has not done anything.'

    b. *Ningú (no)* ha vist en Joan.

      nobody (not) has seen John

      'Nobody has seen John.'

The data in (20) are accounted for by the following ranking: MaxNeg >> NegFirst >> MaxSN <<>> *Neg. Suppose that MaxSN and *Neg are ranked equally high (i.e., <<>> in ordinal OT) or have a strongly overlapping range (in stochastic OT). Given that NegFirst is higher than either one, we generate a preverbal marker of sentential negation with postverbal n-words, just like in a type III language (20a, tableau 12). With preverbal n-words (20b), the equal position of MaxSN and *Neg generates two optimal outputs. This is illustrated in tableau (13):

Tableau 12: Generation of Catalan with postverbal n-word

Meaning	Form	MaxNeg	NegFirst	MaxSN <	> *Neg	IntNeg
¬∨∃x	V neg		*	*	*	
☞	SN V neg				**	

Tableau 13: Generation of Catalan with preverbal n-word

Meaning	Form	MaxNeg	NegFirst	MaxSN <	> *Neg	IntNeg
$\neg\exists x_1 \lor \exists x_2$ ☞	neg V neg			*	**	
☞	neg SN V neg				***	

The difference between preverbal and postverbal n-words is accounted for by the high ranking of NegFirst. However, Catalan is not a full type III language, because MaxSN is not ranked (strictly) below *Neg. It shares features with type I languages in allowing rankings in which MaxSN wins over *Neg. Thus a marker of sentential negation optionally shows up in outputs for the expression of preverbal n-words. As far as interpretation is concerned, we predict that the presence or absence of a marker of sentential negation is irrelevant. As long as *Neg is ranked above IntNeg, all negative meanings will be collapsed into a single negation. As pointed out by Vallduví (1994), the optionality of a preverbal marker of sentential negation in combination with a preverbal n-word does not have a semantic effect.

Haspelmath (1997, 211, 213) observes that the pattern we find in Catalan is also found in Old Church Slavonic and in several (mostly African American) dialects of English. Haspelmath quotes the following examples from Labov (1972, 785–6):

(21) a. *Nobody* don*'t* know where it's at.   African American English

b. *Nobody* fights fair.

We conclude that these are mixed cases of type I and type III languages, which nevertheless represent balanced systems that reflect the interaction of NegFirst and MaxSN.

6. Conclusion

The conclusion I draw from this investigation of the marking and interpretation of negation is that a bidirectional version of Optimality Theory offers new perspectives on the range of variation we find in natural language for the expression and meaning of negation and negative indefinites. Patterns that are found frequently in natural language but that are not absolute can be fruitfully described in a framework that allows constraints to be violable. The bidirectionality is especially important to our analysis, because it relates the semantic compositionality problems raised by negative concord to the functional tendencies to formally mark the scope and focus of negation, in accordance with the view on compositionality advanced by Blutner (2000), and Blutner, Hendriks, and de Hoop (2003). Our OT analysis confirms the insight from de Swart and Sag (2002) that the position and distribution of the marker of sentential negation in negative concord are relevant for syntax but do not affect the semantics. ∎

ACKNOWLEDGMENTS
Many thanks for helpful comments and feedback from audiences at Utrecht University, Radboud University, the University of Amsterdam, Georgetown University, the University of California at Santa Cruz, Hopkins University, and the University of Leuven, and from the editors of this volume. All remaining errors are of course my own. The financial support of the Netherlands Organization for Scientific Research (grant 051-02-070 for the cognition project "Conflicts in Interpretation") is hereby gratefully acknowledged.

NOTES

1. This observation holds modulo the observations about inverse scope made by de Swart (1998).

2. Obviously, this criterion is applicable only in languages that do not require the presence of a marker of sentential negation in all negative sentences. In such languages (labeled class I languages in section 5 below), this criterion is not falsified but cannot be tested.

REFERENCES

Bernini, G., and P. Ramat. 1996. *Negative sentences in the languages of Europe.* Berlin: Mouton de Gruyter.

Besten, J. den. 1986. Double negation and the genesis of Afrikaans. In *Substrata versus universals in Creole languages,* ed. P. Muysken and N. Smith, 185–230. Amsterdam: John Benjamins.

Blutner, R. 2000. Some aspects of optimality in natural language interpretation. *Journal of Semantics* 17: 189–216.

Blutner, R., P. Hendriks, and H. de Hoop. 2003. A new hypothesis on compositionality. *Proceedings of the Joint International Conference on Cognitive Science,* ed. P. Slezak, 53–57. Sidney, Australia: ICCS/ASCS.

Boersma P. 1998. Functional phonology. PhD diss., University of Amsterdam.

Boersma, P., and B. Hayes. 2001. Empirical tests of the gradual learning algorithm. *Linguistic Inquiry* 32: 45–86.

Corblin, F. 1996. Multiple negation processing in natural language. *Theoria* 17: 214–59.

Corblin, F., and L. Tovena. 2003. L'expression de la négation dans les languages romanes. In *Les langues romanes: problème de la phrase simple,* ed. D. Godard, 279–342. Paris: CNRS Editions.

Corblin, F., V. Déprez, H. de Swart, and L. Tovena. 2004. Negative concord. In *Handbook of French semantics,* ed. F. Corblin and H. de Swart, 417–52. Stanford, CA: CSLI.

Dahl, Ö. 1979. Typology of sentence negation. *Linguistics* 17: 79–106.

Déprez, V. 1997. Two types of negative concord. *Probus* 9: 104–43.

———. 2000. Parallel (a)symmetries and the internal structure of negative expressions. *Natural Language and Linguistic Theory* 18: 253–342.

de Swart, H. 1998. Licensing of negative polarity items under inverse scope. *Lingua* 105: 175–200.

de Swart, H., and I. Sag. 2002. Negation and negative concord in Romance. *Linguistics and Philosophy* 25: 373–417.

Fauconnier, G. 1975. Pragmatic scales and logical structures. *Linguistic Inquiry* 6: 353–75.

———. 1979. Implication reversal in a natural language. In *Formal semantics and pragmatics for natural languages,* ed. F. Günther and S.J. Schmidt, 289–301. Dordrecht: D. Reidel.

Giannakidou, A. 1998. *Polarity sensitivity as (non)veridical dependency.* Amsterdam: John Benjamins.

———. 2000. Negative . . . concord. *Natural Language and Linguistic Theory* 18: 457–523.

Haspelmath, M. 1997. *Indefinite pronouns.* Oxford: Clarendon Press.

Herburger, E. 2001. The negative concord puzzle revisited. *Natural Language Semantics* 9: 289–333.

Hoeksema, J. 1997. Negation and negative concord in middle Dutch. In *Negation and polarity: Syntax and semantics,* ed. D. Forget, P. Hirschbühler, F. Martineau, and M.-L. Rivero, 139–58. Amsterdam: John Benjamins.

Hoop, H. de. 2004. The problem of unintelligibility. In *The composition of meaning. From lexeme to discourse,* ed. A. ter Meulen and W. Abraham, 69–81. Amsterdam: John Benjamins.

Horn, L. 1989. *A natural history of negation.* Chicago: University of Chicago Press.

Israel, M. 1996. Polarity sensitivity as lexical semantics. *Linguistics and Philosophy* 19: 619–66.

Jespersen, O. [1917/1962. *Negation in English and other languages.* Copenhagen: A.F. Høst. Repr. in: *Selected writings of Otto Jespersen,* 3–151. London: Allen and Unwin.

———. [1933/1964. *Essentials of English grammar.* Repr. Tuscaloosa: University of Alabama Press.

Kadmon, N., and F. Landman. 1993. *Any. Linguistics and Philosophy* 16: 353–422.

Keenan, E., and D. Westerståhl. 1997. Generalized quantifiers in linguistics and logic. In *Handbook of logic and language,* ed. J.van Benthem and A. ter Meulen, 837–93. Amsterdam: Elsevier.

Krifka, M. 1995. The semantics and pragmatics of polarity items. *Linguistic Analysis* 25: 209–57.

Labov, W. 1972. Negative attraction and negative concord in English grammar. *Language* 48: 773–818.

Ladusaw, W. 1979. Polarity sensitivity as inherent scope relations. PhD diss., University of Texas at Austin. Repr., New York: Garland Press, 1980.

———. 1992. Expressing negation. In *Proceedings of SALT 2,* ed. C. Barker and D. Dowty, 237–59. Columbus: Department of Linguistics, The Ohio State University.

———. 1996. Negation and polarity items. In *The handbook of contemporary semantic theory,* ed. Shalom Lappin, 321–41. Oxford: Blackwell.

Manning, C., I. Sag, and M. Iida. 1999. The lexical integrity of Japanese causatives. *Nordic Journal of Linguistics* 21: 107–44.

Payne, J. 1985. Negation. In *Clause structure.*Vol. 1 of *Language typology and syntactic description,* , ed. T. Shopen, 187–242. Cambridge: Cambridge University Press.

Portner, P., and R. Zanuttini. 2003. Exclamative clauses: At the syntax-semantic interface. *Language* 79: 39–81.

Posner, R. 1984. Double negatives, negative polarity and negative incorporation in Romance: a historical and comparative view. *Transactions of the Philological Society* 1984: 1–26.

Tanaka, S. 1994. Die Mehrfachnegation: ein Sprachgut der Unraffinierten? In *Sprache—Sprechen—Handeln: Akten des 28 Linguistischen Kolloquiums, Graz 1993,* ed. D. W. Halwachs and I. Stütz, 191–98. Tübingen: Niemeyer.

Vallduví, E. 1994. Polarity items, n-words and minimizers in Catalan and Spanish. *Probus* 6: 263–94.

Wouden, A. van der. 1997. *Negative contexts: Collocation, polarity and multiple negation.* London: Routledge.

Wouden, A. van der., and F. Zwarts. 1993. A semantic analysis of negative concord. In *Proceedings of SALT* 3, ed. U. Lahiri and A. Z. Wyner, 202–19. Ithaca, NY: CLC Publications, Cornell University.

Zanuttini, R. 1991. Syntactic properties of sentential negation. PhD diss., University of Pennsylvania.

Zeevat, H. 2000. The asymmetry of optimality theoretic syntax and semantics. *Journal of Semantics* 17: 243–62.

Zwarts, F. 1986. Categorial grammatica en algebraïsche semantiek: een studie naar negatie en polariteit in het Nederlands. PhD diss., Groningen University.

Tense and Aspect

9

Cohesion in Temporal Context
Aspectual Adverbs as Dynamic Indexicals

ALICE G. B. TER MEULEN
Center for Language and Cognition, University of Groningen, The Netherlands

1. Introduction

In dynamic semantics of natural language, communicating agents are represented by information states, understood to capture the information they hold at any one time to be true. Communicating information between agents is accordingly analyzed as an algorithmic update procedure adding new information to the given information state of its recipient. The widened perspectives of this research program open up new pathways to integrate issues of information sharing, commonly considered pragmatic in nature, with the more classical concerns of natural language semantics analyzing only truth-functional aspects of meaning and interpretation. Mere consistency of an information state (= truth of all sentences in a model) no longer suffices to properly characterize human communication. Coherence is the more interesting structural notion to be understood as a property of information states and their dynamic relations. The present chapter sketches some novel insights into the relation between the factual descriptive content of aspectual adverbs and their usage indicating the user's subjective attitudes towards the course of events described. It is of increasing importance to understand how supposedly objective content interacts with subjective information dependent on users' attitudes, creating new kinds of informational dependencies and affecting contextually constrained inferences, presuppositions, and entailments. The chapter is intended to contribute to the general question how asserting information differs in its dynamics from presupposed, entailed, or otherwise inferred information a user may also have access to. Studying the way communication situates its users in time may get us one step closer towards a generally desired dynamic logic of indexicals.

The truth-functional, static semantics of aspectual adverbs captures the indexical interaction between reference times, polarity transitions START and END, and their temporal anaphoric dependencies created by the adverbs SINCE and UNTIL (see Smessaert and ter Meulen, 2004). For instance, if John is not yet asleep, this means that John is falling asleep and hence will be asleep later (1a). If r_0 represents the current reference time, it must be temporally included in the event of John not sleeping $sleeping'(e, j, -)$, while a future reference time r_1 represents the polarity transition ending John's not sleeping, when John has fallen asleep. The indexical, context-dependent nature of the temporal adverbs *since* and *until* is captured by relating them to these reference times, binding in effect the first moment after r_0 at which John is asleep and discarding any later times at which he may also fall asleep as irrelevant or not cohesive. Similarly, if John is already asleep, he must have fallen asleep in the past, and been asleep since (1b). The aspectual adverbs *still* and *not anymore* are the obvious logical counterparts to these analyses of *not yet* and *already*, respectively (1c, d). (Argument *y* of the predicate P' interpreting the verb P inside the VP scope at LF is represented by a choice-function f on the subject argument *x*.)

(1) Basic aspectual adverbs

    a. $[_{IP} \text{ x } [_{INFL} \text{ not yet } [_{VP} \lambda \text{ y P (y)}]]] \rightarrow$
        $[r_0, r_1, e, x, f \mid P'(e, x, f(x), -) \, \& \, e \supseteq r_0 \, \&$
        $r_1 \supseteq \text{END} (P'(e, x, f(x), -)) \, \& \, r_0 < r_1 \, \& \text{UNTIL}(r_1, (P'(e, x, f(x), -))) \supseteq r_0]$

    b. $[_{IP} \text{ x } [_{INFL} \text{ already } [_{VP} \lambda \text{ y P (y)}]]] \rightarrow$
        $[r_0, r_1, e, x, f \mid P'(e, x, f(x), +) \, \& \, e \supseteq r_0 \, \&$
        $r_1 \supseteq \text{START}(P'(e, x, f(x), +)) \, \& \, r_1 < r_0 \, \& \text{SINCE}(r_1, (P'(e, x, f(x), +))) \supseteq r_0]$

    c. $[_{IP} \text{ x } [_{INFL} \text{ still } [_{VP} \lambda \text{ y P (y)}]]] \rightarrow$
        $[r_0, r_1, e, x, f \mid P'(e, x, f(x), +) \, \& \, e \supseteq r_0 \, \&$
        $r_1 \supseteq \text{END} (P'(e, x, f(x), +)) \, \& \, r_0 < r_1 \, \&$
        $\text{UNTIL}(r_1, (P'(e, x, f(x), +))) \supseteq r_0]$

    d. $[_{IP} \text{ x } [_{INFL} \text{ not } [_{VP} \lambda \text{ y P (y)}] \text{ anymore}]] \rightarrow$
        $[r_0, r_1, e, x, f \mid P'(e, x, f(x), -) \, \& \, e \supseteq r_0 \, \&$
        $r_1 \supseteq \text{START} (P'(e, x, f(x), -)) \, \& \, r_1 < r_0 \, \&$
        $\text{SINCE}(r_1, (P'(e, x, f(x), -))) \supseteq r_0]$

These four basic aspectual adverbs constitute a logical polarity square in the temporal domain of events. Limitations of space prevent me from discussing other accounts of the semantics of aspectual adverbs in the literature in requisite detail here. The interested reader is referred to Smessaert and ter Meulen (2004) for our arguments in support of this account and our rebuttal of different analyses.

In English, aspectual adverbs may be effectively used to express not only factual information about the onset of an event or its termination, but, if uttered with marked prosody, they also convey the speaker's attitude regarding the flow of events or its perceived speed. Other languages may express this mix of factual and subjective information differently with aspectual verbs, using, for instance, lexical composition (Dutch) or word order variation (German). A host of interesting crosslinguistic issues must be addressed in studying the expressive variability of such mixed temporal information, but this chapter is limited to very simple cases of English aspectual adverbs. If a speaker feels annoyed or surprised that something is not yet the case, he or she may of course describe his or her emotive attitude explicitly stating in a full clause that he or she is annoyed, surprised, or whatever at its not yet being the case. But in English, such emotive attitudes may be very effectively marked with high pitch prosody on the aspectual adverbs. Though the basic externally negated aspectual adverb *not yet* may accept certain marked prosody other than high pitch, its logically equivalent counterpart with internal negation *still not* readily accepts marked high pitch, here simply indicated with uppercase letters as *STILL not.* Pitch marking of expressions is well known in studies on focus and information structure, where it serves to demarcate given and new information. Along similar lines, the informational purpose of pitch marking aspectual adverbs is to present the subjective content as new, relegating all other supposedly factive information to the background as topic, as if it were already common ground and familiar, hence not at issue in the communication. Speakers use pitch-marked *STILL not* when they had expected for one reason or another the topical event to have started earlier and wish to express their dismay or surprise at it not yet being the case. For instance, if I say that John is STILL not asleep, I must counterfactually have expected John to be asleep by now, hence to have started sleeping or to have fallen asleep in the past. To capture this counterfactual expectation of the speaker in terms of truth-functional operators, the new modal/temporal operator CON quantifies over all possible CONtinuations of the course of events at the given current reference time r_0 relative to the speaker (*sp*). In (2a), all possible endpoints r_1 of the continuing current ($e \supseteq r_0$) negative phase of the P-event ($P'(e, x, f(x), -)$) would be past ($r_1 < r_0$) instead of future ($r_0 < r_1$), relative to the speaker's ALTernative course of events. Similarly, if speakers pitch mark *alREADY*, they indicate that the onset of the current positive phase of P took place earlier than they had expected. Again, the pitch-marked version *STILL* is a polar counterpart to *STILL not,* and *no LONGER* lexicalizes the pitch-marked version of *not anymore* in (2). The analysis is more fully explained in ter Meulen (2000), with some minor differences in the formal details.

(2) Pitch-marked aspectual adverbs

    a. $[_{IP}$ x $[_{INFL}$ *STILL not* $[_{VP}$ λ y P (y)]]] →
        $[r_0,$ e, x, f, **sp** | $P'(e, x, f(x), -)$ & $e \supseteq r_0$ &
        CON(sp, r_0, $[\mathbf{r_1}|$ $r_1 \supseteq$ END ($P'(e, x, f(x), -)$) & $r_0 < r_1$
        & UNTIL(r_1, $P'(e, x, f(x), -))$ $\supseteq r_0]$
        → **ALT**(sp, r_0, $[- |$ $r_1 < r_0$ & SINCE(r_1, $P'(e, x, f(x), +))$ $\supseteq r_0]$))]

    b. $[_{IP}$ x $[_{INFL}$ *alREADY* $[_{VP}$ λ y P (y)]]] →
        $[r_0, \mathbf{r_1}$, e, x, f, **sp** | $P'(e, x, f(x), +)$ & $e \supseteq r_0$ &
        $r_1 \supseteq$ START ($P'(e, x, f(x), +))$ & $r_1 < r_0$ &
        SINCE(r_1, $P'(e, x, f(x), +))$ $\supseteq r_0$ &
        ALT(sp, r_0, $[- |$ $r_0 < r_1$ & UNTIL(r_1, $P'(e, x, f(x), -))$ $\supseteq r_0]$)]

    c. $[_{IP}$ x $[_{INFL}$ *STILL* $[_{VP}$ λ y P (y)]]] →
        $[r_0,$ e, x, f, **sp** | $P'(e, x, f(x), +)$ & $e \supseteq r_0$ &
        CON(sp, r_0, $[\mathbf{r_1}|$ $r_1 \supseteq$ END($P'(e, x, f(x), +))$ &
        $r_0 < r_1$ & UNTIL(r_1, $P'(e, x, f(x), +))$ $\supseteq r_0]$
        → **ALT**(sp, r_0, $[- |$ $r_1 < r_0$ & SINCE(r_1, $P'(e, x, f(x), -))$ $\supseteq r_0]$))]

    d. $[_{IP}$ x $[_{INFL}$ *no LONGER* $[_{VP}$ λ y P (y)]]] →
        $[r_0, \mathbf{r_1}$, e, x, f, **sp** | $P'(e, x, f(x), -)$ & $e \supseteq r_0$ &
        $r_1 \supseteq$ START ($P'(e, x, f(x), -))$ & $r_1 < r_0$ &
        SINCE(r_1, $P'(e, x, f(x), -))$ $\supseteq r_0$ &
        ALT(sp, r_0, $[- |$ $r_0 < r_1$ & UNTIL(r_1, $P'(e, x, f(x), +)))$ $\supseteq r_0]$)]

Assuming this static semantics of aspectual adverbs in (1) and the additional information their pitch marked variants express in (2), the remainder of this chapter is
concerned with applications of their semantic properties in question-answer dialogue
and the constraints they induce on the accommodation of presupposed information in
a given context. The chapter concludes with a discussion of the notion of logical consequence in a dynamic logic with structured information states, arguing that only
states described by perfect tense clauses with locally consistent presuppositions may
always be coherently asserted in context, since they lack the dynamic power to affect
context change. Different contexts impose assertability constraints associated with
simple past tense clauses referring to events. Asserting information that is already
presupposed, entailed, or otherwise part of the common ground is also considered
much more constrained, if preservation of coherence is required. Sharing information must be represented by an onion-layered common ground with constraints on
how deep down into the different layers speakers may have access to revise their
information.

2. Aspectual Adverbs in Dialogue

Proper or felicitous answers to polarity questions with aspectual adverbs must of
course share the presuppositions of the question, as in (3a, b). If the presuppositions
of the questioner A are not acceptable to the answerer B, B must use another, stronger form of negation, that is, denial (3d), to cancel A's presuppositions. In (3a, b) *still*
and *no longer* share the presupposed information that John was asleep before Mary
arrived, not shared by *already* in (3c), and cancelled with *not yet* in (3d). The questioner A requests an update from B about the temporal relation between the endpoint
of John's sleeping and Mary's arrival, positively suggesting John woke up after
Mary's arrival.

(3) a. A: Was John *still* asleep when Mary arrived?

   b. B: No, he was *not* asleep *anymore.*

   c. B: *No, he was *already* asleep.

   d. B: No, he had *not* (even) fallen asleep *yet.*

It should be evident from the relative incoherence of (3a + 3c) that temporal presuppositions of polarity questions cannot simply be canceled by asserting an answer
with partially conflicting presuppositions. A's question (3a) asks B to supply only information about the temporal relation between the two reference times it introduces,
that is, $(r_1 < r_2 \vee r_2 < r_1)$, as indicated in bold face below in (4a). The remaining content of (3a) must be considered common ground, that is, information A assumes is already shared by A and B. The aspectual adverb *still* in (3a) partitions the content of
A's question into very narrow interrogative focus information $?(r_1 < r_2 \vee r_2 < r_1)$, relegating all remaining content to background information, with which A supposes B
to agree already. The questioned focus information is indicated in (4) with $?(r_1 < r_2 \vee
r_2 < r_1)$, informally meaning that the truth value of $(r_1 < r_2)$ or $(r_2 < r_1)$ is requested in
all situations which support the information in the common ground, constituting the

antecedent. The formal semantics of conditionals with background information as antecedent and questioned content as consequent needs to be explicated, but this would lead us much beyond the intended scope of the present chapter.[1] In Situation Semantics, questions could simply be implemented with a parameter for the polarity in the event type to be resolved into true or false by an update with the answer. Whatever precise form the dynamic semantics of interrogatives may take, the insight should be implemented that presuppositions and background information constitute constraints on the situations or worlds that must be satisfied before the focus information is evaluated. Clearly, updating a context with the asserted content requires a more constrained accommodation procedure of its presuppositions than has customarily been adopted.

(4) a. A: $[_{IP}$ John $[_{INFL}$ *still* $[_{VP}$ sleep (j)$]$ $[_{ADVP}$ when M. arrived$]]]] \rightarrow$
$[r_0, r_1, r_2, e, j, m \mid sleep'(e, j, +) \& e \supseteq r_0 \&$
$r_1 \supseteq$ END $(sleep'(e, x, +)) \& r_0 < r_1$ &UNTIL$(r_1, (sleep'(e, x, +))) \supseteq r_0 \&$
$r_2 \supseteq arrive'(m) \rightarrow ?(\mathbf{r_1} < \mathbf{r_2} \mathbf{v} \mathbf{r_2} < \mathbf{r_1})]$

In negatively answering (3a) with (3b), B updates A's information state only by asserting as new information that $r_1 < r_2$, that is, that Mary arrived after John had woken up. Subsequently, A revises his information state by eliminating the other option he held to be possibly true, namely, $r_2 < r_1$. To cancel A's presuppositions by answering with (3d, 4b), B systematically resets the positive polarity parameter in the presupposed information of (3a, 4a), restructuring its content as if its presuppositions were asserted information and relegating the information that Mary arrived to shared information in the common ground, thereby identifying its reference time r_2 with the given reference time r_0. Accordingly, B's answering with (3d, 4b) constitutes a refusal to make the temporal relation between r_1 and r_2 the issue under consideration.

(4) b. B: $[_{IP}$ John $[_{INFL}$ *not yet* $[_{VP}$ sleep'(j)$]]] \rightarrow$
$[r_0, r_1, r_2, e, j, \mid sleep'(e, j, -) \& e \supseteq r_0 \&$
$r_1 \supseteq$ END $(sleep'(e, j, -)) \& r_0 < r_1$ &UNTIL$(r_1, (sleep'(e, j, -))) \supseteq r_0 \&$
$r_2 \supseteq arrive'(m) \& r_0 = r_2]$

The incohesive answer in (3c, 4c) creates havoc with the background/interrogative focus partitioning induced by A's use of *still*.

(4) c. $[_{IP}$ John $[_{INFL}$ *already* $[_{VP}$ sleep (j)$]]] \rightarrow$
$[r_0, r_1, e, j \mid sleep'(e, x, +) \& e \supseteq r_0 \&$
$r_1 \supseteq$ START$(sleep'(e, x, +)) \& r_1 < r_0$ &SINCE$(r_1, (sleep'(e, x, +))) \supseteq r_0]$

In (3c, 4c), B informs A that A is right on only some presupposed information, that is, that John was asleep at the given reference time r_0, *sleep' (e, x, +) & e $\supseteq r_0$*, but B also indicates that A was wrong in questioning the end point of *e*. B corrects A by adding information about the past starting point of event *e*, that is, John's falling asleep. A had not intended to make an issue of the temporal relations of the starting point, although A obviously also secondarily presupposed it. Such secondary presuppositions of presuppositions cannot be canceled by asserting (3c, 4c), since B's correction of A's presuppositions creates incoherence in the context. If secondary presuppositions must be addressed, they must be brought to the foreground by restructuring the relevant information in the common ground using other, more direct communicative means.

Characteristically, English aspectual adverbs may also be used interrogatively in dialogue with marked prosody, in B's reaction to A's assertion describing a current factual state. In (5b) the questioner B seeks A's agreement with B's subjective assessment of the timing of what A described as the factual course of events.

(5) a. A: John is sleeping,

    b. B: alREADY?

    c. B: STILL?

In (5a + 5b), B conditionally accepts A's assertion into the common ground and solicits A's agreement with B's subjective perception that John was early to fall asleep. In uttering (5b), B wants A to agree with B's first envisaged, but now counterfactual, view that John should have been awake at the current reference time. In responding with the question (5c), B wants A to share B's view that John is late to wake up. To develop the dynamic semantics of this interrogative usage of aspectual adverbs in discourse would take us much beyond the present chapter, but in outline, it should be quite clear already. Pitch-marked aspectual adverbs apparently manage to do a lot of dynamic work in (re)structuring factual and subjective information states to partition the common ground and new information extremely effectively.

3. Coherence and Constraints on Accommodation

If (6a) is assumed to constitute a coherent continuous monologue, the presupposition (*John fell asleep*) of the first clause (*John was already asleep*) cannot apparently be felicitously asserted in a subsequent simple past tense sentence, even though the information it contains must either already be part of the common ground or introduce a new, later reference time at which John fell asleep again. (See Beaver 1997 for a review of different systems of presupposition and accommodation in dynamic semantics. My claims will be neutral as to which system is adopted.) Analogously, in (6b), asserting first that John was no longer asleep prevents the speaker from coherently asserting again what has already been presupposed. It is not straightforwardly possible to interpret (6b) as describing two distinct episodes of John's sleeping, separated by a period of his being awake, unless either the presuppositional adverb *again* is used to make the disjoint temporal reference explicit or the monologue itself is temporally discontinuous.

(6) a. ?*John was already asleep. John fell asleep.

    b. ?*John was no longer asleep. John was asleep.

What information may be accommodated or asserted is apparently constrained by aspectual adverbs, as (6a) could not be interpreted to mean that John was asleep twice, coercing accommodation of the presuppositions of the second clause. Cohesion of the discourse in (6a, b) is easily restored by explicitly asserting a polarity reversal (*he woke up*/*he fell asleep*) to shift to a new reference time in (7a, b). Only such asserted information can coerce disjoint temporal reference of the clauses to ensure that the second clause no longer constitutes the presupposition of the first clause but describes a new, later event of the same event type.

(7) a. John was already asleep. He woke up and fell asleep (again).

    b. John was no longer asleep. He fell asleep (again). He was asleep.

The presuppositions of adverbs like *again* serve to coerce such temporal disjoint reference, but their dynamic force is not sufficient to restore cohesion when added to (6a) or (6b). In the perfect clause (8), which describes the state resulting from the corresponding event, *again* takes widest scope to introduce two events of the same type, that is, John falling asleep, where the current reference time is included in the state resulting from the later event. The aspectual adverb *already* in (8) indicates that this second event occurred earlier than expected. In English, aspectual adverbs are odd, if not downright unacceptable, with *again* in the lexically stative clauses (9) and (10). In the richer adverbial structure of Dutch, the morphologically complex *alweer* 'already-again' is perfectly acceptable in either the aspectually stative perfect clause (8), the lexically stative (9), and even in the composition of aspectual adverbs with *again* in (10).

(8) E: John has already fallen asleep again.

    D: Jan is alweer   in slaap gevallen

    J.   is already-again in sleep fallen-PERF PART

(9) E: ??John is already asleep again.

    D: Jan slaapt alweer.

    J.   sleeps already-again

(10) E: *?John is {again no longer asleep/no longer asleep again}.

    D: Jan slaapt (al)weer   niet meer.

    J.   sleeps (already) again no more.

Assuming an overall constraint of local coherence of contexts, updating the common ground by presupposition accommodation must hence be sharply distinguished from updating it by asserting information. Asserting information that is already entailed or presupposed by the immediately preceding clause creates temporal incoherence. In other words, updating with asserted information is only possible when the information to be added is genuinely new. Accordingly, coercion by context shift is not a realistic strategy in natural language semantics to ensure that updating with asserted information remains always possible.

4. Logical Consequence in Dynamic Semantics

The classical notion of logical consequence in Discourse Representation Theory (DRT) in (11) explains why dynamic temporal presuppositions cannot be asserted at the reference time of the subsequent state, even though they are entailed, as logical entailments may never introduce new reference times (see Kamp and Reyle 1993; van Eijck and Kamp 1997 provide good introductions to DRT).

(11) DRT definition of logical consequence

> Let K, K′ be pure . . . Discourse Representation Structures (DRSs). K′ is a logical consequence of K (K |= K′) iff. the following condition holds: Suppose M is a model and f is a function from $U_K \cup \text{Fr}(K) \cup \text{Fr}(K')$ into U_M, s.t. $M |=_f K$, then there is a function $g \supseteq U_{K'}$ f such that $M |=_g K'$. (Kamp and Reyle 1993, 305)

When an event is described again in a later context, one may always do so using static perfect tense clauses in a continuous, coherent monologue, for perfect tense clauses are immune to shifting the reference time, as in (12a, b). The perfect state that results once an event terminates endures forever after, and describing it will never affect the reference time. For instance, that John had fallen asleep remains true not only during John's sleep but also at any arbitrarily distant moment after he woke up. The semantics of the past perfect requires merely that the event causing the perfect state must precede the speech time as well as the contextually determined reference time. Hence in (12a) the second past perfect clause *he had fallen asleep* entails the existence of an arbitrary past event of John's falling asleep. To understand (12a) as cohesive discourse, that arbitrary event is identified as the onset of the state described by the first simple past tense clause *John was already asleep,* and it is claimed by the speaker to have occurred early. Logically, the first clause entails the second one, but the second only entails the existence of some prior event of falling asleep.

(12) a. John was already asleep. He had fallen asleep.

　　 b. John was no longer asleep. He had been asleep.

Preserving coherence, the assertability constraints associated with states described by perfect tense clauses must be distinguished from those associated with states described by simple past tense clauses. Only the perfect tense clauses may always coherently be asserted regardless of the common ground, even when their content is already logically entailed.

This outline of the dynamic semantics of tense, aspect, and aspectual adverbs and its associated, classical notion of logical consequence still needs to be supplemented with a module containing natural deduction-style inference rules to reason with DRSs. The inference rule "PERF introduction" should characterize which transformations of contexts updated by past tense clauses are required to report their content using past perfect tense (see ter Meulen 1995, 2000). In this natural deduction system for DRT, validity of temporal reasoning may be characterized without having to appeal to slippery notions such as a "normal" course of events, to rhetorical relations, or to common sense about what the world is like or any understanding of causality.[2] ■

APPENDIX

Two operators, CON and ALT, have been used in the chapter; their semantics is as follows:

■ Given a model *M,* and DRS *K,* and an assignment *f* such that *f(sp)* = speaker of M and *f(r₀)* is the current reference time in M, then *f(CON (sp, r₀, K))* is true in M iff. the speaker envisages r_0 to change into a state at which all conditions of K are verified by any extension of *f.*

■ Given a model M, and DRS K, and an assignment f such that $f(sp)$ = speaker of M and $f(r_0)$ is the current reference time in M, then $f(ALT\ (sp,\ r_0,\ K))$ is true in M iff. the speaker had assumed the conditions in K to be verified by any extension of f, over the conditions f actually does verify.

NOTES

1. See Lascarides and Asher (1998) for an excellent exposition of various dynamic semantics of questions in dialogue. Their Structured Discourse Representation Theory (SDRT) account would fit well with my analysis.

2. Lascarides and Asher (1993) argues for the need of rhetoric relations and default inference in accounting for temporal anaphora. The Dynamic Aspect Tree (DAT) representation of ter Meulen (1995, 2000) allows stative information to spread to other nodes, modeling to a certain extent the preservation of information in context change, avoiding usage of a special notion of inference dependent upon normal worlds.

REFERENCES

Beaver, D. 1997. Presupposition. In *Handbook of logic and language,* ed. J. van Benthem and A. ter Meulen, 939–1008. Amsterdam: Elsevier; Cambridge, MA: MIT Press.

Kamp, H., and U. Reyle. 1993. *From discourse to logic.* Dordrecht: Kluwer.

Lascarides, A., and N. Asher. 1993. Temporal interpretation, discourse relations and commonsense entailment. *Linguistics and Philosophy* 16 (5): 437–93.

———. 1998. Questions in Dialogue. *Linguistics and Philosophy* 21: 237–309.

———. 2000. Chronoscopes: The dynamic representation of facts and events. In *Speaking about events,* ed. J. Higginbotham, F. Pianesi, and A. C. Varzi, 151–68. Oxford: Oxford University Press.

Smessaert, H., and A. ter Meulen. 2004. Dynamic reasoning with aspectual adverbs. *Linguistics and Philosophy* 27 (2): 209–61.

ter Meulen, A. 1995. *Representing time in natural language. The dynamic interpretation of tense and aspect.* Cambridge, MA: MIT Press.

van Benthem, J., and A. ter Meulen, eds. 1997. *Handbook of logic and language.* Amsterdam: Elsevier; Cambridge, MA: MIT Press.

van Eijck, J., and H. Kamp. 1997. Representing discourse in context. In *Handbook of logic and language,* ed. J. van Benthem and A. ter Meulen, 179–237. Amsterdam: Elsevier; Cambridge, MA: MIT Press.

10

▪ Tense, Adverbials, and Quantification

TOSHIYUKI OGIHARA
University of Washington

1. Introduction

This chapter addresses the issue of how to account for the interaction of tense morphemes and temporal PPs (henceforth, tPPs) in a compositional manner. The main focus of the chapter is the behavior of quantified tPPs such as *during every meeting, on a Sunday*. This is a response to Pratt and Francez (2001) and von Stechow (2002), who are both concerned with the same issue. I will contend that past tense sentences like (1a) contain a covert adverbial (e.g., *on Monday last week, in the past*) that restricts the extension of the temporal noun *meeting* to a past interval. That is, when (1a) is interpreted at LF, it looks like (1b). This guarantees that the meetings in question are restricted to past meetings. I shall argue that this account is preferable to an alternative according to which tense directly restricts the meeting times.

> (1) a. John kissed Mary during every meeting.
>
> b. John kissed Mary during every meeting in the past.

I will also show that in order to account for the behavior of quantified tPPs, it is not sufficient to assume that the denotation of each common noun is restricted by the context. At first sight, it appears that we can simply assume that the inherent restriction upon the denotation of each noun accounts for the semantics of (1a). For example, the noun *student* in (2) is understood to mean the set of students under discussion and not the set of all students in the world. Similarly, it seems natural to assume that the noun *meeting* in (1a) denotes the set of meetings under discussion (i.e., those that occurred within a particular past interval), not the set of all meetings with no contextual restriction. We can then say that the meetings in question must be past meetings because the sentence would be necessarily false otherwise.

> (2) Every student passed the exam.

Despite the initial plausibility of this hypothesis, it turns out that it is not tenable. This point will be elaborated later in the chapter. With this rough outline in mind, let us start with some fundamental issues having to do with tense and adverbials.

What is the source of the existential quantification over past times in a declarative sentence in the past tense? Is it the past tense morpheme, an (overt or covert) adverbial, or some other independently available mechanism? The traditional view, due to Prior (1967), is that the source is the past tense morpheme. The sentence in (3a) is rendered as in (3b) in Prior's tense logic. In tense logic, a predicate only has nominal arguments, and there are no temporal arguments or predicates. The interpretation in (3c), on the other hand, is expressed in a different logical language that explicitly represents existential quantification over times. That is, temporal variables and constants are used overtly in this system.

(3) a. John graduated from Harvard.[1]

b. P [graduates_from_Harvard(j)]

c. $\exists t$ [t < now $\wedge$ graduates_from_Harvard(j, t)]

With appropriate interpretations of the predicates used in (3b) and (3c), we can make sure that (3b) and (3c) are semantically equivalent. But it has been shown by Dowty (1979) and others that the system used in (3c) is preferred over the one used in (3b). For example, natural language has constants that refer to intervals (or instants) such as *2004* (the name of the year), *January, today,* and so forth. Temporal quantifiers abound (e.g., *always, often, sometimes, every time*). Although it is not impossible to use systems in which quantification is represented in the metalanguage, it is more convenient for us to adopt a system that yields formulas like (3c) because essential temporal meanings can be read off logical formulas. I thus adopt a system yields formulas like (3c).

Prior's logical system for tense has been challenged by many researchers. By citing the famous stove example in (4a), Partee (1973) claims that tense is more like a free pronoun than an existential quantifier. The scenario assumed here is that (4a) is uttered when the speaker is driving on the freeway after leaving the house without turning off the stove.

(4) a. I didn't turn off the stove.

b. $\exists t$ [t < now $\wedge \neg$ I turn off the stove at t]

c. $\neg \exists t$ [t < now $\wedge$ I turn off the stove at t]

d. t_R < now $\wedge \neg$ I turn off the stove at t_R (t_R = reference time)

According to Partee, (4a) should be rendered as (4d) rather than as (4b) or (4c). The variable t_R here represents what can be referred to as a reference time (due to Reichenbach 1947)—a contextually salient time. The idea is that in (4a) the tense morpheme behaves like a free pronoun that refers to a contextually salient past time. Interpretation (4d) says that a particular contextually salient time indicated by t_R lies before now and that the speaker fails to turn off the stove at t_R. The past-tense morpheme is like a free variable in that its denotation is recovered from the context. In this case, it refers to the time when the stove should have been turned off.

English has adverbials like *then* and *right at that moment* that appear to refer to moments. When such adverbials are used as in (5a, b), it seems that positing an existential quantifier for the tense is counterintuitive or at least redundant. This supports Partee's (1973) argument.

(5) a. John arrived at the room then.

b. Right at that moment, the bell rang.

On the other hand, most declarative sentences in the past tense appear to involve existential quantification. As shown by Ogihara (1996), past tense sentences in general must involve existential quantification over times even if a particular salient past interval is involved in determining their interpretation.[2] Consider (6).

> (6) John: Did you eat lunch?
>
> Bill: Yes, I did.

Bill's answer in (6) is taken to mean that he ate lunch *within* some salient past interval, say the lunch hour (12:00–1:00). It is certainly not required for him to use up all of his lunch hour to eat his lunch. He could have eaten a sandwich in ten minutes within this period and still utter the sentence truthfully. This means that an existential quantifier is necessary in order to represent the right semantic content of Bill's utterance, as in (7).

> (7) $\exists t\ [t < now\ \&\ t \subseteq t_R\ \&\ Bill\ eats\ lunch\ at\ t]$

Some comments are in order here. Even if we accept the contention that Bill's utterance in (6) requires existential quantification over past times, this does not necessarily mean that an existential is part of the lexical meaning of the past tense morpheme. The following alternative accounts come to mind: (i) adopt a default truth definition that introduces an existential quantifier (Stump 1985) or an embedding function as in Discourse Representation Theory (DRT; Kamp and Reyle 1993), or (ii) change the semantic interpretation of a temporal term used in a time-sensitive predicate, as in (8).

> (8) a. When interpreting a time-sensitive predicate (e.g., verbs, adjectives, common nouns), the semantic contribution of its temporal argument is understood in such a way that whatever is being described holds within the time in question rather than at that time.
>
> b. $[\![eats\_lunch(John,\ t)]\!]^g = 1$

According to (8a), (8b) holds just in case an event of John's eating lunch takes place *within* $g(t)$ (where g is an assignment). This interpretation has an implicit existential quantifier, though this is not obvious from the formula. Partee (1984) acknowledges that an existential quantifier reading is required with most past tense sentences, which I believe is the most empirically accurate position regarding the semantics of tense.

2. Some Scope-Related Issues

From the discussion in section 1, it seems fair to say that most English declarative sentences in the past tense semantically require existential quantification over past times, though the quantificational force is often restricted by overt or covert adverbials. Assuming for the sake of argument that a past tense sentence involves existential quantification, we still need to determine what is responsible for it. Bäuerle and von Stechow (1980) show that having two existential quantifiers (one contributed by the tense morpheme, the other by the adverbial) in the interpretation of a single clause would yield the wrong semantic result. For example, consider (9a) and (9b). If (9b) is taken to mean (10a), then it is never true because as soon as there is at least one relevant hitting event, there are an infinite number of times that contain this event. In other words, the truth condition stated in (10a) is never satisfied. On the other hand, assuming that (9b) means (10b) is also problematic. If (10b) is satisfied, then (10c) is also satisfied. This would mean that (9b) entails (9a), which is clearly undesirable.

(9) a. John hit the target exactly twice.

   b. John hit the target exactly three times.

(10) a. There are exactly three times $t <$ now such that there is a time t' within t such that John hits the target at t'.

   b. There is a time $t <$ now such that there are exactly three times t' within t & John hits the target at t'.

   c. There is a time $t <$ now such that there are exactly two times t' within t & John hits the target at t'.

One could perhaps correct the first problem by stipulating that the three times must be nonoverlapping. But that would still not be good enough, because each nonoverlapping interval could contain more than one event of John's hitting the target. Thus, the prediction is that (9b) is true when John hits the target more than three times. In this way, Bäuerle and von Stechow (1980) conclude that an existential quantifier is not contributed by a tense morpheme or a default truth definition. Rather an existential is contributed by an overt or covert adverbial. When there is no overt frequency adverbial, a covert adverbial meaning *at least once* yields an existential quantifier meaning.

Dowty (1979) independently arrived at approximately the same conclusion. Dowty discusses examples like (11a). In Dowty's system, (11a) translates as in (11b).[3]

(11) a. John cried yesterday.

   b. $\exists t$ [t $<$ now $\land$ John cries at t $\land$ t $\subseteq$ yesterday]

Dowty's (1979) proposal has it that a tense and an adverbial are introduced simultaneously. The resulting translation contains an existential quantifier over times. This appears to represent the idea that a tense and an adverbial jointly introduce an existential, which is possible in a system like Dowty's. Dowty's proposal accommodates sentences in which frequency adverbials like *exactly twice* or *exactly three times* occur. That is, we can maintain that *exactly twice* denotes either (12a) or (12b). Roughly put, (12a) corresponds to "past . . . exactly twice", and (12b) to "future . . . exactly twice." Just as *today* is three ways ambiguous in Dowty's proposal, *exactly twice* is at least two ways ambiguous between (12a) and (12b).

(12) a. $\lambda P_t \exists_{2!} t$ [t $<$ now $\land P_t(t)$]

   b. $\lambda P_t \exists_{2!} t$ [now $< t \land P_t(t)$]

   Note: $\exists_{2!} t$ reads "there are exactly two distinct times t such that . . ." P_t is a variable for predicate of times.

Since Dowty introduces an adverbial and tense simultaneously in the syntax, he does not have to commit himself to the source of the existential quantifier. However, Dowty's proposal suffers from the general problem of not being able to have multiple temporal adverbials. Therefore, sentences like (13) are problematic for him.

(13) John coughed exactly three times yesterday.

Stump's (1985) proposal enables us to introduce multiple adverbials in a sentence, which solves the problem with Dowty's proposal. In Stump's proposal, existential quantifiers are not introduced by adverbials or tense morphemes. Stump posits a rule for existential closure, which introduces an existential quantifier at the top level after all adverbials have been processed. Stump's proposal still does not account for examples like (13). This is because if *exactly three times* is an existential quantifier, which we assume it is, we end up with two existentials. Stump's proposal may be rescued, however, by adopting the idea that frequency adverbials like *exactly three times* are not quantifiers. It may be a modifier of event predicates as suggested by Krifka (1989).

Let us now turn to yet another controversial scope-related issue associated with tense and adverbials. This issue, which was discussed by Ogihara (1994), concerns quantificational temporal prepositional phrases (tPPs) such as *during every meeting* and is very important for the purpose of this chapter. For example, in (14a), if *every Sunday* has maximal scope, and the past tense is understood to involve existential quantification over past times (or events), then we get the wrong interpretation. That is, (14a) is understood to mean (14b), which gives us the wrong interpretation because no future Sunday contains past times. How is this wrong reading obtained compositionally? We first of all assume that *every Sunday* means 'on (i.e., within) every Sunday' and that the invisible preposition *on* justifies the part-of relation. If we adopt Bäuerle and von Stechow's (1980) position that each sentence involves a covert or overt frequency adverbial (an existential one, that is), then we could say that (14a) actually contains a covert adverbial that means *at least once,* which occurs overtly in (14c). If we furthermore assume that *every Sunday* is scoped over *at least once,* then (14a) is interpreted to mean (14b). On the other hand, letting *at least once* and the essential meaning of past tense (i.e., $t < now$) have scope over *every Sunday* would not provide us with the right result, as shown in (14d). The interpretation in (14d) means that there is a past time t which every Sunday contains and at which John cries, which is clearly the wrong reading.

(14) a. John cried every Sunday.

 b. $\forall x[\text{Sunday}(x) \rightarrow \exists t\ [t < now \wedge t \subseteq \text{TIME}(x) \wedge \text{John cries at } t]]$

 c. John cried at least once every Sunday.

 d. $\exists t\ [t < now \wedge \forall x[\text{Sunday}(x) \rightarrow [t \subseteq \text{TIME}(x) \wedge \text{John cries at } t]]]$

 Note: TIME is the temporal trace function from event individuals into intervals. For example, TIME(x) means 'the temporal duration of the event x.'

In order to obtain the right reading, we would need an additional existential quantifier within the scope of *every Sunday* as in (15a) and (15b), which are two alternative ways of symbolizing the reading that (14a) actually has. The trouble is that we do not know where the narrow scope existential comes from. Also problematic is the fact that an inclusion relation is needed between the past time variable t_1 and the time of x. The source of this inclusion relation is not clear.

(15) a. $\exists t_1 [t_1 < now \wedge \forall x[[Sunday(x) \wedge \text{TIME}(x) \subseteq t_1] \rightarrow$
$\exists t [t \subseteq Time(x) \wedge John \text{ cries at } t]]]$

b. $\forall x[[Sunday(x) \wedge Time(x) \subseteq t_R \wedge t_R < now] \rightarrow$
$\exists t [t \subseteq \text{TIME}(x) \wedge John \text{ cries at } t]]$

One might object to the above line of reasoning by pointing out that the denotation of any noun is restricted by the context of use and that this is sufficient to account for the above data.[4] For example, (16a) almost never means that every student in the world had a good time. The common noun *student* as used in (16a) refers to the set of all students that are salient in the context. In general, the actual denotation of a common noun is a proper subset of its lexical meaning. The idea can be symbolized as in (16b). C is assumed to be the set of contextually salient individuals. This is the notation used by von Fintel (1994, 31). As a whole, (16b) says that every student that is salient in the context had a good time.

(16) a. Every student had a good time.

b. [every student had a good time] $= 1$ iff
[[every] ([student] $\cap C$)]([had a good time])

Many researchers argue for the idea that contextual restriction upon the quantificational domain is needed for any quantifier (e.g., von Fintel 1994; Stanley and Szabó 2000). If (16a) is uttered suddenly by an unknown speaker, then the hearer has no idea what C is. This means that the determination of C is made solely in terms of the information available in the context. If we extend this idea to time-sensitive nominal expressions such as *every Sunday,* we can assume that (17a) is rendered as in (17b).

(17) a. Mary kissed John (on) every Sunday.

b. [[[every Sunday]$_1$[Mary kissed John (on) t_1]]] $= 1$ iff
[every] ([Sunday] $\cap C$)(λx . there is a time t_1: Mary kisses John at t_1 & t_1
$< now$ & $t_1 \subseteq \text{TIME}(x)$)

C is understood to be the contextually salient set of intervals. Example (17a) is like (16a) except that C must be a set of past intervals. That is, (17a) can only be uttered in a context in which C is already restricted to past intervals. This appears to be an unnatural restriction. Enç (1986) shows that temporal properties of time-sensitive nouns do not always go with the tense. For example, (18) shows that *fugitive* must denote a set of fugitives at a past time in order to avoid a necessarily false statement.

(18) Every fugitive is now in jail.

Thus, the fact the relevant Sundays in (17a) can only include past Sundays must be explained. The simplest account would be that for (17a) to be true, the relevant

Sundays must be restricted to past Sundays. In other words, it seems that it is sufficient to appeal to the pragmatic principle that the speaker avoids necessarily false statements.

Unfortunately, this proposal too suffers from some empirical problems. Consider (19a).

(19) a. Mary kissed John before every meeting.

b. $[\![[[\text{every meeting}]_1 [\text{Mary kissed John before } t_1]]]\!] = 1$ iff
$[\![\text{every}]\!]([\![\text{meeting}]\!] \cap C)(\lambda x \,.\, \text{there is a time } t_1: \text{Mary kisses John at } t_1 \,\&\, t_1 < \text{now} \,\&\, t_1 < \text{TIME}(x))$

Our intuition says that the relevant meetings in (19a) must all be located in the past of the utterance time. However, according to (19b), if the restriction upon the meaning of *meeting* is imposed by the context alone (and not by the tense form), then C could contain a future interval and (19a) could still be true. In fact, (19a) can be true in a context in which C consists solely of future intervals. Let me show why this is the case. In the proposal under discussion, the only requirement for the truth of (19a) is that each relevant meeting is preceded by a past event of Mary's kissing John. It is therefore possible that all relevant meetings take place in the future of the utterance time, whereas all relevant kissings take place in the past of now. According to the scenario depicted in (20), for each meeting, there is an earlier kissing event that occurred in the past of now. Thus, despite the fact that $[\![\text{meeting}]\!] \cap C$ is a set of future meetings, (19a) is predicted to be true in this situation. This is counterintuitive.

(20)

[kissing$_1$] [kissing$_2$]   speech time   [meeting$_1$] [meeting$_2$]

The actual interpretation of (19a) requires that the meetings be restricted to past meetings. Moreover, for each meeting, a relevant *before*-interval must be defined because for each meeting, a relevant kissing must be found within an interval that is relatively short and immediately precedes the meeting. Obviously, it is not sufficient to restrict the relevant meetings to those meetings that occur within a particular past interval. For example, a natural reading of (19a) involves meetings that concern a particular project and occurred within a particular past interval. What is important here is that (19a) requires that the relevant meetings be restricted to past meetings. This fact cannot be accounted for by the idea that the speaker always avoids uttering a necessarily false sentence. Thus, we must posit something in addition to the default assumption that the denotation of each noun is contextually restricted. Under the traditional account, the scope problem mentioned above is indeed a problem. A satisfactory account of the semantic relation between tense and tPP requires a new proposal.

The semantics of tPPs is discussed in DRT as well. For example, Kamp and Reyle (1993) describe all relevant readings correctly in their discourse representation structures, but it is not clear what contributes the inclusion relation that occurs in the translation of the universal NP and why it has access to the salient past time. For example, (21a) is represented by the Discourse Representation Structure given in (21b). In this particular example, one could argue that the subpart relation between t'' and t (i.e., $t'' \subseteq t$) given in the antecedent box stems from the preposition *in* in *in 1985*. However, the same subpart relation must hold even when there is no such tPP that denotes a definite interval, as in (21c); the mornings in question must be restricted to past mornings.

(21) a. In 1985 Mary went swimming every morning.

b.
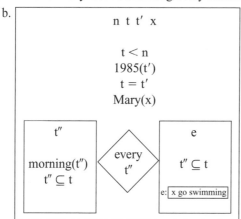

c. Mary went swimming every morning.

Thus, from the viewpoint of compositionality, Kamp and Reyle's analysis needs some improvement.

3. Adverbial Clauses and Adverbs of Quantification

Lewis (1975) shows that what he calls adverbs of quantification (e.g., *always, sometimes, often*) are often used as quantifiers over "cases" rather than over times per se. Lewis formally analyzes them as unselective quantifiers. This idea was adopted by Kamp (1981) and Heim (1982) and was incorporated into DRT.

This short section discusses the import of Lewis's analysis of quantificational adverbs in connection with quantificational tPPs (e.g., *every Sunday*). Following Lewis's analysis, all sentences containing adverbs of quantification require (at least semantically) a restrictive clause and a consequent clause. Since an adverb of quantification is regarded as an unselective quantifier, it does not always quantify over times. For example, in (22a) *always* is said to quantify over farmer-donkey pairs. On the other hand, in (22b), *always* quantifies over times (or events), since there is no other free variable in the antecedent clause.

(22) a. If a farmer owns a donkey, he always beats it.

b. When Mary thinks about his friends, she always calls him in advance.

But the situation is a little more complicated when the sentence in question is in the past or future tense. When the antecedent clause contains a tense morpheme as in

(23a), one could gather that this is why *always* quantifies over past times of John's thinking about his friends. However, the antecedent clause does not always have a tense morpheme as shown in (23b, c).

(23) a. When John thought about his friends, he was always happy.
      b. When thinking about his friends, John was always happy.
      c. When thinking about his friends, John will always be happy.

The time of thinking about his friends in (23b) is restricted to past times, and this information can only come from the past tense in the matrix clause. On the other hand, the time of thinking about his friends must be restricted to future times in (23c). This is clearly determined by the future tense in the matrix clause. This means that when the restrictive clause contains a time-sensitive expression, its correct interpretation requires access to the matrix tense. But it is not easy to do this in a compositional manner. This problem is quite similar to the case of tPPs discussed above in that both constructions involve quantified temporal adverbials. Let us now turn to Pratt and Francez's (2001) discussion of how to deal with quantified tPPs such as *during every meeting*.

4. Pratt and Francez (2001)

We now tackle the sticky problem of how to make sure in a compositional way that the meaning of the tPP with widest scope is restricted by the past reference time for the sentence. Since we do not know in advance which tPP receives a widest scope interpretation, Pratt and Francez (2001) set up their system in such a way that each time-sensitive predicate contains what they call a temporal context variable (as part of its lexical meaning), which could then assume the value of the reference time when the expression in question has widest scope. Example (24) shows how Pratt and Francez's system works. The notation here is that of Heim and Kratzer (1998).

(24) Mary kissed John during every meeting.
     a. $[\![$during every meeting$]\!] = \lambda P \in D_{\langle i,t \rangle} \, . \, [\lambda I \in D_i \, . \,$ every meeting x such that $\text{TIME}(x) \subseteq I$ is such that $P(\text{TIME}(x)) = 1]$
     b. $[\![$Mary kissed John$]\!] = \lambda t \in D_i \, . \,$ an event of Mary's kissing John occurs within t
     c. $[\![$Mary kissed John during every meeting$]\!] = \lambda P \in D_{\langle i,t \rangle} \, . \, [\lambda I \in D_i \, . \,$ every meeting x such that $\text{TIME}(x) \subseteq I$ is such that $P(\text{TIME}(x)) = 1]$
        $(\lambda t \in D_i \, . \,$ an event of Mary's kissing John occurs within t)
     d. $\lambda I \in D_i \, . \,$ every meeting x such that $\text{TIME}(x) \subseteq I$ is such that an event of Mary's kissing John occurs within $\text{TIME}(x)$

After applying (24a) to a contextually salient past interval $PAST_R$, we get the following truth condition for the sentence: every meeting x such that $TIME(x) \subseteq PAST_R$ is such that an event of Mary's kissing John occurs within $\text{TIME}(x)$. This is the right interpretation. The most important feature of Pratt and Francez's proposal is that the translation of each event-denoting noun involves a temporal context variable (i.e., I in [25]) and that the event associated with the predicate is required to occur within this contextually salient time, as in (25). Let us refer to this assumption as Assumption 1.

(25) $[\![meeting]\!] = \lambda x \lambda I[meeting(x) \wedge \text{TIME}(x) \subseteq I]$

The second important assumption (Assumption 2) made by Pratt and Francez is that there are two sources of existential quantification. One is a quantifier (existential or universal) induced at the matrix-clause level by an adverbial (such as a tPP), and the other is an existential quantifier over event variables. The latter implements Davidson's (1967) idea. When a quantificational adverbial (e.g., *during every meeting*) is present, the existential over the main predicate events is scoped under it. When there is no adverbial, the existential over the main predicate events is the only temporal quantifier in the sentence. Let us discuss these two points one by one.

I object to Assumption 1 for two reasons. First, adoping this assumption does not seem to provide a fully compositional semantics to tPPs such as *during the meeting* because the meaning that is intuitively associated with *during* is already expressed by the lexical meaning of *meeting*. It would be like saying that *meeting* itself means 'meeting during,' and *John kisses Mary* means 'John kisses Mary during.' Second, adopting this assumption means that we accept a fundamental difference between (regular) individual arguments and temporal arguments. For example, in (25), for any individual a_1 and interval i_1 if $[\![meeting]\!](a_1)(i_1) = 1$, then for any interval i_2 such that $i_1 \subseteq i_2$ $[\![meeting]\!](a_1)(i_2) = 1$. However, for any group individual a_2 such that a_1 is part of a_2, $[\![meeting]\!](a_2)(i_1) = 1$ does not necessarily hold. Assumption 2 (assuming two sources of existential quantification) would produce the same problem that Bäuerle and von Stechow (1980) present with regard to frequency adverbs such as *exactly three times*. (This was discussed in section 2.) Note also that there are overt existentials like *sometime between 5:00 and 6:00*. Therefore, it seems wise to attribute the existential quantifier to an adverbial.

Pratt and Francez propose Assumption 1 primarily because they want the inclusion relation between the time of the event and the (past) time specified by the context. For example, in (14a), repeated here as (26a), every relevant Sunday must be part of the salient past time and must not be equivalent to it. Otherwise, we would get the wrong interpretation, as shown in (26b, c). If an existential quantifier associated with the past tense has widest scope and this time is equivalent to the time of crying, we obtain the reading in (26b). This is the wrong interpretation because it forces us to think about a set of Sundays that take place at the same time. On the other hand, if the existential quantifier is scoped under the universal quantifier, then (26a) is predicted to mean (26c). It entails, among other things, that every Sunday is in the past. Either way, we obtain the wrong result. Thus, the part-of relation is crucial.

(26) a. John cried every Sunday.
   b. $\exists t \ [\ t < now \wedge \forall x \ [[\text{Sunday}(x) \wedge \text{TIME}(x) = t \ ] \rightarrow \exists t_1 \ [\text{John cries at } t_1 \wedge t_1 \subseteq t]]$
   c. $\forall x \ [\text{Sunday}(x) \rightarrow \exists t \ [\ t < now \wedge \text{TIME}(x) = t \wedge \exists t_1 \ [\text{John cries at } t_1 \wedge t_1 \subseteq t]]]$

Pratt and Francez's (2001) idea is to make such a contextual restriction part of the lexical meaning of each event noun so that the time of each relevant event is within the value of this temporal variable. This enables us to obtain interpretations like (15a, b) for (26a), and this is why Pratt and Francez wish to adopt Assumption 1. However, the correct empirical result is obtained by positing a major difference between "regular individuals" and temporal individuals as suggested above. Prima facie, it would be better if we could make the same empirical prediction without positing this type of asymmetry between individual arguments and temporal arguments. The proposal I defend does just that.

5. Toward a More Compositional Account of Quantified Temporal Adverbials

In this section, I propose an account of the data discussed by Pratt and Francez (2001) that avoids the use of temporal context variables. My account is based upon von Stechow's (2002) proposal and resembles it in many ways, including the way in which syntactic movements at LF are exploited in the semantics. However, it contains what I consider to be an important new idea: an overt or covert tPP *in the past* or some other adverbial that denotes a specific part of the entire past interval such as *during last summer* must occur in a past tense sentence. Unlike Pratt and Frances (2001) or von Stechow (2002), my proposal posits no temporal context variable in the lexical meaning of a verb or time-sensitive common noun. The idea is that the anteriority meaning associated with a past tense sentence is borne by an appropriate overt or covert past-oriented adverbial and not by the tense morpheme.[5]

First and foremost, we should note that tPPs like *in the past* do occur in tensed sentences as in (27a, b), which are found on the Web.

(27) a. In the past, because of its size and fragility, and the modest artistic
    aspirations of many of its composers, sheet music was often considered
    ephemera by music libraries and seldom formed a part of their
    permanent collections.
    (www.collectionscanada.ca/sheetmusic/index-e.html)

  b. At some time in the past there was clearly some sort of fluid on the
    surface.
    (www.nineplanets.org/mars.html)

Given these examples, one needs only a small extra step to conclude that when no such tPP is overtly present in a past tense sentence, a covert one with the same semantic content is there.[6] This enables us to provide a more natural way of accounting for the behavior of tPPs in past tense (or future tense) sentences than Pratt and Francez (2001) or von Stechow (2002). The main points of my proposal are summarized in (28).[7]

(28) a. A sentence abstract (a tensed sentence with no temporal adverbials) is
    of type $<i,t>$ (set of intervals).

  b. A temporal preposition (e.g., *on, in, during*) is of type $<e, <<i,t>,t>>$
    E.g., $[\![on]\!] = \lambda x \in D_e . [\lambda P \in D_{<i,t>} . [\text{there is } t \in D_i. P(t) \& t \subseteq \text{TIME}(x)]]$

c. A temporal PP (tPP) is of type $<<i,t>,t>$

d. A cascade of tPPs (a tPP that possibly embeds some additional tPPs) (e.g., *during every meeting on a Sunday*) is anchored by an overt or covert tPP that indicates a definite past time (e.g., *in the past*) when the sentence in question is in the past tense. (Similarly for future tense sentences.) A tPP α is an anchor iff there is no tPP β such that α contains β.

Given this proposal, the past tense looks as though it is semantically empty. It is assumed in the traditional account that tense carries an anteriority meaning. However, the proposed account posits an adverbial that conveys that information. Thus, I contend with Vlach (1993) that the past tense morpheme has no meaning of its own; it instead syntactically requires that an overt or covert past-oriented tPP such as *in the past* be present in the same clause. An exact syntactic mechanism that brings about this effect is left for another occasion, but I hope the idea is clear. This is analogous to Bäuerle and von Stechow's (1980) view about the existential quantification meaning associated with a past tense sentence, which was discussed above.

In the proposal being defended, statements like $TIME(e) \subseteq t$ are not part of the lexical meaning of any verb or noun. Thus, Pratt and Francez's Assumption 1 is rejected. Since all quantifiers are introduced by adverbials, their Assumption 2 is also abandoned. Example (30) shows how the sentence (29a) with the LF structure (29b) is interpreted compositionally in the system being proposed.

(29) a. Mary kissed John during every meeting on (a) Sunday (in the past)

b. LF: $[_S [_{NP}$ a Sunday in the past$]_2 [_S[_{NP}$ every meeting (on) $e_2]_1 [_S$ Mary kissed John (at least once) during $e_1]]]$

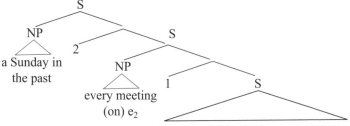

(30) a. ⟦Mary kissed John⟧ = $\lambda t \in D_i$. Mary kisses John at t

b. ⟦during e_1⟧ = $\lambda P \in D_{<i,t>}$. there is a $t \in D_i$ such that $P(t) = 1$ & $t \subseteq TIME(x_1)$

c. ⟦Mary kissed John (at least once) during e_1⟧ = | iff there is a time t & Mary kisses John at t & $t \subseteq TIME(x_1)$[8]

d. ⟦meeting⟧ = $\lambda x \in D_e$. $\lambda t \in D_i$. x is a meeting at t

e. ⟦on e_2⟧ = $\lambda P \in D_{<i,t>}$. there is a time t such that $P(t) = 1$ & $t \subseteq TIME(x_2)$

f. ⟦meeting on e_2⟧ = $\lambda y \in D_e$. ⟦on e_2⟧ (⟦meeting⟧(y)) = $\lambda y \in D_e$. [there is a $t \in D_i$ such that y is a meeting at t & $t \subseteq TIME(x_2)$]

g. ⟦every⟧ = $\lambda f \in D<e,t>$. $\lambda g \in D_{<e,t>}$. every $z \in D_e$ such that $f(z) = 1$ is $g(z) = 1$

h. $[\![$ every meeting on $e_2]\!] = \lambda g \in D_{<e,t>}$. every $z \in D_e$ such that $\exists t$ such that z is a meeting at t & $t \subseteq$ TIME(x_2) is $g(z) = 1$

i. $[\![[$ every meeting on $e_2]$ 1[Mary kissed John during $e_1]]\!] = \ |$ iff every meeting $z \in D_e$ such that there is a time t such that TIME$(z) = t$ & $t \subseteq$ TIME(x_2) is such that there is a time t_1: Mary kisses John at t_1 & $t_1 \subseteq$ TIME(z)

j. every meeting $z \in D_e$ such that TIME$(z) \subseteq$ TIME(x_2) is such that there is a time t_1: Mary kisses John at t_1 & $t_1 \subseteq$ TIME(z)

k. $[\![$ the past $]\!] = \{t \mid t < \text{now}\}$

l. $[\![$ a Sunday in the past $]\!] = \lambda g \in D_{<e,t>}$. there is a Sunday $z \in D_e$ such that TIME$(z) \in \{t \mid t < \text{now}\}$ & $g(z) = 1$

m. $[\![[$ a Sunday in the past $]$ 2[every meeting on $e_2]$ 1[Mary kissed John during $e_1]]\!] = \lambda g \in D_{<e,t>}$. there is some Sunday $z \in D_e$ such that TIME$(z) \in \{t \mid t < \text{now}\}$ & $g(z) = 1$

   $(\lambda x_2$. every meeting $y \in D_e$ such that TIME$(y) \subseteq$ TIME(x_2) is such that there is a time t_1: Mary kisses John at t_1 & $t_1 \subseteq$ TIME$(y))$

n. There is a past Sunday $z \in D_e$ such that every meeting y that takes place within TIME(z) is such that Mary kisses John within TIME(y)

The line in (30n) provides the right interpretation of (29a) with the LF structure (29b). Note that the past tense morpheme has no semantic content.

What I have attempted to accomplish in this chapter is much more restricted in scope than Pratt and Francez (2001) or von Stechow (2002). But I believe that the basic idea I propose here is novel and is worth pursuing. I assume that certain syntactic features are responsible for the occurrence of desired tPPs in tensed English sentences.

6. An Alternative Account

It is often assumed in the literature that the contribution made by tense is a presupposition and not an assertion. For example, Kratzer (1998) assumes what is given in (31).

(31) $[\![$ past $]\!]^{g,c}$ is defined only if c provides an interval t that precedes t_0 (the utterance time). If defined, $[\![$ past $]\!]^{g,c} = t$.

I do not believe that the anteriority meaning associated with a past tense sentence is always presuppositional, but I concede that this is true most of the time. If I had so wished, I could have incorporated (31) into my proposal. For example, one could say that the phonetically null temporal NP (i.e., tNP) is presupposed to denote the entire past interval. Thus, I could go along with Kratzer's idea without agreeing that the tense morpheme carries this presupposition.

We could, alternatively, adopt Kratzer's proposal and assume that past tense is presupposed to denote some past interval and that this constrains the denotation of the main verb. Then we could perhaps account for the fact that the temporal interpretation of any tPP harmonizes with the co-ocurring tense morpheme in terms of presupposition projection as suggested by Heim (1997). Heim's (1997) idea is this: the presupposition imposed upon a time argument by a semantic tense is projected to a time argument occurring in the restriction of a temporal quantifier that binds this variable. Heim's suggestion is not formalized. But suppose it is. Then, this account would allow us to keep the standard assumption that tense only regulates the time of the verb obligatorily. Therefore, it is prima facie a very promising hypothesis. To examine its consequences, let me present a simple example. Consider (32a).

(32) a. When watching TV, Mary always sat on the sofa.

b. always$_t$ [PRO watches TV at t][Mary sits on the sofa at t]

c. always$_t$ [PRO watches TV at t & t $<$ now][Mary sits on the sofa at t & t $<$ now]

When interpreting (32a), we must restrict our attention to past events of Mary's watching TV. This is explained in terms of Heim's account as follows. Her semantic representation of (32a) would be (32b). The tense imposes the restriction upon the variable t that occurs in the nuclear scope of *always*, which is that $[\![t]\!]^g$ is defined only if $g(t) <$ now (where g is an assignment). Heim's idea is that the same restriction is imposed upon the occurrences of the same variable t in the antecedent clause. Given this presuppositional analysis of the variable t in (32b), (32b) is essentially equivalent to (32c) (ignoring the difference between presupposition and assertion). This results in an empirically correct result. As von Stechow (2002) says, this may be the right approach, but the presupposition in question is often represented overtly by an adverbial. So it seems better to posit a covert adverbial rather than a presupposition projection mechanism that is sometimes redundant.

7. Some Residual Issues

In addition to the conceptual problem addressed above, Pratt and Francez's (2001) proposal suffers from some empirical problems. When discussing the semantics of *before* and *after,* Pratt and Francez specify the truth condition of (33a) as in (33b).

(33) a. Mary kissed John before the meeting.

b. The meeting x within $PAST_R$ is such that there is an event e of Mary kissing John & e occurs before x and within $PAST_R$.

By extending this analysis to (34a), Pratt and Francez would obtain (34b) as its interpretation.

(34) a. Mary kissed John before every meeting.

b. Every meeting x within $PAST_R$ is such that there is an event e of Mary kissing John & e occurs before x and within $PAST_R$.

The interpretation (34b) is subject to the problem discussed by Ogihara (1995). That is, (34b) predicts that (34a) is true even when there is only one event of Mary's kissing John that precedes all relevant meetings as long as this kissing event falls within the contextually salient past interval indicated by $PAST_R$. Since this goes against our intuitions regarding (34a), we must make the interpretation of *before every meeting* even more context sensitive. Sentence (34a) is analyzed syntactically as in (35a, b), and the semantic interpretation of (35b) is obtained as in (36).

(35) a. Mary kissed John before every meeting (in the past).

    b. LF: [$_S$ [$_{NP}$ every meeting in the past]1 [$_S$ Mary kissed John before t_1]]

(36) a. [Mary kissed John before t_1] = | iff there is a time t such that Mary kisses John at t & t $\subseteq$ BEFORE(x_1)

    b. [every meeting in the past] = $\lambda P \in D_{<e,t>}$. every meeting x such that TIME(x) < now is such that P(x) = 1

    c. [[$_S$ [$_{NP}$ every meeting in the past]1 [$_S$ Mary kissed John before t_1]]] = $\lambda P \in D_{<e,t>}$. every meeting x such that TIME(x) < now is such that P(x) = 1 ($\lambda y \in D_e$. there is a time t such that Mary kisses John at t & t $\subseteq$ BEFORE(y))

    d. Every meeting x such that TIME(x) < now is such that there is a time t such that Mary kisses John at t & t $\subseteq$ BEFORE(x)

The important point here is that BEFORE is a context-dependent choice function from individuals (i.e., events) to intervals which supplies a *before*-interval for any event *x*. This interval is understood to be the interval within which a relevant kissing event occurs in relation to the meeting in question. The assumption is that each interval provided by this function for an event is a relatively short interval that precedes and abuts this event. This practically eliminates the possibility that one kissing event that precedes all the relevant meetings would make (35a) true. This solution could be incorporated into Pratt and Francez's proposal as well. So this issue having to do with the semantics of *before* is independent of the choice between my proposal and theirs.

Finally, note that the temporal conjunction *before* gives rise to a different type of problem discussed in Ogihara (1995). It is a problem associated with nonfactual *before* exemplified by (37a, b). (37a) does not entail that there is a past time at which *he* committed suicide. The situation is similar for (37b).

(37) a. Mary always came to his rescue before he committed suicide.

    b. John died before he saw his grandchildren.

The proposal defended here can be augmented by the modal analysis of nonfactual *before* presented in Ogihara (1995).   ▪

ACKNOWLEDGMENTS
I thank the committee members of GURT 2004, in particular Rafaella Zanuttini, Paul Portner, and Elena Herburger, for organizing it and for giving me a chance present my work there. I thank Paul Portner and Elena Herburger for detailed comments and suggestions on an earlier draft of this chapter. Earlier versions were also presented at Hosei University, University of Washington, University of Calgary, Tohoku University, Tokyo University, Yokohama National University, and Tsukuba University. I thank the audiences of these colloquia presentations, in particular Yukiko Alam Sasaki, Hotze Rullman, Paul Portner, Ora Matushansky, Kei Yoshimoto, Kaoru Horie, Christopher Tancredi, Makoto Kanazawa, Hidetoshi Shirai, Yoshio Endo, Yoshiki Mori, and Koichi Takezawa. All errors and inadequacies are mine.

NOTES

    1. For (3a) to receive a purely existential reading, we need a context like the one given in (i). The idea is that B's utterance is used to show that John is smart (or that is what people expect from Harvard

graduates). B does not intend to assert that John's graduation from Harvard falls within a particular past interval.

(i) A: Is John smart?
B: Well, he graduated from Harvard.

2. A similar point is made in Kuhn and Portner (2002).
3. Strictly speaking, this notation differs slightly from Dowty's original, but the differences do not give rise to any interpretive differences.
4. Hotze Rullman, Ora Matushansky, and Paul Portner (pers. comm.) independently suggested this possibility.
5. As far as the existential quantifier meaning associated with a tensed sentence, I follow Bäuerle and von Stechow (1980) in assuming that a frequency adverbial such as *at least once* (overt or covert) is responsible for it.
6. Portner (2003) supports this idea indirectly by arguing for the view that the present perfect requires an 'Extended Now' interval (or an adverb that denotes an 'Extended Now' interval), not that the present perfect itself denotes this type of interval.
7. The type system I assume here is the standard one: type e for individuals; type t for truth values; type i for intervals.
8. I follow Bäuerle and von Stechow (1980) and assume that the existential quantification over times originates in the covert adverbial *at least once.*

REFERENCES
Bäuerle, R., and A. von Stechow. 1980. Finite and non-finite temporal constructions in German. In *Time, tense, and quantifiers,* ed. C.Rohrer, 375–421. Tübingen: Niemeyer.
Davidson, D. 1967. The logical form of action sentences. In *The logic of decision and action,* ed. N. Rescher, 81–120. Pittsburgh, PA: University of Pittsburgh Press.
Dowty, D. 1979. *Word meaning and Montague grammar: The semantics of verbs and times in generative semantics and in Montague's PTQ.* Dordrecht: D. Reidel.
Enç, M. 1986. Towards a referential analysis of temporal expressions. *Linguistics and Philosophy* 9: 405–26.
Heim, I. 1982. *The semantics of definite and indefinite noun phrases,* PhD diss, University of Massachusetts, Amherst.
———. 1997. Comments on Abusch's theory of tense. Unpublished manuscript, Massachusetts Institute of Technology.
Heim, I., and A. Kratzer. 1998. *Semantics in generative grammar.* Oxford: Blackwell.
Kamp, H. 1981. A theory of truth and semantic representation. In *Formal Methods in the Study of Language,* ed. J. Groenendijk, T. Janssen, and M. Stokhof. Amsterdam: Mathematical Centre. Repr. in *Truth, Interpretation and Information. Selected Papers from the Third Amsterdam Colloquium,* ed. J. Groenendijk, T. Janssen, and M. Stokhof, 1–41. Dordrecht: Foris, 1984.
Kamp, H., and U. Reyle. 1993. *From discourse to logic.* Dordrecht: Kluwer.
Kratzer, A. 1998. More structural analogies between pronouns and tenses. *Proceedings of Salt 8,* ed. D. Strolovitch and A. Lawson, 92–110. Ithaca, NY: CLC Publications, Cornell University.
Krifka, M. 1989. *Nominalreferenz und Zeitkonstitution. Zur Semantik von Massentermen, Pluraltermen und Aspektklassen.* Munich: Fink.
Kuhn, S., and P. Portner. 2002. Tense and time. In *The handbook of philosophical logic,* Vol. VII, 2nd ed., ed. D. Gabbay and F. Guenthner, 277–346. Dordrecht: Kluwer.
Lewis, D. 1975. Adverbs of quantification. In *Formal semantics of natural language,* ed. E. Keenan. Cambridge: Cambridge University Press.
Ogihara, T. 1994. Adverbs of quantification and sequence of tense phenomena. In *Proceedings from semantics and linguistic theory IV,* ed. M. Harvey and L. Santelmann, 251–67. Ithaca, NY: CLC Publications, Cornell University.
———. 1995. Non-factual *before* and adverbs of quantification. In *Proceedings of Salt 5,* ed. M. Simons and T. Galloway, 273–91. Ithaca, NY: CLC Publications, Cornell University.

————. 1996. *Tense, attitudes, and scope.* Dordrecht: Kluwer.

Partee, B.H. 1984. Nominal and temporal anaphora. *Linguistics and Philosophy* 7: 243–86.

Portner, P. 2003. The (temporal) semantics and (modal) pragmatics of the perfect. *Linguistics and Philosophy* 26: 459–510.

Pratt, J., and N. Francez. 2001. Temporal prepositions and temporal generalized quantifiers. *Linguistics and Philosophy* 24: 187–222.

Prior, A. 1967. *Past, present and future.* Oxford: Clarendon Press.

Reichenbach, H. 1947. *Elements of symbolic logic.* New York: Macmillan.

Stanley, J., and Z. Szabó. 2000. On quantifier domain restriction. *Mind and Language* 15: 219–61.

Stump, G. 1985. *The semantic variability of absolute constructions.* Dordrecht: D. Reidel.

Vlach, F. 1993. Temporal adverbials, tenses and the perfect. *Linguistics and Philosophy* 16: 231–83.

von Fintel, K. 1994. *Restrictions on quantifier domains.* PhD diss., University of Massachusetts, Amherst.

von Stechow, A. 2002. Temporal prepositional phrases with quantifiers: Some additions to Pratt and Francez (2001). *Linguistics and Philosophy* 25: 755–800.